DISCARD

WORLD LITERATURE
IN TRANSLATION

HENRIK IBSEN

CATILINE
AND
THE BURIAL MOUND

Translated from Dano-Norwegian, with Introductions, by
THOMAS F. VAN LAAN

GARLAND PUBLISHING, INC.
NEW YORK & LONDON 1992

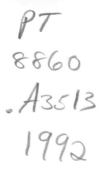
Library of Congress Cataloging-in-Publication Data

Ibsen, Henrik, 1828–1906
   [Catilina. English]
     Catiline; and, The Burial mound/Henrik Ibsen ; translated, with
introductions, by Thomas F. Van Laan.
     p. cm.—(Garland library of world literature in translation ; v. 11)
     Translation of Catilina and Kjæmpehøien.

     Includes bibliographical references.

     ISBN 0-8240-2997-6

     1. Ibsen, Henrik, 1828–1906—Translations, English. I. Ibsen,
Henrik, 1828–1906. Kjæmpehøien. English. 1990. II. Title. III. Title:
Catiline. IV. Title: Burial mound.
PT8860.A35   1990
839.8'226—dc20   90-3257

To Anna, with love—
even though she wouldn't hear of
naming her new kitten "Catiline"

Contents

Preface

This book contains new translations of Henrik Ibsen's first two plays, *Catilina* and *Kjæmpehøien* (*The Burial Mound*, also known in English translation as *The Warrior's Barrow*). Ibsen wrote *Catiline*, a three-act tragedy, in the early months of 1849, it was published in 1850, and in 1874–75 Ibsen revised it for a second edition, which appeared in 1875, accompanied by Ibsen's Preface. He completed *The Burial Mound*, a one-act play, in 1850, and during the same year it was performed at the Christiania Theater in Christiania (now Oslo), Norway; in 1853, he extensively revised *The Burial Mound* for performance at the Norwegian Theater in Bergen, where it was produced on January 2, 1854; the text of this version was published in four successive numbers of a newspaper, the *Bergenske Blade*, during the end of January and the beginning of February of the same year.

I have translated both versions of both plays as well as Ibsen's 1875 Preface to the second edition of *Catiline*. My main source for the original texts is Volume I of the definitive original-language edition of Ibsen's works, the Hundreårsutgave, but in all cases except the revised version of *Catiline* I have consulted the original manuscripts and publications, and as a result I have incorporated some changes that seem to me appropriate, especially in punctuation. The primary medium of both plays is blank verse, but they also contain numerous and extensive passages in rhyme; furthermore, the first version of *Catiline*, written in haste and not corrected by Ibsen when it was published, has many lines that are ragged metrically or that have too many or too few syllables. My aim has been to provide as close as possible a rendering in English of what Ibsen wrote in Dano-Norwegian, and so I have reproduced the metrical irregularities of the first version of *Catiline*, rhymed the passages that rhyme in Ibsen's original texts, and in each case keyed the translation of the second version of the play to the translation of the first, as if the former were a revision of the latter—although this last practice is not nearly so significant for *The Burial Mound*, which Ibsen rewrote more extensively than he did *Catiline*.

In most of these respects, the translations in this book are unique. Except for a nineteenth-century version of the first act of *Catiline*, there have been only two previous renderings of these plays into English. Graham Orton, whose work appears in Volume I of the Oxford *Ibsen* (1970), has provided a complete translation of the first version of *Catiline* but only a partial translation of the second version, from the middle of its final act to its conclusion; he reproduces the metrical irregularities of the first version, but he does not reproduce the rhymes for either version. Anders Orbeck, whose work appears in *Early Plays by Henrik Ibsen* (1921), translates only the second version of *Catiline*, reproducing its rhymes. James Walter McFarlane, also in Volume I of the Oxford *Ibsen*, translates both versions of *The Burial Mound* in full, but, like Orton, he does not reproduce the rhymes. Orbeck translates only the second version of *The Burial Mound*, as *The Warrior's Barrow*; he reproduces its rhymes, but they are less extensive than the rhymes of the first version.

In adopting my own practices, I have hoped to give the reader without Dano-Norwegian an opportunity to study Ibsen's earliest dramatic works as he first wrote them and to observe him at work in revising his own texts. For the reader who is less interested in Ibsen's development and prefers to read only one version of *Catiline*, I recommend the second as the more finished product; the two versions of *The Burial Mound* are sufficiently different to warrant reading both of them.

This book also includes extensive introductions for both plays, in which I discuss their composition, reception, and sources, offer analyses and evaluations of them, address the primary changes made in revision, and add further comments on my translations. Everyone has his or her own method of reading introductions, including skipping them, but thinking in terms of my expectations about the reader's knowledge as I wrote them, I recommend that the first and last section of each introduction be read first, then the first version of the relevant play, then my discussions of its sources and my analysis and evaluation of it, then the second version of the play, followed by my comments on the changes Ibsen made in it.

Catiline and *The Burial Mound* belong together in a single volume because of a peculiarity they share. Ibsen called *The Burial Mound* a "dramatic poem," and the term is equally applicable to *Catiline*. In genuine poetic drama, including Ibsen's own later verse plays, the poetry serves the drama and the drama serves the poetry, as the two interact to form a seamless whole. In *Catiline* and the *The Burial Mound* (especially its first version), however, poetry takes on greater prominence, for the particular effects of these plays result more from poetic devices than dramatic ones. That is why, for example, experiencing the rhymes is crucial to a proper appreciation—and to some extent even an understanding—of these plays. Their belonging to the same form gives this book its unity; it also has an argument, which I conduct implicitly throughout and address most explicitly in my introduction to *The Burial Mound*. And this argument is that although Ibsen began as a writer of dramatic poems his revision of *The Burial Mound* was a highly significant act in which he abandoned his earliest dramatic form and pretty much discovered his mature voice as a dramatist.

In preparing this book, I have benefited from the encouragement and often the invaluable advice of kind friends and colleagues. Barry Jacobs, Joan D. Peters, Otto Reinert, and—especially—Derek Attridge have been influential in making my translations far better than they would otherwise be. Sandra Saari and Andrew and Susan Welsh listened patiently to many of my ideas for the introductions and helped me thrash them out into final form. William Walling, during a very busy time, read the introduction to *Catiline* with devotion and with a sure eye, forcing me to remove numerous infelicities of style and to clarify its thought. Joan D. Peters has been similarly helpful with the introduction to *The Burial Mound*. I am also grateful to the Research Council of Rutgers, the State University of New Jersey, for a grant enabling me to go to Oslo to study the original texts of these plays as well as to conduct other related research, and to the librarians of the Universitetsbibliotek in Oslo for their assistance and especially for the patience with which they dealt with a visitor whose command of spoken Norwegian is much weaker than his ability to read the language. Finally, I would like to thank those at Garland who were involved in the production of this book, particularly Chuck Bartelt, Heidi Christein, and Elspeth Hart.

New Brunswick, New Jersey
December 29, 1989

Key to References in the Introductions

The following is a list of references that I employ more than once and at widely-spaced intervals in the introductions. In each case, I give full citation, in the text or a note, when the reference is first used, but in subsequent uses I employ only the short form given below.

Anker: Henrik Ibsen, *Brev 1845–1905, Ny Samling*, edited by Øyvind Anker, *Ibsenårbok*, 1979 (Oslo: Universitetsforlaget, 1979).

Bull: See Hundreårsutgave.

Cox: Jeffrey N. Cox, *In the Shadows of Romance: Romantic Tragic Drama in Germany, England, and France* (Athens, OH: Ohio University Press, 1987).

Dahl: Per Kristian Heggelund Dahl, "Ibsen-data fra Skien og Grimstad," *Ibsenårbok*, 1985/86, 207–14.

Eitrem: Hans Eitrem, *Ibsen og Grimstad* (Oslo: H. Aschehoug & Co. [W. Nygaard], 1940).

Fraenkl: Pavel Fraenkl, *Ibsens Vei til Drama: En undersøkelse av dramatikerens genesis* (Oslo: Gyldendal Norsk Forlag, 1955).

Haakonsen: Daniel Haakonsen, *Henrik Ibsen, mennesket og kunstneren* (Oslo: H. Aschehoug & Co. [W. Nygaard], 1981).

Haugholt: Karl Haugholt, "Samtidens kritikk av Ibsens *Catilina*," *Edda*, 52 (1952), 74–94.

Hundreårsutgave: Henrik Ibsen, *Samlede Verker*, Hundreårsutgave, edited by Francis Bull, Halvdan Koht, and Didrik Arup Seip, 21 Volumes (Oslo: Gyldendal Norsk Forlag, 1928–1957). Volume I (1928) contains both versions of *Catiline* and *The Burial Mound*, Bull's introductions to the two plays, and Seip's textual notes for both (pp. 207–42 for *Catiline*, and pp. 311–15 for *The Burial Mound*).

KEY TO REFERENCES IN THE INTRODUCTIONS

Johnston: Brian Johnston, *To the Third Empire: Ibsen's Early Drama* (Minneapolis: University of Minnesota Press, 1980).

Koht: Halvdan Koht, *Henrik Ibsen, eit diktarliv*, Ny, omarbeidd utgåve, 2 vols. (Oslo: H. Aschehoug & Co. [W. Nygaard], 1954).

McFarlane: James Walter McFarlane, editor and principal translator of the Oxford *Ibsen*; Volume I, *Early Plays* (London: Oxford University Press, 1970), co-edited with Graham Orton, includes Orton's translations of *Catiline* and his Appendix I, "*Catiline*: Commentary" (pp. 575–84) and McFarlane's "Introduction" (pp. 1–34), his translations of *The Burial Mound*, and his Appendix III, "*The Burial Mound*: Commentary" (pp. 604–06).

McLellan: Samuel G. McLellan, "On *Catilina*: A Structural Examination of Ibsen's First Play and Its Sources," *Scandinavian Studies*, 55 (1983), 39–54 (for the introduction to *Catiline*); "Ibsen's Expanded Idea in Kjæmpehøien," *Edda*, 82 (1982), 273–80 (for the introduction to *The Burial Mound*).

Meyer: Michael Meyer, *Ibsen, A Biography* (Garden City, NY: Doubleday & Company, Inc., 1971).

Orbeck: Anders Orbeck, translator, Henrik Ibsen, *Early Plays: Catiline, The Warrior's Barrow, Olaf Liljekrans* (New York: The American-Scandinavian Foundation, 1921 [Kraus Reprints, 1971]).

Orton: See McFarlane.

Seip: See Hundreårsutgave.

Skard: Eiliv Skard, "Kjeldone til Ibsens *Catilina*," *Edda*, 21 (1924), 70–90.

Thuesen: Arthur Thuesen, "Om Førsteutgaven av Ibsens *Catilina*" (Kristiania, 1922).

Introduction to *Catiline*

Composition and Reception

Ibsen's Preface to the second edition of *Catiline* provides a good, and interesting, account of the circumstances under which the play was conceived and written, the details of its composition, publication, and initial reception, and the occasion of the 1875 revision. The Preface gives only the broad outlines, however, its tone is that of the older and by then successful author's amused attitude toward his younger self, later research has greatly amplified its details, and, of course, it has nothing to say about the fate of the play subsequent to 1875.[1]

i. Background

The full story of the composition of *Catiline* begins many years before Ibsen wrote it, in Skien, Norway, the town in which he was born. His father, Knud Ibsen, ran a general store with an extensive import business and was fairly well-to-do during Ibsen's early years, being listed in 1832-34 as having the seventeenth largest income in the area (Skien itself had about 2,000 inhabitants at the time). He also enjoyed considerable social prominence, for the Ibsen home was the scene of numerous parties and other gatherings that included the wealthiest families of the town, to many of whom Knud Ibsen was related, especially through marriage. In the middle of 1834, however, for reasons that are not clear, his fortunes abruptly declined: parts of his business were shut down by the authorities, and between 1834 and 1836 he was forced by debt to sell most of his possessions. He did not officially become a bankrupt, but his business had come to an end, his property in town and its expensive furnishings were lost, and he and his family were forced to move, probably in June 1835, to a country place that he still owned, Venstøp, now famous as the site of the model for the attic in *The Wild Duck*.

3

Ibsen's biographers and biographical critics make a great deal of Knud Ibsen's abrupt decline into financial ruin. For Henrik, the oldest surviving child in the family and seven at the time of the move to Venstøp, it is supposed to have been a tremendous blow, giving him the sense of having been cruelly deprived of his rightful place in life by an unjust fate and prompting him to turn inward, to his own imaginative resources, in order to protect himself against the hostile world and especially to maintain his dignity in the face of pitying or contemptuous attitudes from a community highly conscious of the disgrace his family had suffered. Having lost his social standing and his intimacy with the wealthier families of Skien, he refused to accept as equals or to develop any kind of friendship with the poorer children who now formed his appropriate circle of acquaintances. He became at most a spectator, rather than a participant, in their activities. Like his much later self, concealing a mind filled with radical and revolutionary ideas behind an outside covered with a fashionable frock coat and medals and other decorations awarded him by various crowned heads of Europe, he insisted on wearing the most elegant clothes his father could afford to buy for him. He began to develop a distinctly satirical attitude that expressed itself largely in the carica-tures he drew of his siblings and others. So far as is known, his playtime activities—such as his performance of magic tricks and his construction and operation of a small puppet theater—were largely of a sort to give himself complete control and to impress others with his accomplishments.

To what extent this reading of the existing evidence is an accurate one cannot, of course, be fully known, but one consequence for Ibsen of his father's financial ruin seems beyond dispute: the effect it had on his education and the beginning of his working career. What is known of his schooling indicates that it was appropriate for his family's reduced circumstances, and for a while he even took art lessons from a local painter. But if the evidence that he had decided at an early age to become a doctor is true, his schooling was inadequate, for he was not sent to the one school, the Latin school in Skien, that would have qualified him for the necessary University training. Attendance at this school was expensive, but as Koht points out (I, 24) Ibsen could have gone there as a scholarship student, and he speculates that Ibsen did not attend simply because it was the standard practice for children of poor families to break off their schooling when they were confirmed and enter into whatever employment they could find that might earn them an independent living. In any event, Ibsen left school in the spring of 1843, shortly after his fifteenth birthday, he was confirmed in October, and, apparently, just before or just after Christmas he left by boat for Grimstad,[2] a much smaller town (about 800 inhabitants) farther south on the east coast of the Norwegian peninsula, where an acquaintance of his father's, a travelling agent, had found him a position as apprentice to a pharmicist and where, five years later, he was to write *Catiline*.

The life Ibsen entered into in Grimstad was far worse than anything he had experienced in Skien. The work was hard and had to be carried out under the most primitive circumstances. His hours were long, from early in the morning until midnight or later, with only some Sundays free. He had to sleep in the same bedroom with his employer's older sons. The pharmicist's income was small and his family large, and there was seldom enough to eat. Ibsen's own income was completely inadequate, and he soon could no longer maintain his elegant surface appearance, although it is reported that he did his best to do so, often going without underclothing in order to spend what little he had on the clothes that could be seen. For his first years in Grimstad he had virtually no friends, and although he occasionally participated in social activities with acquaintances, there was no question of his being accepted by the town's small but well-insulated aristocracy. What little free time he had was largely spent in solitary walks, painting the local scenery, reading, and early efforts at writing; at some point, exactly when is not known, he began to study the necessary material to enable him to pass a matriculation examination for the University in Christiania (now Oslo), depriving himself of sleep in order to do so. In October 1846, when he was eighteen, he had an illegitimate son by one of the pharmicist's maids, a woman ten years older than himself. Since Ibsen had to help support the child until he reached the age of fourteen, this event made his financial circumstances even worse, and, although the mother went home to have her child, the event also obviously did nothing to improve Ibsen's esteem in the eyes of the "better" families of the town.

During the following year, however, Ibsen's circumstances improved in several important ways. The pharmicist for whom he worked was forced by debts to sell his business, and it soon passed into the hands of one of his assistants, who, backed by his wealthy family, moved it to better quarters, where Ibsen shared a comfortable room with his employer. Ibsen had by this time passed the necessary exams to qualify as a full-fledged assistant, and so he received an increase in salary, some of which he spent for tutoring from two local theological students and for other lessons as his efforts to qualify for the University became more serious. Eating his midday dinner with the family of his new employer gave him a slight entry into a higher—and better educated—social circle. He made the acquaintance, by this means, of Georgiana Crawfurd, an elderly Scottish woman who had immigrated to Grimstad about twenty years before and who had a large private library, from which she frequently loaned Ibsen books by important writers—most likely, the early eighteenth-century Dano-Norwegian poet and comic dramatist Ludvig Holberg, the early nineteenth-century Norwegian poets Henrik Wergeland and J. L. Welhaven, the early nineteenth-century Danish poet-dramatist Adam Oehlenschläger, and perhaps Søren Kierkegaard, a copy of whose *Either-Or* she is said to have owned. It has been speculated that she also must have introduced Ibsen to the greatest writer in her original language, William Shakespeare, but there is no evidence for this, and it seems unlikely that she would have been able to accommodate Ibsen, who knew no English, with a Danish or German translation of Shakespeare. Most important of all, Ibsen also in 1847 finally found some real friends in Grimstad. The first of these was Christopher Due, a year older than Ibsen and a clerk at the local customs house. Due soon introduced him to a new arrival in town of the same age, Ole Carelius Schulerud, son of the new senior customs official. Schulerud was an especially impressive figure, since he had already qualified for the University and had therefore earned the right to call himself "Student Schulerud."

Ibsen, Due, and Schulerud spent as much time as possible together, usually at night in Ibsen's quarters, equipped, when they could afford it (for all three of them were poor), with food and drink. They read literature together, including the poems Ibsen was now writing in greater abundance, and discussed all the latest ideas. Ibsen dominated these sessions, reading aloud his lampoons of local figures, expressing the "bitter ill will" he bore toward what he called "empty brains with full purses,"[3] and, based on his avid reading of Voltaire, haranguing his friends with his attacks on all the conventional ideas about religion, society, and politics then current in Grimstad and throughout Norway. As his reputation for being an atheist and a republican grew—to scandalize the local aristocracy (and, no doubt, most of the rest of the community)—more and more of the young people of the town joined the circle formed by the three friends. In 1848, a new focus absorbed the group as the February Revolution in France shook Europe and inspired further uprisings in Italy, Austria-Hungary, Germany, and even closer to home in Denmark, where the German-speaking duchies of Slesvig and Holstein sought to free themselves from rule by the Danish king.

Ibsen responded to the revolutions of 1848 with enormous enthusiasm. Under their influence, according to Due (42), Ibsen "gradually became a full-blooded Republican. With him as the animating force social gatherings of our friends were put together on various occasions, at which there was much merriment and speeches were given, especially on the topic of the ideals of republicanism. We arranged, for example, after the French pattern, a so-called 'Reform Banquet,' at which Ibsen gave a fire-breathing speech *against* all emperors and kings, those monsters of society, and *for* republicanism, the 'only possible' form of government." Ibsen's 1875 Preface and Due's reminiscences from 1909 suggest that there was a certain amount of humor and late-adolescent high spirits in Ibsen's anti-establishment provocations, but they were no doubt, at bottom, deeply felt. 1847 and 1848 were clearly much better years for Ibsen than those that had preceded them, especially because of the close friendships he had won and his new prominence among the local youth, but he continued to be poor, overworked, and unwelcome in the best social circles of Grimstad, and his earlier years there undoubtedly left deep wounds that would take a long time to heal—if they ever entirely did.

Ibsen's continued—and deep-seated—commitment to his anti-establishment and revolutionary ideas is amply indicated by his activities in 1850-51, after he had arrived in Christiania and while the reaction to the uprisings of 1848 pursued its steady course throughout the continent. In May 1850, a month after he arrived in town, he participated in a demonstration and was one of the signers of a petition to protest the deportation from Norway of Harro Harring, a Slesvig German. Having "fought for both the Greeks in their war of liberation against the Turks, and the Poles in their rebellion against Russia," Harring "had come to Norway in 1849 to seek refuge in his old age," but had outraged the authorities by editing a radical newspaper and by publishing a play that was deemed to have "outstepped the limits of the freedom of the press" (quotations from Meyer, 59). In 1851, Ibsen got involved with several radical periodicals. For one of them, founded by a friend, he wrote theater and literary reviews and was soon contributing political pieces highly critical of the activities of the Storting (the Norwegian Parliament), culminating them with a verse burlesque of Bellini's *Norma*, then popular in Christiania, which he called *Norma, or a Politician's Love* and which lampooned the leading figures in the Storting. He also became involved, through another friend, in writing for the official newspaper of the Workers' Union, which had been started a couple of years earlier by Marcus Thrane, the leading Norwegian radical of the era, in conjunction with his founding the union, Norway's first. In July 1851, the police raided the newspaper office and arrested Thrane and Ibsen's friend, both of whom spent three years in prison awaiting trial before serving four-year terms. Ibsen himself was spared a similar fate by the quick thinking of the printer, who strewed all available manuscripts, including some by Ibsen, on the floor, leading the police to believe that they were merely scrap paper. The treatment of Thrane, however, effectively destroyed his movement.

ii. Composition

While still in Grimstad and absorbed in the revolutions of 1848, Ibsen, by a fortunate coincidence, also tackled the syllabus of required texts for the Latin portion of his matriculation exam, reading, with the aid of his Latin tutor, Cicero's orations against Catiline and Sallust's narrative account of Catiline's conspiracy. He read these from a perspective formed by the political events of 1848 and his own financial and social circumstances, and he developed a completely different view of Catiline from the one Sallust and Cicero had sought to convey; their main impact on him seems to have been a negative reaction inspired by their ferocity. More important, in the process he also discovered his first subject for a drama. His introduction to Catiline probably came late in the year, for during the first three months of 1849 he wrote the play with remarkable speed—working on it, as he states in his Preface, in the middle of the night after a long day's work, in hours stolen from the time he had set aside to prepare for his matriculation exam (and, of course, from sleep, which he was apparently able to do without to a truly remarkable degree). The manuscript, now in the University of Oslo Library, contains two dates: "1849" on the title page and "25/2—49—" at the end of the second act; there was probably a date at the end of the third act as well, but the final leaf of the manuscript is missing.[4] He completed the play, apparently, shortly before his twenty-first birthday.

The 1849 manuscript of *Catiline* consists of two quarto-sized exercise books, originally of sixteen leaves each. The first of these has a number of smaller pieces of paper laid or pasted in. The final leaf of the second has been cut out, and in its place twelve additional leaves have been sewn in; this addition originally consisted of thirteen leaves, but the last of these has also been cut out. The last page of the first exercise book contains a scene-by-scene synopsis-outline of Act One and the first scene of Act Two, and the preceding page contains a similar synopsis-outline for the three scenes of Act Two; in all probability there was also a synopsis-outline for Act Three on one of the missing leaves of the second exercise book. There are many corrections in the text, which Ibsen seems to have made as he wrote, and signs of a later slight revision consisting of a few changes in what is most likely a different hand and occasional numbers to indicate revised word order, as whoever made the changes apparently sought to devise a more "poetic" language, primarily by placing adjectives after the nouns they modify.[5] The state of the manuscript clearly indicates Ibsen's working methods and the speed with which he composed.

The beginning of the manuscript suggests some fumbling on Ibsen's part in getting started. The play originally opened with the entrance of the Allobrogian ambassadors, but Ibsen quickly decided to add the monologue by Catiline that now precedes it. After writing a good part of the second scene, he crossed it out and added a new version on a separate sheet of paper; the actual changes in the dialogue are few, but many of the speeches are redistributed, with the result that Lentulus assumes slightly more prominence and Cethegus comes into existence, being assigned the "bohemian" speeches originally given to Statilius, who in the revision becomes more sober and much less prominent. It must have been about here that Ibsen wrote his first synopsis-outline, for its accounts of the first two scenes are brief and generally correspond to the scenes as written, while its accounts of scenes three and five still designate Furia by her original name of Fulvia (which Ibsen changed shortly after he wrote the first speech-heading for her), and its account of scene three differs from the scene itself in a way that suggests that Ibsen had possibly not yet thought of Catiline's crime against Furia's sister and Furia's revenge plot.[6] After completing the third scene, Ibsen seems to have hit his stride, for there are no further revisions of any significant length (except for a new version of the song in the second scene of Act Two and, as I discuss below, the addition of Lentulus' final speech in Act Three). The synopsis-outline for Act Two, moreover, contains a new summary of its opening scene, one far more like the scene as Ibsen wrote it, and the composition of Act Two as a whole deviates from the synopsis-outline only on very minor points (such as associating Cethegus rather than Lentulus with the idea of enlisting the support of the Allobroges).[7]

The chief signs of the speed with which Ibsen composed are the revisions in the play's rhyming passages and the punctuation at the end of individual lines. The revisions in the rhyming passages invariably affect the line ending with the *first* of the two rhyming words. It seems clear that as Ibsen got to the second rhyming word (usually two lines later in the frequent abab pattern of the rhyming passages of the first two acts) and found what he wanted to write he quickly went back and changed a word or phrase to accommodate the new rhyme, and it is this evidence that prompts me to speculate that most of the other changes in words and phrases were also made, as it were, on the fly. The punctuation at the end of the lines provides even better evidence of haste. The internal punctuation is fairly normal (though Ibsen often omitted commas and sometimes forgot to follow his usual practice of placing exclamation points after the text's abundant "Ha"s and names used vocatively), but the punctuation ending lines has an entirely different character. A few of the lines end with the commas, semicolons, periods, question marks, and exclamation points that one would expect to find, but the vast majority of them end either with dashes or no punctuation at all. Setting aside the lines that require no end punctuation, it looks as if, in the heat of composition, Ibsen used no punctuation when a comma or period was called for and—as if he could not take the time to decide—a dash when a semicolon, question mark, exclamation point, or even an actual dash was needed. Given the obvious speed with which he wrote, it is clear that Ibsen already possessed a well-developed facility for composing in meter; it is also astonishing that the play's metrical flaws are not even more extensive.

Ibsen shared the play with Due and Schulerud as he wrote it, reading aloud to them on various evenings what he had composed since last seeing them (Due, 46). They were extremely enthusiastic, and on Due devolved the "honor," as he calls it (47), of making a fair copy so that the play could be submitted to the theater in Christiania and then published. Due's fair copy, from which the first version of *Catiline* was eventually printed, no longer exists, but some sense of its nature can be determined by comparing the manuscript with the printed version.

The single largest discrepancy between the two involves Lentulus's exit speech in Act Three, which is not in the manuscript. It seems clear that, after completing the manuscript as we now have it, Ibsen did some further work on the role of Lentulus, which had already been undergoing evolution. In Act Two, when Catiline enters to accept the leadership of the conspiracy despite his earlier refusal, Lentulus, who has just proposed himself for the vacant post, speaks an aside in which he curses in anger and frustration. In the manuscript, however, he is evidently included in the "ALL" who agree to follow Catiline, even though a bit later, in a speech that Catiline apparently cannot hear, Lentulus disassociates himself from Catiline's noble motives. By Act Three of the manuscript in its first form, Lentulus has decided to hire two Gladiators to murder Catiline so that he can assume the post that was once almost his. The Gladiators flee and Catiline disarms Lentulus but then, despite his treachery, allows him the opportunity to try to save himself from the destruction now facing the conspirators. Lentulus, according to the original stage direction, is "moved" by this, but one of the late manuscript revisions written in a different hand (which is assumed to be Due's) changes "moved" to "with dissimulation." The printed version of the play has two further changes in Lentulus' role: the addition of "except Lentulus" to the "ALL" that serves as the heading for the speech of Act Two in which the conspirators agree to follow Catiline and—as I have already indicated—the addition of Lentulus' final speech, in which the serpent that Catiline would haughtily trample in the dust insists that he has not yet lost his sting and decides to help the Roman army find Catiline's camp more easily than it otherwise might.

If these two additions, especially the second, were actually made in Due's fair copy, then Ibsen obviously participated in the making of it, and we can attribute to him with some assurance certain other discrepancies between the manuscript and the printed version that could well be the result of deliberate changes by him.[8] On the other hand, Lentulus' final speech may have been written down on a separate piece of paper that has subsequently become separated from the manuscript. This possibility is strongly supported by the majority of the discrepancies, which indicate that if Ibsen did look at Due's fair copy, he did so with a very careless eye.[9]

These other discrepancies are of several kinds. The printed version changes Ibsen's spelling by uniformly capitalizing personal pronouns and "collective" pronouns like "everything" (and spacing them after exclamation points so that they seem to be introducing new sentences where they do not in the manuscript) and by modernizing some of Ibsen's by then antiquated orthographical usages. On the other hand, it "corrects" his reformed renderings of certain verbal forms by using apostrophes to indicate omitted syllables. It frequently adjusts the internal punctuation of his lines, making it conform to standard practice in Scandinavia at the time by adding commas and semicolons to his dashes and dashes to some of his commas and semicolons. It considerably increases the number of dashes in the text, most usually by an odd practice (consistent in the first two acts but less so in the third) whereby in lines divided between two speakers the speech of the first ends with two dashes (and no other end punctuation) and that of the second begins with two dashes (followed by a capital letter).

More serious discrepancies consist of the omission of words and stage directions, the failure to incorporate some of the changes in the manuscript, the creation of numerous metrically defective lines through the addition or omission of words and syllables or the mangling of word order, and a number of changes that make no sense (unless they constitute another attempt to make the language more "poetic"), such as having Catiline, in speaking of himself, mention "his name" rather than "my name" and telling himself that this day is "the last" rather than "your last" (a possible confusion, in Norwegian, of "*den*" for "*din*"). Furthermore, the punctuation at the end of the lines in the printed version is a real hash. Someone has made a feeble effort to provide end punctuation without having much sense of what Ibsen seemed to have had in mind or, indeed, without any very systematic sense of punctuation itself. Many of the dashes have been left alone, others have had punctuation added to them, others have been replaced by genuine (but not always appropriate) punctuation. Sometimes lines end with commas or semicolons while the succeeding lines begin with capital letters. Sometimes, in a similar kind of carelessness, initial capital letters have been changed to lower case even though the dashes ending the preceding lines remain unaltered. All in all, as a result, it is often impossible to reconstruct Ibsen's sentences from the printed version.

The first few discrepancies I have mentioned are probably the work of the printers, who may also, of course, be responsible for some of the more serious discrepancies. But on the whole the evidence suggests that Due did a pretty bad job, that his copy was not very "fair" after all, and that Ibsen, for whatever reasons, did not give it the kind of attention it needed.

iii. Publication and Reception of the 1850 Version

This was, however, the copy that Schulerud took with him when he left Grimstad for Christiania around the first of September 1849, in part to market *Catiline* so that the three friends could begin to make their fortune. By this time, for reasons that have never been satisfactorily explained, the play was attributed to one Brynjolf Bjarme, a pseudonym that Ibsen used pretty consistently for his signed published and performed work until June 1851. Ibsen and his friends expected immediate success with Schulerud's enterprise, and, in his impatience and frustration at not soon hearing that *Catiline* had been accepted by the Christiania Theater, Ibsen sent his friend a harsh and accusing letter, which we know about only from his next letter to Schulerud, in which, in a calmer state, he apologized and asked that his earlier letter be destroyed. Ibsen's new frame of mind may very well have resulted from a signal success that seemed to bode well for the fate of *Catiline*: Due had sent one of Ibsen's poems, "In Autumn," to the *Christiania-Post* (for which he served as local correspondent), and the poem appeared in that paper on September 28, the first composition by Ibsen to be published. This was, however, no more than a false spring; things dragged on in Christiania until December, when the Theater, courteously but firmly, rejected the play. Schulerud assured Ibsen, in reporting this outcome to him, that it was probably for the best, that they would be better off by selling publishing rights for the play to the highest bidder, and in his response (on January 5, 1850) Ibsen, despite referring to what had happened as "*Catiline*'s death sentence," agreed with his friend's judgment and urged him to act accordingly. Later in this letter Ibsen adds, "I think it is necessary to provide *Catiline* with some introductory remarks, and I therefore ask you to copy and attach the following"

FOREWORD

This play was originally intended for the stage, but the theater management did not find it suitable for this purpose. Although the author has grounds to suppose that the main causes of the rejection of the play do not stem from any internal defects in it, it is nonetheless not without a very natural anxiety that he presents his work to the public, from whom however he expects the forbearing judgment that a beginner's first appearance can, in all fairness, lay claim to.

But this Foreword was not included when the play was printed. Ibsen ends the letter, sadly, with a plea to his friend (prefaced with "N. B.") not to let any "printing errors sneak in"—a plea made ironic by the state of the text that Schulerud had taken with him.[10]

Schulerud found no bidders for *Catiline*, high or low, among the publishers in Christiania and had to arrange with one of them, P. F. Steensballe, to print it for a fee, which Schulerud paid from a small inheritance of his own, partly out of devotion to his friend and partly on the assumption that he would be amply rewarded from the profits of this venture and of similar ones in the years to come, as he continued to act as Ibsen's literary agent. Thus *Catiline* appeared in Steensballe's bookstore in Christiania on April 12, 1850, the same day that Ibsen, having decided to go to Christiania to finish studying for his matriculation exams, left Grimstad on his way to Skien for a last visit with his family before heading on to the capital.[11] *Catiline* was the first Norwegian play to have been published in seven years and, when it appeared, the best Norwegian play ever to have been published. Given the existing conditions for reviewing books in 1850 Christiania (the number of possible outlets, the tendencies of the reviewers, and the prevailing taste in literary matters) as well as its own ultimate merits, *Catiline* came close to arousing the kind of attention it should have. It was still not accepted for production in the theater, however, and the book-purchasing public was much less responsive than it might have been.

The eagerness with which at least a certain informed portion of the Christiania public was ready to welcome a literary work by a new author is dramatically indicated by the appearance of the first review of the play on the day after it was published. This review, a favorable one, appeared in the Student Association's hand-written newspaper and was produced by its editor, a widely read and well-informed critic named Paul Botten Hansen, who was twenty-five or twenty-six years old and was later to become one of Ibsen's closest friends. Botten Hansen begins by lamenting the absence of any published Norwegian plays for the preceding seven years and even more so the appearance, during the same time period, of numerous poem-collections with their all-too-familiar clichés. "The more seldom it thus is," he continues,

> that there is published in this country a literary work that seeks to win a foothold not by sounding the false strings of the conditions of the times and the taste of the day but only through its poetic essence, the more gratifying it has to be to see a work like *Catiline*, whose author employs no artifices whatever to ingratiate himself with the public but through true and sound poetry seeks to win a few—not easily losable—friends. It is gratifying to discover a Norwegian author who, given his talent for drama, *ought to* win recognition on the stage but perhaps *will not*, because he visibly proclaims a certain Shakespearean power

and seriousness that no audience as a whole can understand and sympathize with.

He speculates that the play will have difficulty winning recognition because its author has neglected to concern himself with "national material" (a reference to the then fashionable "National Romanticism," which focused on Norwegian topics, scenery, and life and glorified Norway's mighty but distant past) or to choose a subject "suited to our time." But he dismisses the first objection by mocking National Romanticism, and he dismisses the second by alluding to authors like Milton, Dante, and Goethe and by pointing out how Roman history—"equally as well in *Catiline* as in Shakespeare's *Coriolanus*"—constantly displays important human characteristics of the sort that precipitated the French Revolution, that remain current, and that "will be interpreted and put into practice in various ways in life's shifting forms until the Republican, on tyranny's and perhaps also the world's Last Day, will sing his hymn of triumph over the last despot's grave."

That Ibsen was not tempted to make Cicero a central figure—as most dramatists would have and as Crébillon certainly did in writing his *Catiline*—Botten Hansen takes as a sign of considerable "scenic-poetic ability." He praises the author for

> not letting Cicero appear among the characters but letting us merely sense that he is involved in the action without our being tempted to ask for him. It is not fortune and Cicero that topple Catiline before our eyes but the whole course of his life. In his deeply divided, richly gifted soul ferment two contending forces, the good and the evil; the former must gradually go under in a visible struggle with the latter, and the tragic fall becomes a tragic consequence of this. In order to give this struggle lucidity the author has—with considerable success—allowed the representative of evil, the Vestal Furia, to stand in opposition to Catiline's kind wife, Aurelia, who always calls the better but foundering soul-forces back to life in his bosom.

Botten Hansen then briefly describes the action, pausing to admire both "the successfully rendered scene of horror" in which Furia unwittingly gets Catiline to swear vengeance against himself and the use of the supernatural in Act Three, especially the appearance of Sulla's ghost and, in part, the events of the conclusion. He adds, however, that Catiline and Aurelia "do not die immediately, but a reconciliation takes place, which is why the author, quite properly, has not called his play a tragedy but a drama. Although the final speeches, as well as, particularly, the entire conclusion of the play, are very poetically beautiful, I nonetheless think that they delay too much the death of the mortally wounded pair." He also feels that Shakespeare would have done much more with the minor characters by making them ridiculous, thereby giving the play as a whole more life. But, he concludes, "in a play that demonstrates so much talent, I will not give undue emphasis to pettinesses; I will, however, call attention to the frequent transitions to alexandrines from the iambic pentameter that is the verse-form used almost entirely throughout. On the whole the author is not strong in his metrics."[12]

The Student Association's hand-written newspaper was normally available only to members—Koht (I, 57) reports that Botten Hansen's account was read aloud to them at an evening meeting on the day it appeared—and so the first genuinely public review of *Catiline* came out a little over a month later, on May 16, in the *Christiania-Post*. This review, a leading article on the newspaper's first page, was unsigned, but its author has been identified as F. L. Vibe, a classical philologist. Vibe begins by focusing on the Catiline of history, as presented by Sallust, a figure "more likely to play the role of the villain in a drama than that of the hero." He shows some impatience with Ibsen's treating the historical material "with the most unrestricted freedom": "The critic is never fond of this divergence from history, the prominent events of which are grounded in an inner necessity and always contain their own poetry, which one must be extremely cautious in thrusting aside." Nonetheless, he seems to accept the author's decision to "go his own way" in making Catiline the hero, adding that he "may lay claim to having his work considered in and of itself without regard to the historical facts." Furthermore, "although Catiline is the figure on whom our interest is focused, the author has indeed taken care not to let him be encircled by any saint's halo. Catiline is infected with the corruption of the times, has lived a dissolute youth, and even makes use of bribes in order to obtain the consulship, but with all this he is a tragic hero, for he despises the wretchedness of the times, he yearns to see Rome strong and feels within himself the urge for something higher, the urge to raise Rome from its degradation, but obstacles tower up before him, he struggles without being able to overcome them, and he must fall."

Vibe then provides a fairly detailed summary of the action, pausing to call the scene of Act One in which Aurelia urges Catiline to leave Rome with her "one of the most beautiful in the entire drama": "The gentle, feminine, almost Nordic Aurelia, who sticks by Catiline with her whole soul, emerges sharply depicted alongside the dark man, who stands there inconsolable about his situation, brooding on his fateful plans; melancholy and gentleness, light and gloom are here splendidly set in opposition to one another." He is shrewd on Furia, noticing what Ibsen seems to have intended but did not fully carry off ("she must follow Catiline everywhere, partly because she cannot live without seeing him and partly as his goddess of revenge") and capturing her ambivalence in pursuing her goal: "It is no finely conceived plan by Furia . . . through which she can bring about Catiline's fall and satisfy her desire for revenge, no, here [when, in Act Two, she persuades Catiline to participate in the conspiracy] her hysterical enthusiasm runs away with her, she sees herself in this moment as really leading Catiline to greatness, and it is only later that her second thoughts awaken and she plans to topple him."

Vibe does not, however, like the ending of the play:

> When the author, in order rightly to evoke a tragic effect, lets Furia seduce Catiline into killing Aurelia, our interest in Catiline decreases considerably, and he is clearly performing a pointless atrocity. It makes an extremely unpleasant impression to imagine Aurelia bloodily dragging herself forth in order to die with Catiline. Could she not without this have been by his side like a good angel, consoling him in his hour of death? The author will perhaps say that this is necessary for conveying the triumph of the evil genius—Furia—over the good Aurelia, but her triumph is complete enough when she manages to break Aurelia's heart and to thrust the dagger into Catiline's, and besides it is nonetheless, finally, the good who triumph. Something the author cannot manage without allowing Aurelia to continue living a moment in order to direct Catiline to something higher.

And he adds: "If the author was that determined to regard her life as so connected with Catiline's that she necessarily had to die with him, he should likewise have let Furia die, for she too has fulfilled her call, but in that case there would have been a catastrophe as in *Love without Stockings*," a reference to a 1772 play by the Norwegian Johan Herman Wessel that burlesques neoclassical tragedy and was still much esteemed in mid-nineteenth-century Scandinavia. Another thing Vibe dislikes "is the ghost of Sulla, a garrulous creature who appears in Act Three and in a veiled manner prophecies Catiline's future but who is nonetheless quite superfluous. Ghosts should not without overwhelming necessity be brought forth on the stage."

In his three concluding paragraphs, Vibe turns to more general considerations, with mixed but on the whole positive results. He begins with praise of the highest sort: "The author has an unusual ability to rise to tragic height and power, he has an unusual ability to allow the passions to emerge in their full strength, and his language is of a purity such as we seldom encounter. On the other hand," he continues, "his flaw is an occasional conspicuous hysterical pathos, in which the heroes 'strike attitudes and declaim.' Brynjolf Bjarme would benefit from familiarizing himself with *Love without Stockings*. In particular, there is a scene that strongly reminds one of the oath with the yellow peas, in which Furia exhorts Catiline to swear eternal hatred toward her enemy." He then quotes a lengthy passage from this scene, one with the usual abundance of "Ha"s, and remarks: "A particular manifestation of this pathos are these 'Ha's, which incessantly come thumping along." He finds the play's verses "beautiful and melodious," adding, "the only thing I have to observe is that the rhymed verses with which the author varies the usual meter ought to have been used more sparingly. Where Catiline tells his dream, they are effective, since this forms a kind of rounded whole, but it is open to question as to whether they do not usually confuse and weaken the impression rather than strengthen it." And he concludes: "With all this one nonetheless sets *Catiline* aside with satisfaction, for there is manifested in it an unmistakable talent, and with a young author there must necessarily be something to trim away. The play is scarcely suitable for performance; for that the changes in setting, especially in Act One, are much too frequent. As a deplorable sign of the times, it must be noted that the author has not been able to find a publisher;

it would be too bad if he has had to suffer a loss in order to get his book into print."[13]

An even longer review of *Catiline*, signed only with the initial "A," appeared in *Morgenbladet* on June 5. A. states that the work under consideration "must make a claim on our attention in a time likes ours that is on the whole so impoverished in works of its kind," adding that it has already "aroused a not inconsiderable sensation in our literary world, to which its pseudonymity has contributed its share." He then wittily explains why the third of Christiania's three major newspapers, *Dagbladet*, had not as yet reviewed the play (which, by the way, it never did): "That it hitherto has not been the object of public criticism (with the exception, if we are not mistaken, of a short review in the *Christiania-Post*) may well be owing to *Dagbladet*'s abundant bustling in the realm of politics and the relative lack of critical journals." Pointing out that considerations of space prevent his exceeding the bounds of a newspaper review, he assures his readership that they can expect a more comprehensive criticism of the play in Lange's *Norsk Tidsskrift*. He turns to the play itself by pontificating on the nature of drama and then indicating how the author has tried to meet the demands of the form by personifying the good and evil forces in his hero's soul through Aurelia and Furia. "The over-all idea of the play," he adds, "emerges in general with clarity but most readily and comprehensibly in the conclusion of Act Three through the following sections in the same meter: Catiline's dream, the scene between Aurelia and Furia (the conflict), and the play's concluding scene (the reconciliation)." He then provides the most thorough summary of the action so far in these reviews, pausing after a detailed account of Catiline's first scene with Furia to note that "Catiline's own oath and Furia's desire for revenge are now the impelling elements in the play. By them he is led forth to his criminal plans, which nonetheless always retain an elevated touch and noble motives."

A.'s explicit evaluations are at first quite positive. He notes the play's "large divergences from the historical facts as we during our schooling read about them in Sallustius," but he adds that the author is not to be absolutely censured for this:

> Not to mention the customary *licentia poetica*, to the use of which
> he like any other writer is justified, it has to be quite clear to the

more mature reader of Sallust that his book, so excellent in terms of its representation, was written under the influence of party-politics, and Catiline may very well have been a hero and have had honest intentions with regard to his fatherland, even if Sallust represents him as a Marcus Thrane. One needs only to imagine how differently Catiline would have been judged if his undertaking had succeeded!

A. likes the play's design, particularly approving the decision of the author—unlike Crébillon—to dispense with Cicero and the Senate: "he has thereby avoided great dramatic difficulties. Cicero outside the Senate is not Cicero, and Cicero in the Senate is undramatic."

At this point, however, A.'s judgments grow more negative:

> It is to be wished that the author had shown the same discretion in his characterizations. But these are to a high degree over-wrought. Furia—it is characteristic, to be sure, that he changes the name Fulvia from Sallust into Furia—is throughout quite impossible and, we could perhaps also add, unesthetic. Catiline's love for both Aurelia and Furia is likewise either an impossibility or an unesthetic banality. With respect to the play's minor characters we could, I think, have desired a stronger and more definite accentuation of the bad morality that then ruled in Rome, which perhaps would have placed Catiline's character in an even stronger light. The naiveté and simplicity of the Allobrogian ambassadors are quite graphically portrayed.

"The speeches," he continues, "are not lacking in poetic strength; in particular this is the case with those that have been placed in Aurelia's mouth, on whose character the author seems to have lingered with love. At the same time, the beginner betrays himself in a far too strong inclination for pathos." A. then devotes several paragraphs to the play's flaws in language, noting the incessant "Ha!"s, objecting to and illustrating occasional insufficient nobility in the diction, jarring and defective versification, the absence of initial unstressed syllables so that the lines in question become trochaic, and, in terms of the meter, words accented on the wrong syllable. He notes the frequent shifts into rhymed passages and describes carefully the meter of the rhymed passages in Act Three—which he rather likes, except that he finds that the rhymes in these passages are not always correct.

But A. also concludes on a generally positive note:

> In setting forth these weaknesses, however, we have not intended to have pronounced an over-all unfavorable judgment of the work. It betrays the beginner, but with that a beginner with uncommon talent, and the flaws of which we have complained are all of the sort that the ambitious poet with properly employed self-criticism can liberate himself from. We dare assure that anyone who usually finds pleasure in poetic literature will read through this writing not without interest and therefore highly recommend it, as we likewise encourage the author to continue the path on which he has stepped and next time, if possible, to try his strength in a more worthwhile sphere, namely the history of our fatherland.

The more comprehensive review promised by A. appeared in October in *Norsk Tidsskrift*, the most important Norwegian literary journal of the time (Haugholt, 74, says it was the only one). It was written by another classical philologist, Carl Müller, who manifests his profession in a number of Latin tags (from Cicero's orations against Catiline and elsewhere), other bits of pedantry, and—perhaps—the sarcasm and general tone of superiority with which he discusses the play. He begins with a long paragraph in which he laments the lot of the reviewer assigned to discuss a young author's work ("which as a rule must have a good deal to censure and find fault with"), hopes that the attention the play has already aroused will have led to the formation of a general opinion so that his own contribution may be regarded as an expression of it ("furnished primarily for the author's own use"), and claims that he "supposes Brynjolf Bjarme to be already worth the attention of the public and to be an author about whom one can entertain good expectations."

He then turns to the subject that takes up four of his six and a half pages (as the review is printed in Haugholt's article), the character of the play's hero. The name Catiline, he informs us, has, like Alexander,

Caesar, and others, become a concept, the expression of a certain structure of ideas and character traits. Thus the "large words" of Ibsen's concluding notes, which seek indulgence for allowing historical names to be associated with unhistorical actions and characteristics, gave him some pause:

> I expected, to be sure, that the poet, whose call, after all, is to reconcile us with life, would provide a less ignoble motive where history indicates sheer wickedness, that he would show us some of the great qualities that according to contemporary judgment perished in him, in short, that he would touch up his painting with a noble characteristic or two in order to light up its lamentable gloom; nevertheless I expected, all things considered, to recognize Catiline, and was better prepared to shudder at him as evil than to pity him as characterless and weak.

Yet this is the "remodeling" that the author has thought it necessary to produce in order to use Catiline as his hero, and from it stem "major flaws in the progress of the drama as a whole."

Müller then provides a detailed survey of the play's action, focusing on the behavior of Catiline, in which he relentlessly, and with considerable sarcasm, delineates what he takes to be Catiline's vacillations, inconsistencies, and general lack of any clear intentions or real substance. He is on reasonable ground when he notes that because of the impact on him of Aurelia and Furia Catiline is a character who neither makes decisions nor acts on his own volition, but most of the vacillations and inconsistencies Müller delineates are so petty, exaggerated, or distorted that he seems incapable of imagining a character with a divided soul or—worse—determined to give this character as savagely critical a treatment as he can. In any event, he finds Lentulus, Cethegus, and the other conspirators superior to Catiline, because they, at least, know from the beginning what they want. He also finds the hero unsuitable for tragedy since "the tragic heroes of the ancient stage are, by the incontestable power of fate, driven forth on their courses until the measure is full." "It is not obvious," he sums up, "why the author has preferred to deprive him of hues rather than allow him to appear with those he had; what from history could and ought to have been used for the drama has in this manner entirely vanished, and if the author did not believe he could use any of it, then he ought not to have used the name." Müller concludes this part of his discussion by finding one other element in the play as poorly motivated as the actions of its hero: "the scene in which the ghost of Sulla appears; the author is surely aware of the rule that one ought not to conjure up ghosts, *nisi dignus vindice nodus.*"

Müller likes the characterizations of Furia and Aurelia, for these two also know what they want—although, he adds, this is not really true of Furia in her first scene—and because of this he also finds several of the scenes in which they appear "successful." He also believes that "with regard to the language and the over-all poetic form" he is able "to congratulate the author." He then, however, provides a lengthy list of flaws in these areas. Ibsen is "often addicted to singing in grandiloquent [*"hastemte"*] notes, and the word 'Ha' itself occurs in individual speeches in much too superfluous a quantity." In the scene of Furia's urging Catiline to swear vengeance, he feels, "the cothurnus totters to a high degree under both of them." "The frequent rhyming that often commences and is again abandoned without apparent reason" he could "in most places wish away," and he adds that "now and then the shape of the verses emerges much too sharply because the unrhymed verses also often end alternately on one- and two-syllable words, whereby the whole thing becomes a sort of collection of *disticha.*" He cites several lines that cannot be scanned, notes that both "Proserpina" and "Icarus" are accented on the wrong syllables, and concludes with some samples of the play's "*incuriae*" ("carelessnesses"), such as Furia's asking Catiline if he lacks "the strength and courage / to fight against what you have called your fate?": "Here Furia, who is not speaking ironically, seems to demand too much."

Nevertheless, Müller also ends with the customary positive concluding paragraph, although his is less positive than the others':

> The author has then, in the reviewer's opinion, with this his first appearance presented something that to be sure is not fully satisfying but nonetheless pleases in some particulars and, what is most important, gives one hope that he, when in time he manages to succeed, will be capable of presenting something closer to perfection. No one will be able to deny that he has

chosen for himself a difficult subject; and that he, even if he has been cautious where it concerns Catiline's character, has been bold where it concerns Furia. That he has not succumbed completely may be for him a spur for seeking to develop himself further.[14]

Fortunately for Ibsen's feelings, the editor of *Norsk Tidsskrift*, M. J. Monrad, a professor of philosophy at the university and at the time Norway's most authoritative voice in literary matters, added to Müller's piece a postscript almost one third as long as the review itself. Monrad wants to make it clear that, given the policy of anonymity for reviews, this one was not written by him, and he takes issue with its judgments, conveying in the process a much better understanding than Müller of the play's design and dramaturgy. Monrad finds that— what for him is the most crucial quality of a literary work—"the central idea of the poem is both clear and beautiful," even if

the execution in some of its particulars, truly enough, suffers from many imperfections, carelessness in versification, broad and rhetorical pomp in expression, and so forth—on the whole, signs of an unpracticed pen. And exactly therefore, I find, Brynjolf Bjarme promises something—in contrast to the poetic rabble, particularly those who begin by writing for the theater and as a rule possess a certain ease and polish in expression and have a few good fancies but are not capable of grasping a single complete or grand idea. It is better that the growth should begin from within, from the idea; where this stirs powerfully, it will certainly at last find its form.

The "beautiful central idea of the poem," according to Monrad, is "the sharply emphasized opposition between the moral, the principles associated with the existing moral forces, and the individual's obscure longing for independence, which, although originating in moral corruption, yea, demonic in its origin, nevertheless in its enthusiasm for freedom, its passion for the bygone, even its opposition to the general corruption in which it has its roots, seeks an association with and an appearance of justification. In order to represent this conflict in its full significance," he continues, "the poet needed a period in which corruption was common and the moral bonds on the whole loosened; for only when depravity is common has the opposition of the individual against the whole that appearance of justification whereby it becomes a respectable force and thus tragic." Since the last years of the Roman Republic formed such a period and the Catilinian conspiracy was in this respect a characteristic event, "the historical basis of the play—although the historical here is only a means and a side-issue—is essentially true." Monrad then notes how, "in the interest of poetic lucidity," the two conflicting principles are "objectified in the half-allegorical women," Aurelia and Furia, adding, significantly, that

> these principles are also essentially internal, subjective; both have their home in Catiline's breast. Hence the vacillating, the contradictions in his actions, hence the violently driven and, as it sometimes seems, unmotivated powerful utterances in both directions—characteristics that on the whole are undoubtedly correct psychologically. Even the rhetorically bombastic language Catiline produces one can to some extent—although it sometimes certainly goes rather far—find suited to the idealistic substance of his character, just as in general a rhetorical tone is genuinely Roman.

Nevertheless, because of the play's seriousness, its length, its formal imperfections, its allegorizing, and its all too well-known subject-matter, Monrad is inclined to agree with the reviewer in doubting that it would succeed on the stage, "even with a sounder and more patient audience than ours."

Given *Dagbladet*'s abundant bustling in the political sphere, *Catiline* received as much attention in the outlets for reviewing available in Christiania as could be desired, and setting aside such things as Müller's denseness or meanness, A.'s preference for works of National Romanticism, the reviewers' conflicting judgments about specific scenes, and—in spite of Monrad—a general failure to perceive exactly what sort of work Ibsen had written, it got on the whole a rather fair and intelligent treatment. Despite this, sales of the book came nowhere near meeting the expectations of Ibsen and his friends. It is generally assumed that about 45 copies were sold within the first year after its publication, a figure that is based on a printing of 250 copies and an inventory a year later of 205 as yet unsold. But 45 may be too high a figure: if, as Meyer speculates (63), it was probably sometime in the summer or autumn of 1850 that Ibsen and Schulerud, in order to be able to buy food, disposed of the copies of *Catiline* that Schulerud had in his keeping, then these copies could not have been included in the inventory of 1851. On the other hand, Arthur Thuesen has speculated, on the basis of the existing evidence and his knowledge of the habits of nineteenth-century publishers, that the original printing probably consisted of more than the 250 copies that have been reported.[15] In any event, even at the highest possible estimate, not many copies were sold, and at 48 shillings each, or 1.60 Norwegian kroner (Thuesen, 13; this would be about $0.24 at today's rate of exchange), the proceeds would not have kept Ibsen, who was otherwise unemployed, for very long. Nor, given this selling-price, is it likely that it was the book's cost that prevented it from finding favor with the public.

According to Thuesen (10–14), despite the prevailing idea that the bulk of the first edition of *Catiline* was destroyed, copies of it continued to be available and were sold through bookstores in both Christiania and Copenhagen (including the one Ibsen requested for himself in 1874) right up to the appearance of the second edition in 1875, and on February 17 of that year, shortly before they were disposed of as waste paper, fifty-five copies of Steensballe's original printing still remained unsold. Thuesen claims (11) to have himself seen 42 copies of the first edition and speculates from this that at the time he was writing (1922) 70–80—perhaps even 100—still existed. He also speculates that the original price held until 1875; somewhat later, however, as bibliophiles began seeking the book, the selling-price of an uncut copy (which says something about those who actually bought *Catiline*) rose sharply, reaching 5 kroner at the turn-of-the-century, 20 in 1912, 30 in 1914, 75 in 1915, 100 to 130 in 1917, and 200 in 1918, with a copy being sold in Copenhagen in the spring of 1918 for 400 (13).

Since Thuesen completed his research, the price has continued to soar. I have been informed by a rare- and used-book dealer in Oslo that the current selling-price for a copy of the 1850 *Catiline* would be somewhere between 20,000 and 40,000 kroner (approximately $2,900 to $5,800), with the highest price being commanded by an uncut copy in a special yellow and white wrapper that was used for a small portion of the edition, the next highest price (still very close) for an uncut copy in the standard blue and green wrapper, and so on down, depending on the condition of the book and whether or not the original purchaser had been so foolhardy as to have the book bound or—worse yet—cut the pages so that he could read it. Even today, moreover, copies are not that rare; my informant told me that another Oslo dealer, who has been in the business for fifty years, claims to have sold some 80 copies in his time. In addition to good profits—which Ibsen could certainly have used in his hungry days in Christiania—the rarity of the 1850 *Catiline*, along with its appearing under the pseudonym Brynjolf Bjarme, seems also to have generated an example of what is known as an "urban myth." My informant took pleasure in telling me an amusing anecdote related to my inquiries, that a few years ago the other dealer was approached by someone who had picked up a copy of the first edition of *Catiline* for a few kroner while browsing over the sale books in a trough outside a bookstore in Stockholm, put there by a dealer who obviously had no idea who Brynjolf Bjarme was. Two days previously, although I had not told my informant of this, I had read the same anecdote in Thuesen—only in this case the bookstore was in a city in Germany.

iv. The 1875 Version and its Reception

Ibsen had the manuscript of *Catiline* (and possibly a copy or copies of the printed text) in his possession until he left Norway in April 1864, putting his manuscripts and other papers in the keeping of the Norwegian Theater in Christiania, which he had served as artistic director from 1857 until its failure in 1862. Two and a half years later, in the fall of 1866 and while Ibsen was in Rome, the property he had left behind in Norway, including his manuscripts, was sold at auction for debts he had incurred in Christiania, and Ibsen never got his manuscripts back. In 1901, they were purchased from their then owner by the University of Christiania library, where they still remain (Seip, 207). Ibsen seems to have done nothing with *Catiline* during the fourteen years after its publication that he remained in Norway. In 1853, he revised his second play, *The Burial Mound* (first written in 1850 and produced at the Christiania Theater in the same year), in order to fulfill his contractual obligation to provide a new play annually for the Norwegian Theater at Bergen, where he was employed from 1851 to 1857 as house dramatist and technical director. He did not, however, do this with *Catiline*, and the probable explanation is that he was by then trying to make his way as a dramatist by satisfying the current taste for works of National Romanticism. Nor, and probably for much the same reason, did he produce *Catiline* during his stint as artistic director of the Norwegian Theater in Christiania, although he had no qualms about staging *The Vikings at Helgeland* there in 1858.

After leaving Norway in 1864, Ibsen most likely had no access to any copy of *Catiline* for the next ten years, although it is known that the Scandinavian Club in Rome had a copy of the first edition in its library, and on one of his stays in Rome—which *may* have been the one from 1864 to 1868—he struck out the name Brynjolf Bjarme on the title page and wrote his own name in its place. Ibsen did not, however, forget his first play, and in a letter to Peter Hansen on October 28, 1870, in which he briefly discusses all of the plays he had written up to and including *The League of Youth* (except for some early ones he had decided to disown), he talks about *Catiline* in a way that nicely supplements what he was later to write in the Preface to the second edition: "*Catiline* was written in a little philistine town where it was not in my power to give vent to everything that was fermenting within me, except through crazy pranks and riots that brought on me the ill will of all the respectable citizens, who were unable to enter into the world that I knew and struggled with alone."

Ibsen at last decided to do something about *Catiline* in 1874. By this time, through the publication of *Brand*, *Peer Gynt*, *The League of Youth*, *Emperor and Galilean*, and a volume of his poems, he had become the most famous and the most important author in Dano-Norwegian and was already beginning to win some fame in Germany. As a result, Frederik Hegel, the Copenhagen publisher he had acquired upon writing *Brand*, had begun issuing some of his earlier plays in new editions. *Love's Comedy* appeared in 1867, *The Pretenders* in 1870, *The Vikings at Helgeland* in 1873, and *Lady Inger of Østråt* in 1874. And it occurred to Ibsen—even before the appearance of the second edition of *Lady Inger*—that a new edition of *Catiline* might well be in order. His somewhat ambiguous account of this in his Preface seems to imply that the idea came to him, and that he got a copy of the play, during his first return visit to Norway, in August and September of 1874, but in making his proposal to Hegel he also asks him to borrow a copy of *Catiline* so that he may use it in making his revisions. In his letter to Hegel, dated November 23, 1874, he wrote the following:

But now I have another proposal to submit for your consideration. Next year I celebrate the twenty-fifth anniversary both of my becoming a student and my becoming an author. For in March 1850 [Ibsen's memory has failed him here], *Catiline*, a drama in three acts, was published, the first book of mine to be printed. This work contains quite a bit that is good alongside quite a bit that is immature; in recent years critics have often stressed that it is characteristic of me to have made my debut with this play; and I myself must agree with this, since I now feel that it is closely connected to my circumstances at the time and that it contains the seeds of a good deal that has subsequently emerged in my writing.

This and other matters I have been thinking about giving an account of in a preface and along with that seeing to a new, corrected edition of the book. The thoughts and the ideas would not be touched, but only the language in which they are expressed; for the verses are, as Brandes has said somewhere, bad, which is owing to the fact that my first, loosely dashed-off manuscript was used uncorrected when the book was printed.

I for my part believe that this poem will be received with a good deal of interest and that those who possess my other works will also buy this one. The book is now known to the public only by repute; it was in its time circulated in no more than 60–100 copies, and I myself have been witness to the rest of the issue being reduced to waste paper.

I would like to hear your frank opinion about this proposal. If you have doubts about its appropriateness, please say so. If you agree to it, I would be very grateful if you could obtain a copy of the book for me as soon as possible; for a complete copy will have to be made to print from, because of the many corrections and revisions; and the new edition should, of course, preferably be published at the same time of the year as the first. The borrowed

copy shall be returned in undamaged condition; I assume it will
be possible to get one from one of the big libraries.

Hegel readily agreed to this proposal, Ibsen revised quickly, sending Hegel the text on January 27, 1875, and the book was published in March, a couple of weeks short of the twenty-fifth anniversary of the publication of the first edition. The day after sending the text, Ibsen, "in all haste," wrote again to Hegel, enclosing a letter to be forwarded to Steensballe (presumably about disposing of the remainder of the first edition) and asking Hegel "kindly to take care of everything else concerning the recalling and destruction of the old copies." In a letter to Ludvig Daae on February 4, Ibsen associates the timing of the publication of the second edition with his birthday (March 20), which, he writes, could be regarded as the twenty-fifth anniversary of the beginning of his career as an author "since *Catiline* appeared in the bookstore on about this date in 1850." In early March, Ibsen sent Hegel a number of letters to accompany presentation copies of the new edition for, among others, the King of Sweden-Norway, the Prime Minister (both of these in relation to the author's pension Ibsen now enjoyed), Monrad, and Christopher Due. In one of these letters, Ibsen assures Erik af Edholm, head of the Royal Dramatic Theater in Stockholm, that the play is meant for his private library and is not being officially submitted to the Theater since "it is not suitable for performance."[16] With the publication of the second edition and the destruction of the remaining copies of the first, the history of the reception of *Catiline* becomes, except for a few details, that of the 1875 version.

I have been able to find three reviews of the second edition, all from Christiania and Copenhagen, and although Ibsen was already somewhat known in Germany, it is doubtful that it was reviewed elsewhere. Georg Brandes, who had met Ibsen, already written a good deal about his work, and been in frequent friendly correspondence with him for several years, reviewed it in the literary journal he edited, *The Nineteenth Century*.[17] He devotes some attention to the Preface, which he calls a "humorous little piece of autobiography . . . describing the droll tragicomic circumstances in which the book came to be," but by far the bulk of the review focuses on the meter and the diction of the new version. Having once described the iambics of

Catiline as "horribly bad" (in his *Æsthetiske Studier*, 1868), Brandes wants his readers to realize that he was by no means referring to "the sonorous and powerful verse they now have in view." The play's action and characterizations have remained unchanged, he notes, "but its diction has been subjected to such a thorough improvement that it has acquired an entirely new character, and every living and well-formed verse in the old drama has been carefully transferred into the new one." Despite what Ibsen claims in his Preface, Brandes adds, he could not have written this well back then had he had the time, for "the old diction is an enfeebled echo of that characteristic of Oehlenschläger and Hauch, while the new, through a quite light but superb retouching, has been transformed into Ibsen's own well-known diction." Brandes then provides a series of comparisons to demonstrate "the artistic skill and acuteness with which Ibsen has undertaken his corrections." "All awkwardness in expression," he concludes, "is as it were swept away, and in its place now stands, purified of all external flaws and blemishes, the curious and promising piece of juvenilia that was to be followed by *The Pretenders* and continued with *Brand* and whose poet was to contain so infinitely much more than with this first effort he had promised."

A more searching review of the second edition of *Catiline* as a play was written by Ludvig K. Daa, a Norwegian historian, for his journal *Chronological Tables*.[18] "With this reworking of his first youthful effort," Daa states, "the famous writer has given us a rare treat. We have here a drama in the same brilliant language and the same harmonious versification that we are accustomed to being delighted by in the writing of his more mature age. We admire the same fine portraying of the play's gigantic characters and their wild passions. And yet," he continues, "the greatest interest is owing to its being a reflection of the author's development. It bears the unmistakable stamp of being, as the author tells us, written by a twenty-one year-old youth. . . . The gift for writing poetry is the same, but in *Emperor and Galilean* we see it in association with the more mature thoughts of manhood and in *Catiline* those of the still quite inexperienced and naive youth." The development he has in mind, he adds, is much like Schiller's between *Die Räuber* and *Wallenstein* or *Don Carlos*, and, like *Die Räuber*, *Catiline* is deficient in providing its heroic figures an authentic and well-defined historical and geographical background.

The rest of Daa's discussion illustrates this deficiency at length. We are told that we are in Rome, he remarks, and there are some Latin names, but we do not get to see much more than this that is Roman. The play's Lentulus is a figure completely unrelated to the possibilities for dramatizing him offered by the information in Sallust. The absence of motives and intentions on the part of the other conspirators makes them mere villains who want to burn and plunder. And "Ibsen is certainly wrong in indicating that, for either Catiline or any other Roman, the aim of the struggle was freedom for Rome's citizens. That is in no way appropriate to a period that knew only aristocrats and slaves or rulers and subjugated." "When the historical researcher," he adds, "confronts the palpable contradictions and conspicuous absurdities with which party spirit and a genius for advocacy has sullied Catiline, he gets a suspicion of being in the presence of one of those numerous commonly believed falsehoods. But he should not, nonetheless, substitute for it unprovable suppositions from his own head." The Ibsen of 1875, Daa concludes, would have a much better sense of how to dramatize this material.

The third, and least positive, of the reviews appeared on April 18, 1875, in the Danish journal Nær og Fjern [Near and Far], along with a discussion of the also recently released second edition of Lady Inger (11–13). The reviewer, whose name is not given, begins with a fairly detailed recounting of the "very interesting little Preface . . . which will surely be sufficient by itself to win the book a wide circulation" and then turns to the revisions, which show, he states, that the poet has sought throughout a more elevated but sometimes also a more traditionally pathetic expression. He discusses the advisability of an author's revising his early work, pointing out that while some have improved it others have not. "As far as Ibsen and Catiline are concerned," he continues, "it cannot be denied that the changes are not only improvements but that they were also for the most part necessary if the play was to be newly published, and yet a literary historian will always go back to Brynjolf Bjarme's modest original, because in so many ways it is characteristic of the history of the poet's development." The reviewer is willing to grant Ibsen his claims about the play's relevance to his later work and finds it interesting to see Ibsen writing that even now he maintains much the same view of Catiline's character and reputation, but on the whole, the reviewer believes,

"*Catiline*, even in its new form, scarcely assumes any position of eminence in the Norwegian literature of our time."

This reviewer also links *Catiline* with Schiller's *Die Räuber*, but to its detriment, for, he says, it clearly pales by comparison with Schiller's maiden effort, "as well in the fire of inspiration as in the poetic worth of its contents." Catiline himself "consists more of declamation than of genuine passion, and even dramatic life and action, the main characteristics of the later Ibsen, are in short supply here." He wonders whether it is desirable for a talent for writing "to spring fully armed from the brow of Zeus," adding that Ibsen's "in any case has not done so. Even a whole six years after *Catiline* the poet had gotten no farther than imitating *Svend Dyring's House* in his *The Feast at Solhaug*."[19] The reviewer admits that Ibsen's two subsequent works, *Lady Inger* (actually, *Lady Inger* was written the year before *The Feast at Solhaug*) and *The Vikings at Helgeland*, constitute major advances, "and yet," he adds, "we have recently, in our review of the production in our theater of the latter play, had the opportunity to show how dependent the poet still was on the models from which he borrowed. It is only in 1862 that with *Love's Comedy* he gives notice of being able to become the author of *Brand*, *Peer Gynt*, and *The League of Youth*, while his nordic history plays already culminate in 1864 with *The Pretenders*." The reviewer then turns his attention to the second edition of *Lady Inger*, a play that he likes much better than *Catiline* and that he recommends be performed on the Danish stage.

The sales of the second edition of *Catiline* were modest: Ibsen earned 328.50 *spesidaler* (equivalent to 1,314 kroner) from it in 1875, a sum that can be better understood if one realizes that during the same year he earned, for example, 281.25 *spesidaler* from the fourth edition of *The Pretenders*, 243.25 from the second edition of his *Poems*, and 300 from the Christiania Theater for the rights to stage *Lady Inger*. But the over-all sales of the second edition were good enough to occasion a third in 1891. Eleven years before this, on May 31, 1880, Ibsen had written to Hegel with a new proposal:

> I believe I am not mistaken when I seem to have noticed that the
> Preface to the new edition of *Catiline* has been read with a good
> deal of interest. What if I now wrote an entire small book of 10–
> 12 signatures [160–192 pages] containing similar accounts of the

outer and inner circumstances in which each of my various literary works came into existence?

Hegel discouraged this, recommending that Ibsen instead write a more connected autobiography, but when Ibsen proposed doing just that eighteen months later, Hegel was once again discouraging (Meyer, 462). As a result, the only other piece Ibsen wrote that was even remotely similar to the *Catiline* Preface was his Preface for a second edition of *The Feast at Solhaug* in 1883.

Meanwhile, the second edition of *Catiline* had inspired the first staging of the play anywhere, at the New Theater in Stockholm under the direction of Ludvig Josephson on December 3, 1881. In a letter of the following month (January 25, 1882), Ibsen wrote to Josephson, "From your last letter I learn that the performance of *Catiline* in Stockholm did not have the success that you, and I as well, had expected. I am quite fond of this drama and am still of the opinion that it is bound to have a not inconsiderable effect on the stage, if it gets, in all respects and on all points, an outstanding production."

v. Subsequent Reception

The 1875 version of *Catiline* was included in the collected edition of Ibsen's works that Hegel began to issue in 1898 to commemorate Ibsen's seventieth birthday. In a brief preface for this edition ("To My Readers"), Ibsen, who had learned to be very canny in helping along the sales of his books, insists on the importance of *Catiline*, though without explicitly mentioning it:

> Only by comprehending and mastering my entire output as a coherent and continuous totality will one grasp the intended, pertinent impressions of the individual parts.
>
> My friendly appeal to my readers, therefore, is, in short, not to lay any play aside for the time being, nor, for the time being, to skip any of them, but to master these works—to read them through and fully experience [*gennemlæse og gennemleve*] them—in the same order as that in which I composed them.

The 1875 version also appears in all subsequent original-language complete editions of Ibsen's plays. The 1850 version was first reprinted in Volume VII of the Standardutgaven (1918), edited by Didrik Arup Seip. Slightly revised to correct typographical errors and to accept a few readings from the manuscript, the 1850 version was also reprinted in 1928 in Volume I of the standard Norwegian edition of Ibsen, the Hundreårsutgave, along with Ibsen's manuscript synopsis-outlines for Acts One and Two and thorough and excellent textual notes by Seip comparing the printed version to the manuscript and recording the changes Ibsen had made in the manuscript itself.

Through its 1875 version *Catiline* also gradually began to come to the attention of the rest of the world.[20] The first translation into any language was a partial one, into English, by Andrew Johnston, who in 1879 or 1880 provided a rendering of Act One and a brief resumé of the rest of the play in a volume entitled *Translations from the Norse*, which, under the signature B.S.S., was printed in Gloucester, England, for private circulation. The first German translation, authorized by Ibsen, appeared in 1896, and in 1903 a different translation was included in the German edition of Ibsen's complete works. A French translation appeared in 1902, a Russian in 1906, an Italian (in prose) in 1924, a Dutch in 1928, and a Czech at a date not indicated on the title page. William Archer and his colleagues did not translate the play, so *Catiline* does not appear in any of the several editions of Ibsen that Archer produced.[21] A complete English rendering had to wait until 1921, when it appeared in Anders Orbeck's *Early Plays by Henrik Ibsen*, an attempt to provide English versions of the plays Archer had ignored. The only translation of the 1850 version that I know of, by Graham Orton, appeared in 1970 in Volume I of the Oxford *Ibsen*, which also contains Orton's translation of the second half of Act Three of the 1875 version and, in an appendix, a list of the major differences between the two versions.

If the Norwegian and English records provide a good indication— and they no doubt do—*Catiline* has been performed only rarely after its 1881 premiere. It was first produced in Norway in August 1935 at the New Theater in Oslo, when, according to Orton, "Stein Bügge, the producer, treated the play in twentieth-century terms: drunken Romans entered the stage to jazz music, clad in togas and tophats, and Catiline and the conspirators wore German steel helmets" (583); this was, or was to become, in the thirties a common method of sprucing up older plays, especially those based on history—a famous American example is Orson Welles's 1937 "no-scenery" production of *Julius Caesar*, with its allusions to contemporary Italian fascism. Stein Bügge also directed a British production with Donald Wolfit as Catiline; this opened on January 27, 1936, at the Croydon Repertory Theatre, and after a week's run it was transferred to the Royalty Theatre in London. According to Orton,

> In a review on 1 February 1936 the *Croydon Advertiser*, reiterating an introductory speech by the producer, found that there "seems to be manifest a tendency towards softer emotional colours than those to which we are accustomed in his mature work." The reviewer made no mention of audience reaction, but of the play itself wrote: "in its mould *Catiline* derives directly from the Greek tragic drama, exemplified here and there in detailed imitation. . . . It is in the essential treatment of the theme that the classical conception is apparent. Nemesis broods over the action from the very first scene, as dominating an influence as in *Oedipus Tyrannus* and *Macbeth*, and the technical devices of the Greek school are exploited in other ways with telling effect. That stress should be laid on the postulate that man's fate is determined by the elements of his own personality is the natural outcome of a nineteenth-century genius expressed in Athenian terms and thence too arises that moving picture of the entirely human love of Aurelia for her self-contradictory husband." (583–84).

The height of the *Catiline* boom came in the early seventies when two separate adaptations of the play were produced in Norway (in 1972–73 and 1975–76). So far as I have been able to find out, *Catiline* has never been produced in America, nor, so far as I have been able to find out, has there ever been a production of the 1850 version.

Two factors—aside from the actual merits of the play—help account for the paucity of productions after the appearance of the revised version. One is that Ibsen, who had risen to eminence largely through *Brand*, *Peer Gynt*, and *Emperor and Galilean*, was not yet generally thought of as a dramatist whose plays demanded to be staged, both immediately and often. The other, and far more important, factor is that Ibsen himself helped make the staging of a play like *Catiline* a rather unlikely possibility. Two years after the second edition of *Catiline*, he published *Pillars of Society* and two years after that *A Doll House*, taking his own work into a completely new mode from most of what he had done before and almost single-handedly transforming the kind of thing audiences expected when they were willing to experience a serious play in the theater. For the theater of today, as a result, Ibsen pretty much means *Peer Gynt* and the twelve prose dramas of contemporary middle-class life from the second half of his career. *Catiline* and most of the other early plays are ignored—and remain virtually unknown—in contrast, for example, to early Shakespeare plays like *Titus Andronicus, King John,* and the three parts of *Henry VI*, which theaters have been inclined to produce—thus showing their considerable power—because they are in much the same mode as the masterpieces Shakespeare wrote later. By writing *Pillars of Society, A Doll House,* and the plays that followed, Ibsen prevented a similar treatment of his own early work. The chief victim of this phenomenon, however, has been not *Catiline* but his first unequivocal masterpiece, *The Pretenders.*

The current evaluation of *Catiline* by scholars and critics, a topic that shifts the focus back to the 1850 version, is to some extent indicated, no doubt, by a tendency to ignore the play, even in the case of those who feel it necessary to go back behind the last twelve "modern" plays in order to give a comprehensive overview on Ibsen. Most of them go back no farther than *Peer Gynt,* or *Brand,* or *Love's Comedy* and, out of conviction or ignorance, leave *Catiline* undiscussed. Maurice Valency, for example, begins his important and influential discussion of Ibsen in *The Flower and the Castle* (1963) essentially with *Brand* and mentions *Catiline* once only:

> It would be senseless to suggest that Ibsen was born as a playwright at the age of fifty-one. *Brand* and *Peer Gynt* are unique masterpieces. All the same, had Ibsen written nothing before 1879, his status as a dramatist, outside the Scandinavian countries, would hardly be diminished. The current critical tendency is to place more and more emphasis on the early Ibsen, particularly on *Catilina* and *The Pretenders,* perhaps because of a feeling that there remains nothing more to be said about his later works. But Weigand [Hermann J. Weigand, author of *The Modern Ibsen,* 1925] was doubtless justified in limiting his

detailed analysis of Ibsen's plays to the period beginning with
Pillars of Society.[22]

Some who do discuss *Catiline,* such as the biographers and the
editors of the Hundreårsutgave and the Oxford *Ibsen,* are clearly in
part responding to an obligation to be thorough. Many of those who
seem to be discussing it out of an awareness of its importance, such as
G. Wilson Knight in *Henrik Ibsen* (New York: Grove Press, Evergreen
Pilot Books, 1962) and Daniel Haakonsen in *Henrik Ibsen, mennesket
og kunstneren* (Oslo: H. Aschehoug & Co. [W. Nygaard], 1981), say
almost nothing explicit about its merits. Instead, like most who
comment on *Catiline,* they imply that it is of value mainly for its
expression of Ibsen's own inner experience at the time he wrote it and
for its anticipations of specific themes, characters, and dramatic
devices in his later plays, ideas about *Catiline* that go back at least as
far as Brandes' first substantial discussion of Ibsen in 1867. Explicit
evaluations of *Catiline,* as a result, are in fairly short supply. Koht (I,
43) wrote in 1954:

> As imperfect as the play in many respects is—often awkward in
> its construction of individual scenes, with very little in the way
> of individualized character-portrayal, and with numerous large
> and strong words that all too often develop into thundering
> declamation—it is nevertheless infused with a dramatic passion
> that above all manifests itself in the strong framework of the
> structure, but which also time after time emerges in words and
> lines of genuine Shakespearean power and antithetical force.
> There is no doubt about it: it is an authentic dramatist who is
> making his beginning here.

Meyer (43) wrote in 1967:

> *Catiline* is far from being a mere pastiche. Apart from the
> considerable skill of the verse, a signpost to the flexible and
> muscular dramatic poetry that was to come in *Love's Comedy,*
> *Brand,* and *Peer Gynt,* the sharpness of the characterization, the
> continuous movement of the plot and, rarest of talents in a
> playwright, the ability to construct and develop not merely a

character but a human relationship, are all evidence of uncommon maturity in a largely self-educated youth approaching his twenty-first birthday.

McFarlane, in his 1970 introduction to Volume I of the Oxford *Ibsen*, wrote of all the plays in the volume, "by any standards, let alone when measured against the towering stature of [Ibsen's] later dramas, the achievement of these early works was modest indeed, and very uneven. All was promise." And he distinguishes *Catiline* from the others in this respect essentially only in its being "as yet free of the obtrusive nationalism that was very shortly to overwhelm [Ibsen's] work" (1, 8).

The two most thorough of the recent assessments, by Arild Haaland in 1978 and Brian Johnston in 1980, are—as one might expect, given the play's genuine weaknesses—the most severe. Haaland chooses *Catiline* as one of the six plays he discusses in detail to make his argument about Ibsen, but he admits that the reason it has not been performed more often is that it is poorly suited for the stage. One problem for Haaland is its sheer abundance of effects that are never brought into a coherent pattern, by which he means both the sudden and unexpected shifts in the characters' behavior, especially that of the hero, and the lack of sufficient connections among the various dramatic motifs, especially in Ibsen's failure to work out a link between the criticism of the social order and the actual motives that propel the characters. Another serious problem, he finds, is the "confused" treatment of Aurelia and Furia, for to the extent that they become purely allegorical they fail to achieve independent existence, which is an offense from a feminist as well as a dramatic point of view, and to the extent they do achieve independent existence the hero is deprived of a capacity to will and to act on his own. This last, Haaland feels, keeps *Catiline* from being the tragedy Ibsen intended to write, for it makes the hero a mere victim or a culprit brought to justice by another, as in a detective story, whereas tragedy requires the protagonist's discovering his or her responsibility for what has happened and taking responsibility for the consequences—as in *Ghosts*, where Mrs. Alving "is compelled to carry out retribution with her own hands and with full insight concerning the original offense committed by her in her youth." Furthermore, Haaland concludes, none of the three central figures possesses the sort of richly delineated personality we come to expect in later Ibsen, where characters are endowed with detailed pasts that fully define them.[23]

For Brian Johnston, "*Catiline* is compelling only to the reader or viewer aware of Ibsen's later mastery and of the way in which the play prefigures his later works. The drama seems at once conventional and fumbling as it attempts, with painfully inadequate artistry, to fulfill the terms of the German fate-tragedy and of the Romantic, i.e., Byronic, drama (in the manner of *Manfred*) of the lonely blasted hero bringing himself to destruction." The chief problem for Johnston is the play's "Romantic subjectivity," which "weakens its dramatic impact. The characters, overcharged with immediate symbolic and archetypal implication, belong less to the realm of drama than to that of opera," and the play, "which actually reads much like an opera libretto, has nearly all the deficiencies of the opera form without the one ingredient, music, that could give it artistic unity and authenticity." Johnston also finds the play to be almost entirely lacking in "objective content," by which he means that the background is sketched in only the vaguest of terms, the stage space is "conveniently undefined," so that "characters enter and exit entirely according to thematic convenience," and the characterization is virtually without substance, so that, for example, Catiline's fellow-conspirators are "a mere cloud of unindividualized forms hovering around the Byronic hero." "If," he concludes,

> we valued archetypal content in literature the most and found the presence of compelling archetypes sufficient to guarantee the worth of a work, *Catiline* would be Ibsen's most valuable play, for it contains hardly anything but fervidly archetypal and mythic content, whether we see this as public and Romantic or private and subconscious. But to be truly important, a work of art must significantly objectify its form and content. What so obviously is missing from *Catiline* is not only a subtly felt, rational, objective, and fully human content but also a clear conception of the nature of the conflict it is dramatizing.[24]

My own assessment of the merits of *Catiline* appears in a later section of this introduction, following a discussion of its sources and an analysis of its contents.

Sources

The sources Ibsen drew on in writing *Catiline* are of three basic kinds: (1) The specific texts that he had either literally before him as he wrote or in memory based on recent reading (Sallust and Cicero, as Ibsen himself indicates in his Preface, and a narrative poem by the Danish poet Frederik Paludan-Müller entitled *"Vestalinden"* ["The Vestal"]).[25] (2) The themes and clichés of Romanticism, especially as they are articulated in Romantic drama, particularly tragedy. (3) Ibsen's own experience at the time he wrote the play: the feelings aroused in him by his situation in Grimstad, his responses to the revolutions of 1848, and the non-dramatic poetry he had already been writing, which not only articulates his feelings and attitudes and his sense of his identity but also literally supplied him with source material. The first of these three kinds of sources, especially the historical documents, were read through lenses honed by the other two.

i. Specific Sources

Sallust. The play's primary specific source, without question, is Sallust's monograph-length account of Catiline and his conspiracy—the *Catilinae Coniuratio*, written sometime between 44 and 40 B.C. From this work Ibsen took the basic outline for his story material, the names of most of his characters and some of the information he develops about them, particular details for a few incidents, bits of language for certain speeches, and various hints for many of his deviations from Sallust's version of the story.

The Conspiracy of Catiline begins with a preface of sorts, in which, among other things, Sallust discusses the writing of history, states his purpose in recording this one, and provides a summary characterization of Catiline. Sallust then turns to Catiline's youthful unruly behavior (his "many scandalous intrigues—one with a maiden of noble birth, another with a priestess of Vesta, not to mention similar offences against law and morality") and his first major crime, the murder of his adult son by a previous marriage, so that Aurelia Orestilla, with whom he had fallen in love but who feared his son, would marry him; it was, Sallust claims, "principally this deed that determined him to postpone his criminal attempt no longer . . . so cruelly did remorse torture his frenzied soul."²⁶ This is followed by an account of Catiline's abortive attempts to gain the consulship: his plot to murder the winners of the election in 66 B.C. when, because of a prosecution against him, he could not himself run; his meeting with his various followers during the election campaign of 64, including his speech to them, which Sallust "quotes" in full; his loss of this election, which prompted him to start making preparations for outright rebellion; and his loss of the election again in 63, prompting him to set his plot in motion by sending supporters of his with their armies to various parts of the Italian peninsula, including Manlius to Etruria.

Sallust then recounts the events leading up to the climax of the conspiracy: Catiline's plot to murder Cicero; Cicero's foiling of this, having been warned by an informant within Catiline's group; Cicero's assumption of war powers and his sending armies out to confront Catiline's; Catiline's visit to the Senate, where he is denounced by Cicero in his "First Oration," after which Catiline tries to defend himself, is shouted down by the Senators, and leaves in a rage, promising that "'Since I am encompassed by foes . . . and hounded to desperation, I will check the fire that threatens to consume me by pulling everything down about your ears'" (31; 198–99); Catiline's returning home to ponder deeply on the situation; and his decision to join Manlius and assume leadership of the army in Etruria, leaving many of his most important followers behind him in Rome to "do everything possible to increase the strength of their party, to find an early opportunity of assassinating Cicero, and to make arrangements for massacre, fire-raising, and other violent outrages" in order to prepare Rome for his attack, which was to come shortly (32; 199). Sallust describes the letters Catiline then sent to several members of the aristocracy in order to mislead them about his intentions and quotes one of them in full because, in its differences from the others, it is of unusual interest.

Sallust saves his most detailed accounts for the climactic events: the activities in Rome of Catiline's supporters, including Lentulus' efforts to enlist the support of the Allobrogian ambassadors who had come to Rome seeking redress against "the rapacity of the Roman officials" in their territory (40; 206); the exposure and capture of the conspirators in Rome; the debate in the Senate that led to the decision to execute the captured conspirators, with the speeches by

Julius Caesar and Cato given in full; and, finally, the defeat and death of Catiline in Etruria. Here Sallust tells how Catiline, cut off by one of the Roman armies, decided to engage the other in a final desperate attempt at victory, quotes the speech in which Catiline exhorts his troops, and concludes with an account of the battle, in which the army of the conspirators—and especially its leader—fight bravely but are cut down to the last man: "Catiline himself was found far from his own men among the dead bodies of his adversaries. He was still just breathing, and his face retained the look of haughty defiance that had marked him all through his life. Of that whole army which fought and fled, not a single free-born citizen was taken prisoner: all were as careless of their own as of their enemies' lives" (61; 233).

Ibsen greatly simplifies this narrative by altering Sallust's chronology and by omitting a good deal, with many of the omissions, no doubt, stemming as much, if not more so, from Ibsen's quite different view of Catiline as from his desire to streamline the action. The arrival in Rome of the Allobrogian ambassadors in order to make their appeal to the Senate gives the opening scene of *Catiline* some sense of specificity in terms of time, putting the scene rather late in the narrative as Sallust tells it. But as far as Catiline's own involvement in this scene is concerned, it could be occurring at any point between his becoming fully aware of the frustrations of his situation and the meeting of the Senate during which he is attacked by Cicero. The rest of Act One and all of Act Two, however, clearly take place on the evening and night following this attack, while Act Three passes in a single continuous stretch of time at some later date, the day of the battle in which the conspirators are defeated, although the exact time relationship between this date and the preceding action is not specified. References within the play provide some indication of Catiline's dissolute and wastrel past, but Ibsen considerably mutes this element: he trims away Catiline's worst crimes, such as his murder of his son, and he reduces Catiline's prior attempts to gain the consulship to some references to his once having used bribes for this purpose. The explicit idea of a revolution stems from others, rather than Catiline himself. He is dismayed by the situation in Rome, feels oppressed and threatened by his many enemies, and entertains some very sketchily defined "plans" to do something in response, but he also seems appalled by the conspirators' intentions when Lentulus and

Cethegus inform him of them. He at first refuses to lead the conspiracy, even though Cicero has already attacked him, and finally agrees to do so only under the spell of Furia's perhaps more than human urging. All specific plans for the rebellion are apparently made on the night following Cicero's attack and seem to consist only of Catiline's forming an army in Etruria—though why there is not made clear in the play—and marching on Rome to destroy the oligarchy in power. Ibsen omits all the material about the activities of the conspirators in Rome and the debate in the Senate. These sections in Sallust are at most only obliquely referred to, in Curius' Act-Three response to Catiline's question about his friends in Rome: "they've been imprisoned and perhaps are slain."

But Ibsen also expands on Sallust's narrative, makes some important changes in it, and adds elements of his own. The third scene of Act One, for example, in which Catiline broods on what has happened and confers with Aurelia, apparently grows out of Sallust's brief statement that after the meeting in the Senate Catiline went home to ponder deeply on his situation. The chief narrative changes, besides those mentioned in the preceding paragraph, consist of altered motives for both the betrayal of the conspiracy to the Senate and the defection of the Allobroges, the reduction of the two Roman armies confronting Catiline in Etruria to one, the presence in Etruria of the conspirators who in Sallust remained in Rome, Catiline's deciding to fight in order to die heroically, "with sword in hand," rather than out of hope of still being able to win, and his surviving the battle. The chief additions, some of which seem to have evolved at least in part from details in Sallust, include Catiline's having seduced Furia's sister (and hence Furia's primary motive), most of Furia's involvement in the action, Catiline's temptation to leave the turmoil in Rome and find seclusion in Gaul, most of the involvement in the action of Aurelia (who is closely associated with the idea of retreating to Gaul), Catiline's dream in Act Three, Lentulus' plot against Catiline, and all of the play's conclusion following the battle. I shall discuss some of these changes and additions in more detail, as well as mentioning others, as I consider the relationship between Ibsen's characters and their counterparts in Sallust.

The supernumeries (the attendants of the Allobrogian envoys, the servants in the Temple of Vesta, the Waiters, the "several other young noblemen" present among the conspirators in two scenes of Act Two, the Warriors) and characters with minimal speaking parts (the Vestal, the Old Soldier in Act One, and the Gladiators in Act Three) are for the most part mere lay figures arising from the occasions in which they occur, with only the Gladiators and the Old Soldier reflecting anything in Sallust's narrative: his assumptions about what can be expected of Gladiators and his accounts of how some Romans, sometimes unjustly, had been deprived of property and/or jailed for debt. The two envoys of the Allobroges, Ambiorix and Ollovico, derive from Sallust's primary account of them in sections 40 and 41. Ibsen found names for them in Caesar's *Gallic War*, but he based their dialogue in the opening scene on the complaints Sallust puts in their mouths and their brief exchange toward the end of Act Two on their debate, which Sallust paraphrases, about whether to join the conspiracy or side with Rome. According to Sallust, they concluded that their own interests would be better served by siding with Rome, and so "they communicated all they had been told to Quintus Fabius Sanga, who regularly acted as their patron in Rome," Sanga passed it on to Cicero, and Cicero used them in his successful efforts to get evidence against the conspirators remaining in Rome (41; 207).

The names of four of Catiline's co-conspirators in the play (Lentulus, Cethegus, Statilius, and Gabinius) appear in section 16 of Sallust, which lists several of Catiline's supporters, most of whom Ibsen ignores, and it is more likely that he took the names from Sallust's account of the doings of the conspirators in Rome, where these four are prominently featured, without their praenomens and cognomens, as is also Caeparius, Ibsen's other named co-conspirator (as Coeparius). Ibsen calls them noblemen, but he has made them much younger than they were, more like his own age, and deprived them of their wealth and status. Lentulus, for example, had been consul in 71 B.C., was later expelled from the Senate for immoral conduct, but was elected praetor, for a second time, in 62; and both Lentulus and Cethegus, Sallust makes clear, had ample supporters in the form of freedmen and other dependents. In Ibsen, however, all the co-conspirators derive from a softened portrait of but one of the many groups who, in Sallust, support Catiline: the young, impoverished, somewhat dissolute, and dangerous young men attracted by Catiline's promises of easy wealth, anti-social adventures, and power. The tavern they frequent is strictly of Ibsen's own era, perhaps reflecting something Ibsen knew in Grimstad but more likely an echo of his reading; it smells far more of Schiller's *Die Räuber* than of Sallust. Cethegus' carefree profligacy is also a modification, based on Ibsen's reading of contemporary literature, of one of Sallust's charges against Catiline's supporters. Lentulus' self-interested plotting to usurp Catiline's position as leader, a commonplace of melodrama, may have been in part inspired by Sallust's report that the Allobroges proved Lentulus' guilt to the Senate "by repeating words which he had often used. 'The Sibylline books', he had said, 'prophesied that Rome would be ruled by three Cornelii; Cinna and Sulla had been the first two, and he himself was the third who was destined to be master of the city'" (47; 211).

Some of the details concerning Manlius and Ibsen's wholly positive view of him undoubtedly derive from Sallust's quotation of a statement by Manlius to proconsul Marcius Rex explaining why he is raising an army in Etruria:

> "We call gods and men to witness, sir, that our object in taking
> up arms was not to attack our country or to endanger others, but
> to protect ourselves from wrong. We are poor needy wretches;
> the cruel harshness of moneylenders has robbed most of us of our
> homes, and all of us have lost reputation and fortune. [. . . .] We,
> however, are not seeking dominion or riches—the invariable
> causes of war and quarrelling among human beings—but only
> freedom, which no true man ever surrenders while he lives. We
> beseech you and the Senate to rescue your unhappy fellow
> citizens, to restore to us the legal protection snatched from us by
> the praetor's injustice, and not force us to seek a means of selling
> our life's blood as dearly as we can." (33; 199–200)

On the basis of this statement, Ibsen apparently found it fairly easy to transform the details of Sallust's earlier report on Manlius in such a way as to put him in a much more favorable light: "in Etruria, Manlius was agitating among a populace whose poverty, added to the resentment which they felt at their wrongs, made them eager for revolution; for during Sulla's tyranny they had lost their lands and all the rest of their possessions. He also approached some of the many types of brigands who infested that part of the country, as well as some veteran soldiers from Sulla's 'colonies', whose lavish indulgence of their appetites had exhausted the enormous booty they had brought home" (28; 196). In Ibsen, the "brigands" have disappeared, Sulla's veterans—such as Manlius himself—are no longer to blame for their impoverishment, and, in fact, they have become the victims rather than the beneficiaries of dispossession. Ibsen's Manlius has also acquired the objection to using slaves to augment the army that Sallust attributes to Catiline (44; 209, 56; 228). As for Manlius' past relationship with and present avuncular attitude toward Catiline, they are Ibsen's inventions, no doubt based on his familiarity with literary clichés.

The reference to "Sulla's dictatorship" quoted above is one of several such in Sallust, and these—for example, "After Sulla had used armed force to make himself dictator, and after a good beginning turned out a bad ruler, there was universal robbery and pillage" (11; 182)—would have given Ibsen all he needed to know for the speeches he assigns to Sulla's ghost. His connecting Catiline with Sulla in the past may well have been based on Sallust's first mention of Sulla, in his initial summary characterization of Catiline: "After the dictatorship of Lucius Sulla, Catiline had been possessed by an overmastering desire for despotic power, to gratify which he was prepared to use any and every means" (5; 178).

Curius, Furia, and their jointly engineered betrayal of Catiline's plot all derive from a single paragraph in Sallust, which is worth quoting in full as another example, along with the passage on Manlius given above, of how Ibsen constantly revised what he found in order to meet the needs of his quite different conception of the events:

> Among the conspirators was one Quintus Curius, a man of good birth but sunk over head and ears in infamy and crime, whom the censors had expelled from the Senate for immoral conduct. As unreliable as he was reckless, he could neither hold his tongue about what he heard nor even keep dark his own misdeeds, being utterly regardless of what he said or did. A woman of good family named Fulvia had long been his mistress; and when he found himself less in favour with her because lack of means compelled him to be less lavish with his presents, he suddenly began to talk big and to promise her the earth—the next moment threatening

to stab her unless she complied with his demands. This high and mighty tone was so different from his normal manner that Fulvia insisted on an explanation; and on learning the cause of his arrogant behaviour she decided that such a serious danger to the state must not be concealed. Without mentioning the name of her informant, she told a number of persons the various facts that she had ascertained about Catiline's plot. (23; 191–92)

Sallust subsequently adds further details about Curius and Fulvia passing information to Cicero, but the only other passage from Sallust that Ibsen needed to complete the basic shaping of his love-triangle was the early one in which Sallust gives his two examples of Catiline's many scandalous intrigues in his early days: "one with a maiden of noble birth, another with a priestess of Vesta" (15; 184). By combining Sallust's Fulvia with the "priestess of Vesta," Ibsen makes her Catiline's love object before Curius', and it just may be possible that the "maiden of noble birth" was the germ for Catiline's prior seduction of the Vestal's sister—with the noble birth of both Fulvia and the maiden vanishing in Ibsen's general unwillingness or inability to make much of his characters' aristocratic status. The characterization of Furia, one of the strong points of *Catiline*, is, of course, Ibsen's own contribution, with its distance from Sallust amply denoted by the change of name from Fulvia to Furia. Also Ibsen's own is the kinship and affectionate relationship between Catiline and Curius.

Ibsen's most striking deviation from Sallust in characterization is his conception of Aurelia, whom Sallust mentions only once in his narrative, and in completely negative terms, when he reports Catiline's "falling in love with Aurelia Orestilla, a woman in whom no respectable man ever found anything to praise except her beauty" (15; 185). Ibsen got much more help with her from the letter of Catiline to Quintus Catulus that Sallust quotes, in which Catiline, explaining why he has decided to use force, insists that it was not because of his debts: "'It was not that I could not have paid my personal debts by selling some of my estates—and as for the loans raised on the security of others, the generosity of Orestilla would have discharged them with her own resources and those of her daughter.'" And he concludes the letter with what seems to be an expression of his love for her: "'So for the present I commend Orestilla to you and entrust her to your protection. Shield her from wrong, I beg you in the name of your own children'" (35; 201). As I shall discuss in more detail below, Ibsen's characterization of Aurelia is essentially inspired by Romantic literary pastoral, but he may have derived the initial impulse for this from Sallust. Aurelia's urging Catiline to retire with her into nature and away from Rome's tumult becomes translated, by Act Two, into Catiline's intention to emigrate to "Gaul's far valleys." And this idea perhaps derives from Sallust's claim that in his other letters to members of the aristocracy Catiline wrote "that since he had not been able to withstand the group of enemies who persecuted him with trumped-up charges, he was resigning himself to his lot and going to Marseilles as an exile" (34; 200).

Catiline's expressed reason for this decision ("not because his conscience reproached him with the heinous crime of which he was accused, but in order to preserve the peace of the state and avoid stirring up civil strife by struggling against his fate") is important for what it shows about how Ibsen, in defining his protagonist, seized on whatever he could manage to cull from Sallust. The end of this passage—the remark about "struggling against his fate"—is perhaps the immediate source of one of the major themes in the play, while the rest of it is typical of the kind of detail Ibsen's well-prepared eyes were ready to zero in on in his seeking to find evidence for purer and more ideal motivations on Catiline's part than Sallust normally gives him. Ibsen does use some of the evil actions Sallust attributes to Catiline—even adding a new one in the seduction-rape of Furia's sister—but he suppresses the worst of these, and, for the most part, those he keeps seem somehow merely to sit there, strangely unrelated to Catiline's basic nature as an essentially noble and heroic figure, who in good Romantic fashion seeks greatness for himself but primarily only as a means of furthering the freedom and well-being of his land and its people. Ibsen's desire to portray Catiline in these terms lay behind many of the alterations that I have already described, and it also required further suppressions and alterations in what Sallust specifically records about Catiline's character and motives.

On the other hand, although the portrait of Catiline in Sallust is primarily negative, he was at some pains to provide a balanced account, as can be seen from the positive details in his summary character of Catiline, his careful weighing of evidence in order to reject certain extreme charges against Catiline (such as his having engaged in homosexual practices with his younger followers [184] and his having passed out bowls of human blood mixed with wine when getting his followers to swear an oath of allegiance [191]), his quoting of Catiline's speeches and letters with little or no editorializing, and his presentation of Catiline's behavior in the final battle as heroic and tragic. Ibsen must have felt that in passages like these he was getting in touch with the "real" Catiline, and he found in them virtually all that he needed for his characterization of his hero.

Ibsen's primary method of transforming Sallust's Catiline into his own, then, consisted of an even more extensive sort of "reading between the lines" than that already exemplified in my accounts of some of the other characters. By applying this method lightly to Catiline's quoted letters, more severely to his quoted speeches, and quite strenuously to Sallust's summary characterization, Ibsen could have come up with numerous statements supporting his view of Catiline and—only slightly modified—providing him with many details he could appropriately use (and in certain cases obviously did). The following are some choice examples:

> [From Sallust's summary characterization] Lucius Catiline was of noble birth. He had a powerful intellect and great physical strength. . . . He could endure hunger, cold, and want of sleep to an incredible extent. His mind was daring, crafty and versatile. . . . A man of flaming passions. . . . His headstrong spirit was tormented more and more every day by poverty and a guilty conscience. . . . (5; 177–78)
>
> [From Catiline's first speech to the conspirators] ". . . every passing day kindles my enthusiasm more and more when I think what will be our lot unless we ourselves assert our claim to liberty. Ever since the state came under the jurisdiction and control of a powerful oligarchy. . . . [. . . .] How long, brave comrades, will you endure it? Is it not better to die courageously and have done with it, then to drag out lives of misery and dishonour as the playthings of other men's insolence, until we lose them ignominiously in the end? [. . . .] Use me as your commander or as a soldier in the ranks: my heart and my hands shall be at your service. These are the objects I hope to help you

achieve when I am your consul—unless indeed I deceive myself and you are content to be slaves instead of masters." (20–21; 189–90)

[From Catiline's letter to Quintus Catulus] "I was provoked by wrongs and insults and robbed of the fruits of my painstaking industry, and I found myself unable to maintain a position of dignity. So I openly undertook the championship of the oppressed, as I had often done before. [. . . .] I saw unworthy men promoted to honourable positions, and felt myself treated as an outcast on account of unjust suspicions. That is why I have adopted a course of action, amply justified in my present circumstances, which offers a hope of saving what is left of my honour." (35; 201)

[From Catiline's exhortation to his troops before the battle] "Moreover, soldiers, our adversaries are not impelled by the same necessity as we are. For us, country, freedom, and life are at stake; they, on the other hand, have no particular interest in fighting to keep an oligarchy in power. [. . . .] But if . . . Fortune robs your valour of its just reward, see that you do not sell your lives cheaply. Do not be taken and slaughtered like cattle. Fight like men: let bloodshed and mourning be the price that the enemy will have paid for his victory." (58; 230–31)

His technique of reading between the lines must also have served Ibsen well as he encountered such passages as those stating that none of Catiline's followers betrayed or deserted him despite the promise of large rewards from the Senate (36), that the "city populace" were eager to join his revolt (37; 203), and that during the preceding years "the popular party lost ground and the oligarchy became more powerful" (39; 205).[27]

Ibsen also employed another creative technique in culling from Sallust what he needed for characterizing his hero: he made clever use of Sallust's self-representation in his prefatory remarks. "My earliest inclinations," Sallust writes here,

led me, like many other young men, to throw myself wholeheartedly into politics. There I found many things against me. Self-restraint, integrity, and virtue were disregarded; unscrupulous

conduct, bribery, and profit-seeking were rife. And although,
being a stranger to the vices that I saw practised on every hand,
I looked on them with scorn, I was led astray by ambition and,
with a young man's weakness, could not tear myself away.
However much I tried to dissociate myself from the prevailing
corruption, my craving for advancement exposed me to the same
odium and slander as all my rivals.

After suffering manifold perils and hardships, peace of mind
at last returned to me, and I decided that I must bid farewell to
politics for good. (4; 177)

This portrait of youthful misdeeds as deviations from an essentially
noble and virtuous nature could well be what Ibsen had in mind for
Catiline, especially since Sallust goes on to say that he refused to be
idle in his retreat but instead devoted himself to doing what he could
for the welfare of Rome—i.e., by writing cautionary moral histories.
And, after completing his summary characterization of Catiline, he
then provides an extensive account of how Rome in its present
corruption has sadly fallen away from its glorious, virtuous past, thus
attributing to himself a particular moral point of view that Ibsen
assigns to Catiline as one of his most important character traits.

Cicero. Skard (82) assumes that Ibsen probably read Cicero before
Sallust, since Cicero's Latin is much easier, but there are few specific
traces from the Orations against Catiline in Ibsen's play. This is in
large part no doubt owing to their occasion: Cicero, speaking out of
a sense of immediate urgency and trying to win support for his efforts
to stop Catiline (as well as doing a bit of politicking on his own
behalf), had little interest in compiling a coherent narrative and none
at all in offering even faintly positive statements about his adversary,
whom he characterizes as a monster of perversity. Ibsen's almost total
suppression of Cicero's contribution to the events, his representing
him merely as Catiline's enemy (and for unspecified reasons), his
presentation of the First Oration, delivered in the Senate, as an
unprovoked attack, and his remarks about him in the 1875 Preface
suggest that the main impact on Ibsen of the Orations was one of
violent antagonism (Skard, referring to the Preface, observes that for
Ibsen Cicero became the prototype "of the philistine, the reactionary,
the spokesperson for the 'compact majority,'" 82). This reaction to

Cicero may have been what prompted Ibsen to read Sallust in creative ways in order to dig out the "truth" that Catiline's enemies, led by Cicero, had deliberately suppressed. To this extent, then, Cicero is perhaps the primary inspiration for Ibsen's view of his hero—as well as, insofar as specific details of action and characterization are concerned, essentially a non-source.

A few details in the Orations, nevertheless, suggest that if Ibsen did read Cicero first, he returned to him after getting his primary material from Sallust. Ibsen's treatment of Catiline's co-conspirators may have been affected by Cicero's remarks about Catiline's followers throughout the orations, especially his elaborate analysis of the five classes of them in the Second Oration. The idea of Catiline's leaving for Gaul may have gotten something from Cicero's frequent urgings in the First Oration that Catiline leave Rome in view of the fear and loathing with which so many of its citizens have come to regard him, and surely the many references in this Oration to how those in the Senate are now looking on at Catiline in silent fear and contempt contributed to the account of this event that Ibsen's Catiline gives in the play. Cicero's preoccupation, in the Third Oration, with his own desire for an immortality of fame may—apart from increasing Ibsen's hostility—have helped prompt the similar concern that Ibsen attributes to his hero. To my mind, however, the passage in Cicero that is most likely to have affected Ibsen's treatment of his material is one in the Second Oration, in which Cicero describes the class that includes Manlius:

> The third class is composed of men already affected by old age, but still strong because of their physical exercise. In this class is the scoundrel Manlius, whom Catiline has now joined. These are men from those colonies which Sulla established; those colonies I recognize are entirely composed of very fine citizens and very brave men, but still these are the colonists who have disported themselves too luxuriously and too wantonly in their unexpected and newly-acquired possessions. While they are erecting build-ings like men of wealth, while they are delighting themselves with their choice estates, with large retinues of slaves, with elaborate banquets, they have fallen so deeply in debt that if they would be solvent they must call Sulla back to them from the infernal regions.[28]

This passage associates Manlius with the "old-soldier" motif central to his characterization in the play and, with the appropriate modifications, may also have given Ibsen other details he could use. Even more important, however, is the final clause, the possible inspiration for Ibsen's own decision to "call Sulla back . . . from the infernal regions."

"*Vestalinden.*" This is a narrative poem of about 700 lines by the Danish poet Frederik Paludan-Müller, first published in 1838. It recounts the burying alive (with considerable and apparently authentic detail on the procedure) of a Vestal named Fulvia, her suffering in the hole as the air slowly dies away, and her several dreams as she keeps going in and out of consciousness. Most of these dreams serve as flashbacks, allowing the author to sketch in her background and explain her present situation; they recount her idyllic childhood, her vows to the goddess Vesta, her accidental seeing and falling in love with a knight named Marcellus, and their passionate meeting on a bridge. The last of them, however, is more a hallucination than a dream, in which she finds herself in a ruined temple where the goddess appears to her, tells her she is the cause of the destruction, and shows her a funeral procession conducting the bloody corpse of Marcellus to his grave. The poem ends with a reconciliation of sorts for Fulvia, who prays to the goddess that she may die before the lamp with her in the hole burns out, "and her prayer was fulfilled": the lamp in fact burns more brightly than before and is still casting its radiance on Fulvia's image "as the expression on her face caused by the pangs of death gently relaxes" (110).[29]

There is evidence that Ibsen was generally familiar with Paludan-Müller's poetry when he wrote *Catiline* (see Skard, 87, 90), and although "*Vestalinden*" is essentially sentimental and pathetic in tone and mood, the similarities between it and important elements in *Catiline* are too great to be accounted for by coincidence: Ibsen clearly knew the poem and unquestionably drew on it in developing the role of Furia and, especially, in writing the final scene of Act One with Furia in "the offender's tomb." Ibsen, following Sallust, had originally intended to call his character Fulvia, and it is possible that the coincidence in names with Paludan-Müller's Vestal is what prompted him to unite Sallust's Fulvia and the Vestal with whom, according to Sallust, Catiline had a scandalous intrigue. Skard points out (88–89) that Ibsen was incorrect in having his Vestal buried alive for letting the lamp go out: that punishment was reserved for Vestals who broke their vow of chastity, while the actual punishment for Furia's offense was whipping. Drawing on Ibsen's synopsis-outline for the final scene of Act One, which has "Fulvia" in "despair," unlike Furia in the scene as actually written, Skard speculates that Ibsen originally intended to have his character punished for the same crime as Paludan-Müller's but changed his mind. If so, Skard concludes, he could have been led to his erroneous cause of the punishment by a passage from Fulvia's hallucination, in which the goddess tells her:

> . . . Here Vesta's castle stood
> [. . . .]
> But you have quenched the flame: and the temple fell
> That very moment—but your judge still stands:
> Look behind you, Fulvia! Your punishment is coming. . . . (103)

Skard surprisingly states (89) that there are few verbal borrowings from the poem in *Catiline*, for these, both in Furia's scene and elsewhere in the play, are fairly extensive, enough so as to suggest that Ibsen had the poem at hand as he wrote or retained many of its details in his memory. The diction of the poem constantly suggests that of *Catiline*. To some extent, no doubt, this is because of the similarity of subject matter, which readily explains the numerous turns in both works on "gloom," "death," "graves," "shadows," and the like. But both poets also display considerable fondness for certain words (such as "bosom") and expressions (such as cheeks as "white as marble," eyes that "flame," and eyes that "glaze over" in death) which do not necessarily derive from the subject matter. Furthermore, several passages in the poem seem to have been the objects of more specific borrowings on Ibsen's part.

When the poem's Fulvia is first taken down into the hole, "She stands there like a statue mute and still / Upon the boundary where life and death / Disjoin" (87), the first line of which suggests the posture of Furia at the beginning of Ibsen's scene in the hole, while the rest is echoed by Furia in the first scene of Act Two when she tells Catiline about her experience. The poem's Fulvia is said to be standing "like a Genius / Beside her own grave" (88), which is a possible source for Furia's claim, several times in the first scene of Act

Two and later in the play, to be Catiline's "Genius." After the lid is placed on the hole from outside, Fulvia hears dirt being thrown on it and then "a rumble much like muted thunder" (92), which is the sound of a large stone being rolled in place; this probably accounts for Furia's first line in her tomb, "A hollow boom! it's thundering up there" (and perhaps, incidentally, explains what the already mad Furia is actually hearing in Ibsen's play). In her second dream, Fulvia recalls her first sight of Marcellus, when, from one side of a brook, she "quickly lifted up her eyes" to meet his on the other side ("like two bright lights uniting into one, / Then all at once the eyes of these two met," 100); this seems to be echoed in Catiline's account to Curius of his first notice of Furia while watching the procession of the priestesses of Vesta: "by accident, on one of them I chanced / to fix my glance, and with a fleeting look / her eyes met mine—they pierced right through my soul." Later, as her situation grows more desperate, Fulvia seems to hear another sound from above:

It was as if someone was breaking through
The ceiling of the grave, and Fulvia
Jumps up and turns her eyes unto the sound,
Which now once more comes to an end. She listens—
But nothing more is stirring now. (105)

In Ibsen, of course, Furia also hears a second sound, and in this case it does not simply end, unaccounted for, but is followed by Curius' coming through the iron door to save her. Finally, the resemblance between "Yes, higher than before its light was burning" (110), describing the effect on the lamp of Fulvia's prayer, and Catiline's claim in the second scene of Act Two that the spark of the ancient Roman spirit "shall be fanned up to shining flames, / more clear and high than any time before" suggests that Ibsen was still hearing echoes from "*Vestalinden*" even when he was writing scenes having nothing to do with Furia.

Skard's discussion of the influence of Paludan-Müller's poem focuses almost entirely on the scene of Furia in the offender's tomb, apparently because of his conviction that it has the effect of being merely stuck in. The scene tells us nothing new, nor is the action well served by it, he states, and he all but states that it exists merely because Ibsen knew the poem and wanted to imitate it (86–87). This is an astonishing judgment. Aside from the fact that in writing the scene Ibsen wholly transformed his borrowed material so that in its contents, tone, and mood it could conform to his conception of Furia, the scene is quite essential to the play's literal and symbolic actions and, indeed, enriches them. On the level of the literal action, it shows Furia sinking into full madness and explains why throughout the rest of the play she consistently sees herself as a spirit returned from the grave. It thus also provides a justification, a sort of anchor within the plot, for one of the roles that Ibsen has chosen for her in his symbolic scheme, thereby introducing a technique he was to employ often in his later work with such characters as Ulrik Brendel in *Rosmersholm*, the Stranger in *The Lady from the Sea*, the Rat Wife in *Little Eyolf*, and Irene in *When We Dead Awaken*.

Like so many scenes in Shakespeare, moreover, this scene also works through juxtaposition to convey much more than it explicitly includes. In the scene preceding it, Catiline, by showing his responsiveness to Aurelia's pastoral vision and by instinctively giving the money he has acquired for bribery to a needy old soldier, can once again be recognized by Aurelia as *her* Catiline. In the scene following it, Catiline refuses to accept the leadership of the conspiracy because he is leaving Rome and abandoning his dreams of achieving greatness there. Through its placement, the Furia scene comments in two quite different ways simultaneously. On the one hand, the desperateness of her plight additionally dramatizes the weakness in Catiline at this point of the Furia side of his nature. On the other, this separate focus on her, her continued preoccupation with Catiline, her eagerness to see him ending up in "Proserpine's great hall," and her being saved from the tomb by Curius work together to insist that Catiline will not so easily be able to escape his fate. In pure dramatic terms, in fact, this scene asserts far more powerfully than all the repetitions of the word "fate" the idea of Catiline's destiny being controlled by forces outside himself.

ii. Romanticism

Skard has noted that one major difference between Ibsen's Catiline and Sallust's lies in Ibsen's "entirely modern conception" of Catiline as "a divided character, with '*zwei Seelen*'"; this, he says, Ibsen took from experience and not from classical literature, "where the conception is, of course, rather alien" (84). I shall be considering later to what extent Ibsen's characterization of Catiline derived from his own experience. I am here concerned with a rather different source, however, for Catiline's divided soul is an index of the extent to which, in shaping and developing the material he took from his immediate sources, Ibsen was influenced by the conventions, clichés, thematic patterns, and narratives of literary romanticism and of the thoroughness with which Ibsen, whose reading was much wider than his location and circumstances would lead one to suppose, had absorbed these and made them his own. All of the features of *Catiline*, "even the oddest and most 'archetypal,'" writes Brian Johnston in a statement that is only slightly exaggerated, if at all, "can be traced to the Romantic movement which was Ibsen's immediate cultural inheritance" (29). Johnston particularizes this generalization when he adds, "The light-darkness, height-depth, inner-outer symbolic dualities, the Nature imagery, the characterization of the rebel-hero alienated from a degenerate reality and flanked by contrasting and competing female forces, and the theme of redemptive death—all are major elements of Romantic symbology" (32). I will develop Johnston's generalization even further by briefly discussing a few of the major elements of the play that clearly demonstrate Ibsen's reliance on his "immediate cultural inheritance."

Catiline's divided soul is one aspect of an over-all characterization defining him as a somewhat modified and softened version of the Byronic hero, that "blasted, moody, disenchanted" figure, in Johnston's description, "cut off from his fellowmen and responding only to abysses within himself and to the more awesome and exalted aspects of Nature" (30). Catiline, too, is a figure in relative isolation, unable to make a completely satisfying fit with any of the other characters, at odds with, misunderstood by, and finally rebellious against his society. He, too, is a figure with great passions and yearnings, who carries with him the burden of past crimes and misdeeds and may, in seeking to fulfill his aspirations, be readily drawn to acts of destruction, but who at bottom is nonetheless motivated by the highest and best ideals, and, as a result of *all* his characteristics, is far more appealing and valuable than those he is placed in opposition to, the crudely base and the dully good. The importance of Catiline's divided soul and his inner experience in general require that a valid representation of him must emphasize his interiority, even to the extent of sacrificing a particularized representation of his social and historical context and a vivid and coherent surface action. In this respect, too, *Catiline* responds to romantic convention, the idea that inner experience is truer and more meaningful than outer.

The dream Catiline reports in Act Three, which Johnston, also referring to the subsequent appearance by the ghost of Sulla, calls one of "the two most vivid events in the play," stems from an offshoot of the romantic preoccupation with interiority. Catiline's dream, Johnston writes, is a "sort of 'set piece' or obligatory signaling of the more fantastic and fearful areas of the mind that we find in so much Romantic writing" and "is made up of elements that derive from common Romantic metaphors" (45). It does not tell us anything new, Johnston adds, but "merely elaborates, in Romantic and occult terms, what the action of the play has established; but it thereby insists that we read this drama as a pattern of inward events" (47). When Catiline reports his dream, it seems as if the dark female in it, the Furia figure, has triumphed over the fair, gentle female, the Aurelia figure, but at the very end of the play he finally recalls the actual ending of his dream and the ultimate triumph in it of the forces of light. His dream—and his experience as a whole—have been transformed, and they now coincide with another romantic convention, the one Johnston refers to in his mention of the "theme of redemptive death." This is the tendency of romantic authors to save the heroes with whom their psyches are so deeply involved, even if it requires a salvation beyond catastrophe, through which the hero is finally redeemed and allowed to enjoy something approximating an apotheosis in death. Often, as in *Catiline*, this redemption is justified by and engineered through love, that of the hero for a saint-like woman, who loves him in return.

My mention of the contrasting and opposing figures of Catiline's dream points to what is no doubt the play's most striking reflection of Ibsen's thorough absorbing of the conventions of romanticism: his treatment of Aurelia and Furia. Aurelia, in her language as well as her nature and interests, is an embodiment of sorts of the romantic sentimental pastoral strain that, entirely lacking any of the darkness of a poet like Wordsworth, prettifies nature and rural activity into flowers, meadows, soothing peace and quiet, and pleasant tasks lovingly shared. Furia, in contrast, is an embodiment of the Gothic strain and its obsession with gloom, death, graves, ghosts, the supernatural, the demonic, revenge, and the more savage elements of nature, such as fire, thunder, and lightning. The most important thing about these two characters, however, is the structuring that places them in opposition to one another, battling to possess and control the soul of the hero. As is well known, the pattern in which the hero (or his lyric counterpart) is flanked by two women, the one fair and good, the other dark and evil, both of whom he is attracted to, is a staple of romantic poetry and nineteenth-century melodrama and narrative fiction; there is, however, something unique in Ibsen's employment of it. Koht (I, 42) regards the treatment of Aurelia and Furia as one of the primary instances in *Catiline* of Ibsen's originality: "For here he has created a new dramatic driving force. To be sure, many dramatists before him have placed alongside the central male figures of their plays a woman who, as good or evil, represents something of the man himself and urges him onward or holds him back. But Ibsen has laid bare the inner opposition in the man, his inner discord itself, in two women who personify the forces that are at strife in his soul."[30] And even if Ibsen's representation of this familiar pattern is not so original as Koht claims, it is nonetheless in all likelihood as thorough-going a version of it as we have; if *Catiline* were better known, it would undoubtedly serve as a primary example for literary historians discussing this pattern.

Ibsen's familiarity with romantic conventions and clichés must have derived to some extent from the poets he had read, such as the Norwegians Wergeland and Welhaven and the Dane Paludan-Müller. Quite clearly, however, the major source of his knowledge was romantic tragic drama. In fact, the careful, detailed account of this form and especially of the characteristics of its protagonist that Jeffrey N. Cox has drawn from his study of the romantic tragic drama of Germany, England, and France in large measure reads as if it were a description of *Catiline*, which Cox never mentions and apparently does not know.[31] Central to this form, according to Cox, is a motif that recalls Ibsen's formula in his 1875 Preface of "the opposition between ability and aspiration, between will and possibility": its dramatization of "the nightmare that haunts the imagination's 'dreams of what ought to be,'" that is, the likelihood of the protagonist's being unable to fulfill these dreams and of his destroying himself—both literally through his death and figuratively in wasting his best qualities—in the attempt (16).

The protagonist of romantic tragic drama, Cox writes,

> finds himself seeking heroism in an unheroic world and order in the midst of chaos. Though he lacks the absolute sense of self granted the traditional hero, his heroism lies in his continuing struggle to become heroic, to forge a meaningful order for his own life and for the modern world. This project has two important aspects or phases. Cut off from objective systems of order, the romantic protagonist must first turn inward to discover an inner vision within which he is heroic and his world meaningful. He must then turn outward to act in an attempt to realize this vision. In view of his relationship to his society, this action can only take the form of a revolt waged in the name of his inner ideal. (17–18)

"The inward turn of the romantic protagonist," Cox adds, is not the result of a preoccupation with psychology and character analysis for their own sake; it stemmed from a recognition on the part of the romantic dramatists that "isolation, alienation, sickly subjectivity" were the very problems they needed to confront in their plays. What the romantic protagonist discovers when he turns inward is "a chaos of passion and thought, spiritual longings and physical appetites. Neither providence nor society provides him with the means to structure the complexities of the self. He has no map to chart out the regions of the intellect, the will, and the appetites, nor a role to shape his personality. The hierarchies of the inner life have collapsed with those of the outer world" (20). The romantic protagonist "strains to transform his inner life into a powerful identity . . . an absolute selfhood," and while his "artful identity gestures beyond the alienation and isolation of the present to a fuller humanity . . . it does not reach the visionary point where the imagination transcends the distinction between art and reality" (21). In probing his inner nature, he risks becoming "lost in an inward gaze. Endlessly fixated upon the self, torn between this thought and that desire, he may become a romantic Hamlet, incapable of action." He may "betray his full humanity" by accepting "a reductive sense of himself," he may "adopt a destructive mode of analytic consciousness that defines itself by severing all the ties that link the individual to others," he may even "find himself... under the sway of an unconscious will" (21–22).

"Revolt dominates the action of romantic tragic drama," Cox states, for "while the difficulties of subjectivity lie at the heart of" its characterization, "revolt shapes its plot" (22). The protagonist's "glory and his claim to heroic stature lie in his assertion of his inner ideal against the chaos of a world without God, against the oppression of a powerful but illegitimate political order, against a society that debases the spirit and exalts materialism." This revolt must necessarily fail, however, "for it is in the unheroic present that the protagonist must act. Seeking to forge the future, he must adopt the debased means of the present and thus betray the ideal end for which he fights" (23). His attempt to impose his inner ideal on a world lacking a divine plan leads only to violence, and "violence cannot be purgative in romantic drama as it can be, say, in the plays of Shakespeare. Violence in traditional tragedy can contribute to a larger pattern of order. In romantic tragic drama, man's turn to violence can only compromise the order he would create" (24).

Catiline has been frequently associated with two prominent subtypes of romantic tragic drama and needs to be associated with a third. The first of these is the Gothic drama, the play's affinities to which have been well discussed by Haakonsen (48–52, 66), who focuses on its abundance of "gloom, terror, and horror," the presence of Sulla's ghost and its "evil prophecy," and especially Furia, whose experience turns her into "a representation of terror-romanticism's evil spirit." The other subtype with which *Catiline* has been frequently associated is the German *Schicksalstragödie*, or "fate-tragedy," a kind of verse drama that flourished for a decade or so after being invented in 1808 by Zacharias Werner in *The Twenty-Fourth of February*. *Catiline* is thought to resemble this form because of its Gothic imagery, its constant repetitions of the word "fate" (especially in Catiline's speeches), and its ending in which the lovers, deprived of a chance for happiness in life, can expect to find it beyond the grave—a motif frequently featured in fate-tragedy. It is highly unlikely, however, that Ibsen could have had the opportunity to see or read any examples of fate-tragedy, and in any case, despite its protagonist's preoccupation with fate, *Catiline* does not really observe the form's primary conventions. The writers of fate-tragedy, showing little or no interest in characterization, made fate the driving force of their plays and sought to dramatize its workings through a rigid formula in which coincidence, ignorance, and willful human violence produce catastrophe. Taking Werner's play as an example, the exploitation of coincidence lies in two things: that everything bad that has happened to the family in the play has occurred on February 24 and that on the February 24 on which the play is set the absent son returns to his home, an inn, exactly when his parents, out of desperation inspired by their poverty, have decided to murder and rob the next unknown traveler who stops at their inn for shelter. The ignorance consists of the parents' remaining unaware of the son's real identity, which he keeps hidden from them, not knowing how they will receive him, although he intends to reveal himself to them in the morning and give them a large sum of money that he has brought with him for this purpose. And the willful human action, of course, is that, although reluctant, his parents decide that this rich, unknown traveler ideally suits their purpose, which they proceed to carry out. There is, I suppose, something like these formulaic elements of coincidence and ignorance in Catiline's happening to fall in love with the sister of the woman he has seduced, not knowing that she is her sister, but the play gives these features very little emphasis, and in any case its center of gravity is elsewhere. Certainly, Furia does not act in ignorance when she pursues Catiline, and what he means by fate—a hostile force that frustrates his efforts to strive—is quite different from the all-powerful and malevolent puppet-master of Werner and his imitators. The subtype that *Catiline* needs to be associated with is the monodrama (discussed by Cox, 40, 98). This peculiar dramatic form, designed to emphasize the expression of the passions, is entirely dominated by its protagonist, with the other characters appearing "mainly to draw forth or externalize his internal questionings" (98). Ibsen probably knew no examples of this form either, but his development to their logical extreme of some of the conventions he had absorbed led him to produce a play that at times comes close to reinventing it.

Ibsen's knowledge of romantic tragic drama was undoubtedly fed by a number of sources. He is thought to have known, and drawn on for *Catiline*, Schiller's first play, *Die Räuber*, Goethe's *Iphigenie auf Tauris*, and even Hegel's model for tragedy.[32] Nevertheless, Ibsen could have learned everything he knew about this form from one of the two dramatists (the other being the Dano-Norwegian comic dramatist Ludvig Holberg) he later admitted to having any familiarity with when he wrote *Catiline* (Koht, I, 40–41): the Dane Adam Oehlenschläger, the leading Scandinavian dramatist of the first half of the nineteenth century. Oehlenschläger was also a non-dramatic poet of some note, and as such was responsible for introducing National Romanticism into Dano-Norwegian literature, but his most important work consisted of the many plays, most of them based on the Old Norse sagas, that he began writing in 1803. These include a fine tragedy, *Hakon Jarl* (1805), and several other pieces that are at least enjoyable; many of them continued to be performed throughout the nineteenth century. The young Ibsen paid his respects to him upon his death with a poem called "The Skald in Valhalla," published in the *Christiania-Post* on February 16, 1850. In it the speaker states, "For now the Northland's / Most holy gods have / Lost their one spokesman on earth," and in Valhalla Skulda tells the dead skald, "Singer! your memory / Always shall live on, / Never your lays shall expire!"

Samuel G. McLellan has provided an extensive demonstration of *Catiline*'s probable dependence on one of Oehlenschläger's plays, *Stærkodder* (the name of its main protagonist), written in 1811, published and performed in 1812.[33] He singles out, as likely sources for key elements and moments in *Catiline*, two female characters who resemble, respectively, Aurelia and Furia, and who, in flanking one of the male protagonists, form a triad similar to Ibsen's; a specific scene, in which one of the female characters gets the male character to swear vengeance and which contains several passages that Ibsen seems to be echoing in the third scene of Act One; another, later scene between these same two characters that has similar resemblances to the meeting between Catiline and Furia in the first scene of Act Two; another scene involving the male character that contains several elements that Ibsen might well have drawn on in creating Sulla's ghost and the prophecy it speaks; and numerous other more minor details of language, plot, and characterization.

A weakness of McLellan's demonstration is its being less thorough than it should be, for he overlooks many passages in *Stærkodder* that

Ibsen also seems to have echoed, and he neglects, apparently by concentrating too exclusively on but one of the plot strands in this very complicated play, several of its elements that also must have had an impact on the shaping of *Catiline*. These include the past sin of the titular protagonist, for which he must eventually pay with his life; his failure to find the death he seeks for himself in "heroic battle"; his effort to restore Denmark's past greatness; the dark clothing and Furia-like misery of the character McLellan associates with Furia; a scene in which the current Danish king, the weakling Ingild, yearns at length for an idyllic, rustic, and simple pastoral existence far away from the "empty dream" and constant terrors of kingship; and the old warrior who remains faithfully by Ingild's side in his plight and also suggests Manlius in various other respects. In its constant alternating of masculine and feminine endings, its frequent shifts into rhyme and into various verse forms, *Stærkodder* could also be seen as the model for the similar variations in *Catiline*. This is true even of the thirteen-syllable trochaic couplets Ibsen uses three times in Act Three, for toward the end of his play Oehlenschläger writes a speech in thirteen-syllable couplets with a strong mid-caesura in the lines, which differs from Ibsen's passages only in being iambic. And the occasional alexandrines in *Catiline*, which have the look of being accidents resulting from the speed of composition, may well derive from the more systematic use in *Stærkodder* of extended passages in unrhymed alexandrines—and may therefore have after all been intentional on Ibsen's part.

Another weakness of McLellan's demonstration—which my additions tend to compound—is that, by mentioning no other Oehlenschläger play except the mythological *Balder the Good* (1807), he implies, while not explicitly saying so, that *Stærkodder* is *the* Oehlenschlägerean source for *Catiline*. The fact of the matter is that *Catiline* shows evidence of Ibsen's having been steeped in several of his Danish master's works as well as in his dramaturgy generally, and in addition to *Stærkodder* two other of his plays, *Axel and Valborg* (1808) and *The Vikings in Byzantium* (1827), contain many elements that have unequivocal parallels in *Catiline*.[34] Axel has much in common with Ibsen's protagonist: he is the victim of a past crime that must be expiated, although it was committed by another, not Axel himself; he is constantly talking about the hostile fate that oppresses him and that, as he says at one point, has "wholly crushed [his] courage" and left him "standing by his grave, not at his goal" (269); and he is united only in death with the woman he loves (Valborg) but whom fate has deprived him of during his life.[35] The play also contains, in Act Four, a visit from a supposed ghost who speaks in a distinctive verse form and a typical villain figure who works against the titular characters (for no very good reason) and may have suggested Ibsen's development of Lentulus. And there are throughout this play numerous passages that Ibsen seems to have borrowed to adapt to his own use: for example, a character, not the protagonist, saying, "I feel within my breast an endless seething," and another character asking, "Is that a voice that from the graves is speaking?" (272).

The model for the Aurelia-Catiline-Furia triad that McLellan finds in *Stærkodder* is not really very fully worked-out, and if it was Ibsen's source he needed to use considerable imagination to develop it into the full-scope version in *Catiline*. There is a much better, more fully worked-out model in *The Vikings at Byzantium*, which, while still not as complete as Ibsen's version (for example, this male figure is not really attracted to the dark lady, who loves him in vain), is far closer to it; among other things, it is more central to the action than the model in *Stærkodder* and, unlike that one, it actually puts its opposing figures in dramatic confrontation. At one point, the Furia figure here says, "This little piece of parchment is a pass, / Which will cause Charon at its sight to ply / His pole to shove his pitch-black boat from land, / And furnish him [i.e., the male figure, against whom the speaker now wants revenge] free passage over Lethe" (222–23). At another point, the Aurelia figure is associated with the motif of fleeing to a distant pastoral world—in this case Norway—when she eagerly endorses the protagonist's initiation of it. This triad, however, is only the most obvious and important element of *The Vikings at Byzantium* from the point of view of its being a likely influence on *Catiline*; other elements of the play could well have helped Ibsen with such things, major and minor, as the Old Soldier's apology for his entrance in the fourth scene of Act One, aspects of Manlius' voice, the visit by Sulla's ghost, the swearing scene between Furia and Catiline, and much else. To cite but one example, here is the protagonist vowing to destroy Byzantium: "A mighty heap of stones alone shall mark / Where Babel stood; and, wild as Nastrond's spirits, / the Nordic sons shall trample on its ruins" (240).

The Oehlenschläger plays are not, I believe, to be thought of as sources of the same kind as the three I discussed in the first part of this section—that is, as works that Ibsen had immediately "at hand" as he wrote. But there can be no doubt that he was steeped in their dramaturgy, their characters, their language and imagery, and even specific passages, all of which found reflections in *Catiline*. It is also easy to see how Ibsen could have derived from these plays the extensive familiarity with the conventions and clichés of romanticism for which *Catiline* provides so much evidence.

iii. Ibsen Himself

Except for a mild lampoon preserved in manuscript and another recalled more than five decades later by people who had known Ibsen in Grimstad (no one seems to have memorized the more savage ones), the earliest surviving poem by Ibsen is a short lyric entitled "Resignation," written in 1847. I give it in its entirety because of its relevance to *Catiline*, a relevance that should be apparent even in my rough translation:[36]

> Are they gleams from my soul's night
> That have broken through the darkness,
> And, like lightning flashing bright,
> Born but for oblivion's starkness?—
> Was in vain then all my yearning,
> Was my dream a phantomoid,
> Am I barred the soul's upturning,
> Was my writing cold and void!—
> Silence, then, you undercurrents!—
> If I can't your sense descry,—
> Let me mid life's million servants
> Live forgot, forgotten die!— — —

Anyone fresh from a reading of *Catiline* will immediately focus on the familiar words ("gleams"—or "glimmers," which is perhaps better word-choice but impossible metrically—"soul," "night," "darkness," "lightning," "oblivion," "yearning") ideas (the yearning that has been in vain, the dream that turns out to be mere illusion, the upward striving of the soul, the vague and uncertain stirrings in its depths, the thoughts of living obscurely, without accomplishing anything that might win fame or prominence, and, as a result, dying forgotten) and images (principally that of darkness lit only by flashes of lightning).

Also relevant is the drama of the poem as a whole. The speaker feels stirrings deep in his soul and catches glimpses from it that arouse a yearning in him, a dream of accomplishing something important and valuable, of soaring to the heights and winning fame—in this case through his writing. But he cannot grasp (in either sense) the glimmers from his soul, which are born only to perish into oblivion in the instant, and so his yearning remains unsatisfied, his dream of accomplishment is *only* a dream, and he is left, essentially, with nothing but darkness. He even feels that some force, here undefined, stands in his way, barring his aspiration (literally, denying him the capacity to fulfill it). So he tries to still the stirrings within him, to suppress the glimmers, and resigns himself to living obscurely and dying unknown. This response is, apparently, a passive submission to what he can do nothing about, perhaps a means of consoling himself by seizing on an alternative that would seemingly give him a certain measure of control. On the other hand, partly because of the final exclamation point, partly because of the "if" (it shouldn't be that way, there are other possibilities), I also hear reluctance in the last four lines, even protest. All in all, the speaker's situation, as dramatized in the poem, is not dissimilar to that of Catiline—at least up to the first scene of Act Two, when Furia persuades him to abandon the consoling alternative, the resignation, urged by Aurelia, to defy the force that is frustrating him (in this case, his "fate"), and to strive even more boldly to reach his goal.

"Resignation" is the only poem dated 1847 in "Mixed Poetical Works" ("*Blandede Digtninger*"), a manuscript collection of twenty-five poems that Ibsen had written in Grimstad and that he put together sometime in 1850, apparently after he had arrived in Christiania, with, no doubt, the intention of having it published. During the same year, he also sent to Clara Ebbell, a young Grimstad woman with whom he had been briefly and unsuccessfully enamored, a collection of six poems; one of these is the same as a poem in "Mixed Poetical Works," and the five new ones, which are in several respects similar to the Grimstad poems, may also have been originally written there. As a whole, the poems in these two collections read like preparations for *Catiline*—or, in the sense I am discussing here, like "sources" that Ibsen drew on in much the same manner that he echoed "*Vestalinden*" and the plays of Oehlenschläger. To particularize this characterization of the Grimstad poems, I will first focus on two of the poems from "Mixed Poetical Works" that are dated 1848 and therefore presumably written before *Catiline* ("By the Sea" and "Doubt and Hope"; the third 1848 poem, "The Giant Oak," is important mainly as the first indication of Ibsen's trying his hand at National Romanticism). I will then discuss the other Grimstad poems more generally (since it is impossible to know whether in their earliest versions they anticipate or echo *Catiline*) for their similarities in words, phrases, and images and for their fuller development of the patterns adumbrated in "Resignation" and the two poems from 1848.[37]

The speaker of "By the Sea" addresses the "foaming wave" that, in its "joy in battle," no one can hold back: "To play against [or "waste yourself on": "*spille*"] the cliff / Was always your delight." But, he continues, even in the midst of your fighting and anger, the little sea-flower beckons you to its bosom. Your greatness is as fleeting as the passing moment; your strength soon vanishes and you sink into the "grave" that awaits you in the cleft of the cliffs: "Ha, Wave! is thus ended / Your dream of great feats!" Since nothing remains for you, not even memory, blend your wailing with the song of the surf: "For while in its heaven / Preserved you are dreaming, / In the swarm of the waves / You're long since forgotten!" In this poem, the speaker projects onto the wave his sense of his own situation, which is similar to the one in "Resignation." Here the battle to accomplish great feats is frustrated by a harsh and violent reality that almost instantaneously negates the aspiration and efforts of the striver, rewarding it/him with nothing more than the grave. In contrast is the offer of consolation in the sea-flower's beckoning the striver to its bosom and ultimately in the alternative of dreaming on, preserved in the oblivion of blending with the multitude. But "By the Sea" also ends with the kind of ambiguity I find in the ending of "Resignation," for the final note is on being forgotten—rather than being preserved to dream on—which may be meant as part of the resigned consolation but seems instead, once again, to be more a cry of protesting despair.

In "Doubt and Hope," the speaker evokes the violent storm outside:

> Ha! what a night, so dreadful, dark!
>   [. . . .]
> Ha, come you from the vale of death,
> You yonder shades, that go
> Like spirits above a night-time battlefield
> Endraped in clouds of gray?
>
> And the clang of these thunder-voices
> Now at this midnight hour!—
> Like the triumphant march of gloom. . . .

The storm reminds him of how his frequent scoffing at the horror of Doomsday has brought him only "wild despair." As a child, he prayed and dutifully performed his other devotions, but "Alas, that is long since passed." And now once more he expresses his scorn for Doomsday and the God he does not believe in, but once more he gains only inner turmoil from it:

> Ha, Demon, are you roused again?—
> Get thee behind me, Tempter foul!
> O, like the hurricane's wild chase,
> It's storming in my soul. . . .

He cries out to God that he would give all his worldly wisdom to be able to render Him a child-like prayer—but he is no longer a child and is blind to what the eye of innocence in its faith can see. And once again he acutely feels the threatening storm:

> O, dreadful is this night,
> By lightning only lit,—
> And yet it is a daylight clear
> Against the gloom that's in my breast!

Instead of despairing, however, he will follow the command of the heart, clinging to hope and to faith in his God. So let the hurricane howl; its song will lull him "into a sleep of peace and quiet," from which he will someday waken with his childlike faith reborn. Here, then, the self-assertion of the speaker, now unequivocally rebellion, brings him the terrors of the night and the grave both without and within, and to escape them he seeks a peaceful, oblivious sleep that is clearly that of death.

Like these three, the rest of the Grimstad poems (some probably originating prior to *Catiline*, some concurrently with it, some subsequently) are replete with words and images also found abundantly in the play and often contain longer verbal formulations that, assuming they were written first, can be said to have been, with only minor adjustments, echoed in the play's text. To illustrate this last phenomenon, I cite a few striking examples from the many that might be chosen:

> Out over the churchyard's wasteland
> The night has spread widely its wings;—
> So calmly the dead are there slumbering,
> A slumber not easy to break. . . .
> (From "The Ball of the Dead," [1849], Ibsen's version of the dance of death);

"the forms of air that are my dreams" ("Autumn Evening," 1849); "The cooling sea-breeze fans about my brow" ("A Moonlight Trip on the Sea," 1849); "It is too bright, it is too bright / Where the moon is shining down" ("An Evening's Wandering in the Woods," 1849); "But there beyond the thralldom's night will beam a glorious dawning" ("To Hungary," dated 1849 and, given its content, probably written after the final defeat of the Hungarians on August 11; but the handwriting on the wall for them was already evident by December 1848, and the poem was perhaps initially conceived at that time); "Woe, o woe to you, if you desert in time of danger"; "What the curtain of the future hides still lies / in dimness,—but the veil will shortly burst"; "Soon turns the page in the book of fate" (all three passages from "Wake, Scandinavians!" dated 1849 and presumably responding to the threatened invasion of Denmark by Prussian armies in the spring of that year; but its exhortations are almost equally applicable to a similar situation nine months earlier in 1848); "How splendid in dreams once again / To clasp each memory as a friend"

("In the Night," 1850); "To be able to reach the goal toward which you aspire" ("Youthful Dreams," the first of the six poems sent to Clara Ebbell); "Tear her [your Ideal] out of your soul, and you will meet, / Which way you turn, an endless wasteland!" (number 3 of "Sonnets," the second of the six poems sent to Clara Ebbell.)

The far more important feature of these later Grimstad poems, partly because it is not affected by their individual dating, is that they amplify over and over the details of the little drama sketched out in the three poems from 1847 and 1848. The speaker of these later poems remains constantly preoccupied with his yearnings, sometimes humorously but most often in deadly earnest, frequently in terms of his search for love but also with regard to other matters. He is even more preoccupied, however, with the frustration of his yearnings, with reality's hostile response to his desires for accomplishment and self-fulfillment, with "the image of what fate has given me: / No peace in life, no peace in the grave, / No peace in eternity!—" ("An Evening's Wandering in the Woods"). Again and again, his striving—or even his mere wish—arouses a threatening and terrifying complex of images of night, darkness, storms, and shades rising from their graves. Again and again, to counteract this he seeks refuge in dreams, memories (sometimes even the memories of dreams), and the love of his "heart's ideal" (a dream lady, his "star"), whose "tender, gentle look" brings him "cooling relief" ("Autumn Evening") and who will

> Disperse the black cloud of doubt
> From my sick interior,
> Let a blessed dawn of certainty
> Sparkle through the gloom!— ("To the Star")

And often in these poems the counteracting force evolves into a fully-represented pastoral world. The speaker dreads the demonic force, but he is sometimes strangely attracted to it, and one of the Grimstad poems ("An Evening's Wandering in the Woods") can best be described as a dark, demonic pastoral. Significantly, given the speaker's sense of the hopelessness of his ever being able to fulfill his dreams in the real world, both forces culminate in death, so that frequently the outcome of his drama is his escape from a death of violent horror by seeking instead the peaceful "sleep" of oblivion.

Behind these alternatives, no doubt, lie the hell and heaven of Christianity.

It requires no critical brilliance to perceive the intimate connection between the little drama of the poems and central elements of *Catiline*. Furia is less a dramatic character in the normal sense than a culminating personification of the demonic images, while Aurelia is a similar creation made from the soothing "heart's ideal" and the pastoral world that is an alternative expression of what this ideal embodies. And the situation of the speaker in these poems has provided the major source for dramatizing the experience of the play's protagonist: his initial condition, his conflict, the course of action he pursues, and his ultimate fate.[38] The little drama of the poems quite clearly articulates Ibsen's feelings about his situation in Grimstad, and his recreation of this drama as the core of *Catiline* makes it, especially through the representation of its protagonist, an intensely personal statement.[39]

I have already discussed, in the first section of this introduction, the impact on *Catiline* of Ibsen's response to the uprisings of 1848, but a couple of further observations on that topic are in order here. The first is that his understanding of these events seems to have been rather vague, even confused. His unalloyed enthusiasm for the cause of the Hungarians does not seem to have taken into account that, in addition to trying to free themselves from a subordinate position in the Austro-Hungarian Empire, the Hungarians were also planning to subjugate the several Slavic peoples in their territory, even to the extent of forcing them to abandon their own languages and adopt Hungarian. Similarly, Ibsen's enthusiastic support for tiny Denmark, threatened, as he saw it, with annihilation by the Prussian hordes, pretty well ignores the origin of the trouble in Denmark, the wish of the German-speaking citizens of Slesvig and Holstein to free themselves from what they regarded as domination by a foreign power: the Danes. Ibsen's vagueness about the heady events that so inspired him may account for—as it surely is a corollary of—the essential thinness of genuine historical and political background in his play. He seems to have seen the uprisings of 1848 as a sort of melodrama of oppressed victims heroically seeking to free themselves from or to resist the subjugation of evil tyrants. If this is the case, it helps explain the ease with which he could equate the historical Catiline with the oppressed victims of 1848, the outsider-rebel of romantic narrative, and the unjustly treated, scorned pharmacist's assistant whose inner yearnings assured him that he deserved a better fate.

The other observation is that 1848 was the year not only of the rebellions but also of their quelling. The reaction dragged on into 1849 and even, to some extent, into the next couple of years, but by the end of 1848 it must have been already evident to anyone paying the least bit of attention that most of the rebellions had been fully suppressed and that the rest of them inevitably would be. 1848 could have provided Ibsen, then, with a full mirroring at a grand level of his own little drama, a large-scale confirmation of his fears that those who deserved to fulfill their aspirations were fated to be crushed in the attempt. Hence the importance—verbally, at any rate—of the fate-motif in his play, and hence, too, the full appeal of the story of Catiline, which in its entirety—his defeat as well as his noble attempt—must have seemed to Ibsen to match the course of events on the continent, events that by the end of the year he may well have seen as the tragedy of 1848. "To Hungary" and "Wake, Scandinavians!" (his vigorous, shaming exhortation to the Swedes, Norwegians, and particularly King Oscar of Sweden-Norway to go in aid of their Danish brothers) especially show that Ibsen wanted to do something himself to help the cause of the oppressed, and I will speculate even further by suggesting that to some extent the writing of Catiline was an act in this spirit, an attempt to liberate Catiline from the tyrannical literary subjugation practiced on him by those supporters of the party in power, Sallust and Cicero, who had succeeded in unjustly blackening his reputation for posterity. But since Ibsen's Catiline is largely himself, this act was, of course, an effort at self-liberation as well.

iv. A Note on Julius Caesar

Since I am dealing with the sources of Catiline, I want to try to dispel a notion that has been repeated by so many commentators on the play that it now seems almost taken for granted: that Ibsen must have already been somehow familiar with Shakespeare when he wrote Catiline and that Julius Caesar is one of the play's sources. Most of the commentators merely say so, and the fullest attempt to argue this notion that I have been able to find is by Francis Bull in his Introduction to *Catiline* in Volume I of the Hundreårsutgave:

> ... when one places Shakespeare's *Julius Caesar* and Ibsen's *Catiline* alongside one another, one will easily notice a wealth of substantial common characteristics: both plays take place in ancient Rome toward the end of the Republic and both end with great battles in which the hero (Brutus, Catiline) loses and his cause is destroyed; when he does not succeed in finding death in battle, he kills himself. This hero is in both cases a large-minded, proud, aristocratic Roman, who raises a rebellion against those in power because they seem to him to have degenerated from the ancient Roman virtues and ideals. Brutus has, like Catiline, a noble, self-sacrificing wife but feels constantly dissatisfied, lives "in dissension with himself," and half reluctantly is lured into a conspiracy of which he immediately becomes leader. Prior to the final battle, there appears before both Brutus and Catiline a frightening ghost from Rome's past who is an omen of disaster. (35)

Some of these parallels are obviously coincidences for which history, not the dramatists, are responsible—unless one assumes that the model of *Julius Caesar* prompted Ibsen to seek a similar story in the annals of Rome.[40] And most of the others depend a great deal on their being stated in very general and even vague terms. The evidence tends to indicate that Ibsen was attracted to the story of Catiline merely by the fortuitous chance of his reading the relevant material during the year of revolutions and that he got both the idea of dramatizing it and guidance in doing so from the sources I have discussed. If one accepts this evidence, almost every parallel that Bull lists, however plausible it may seem when the two plays are considered in isolation, takes on the look of mere coincidence.

I say "almost" because of the parallel concerning the ghosts, which is the least easily dismissible point in Bull's argument for *Julius Caesar* as a source for *Catiline*. And yet, as I have shown, Ibsen may easily have gotten his idea for the visit by Sulla's ghost quite independently of Shakespeare, from a suggestion in Cicero and the practice of Oehlenschläger. Both Brutus and Catiline do ask the ghost his identity and urge him to speak, but there are no other verbal parallels, and this seems out of keeping with the way Ibsen worked with sources like "*Vestalinden*" and Oehlenschläger's plays. Furthermore, it seems to me that the influence of Shakespeare, even at this early point, would have prompted Ibsen to try to give more substance to his minor characters and especially to the background of his action, something that seems clearly to have happened when he definitely came to know Shakespeare a few years later. And since the ghost in Ibsen is that of Sulla, its appearance might better be seen as an indication of Ibsen's indebtedness to Ben Jonson, who also raises Sulla's ghost in his *Catiline*; but this is an extreme unlikelihood that, as far as I know, only McLellan (44) has suggested as even a remote possibility.

Analysis and Evaluation

This section concerns only the first version of *Catiline*. I shall briefly discuss the changes Ibsen made in the 1875 revision and evaluate it in the following section.

i. Form

Proper understanding and appreciation of *Catiline* necessitate realizing exactly what kind of literary work it is. All three title pages (of the 1849 manuscript, the 1850 printed text, and the 1875 revision) call it a "Drama," and a number of its features would seem to justify this label. Scenes like those in which Furia compels Catiline to accept leadership of the conspiracy and Curius to betray it, for example, work in the way we expect episodes in drama to work—that is, the pressure of one character on another results in the second character's acting in a way he had not intended to and may even have been determined not to. Equally dramatic in this sense is the episode in which Catiline swears revenge against Furia's enemy only to discover that *he* is that enemy and that his swearing has therefore irrevocably altered his own situation. And, to exemplify another sense in which *Catiline* resembles genuine drama, Manlius, unlike most of the characters, tends to speak, especially in the beginning of Act Three, with a distinctive, plausible voice, so that his characterization is not merely a matter of his possessing a few easily recognizable traits and motives, as is the case with the other co-conspirators. On the whole, however, *Catiline* is much more accurately described by the label Ibsen applied to his second play, *The Burial Mound*: "dramatic poem." In other words, Ibsen's tendency throughout *Catiline*—even to some extent in the episodes I have mentioned—is to shape, heighten, and define his material more through the means of poetry than of drama.

The most obvious indication of this tendency is the play's versification.[41] The primary mode of *Catiline* is blank verse, the verse-form closest to normal speech. From the beginning, however, Ibsen mutes this effect by trying systematically to alternate masculine line-endings with feminine ones, and, more important, he frequently suppresses it altogether by substituting rhyming passages for the blank-verse norm, some of them in meters other than iambic pentameter. Through most of the first two acts, the substitutions consist of sequences rhyming abab.[42] The final speech of Act Two, still iambic pentameter, rhymes in couplets. The Ghost's cryptic prophecy in Act Three is in iambic octosyllabics rhyming abab. And, in by far the most conspicuous substitutions in the play, three long passages in Act Three—one near the beginning, one in the middle, and one at the end—employ thirteen-syllable trochaic couplets with a strong caesura after the eighth syllable in nearly every line (some of the couplets—and a few individual lines—in these sequences contain fifteen syllables per line, with the caesura still occurring after the eighth syllable).

Lervik argues interestingly (278–79) that the rhyming passages signal a powerful emotional interplay between the characters involved, either because of harmony of thought between them or because of one character's strong opposition to what the other is saying. Whatever one makes of this argument, it seems unequivocal that a major function of the rhyming passages is to give added, *poetic*, emphasis to the moments they encompass, thus lending these moments a heightened effect similar to that normally produced in drama by the interaction of characters or of characters and external events. A survey of the moments involved supports this view. The rhyming passages in Acts One and Two encompass Catiline's declaration to the Allobrogian ambassadors (and to the audience) of his being a lover of freedom, hater of tyrants, and champion of the oppressed and of his intention to do something to restore Rome's past glory; the discovery by Catiline and Furia of their spiritual affinity and her urging him to leave Rome with her to found an empire elsewhere; Aurelia's attempt to soothe Catiline with an application of tender comforting and her extended description of the pastoral haven to which she urges him to flee; Furia's winning Catiline back to assume leadership of the conspiracy (brief, intermittent rhyming); Furia's account to Curius, as she assumes full control over his will, of her existence in Death's abode; and the fiery speech by Catiline at the end of Act Two as he imagines the utter destruction of Rome. In Act Three, in addition to the prophecy of the Ghost and the three trochaic passages, already mentioned, there is also a brief rhyming substitution similar in kind to most of those in Acts One and Two as Catiline leads his men out to the plain for the battle that is to determine their destiny.

The three trochaic passages in Act Three constitute the most unequivocal indication that the drama of the play is defined essentially in and by its rhyming sequences. Through their versification, their content, and their relationship to the action they interrupt—or, in the case of the third of them, bring to an extremely heightened close—they define themselves as definite set-pieces. In their connections with one another, moreover, they lay bare and recapitulate the basic action of the entire play. The first of them, Catiline's dream, records in extreme symbolic terms his ultimate situation, his sense of existing in a dark, terrifying vault, with only intermittent glimpses of light and of "a better sphere," and particularly of his being fought over by two diametrically opposed women, one of fairness, gentleness, and radiance, the other a dark and threatening figure by whom he is appalled but toward whom he also feels strangely attracted. He cannot recall the ending of his dream, but at the point where his memory has failed him it looks as if the dark figure is triumphing, for the forces associated with her are clearly besting the fair figure and her forces. The second trochaic passage, a debate between Furia and Aurelia, provides, as it were, an extreme close-up of the contest between the two figures of the dream and stages it as dramatic conflict. Furia begins the debate where the dark figure of the dream left off, definitely in command and confident of ultimate victory. Aurelia at first seems, like the fair figure of the dream, in a position of weakness, but she quickly gains strength, signalling her ability to stand up to Furia by interrupting and completing one of her couplets, and it is Aurelia who has the last words in the exchange, a passionate promise that she will eventually wrest from Furia's grim hands the booty she has seized and "bind him to the realm of light with love's eternal bands." The third trochaic passage transforms the components of the dream fully into dramatic action as Aurelia fulfills her promise while Furia stands by helplessly. Toward the end of this sequence, moreover, Catiline explicitly connects this action to his dream by finally remembering its ending, in which the forces of light overwhelm and eliminate those of darkness.

Numerous additional poetic devices contribute to making *Catiline* a dramatic poem rather than poetic drama, and while some of these are typical of what we expect to find in poetic drama, this is not true of all of them, nor are the ways Ibsen uses them and the extent to which he uses them at all typical. Individual speeches that lack rhyme often gain poetic heightening through strong alliteration (Furia's monologue in Act Three imagining the battlefield after the defeat of the conspirators), rhetorical fervor (Catiline's two long speeches to his co-conspirators in the second scene of Act Two), or careful defining of mood and abundant use of highly pointed imagery (Catiline's monologue in the first scene of Act Two). Imagery itself tends to have throughout the play far more prominence than is the norm in poetic drama, especially in its role in defining individual characters and the relationships linking them. Aurelia and Furia, as I have already indicated, exist primarily as verbal complexes composed of a small number of constantly-repeated images and verbal motifs. Aurelia is defined by images of light (especially the mild, sustained light of stars and the relief-bringing gentle light of dawn as it dispels the darkness of night), flowers, cheerful summer days, cool forest shades, and cooling evening breezes, and by such motifs as kind and tender loving comfort, lulling one into a gentle and restful sleep, rustic peacefulness, and quiet joy. Furia, in contrast, is composed of harsher, threatening images (darkness, the sudden flash of lightning, fire, death, graves, evil spirits, poisonous weeds and other plants) and such motifs as revenge, cataclysmic destruction, oblivion, and relentless striving toward a distant, difficult goal.[43] Catiline, whose nature encompasses both of these extremes, and far more in addition, is often made to show his momentary affinity toward one or the other of the two women by his adopting, or by the association with him otherwise, of the images and verbal motifs characteristic of the one toward whom he is at that point drawn.

Language also becomes virtually self-reflexive in *Catiline* through abundant repetitions, conscious and otherwise, numerous echoes, and the frequent recurrence of key words and key ideas. Catiline consciously and deliberately twice repeats both Furia's outcry when she learns that the man she knows as Lucius is really the Catiline who seduced her sister ("Ha! Nemesis indeed has heard my prayer; / yourself you've called down vengeance over you!"—the second time he repeats only the second line) and the Ghost's prophecy (the second time in Ibsen's original formulation of it). More interesting are the repetitions or near-repetitions of whole lines by characters who were not present when they were originally spoken. When Furia is trying to urge Catiline into action in the first scene of Act Two, she unwittingly repeats a line he had addressed to himself in the monologue with which the play opens ("Despise, despise yourself then, Catiline!"); and when she has succeeded, her "Now once again I know you, Catiline!" is an unwitting near-repetition of the "Now once again I know my Catiline!" spoken by Aurelia at the end of the fourth scene of Act One, when Catiline has given his remaining money to the Old Soldier. The third and last example of this kind of unwitting repetition is Catiline's declaration to his co-conspirators, in the second scene of Act Two, that "a new existence almost beckons to us!", which repeats Aurelia's line from the preceding scene, "A new existence will be dawning for us," where she is speaking of their flight to Gaul. This third example is notable because of its irony, but the effect of the other two examples, Furia's unwitting repetitions, is much more powerful, because they reflect and help dramatize a central feature of the play: the intricate symbolic interconnections among its three main characters.

By "echoes" I mean the characters' unwitting repetitions of individual words, phrases, and images, whether initially spoken by themselves or by others. There are numerous examples of this device, two of which should suffice to illustrate its effects. At the end of the first scene of Act Two, fully roused by Furia's urging, Catiline vows that "soon there shall be spread / a dawn of flames upon the city of

Rome!" His image recalls his speech to the Allobrogian ambassadors at the end of the play's opening scene, in which he uses the image of a sun flaming over the city of Rome to signify the coming of a dawn of freedom to Rome after its present night of slavery. In his Act-Two echo, however, the idea of nobly restoring freedom is entirely absent, and his main preoccupation in the speech as a whole is revenge and utter destruction. A more complex case of echoing, culminating in a similar effect, begins in Catiline's monologue in the opening scene of Act Two, when he expresses his intense desire for great accomplishments worthy of immortality in terms of his being able, just once, "to shine out bright— / and flaming like a meteor!" Later in this scene, after Furia has gone to work on him, he develops this image into "Ha! I shall shine out for the sunken Rome, / and blaze forth in the comet's radiant terror!" And he echoes this development in Act Three, when, after the Ghost of Sulla disappears, he defines for himself the purpose of the Ghost's visit: "He was afraid that I should pillage him, / not his glory, no, the radiance / of terror keeping bright his memory." The upshot of this evolving sequence is the subtle linking of Catiline's desire for personal glory with the pursuit of undying fame through deliberate, unmitigated evil that the Ghost of Sulla has attributed to himself.

The force that Catiline sees as standing in his way, frustrating his desires, and that he constantly refers to—his "fate"—does not get much reinforcement in dramatic terms, and in a different kind of drama one would be inclined to dismiss his references as "mere words." However, given the tendency of the play's language to become, as it were, virtually incarnated, these references necessarily acquire more weight than they would normally have. "Fate" is, in fact, one of the play's "key words," words that, through constant repetition, acquire important thematic relevance and even a kind of dramatic substance. Two other such words are "oblivion" and "goal," both of which are more resonant than the essentially unchanging "fate," the first because it images something that Catiline both desires and fears, the second because the repetitions of it by Furia and the co-conspirators twist it into quite different senses from the one Catiline has in mind. In addition to its "key words," the play also employs a number of "key ideas," most notably the motif of the journey developed and primarily exploited by Furia—presumably as an evolution from the "goal"-

concept—and Catiline's motif of life as a battle, between, as he expresses it in his final formulation of the motif late in Act Three, "the warring forces of the soul."

Finally, to complete this account of the play's form as that of a dramatic poem, I want to take another look at the third act. I have already pointed out that the three passages in trochaic meter comprise individual "set-pieces" isolated from the dramatic action and connected more with one another than with their context. With its alliteration and other poetic devices, Furia's monologue imagining the aftermath of the battle is a virtual set-piece, and much the same can be said of the visit by the Ghost of Sulla, a splendidly conceived poetic display that has no impact on the action. Act Three also contains a number of other passages that can be described as "near set-pieces": Manlius' monologue prior to Catiline's dream (establishing, in his talk of the dark night and the oncoming storm, a mood of foreboding), Catiline's speech to his troops about their having no choice remaining except that between heroic death in open battle and "being hunted down / ferociously like wild beasts of the woods," his account of the battle and of the "sleeping" warriors, and Furia's offering of the various kinds of garlands she is prepared to weave for Catiline. Act Three as a whole, in fact, is essentially a sequence of individual poems—of, be it noted, considerable interest and variety.

ii. Action

The basically static nature of Act Three is one of the qualities of *Catiline* that prompts me to make a distinction I would not ordinarily be inclined to make in analyzing a play, a distinction between its "outer" and its "inner" action. By "outer action" I mean the sequence of events that takes place as a result of decisions made and acts performed by the characters, that determines their destinies, and that we could imagine literally happening in some real world.

The outer action of *Catiline* originates in the nature and circumstances of its protagonist. He is, in several ways, in conflict with both himself and his surroundings. He hears an inner voice urging him on to noble and glorious deeds, but he acts only hesitatingly. He is preoccupied by a whole host of dreams and plans, but they remain unfulfilled. He is a figure of magnanimity, abundantly conscious of a need to help the oppressed, make freedom available to all, and restore

Rome's lost glory, but he also pursues "a simple round of pleasures unrestrained" and has seduced, perhaps raped, a young woman, causing her to commit suicide. He has sold his wife's property in order to bribe his way to the consulship, but he wants this post only as a foothold in his efforts to fulfill his noble aims. He has, then, tried to respond to the inner voice, but his doing so has won him only contempt and infamy, for he is blocked by the wretchedness of his circumstances, the opposition of enemies, and, especially, "fate."

He experiences the attack in the Senate by Cicero as a culmination of the external opposition to him, for it causes even him to shudder in horror and convinces him he has been condemned to an immortality of infamy, but this attack can also be seen as something of an instigating action, prompting an all-out effort now or never. The arrival of the Allobrogian ambassadors and—more significantly—the decision of his friends to do something about their own unhappy lots by rebelling against those they hold responsible provide Catiline with an appropriate opportunity. Before this opportunity fully materializes, however, he slips into the Temple of Vesta, like some debonair, devil-may-care playboy quite different from the serious, brooding figure we have so far come to know, to dally with Furia, a Vestal with whom he has, characteristically, become infatuated. Through her urging, he takes his first real action in the play, swearing to support her in her desire for vengeance against her enemy—who turns out to be himself. Furthermore, by revealing his identity to Furia, he also starts her on her own course of action, which is to exert all of her enormous energy and will toward taking vengeance herself by destroying Catiline and leading him with her into the grave and beyond that to the underworld.

Under the urging of his wife Aurelia, who wants to relieve him of the burden of suffering imposed by his frustrations and the hostility of his surroundings, Catiline agrees to give up his dreams and retreat with her into a peaceful existence far from the temptation of fulfilling his "sensual desires" and the possibility of achieving immortal fame. As a result, when his friends try to get him to lead their rebellion, he refuses. But he remains dissatisfied; his yearnings will not allow him to retreat contentedly. And in this mood he is suddenly confronted by Furia, now insane from having been buried alive and regarding herself as a spirit returned from the dead. Partly out of love for Catiline but mainly to make him vulnerable, she manages to free him from his half-hearted resolve to retreat with Aurelia and not only reawakens within him all his former yearnings but also inspires him to put them fully into action for the first time. Fired up by her, he rushes to accept leadership of the conspiracy, even though he knows his friends are motivated only by desires for power and wealth. Lentulus had proposed himself—and been accepted—for the vacant post, but, after a tense exchange in which the conspirators threaten to kill Catiline and then cravenly back off, they switch their allegiance to him. He then prepares for an attack on Rome, but even as he is doing so, Furia ensures his defeat by seducing Curius into betraying Catiline's intentions to the Senate and by frightening away the Allobroges who had been heading home to get "the whole of Gaul" up in arms in Catiline's support.

In Act Three, Catiline is in Etruria, awaiting the upcoming battle and suffering from bad dreams. He is momentarily shaken by the attempt of the Ghost of Sulla to halt him in his course of action, but he then resolves to continue boldly. Curius arrives, telling Catiline that he has betrayed the conspiracy and that the Roman army is on its way. He begs Catiline to kill him, but, after a moment of despair, Catiline forgives Curius and resolves to meet a heroic death. Lentulus, using two gladiators, tries to kill Catiline so he can fulfill his desire to lead the conspiracy himself, but the gladiators flee at the sight of Catiline, who easily defeats Lentulus and, after momentarily toying with him, magnanimously allows him to get away safely, an opportunity that Lentulus decides to use to assist the Roman army in locating Catiline's camp. The betrayals by Curius and Lentulus provoke in Catiline another moment of despair, but he is cheered by the approach of the conspirators still loyal to him, and, while Aurelia tries to hold him back, Furia spurs him on until he is ready to lead his men into battle. All the other conspirators fall in battle, but Catiline, despite his courageous efforts to join them in death, is spared, and he returns to Furia. She forces him to feel remorse for the death of his friends, the blood of Roman citizens shed by his hands, and— especially—his crime against her sister. He therefore longs to find the "repose" available through Furia's poisonous poppy garland, but he cannot join her in death while Aurelia still lives and holds him as well to life. Furia persuades him to kill Aurelia, and this act frees him to accept the fatal wound from Furia's hand. As he is dying, however, Aurelia heroically drags herself back onstage and fulfills her earlier promise by wresting him from Furia's grim hands and taking him with her into the realm of light, where he is at last to find peace.

This complete, and deliberately over-detailed, account readily demonstrates a number of salient features of the outer action of *Catiline*. There is, really, very little of it, especially in Act Three (until, possibly, after the battle). The typical action of romantic tragic drama, in which the noble dream of the protagonist and he himself are gradually destroyed by his internal conflicts, the flaws in his make-up, and the limitations of the people and conditions in his surroundings, would seem to have been constantly within Ibsen's grasp, but he rejects or ignores it. Much of what he provides instead, such as Catiline's several new resolves in Act Three and Lentulus' attempt on his life, is, at best, pseudo-action. What little there is in the way of genuine action does not stem from the protagonist but from others, especially Furia. And the climax of the action occurs at an unusually early point, the first scene of Act Two, when Furia lures Catiline from Aurelia and persuades him to assume leadership of the conspiracy.

This skimpy, top-heavy, and far from compelling outer action is ultimately little more than a vehicle to make possible the rendering of the play's rich inner action, the dramatization of Catiline's psyche. Ibsen was quite right to alter his original plan by giving Catiline a monologue before the arrival of the Allobroges, for this monologue at once introduces us to the real action of the play and its real setting: Catiline's yearnings, his sense of frustration, and his inner divisions and conflicts, all of which have for "their one arena" the interior of his soul. The voice commanding him "from my soul's depths" that he mentions in the two opening lines of the monologue eventually becomes associated with Furia, and so his reference to it initiates, although very obliquely, the primary device of the inner action, the use of Aurelia and Furia as representations of the two major divisions in his soul. This treatment of the two characters is usually described, in commentary on the play, as "allegorical," but for me the complex and ultimately subtle use that Ibsen makes of it amply justifies the term "symbolic."

Ibsen establishes the links—actually, the virtual identification— between these two characters and forces in Catiline's psyche in a variety of ways, explicit and implicit. Before either of the two appears, or has even been mentioned, Catiline speaks to Curius, in the third scene of Act One, of his two "loves," using the word in such a way that it simultaneously signifies both his internal feelings and the women toward whom they are directed. Soon afterwards Furia describes her lot as one in which her yearning to perform glorious deeds is frustrated by her circumstances as a Vestal, thereby defining herself as a parallel to Catiline; and, like him, she too claims to hear a voice crying out within her. Catiline expresses his recognition of their affinity by stating that her fervent speech "has the music of my own heart's core," and he continues with an extended comparison between Furia and himself adding, a bit later, "a magic force enthralls me to your side." In the next scene, he briefly displays a similar affinity to Aurelia by deeply feeling, like her, that "the quiet life / has pleasures that the raging turmoil lacks." But he cannot tear himself free from the "raging turmoil" (an expression signifying both the difficulties and uncertainties of public life and the "endless ferment" seething in his own bosom) as easily as Aurelia wishes, and it is not until the end of their scene together that his mind has become wholly attuned to hers. Here he states that he is in no mood to take vengeance because his mind has become "a gentle child's" and that "quiet comfort"—such as giving his remaining money to the Old Soldier—"also has rewards." It is at this point that Aurelia makes explicit what has happened: "now once again I know *my* Catiline" (my emphasis).

Furia's representation of one dimension of Catiline's divided soul becomes even more evident in the climactic episode between Catiline and Furia that completes the first scene of Act Two. Catiline initiates this process in his preceding monologue by adopting Furia's imagery of darkness and by focusing anew on his—and her—yearning to accomplish glorious deeds. More important, her entrance introduces a pattern characteristic of all her subsequent entrances, for she appears in response to his monologue, as if she were an embodiment of its thought (in some of her later entrances, such as the one provoked by the Allobroges toward the end of Act Two, she is more an embodiment of scarcely expressed fears). During their exchange, she tells Catiline she is his "genius" (more than once) and must accompany him wherever he may go, adding, "a bond most strange / links us together." Catiline still feels "a mysterious magic force / in all

[her] words and in [her] murky glances," and once again her words echo a corresponding music in him: "There a chord / you struck that touched the deepest part within me, / an echo in their sound your words afford / of what my heart has whispered endlessly!" It is at this point that Furia repeats Aurelia's line about once again knowing Catiline, though without Aurelia's "my." But her most explicit formulation in the episode of her serving to represent one of Catiline's psychic forces comes a bit later when she says, "I am, you see, / an image out of your own soul," a claim that Catiline endorses with fervor ("my genius, you image of my soul") when he gives her his hand in "everlasting league." After this episode, further explicit indications of Furia's symbolic representation of Catiline's own psyche are unnecessary and, in fact, almost non-existent. The two most important of them occur near the end of Act Two and near the end of Act Three. In the first, when Furia appears as if from nowhere to cry "Revenge!" in answer to his momentary doubting question about what he has to gain from the conspiracy, he asks, "Is this voice from my own interior?" In the second, her fatal stabbing of Catiline exactly fulfills the Ghost's prophecy ("By your own hand your fall will come, / and yet another shall you slay"), for she is both someone other than Catiline *and* himself.

Furia's symbolic role also has a further dimension. When she first asks Catiline, in their episode together in Act Two, to give her his hand in "endless league," he hesitates. He is disturbed by the "dreadful gleams" burning in her glance, "like lightning in the night's thick gloom," and by her "foul" smile, which makes him think of Nemesis. She assures him that he will find Nemesis "deep down in your own breast" and reminds him of his oath. She seems, he says, "a spirit of / revenge," and it is in her response to this that she claims to be "an image out of your own soul." Her words make Catiline experience "obscure forebodings / and strange but hazy images" rising "deep within" himself, but he cannot understand them because it is "too dark" there. Nonetheless, after Furia assures them that it must be dark ("darkness is our kingdom") and once more urges him to give her his hand, he fully acknowledges her, prefacing his acceptance of her as "my genius, you image of my soul!" with "O lovely Nemesis!" He clasps her hand and at once feels her touch tearing a passage, like a fire, through his veins: "Blood courses there no more, just raging flames!" Everything about this sequence makes it the most complex moment of the play's inner action.

For one thing, it gives Furia a third level of signification to go with her roles as a particular figure in the outer action and as a representation of one of Catiline's internal dimensions. As Catiline's later speech to Curius linking her with the Furies also indicates, Furia has come, symbolically, to represent Nemesis, the spirit of Revenge shaping Catiline's journey in such a way that his goal must become the grave and, beyond that, the halls of Death. Catiline's ultimate opponent is less the vague "fate" with which he is so preoccupied verbally than the malevolent force of Nemesis lying in wait—and even directing his steps accordingly—to destroy him *as* he seeks to fulfill his desires and *for* doing so. And it is through Furia that Ibsen makes this force genuinely felt. Aurelia also has a corresponding third level of signification. In his monologue, early in Act Two, Catiline calls her his "good spirit," but she does not fully take on this role until the very end of the play, when, in dying, she struggles successfully to free him from darkness and save him in the realm of light.

In assigning Furia her third level of signification, Ibsen is not requiring her to do double duty symbolically. As the climactic passage of the inner action clearly demonstrates, the malevolent force of Nemesis and revenge is as much within Catiline as outside of him. It is, in fact, an aspect of his Furia-side, his aspiration, that dimension of his soul compelling him to act, to impose his will and identity on the external world. For, in the play's full dramatization of it, this impulse is a self-destructive one. Asserting oneself necessarily provokes retaliation, and one would be much better off to retreat, to hide oneself in some quiet, peaceful state of oblivion. Catiline's tragedy is that he cannot accept this alternative. He senses that his yearnings are self-destructive, that acting to fulfill them will make him vulnerable to the malevolent force, but for him this force is also "lovely Nemesis," and so, in the play's inner action at least, he actively embraces the fury/Furia within him.

Ibsen's symbolic treatment of the two women is the primary device of the inner action's dramatization of Catiline's psyche but not the only one. Several echoes in Furia's seduction of Curius in the third scene of Act Two, especially Curius' repetitions of Catiline's first words ("I must, I must") and his sense of being snared in a "magic net," make this episode a replay of her similar seduction of Catiline earlier in the act. The scene thus pertains as much to Catiline as to Curius, and it adds to the representation of Catiline's inner Furia-dimension the suggestion that—symbolically, at any rate—it is he himself who betrays his undertaking. Similarly, although the ostensible reason for the visit by the Ghost of Sulla in Act Three is the dead dictator's obsession with preserving his dearly-bought fame, both the aura of perversity emanating from the Ghost and the parable on the futility of all striving for immortal glory etched out by its speeches reflect on Catiline's immediate intention, and it is tempting to read this episode as a counterpart to the preceding one, Catiline's recitation of his dream—that is, to read it as an expression of Catiline's fears. Catiline's three basic motives for action—to topple tyrants and restore Rome's past glory, to fulfill his aspirations for personal accomplishments worthy of immortal fame, and to exact a terrible vengeance—are presented sequentially in the play, as if changing circumstances were bringing about changing responses. But this effect is misleading, a result of the necessity to represent each of the motives separately to make it fully clear. The inner action is essentially simultaneous, and Catiline's various motives exist side by side in his divided soul—as Ibsen makes clear through Catiline's splendid Icarus-speech at the midpoint of the play.

Act Three is for the most part, especially in the three trochaic passages, a recapitulation of the inner action, cast in more extreme symbolic terms. But the act also provides an ending for the inner action, and in doing so it puts the finishing touch on another of its elements. The time-frame of the inner action is one long continuous night, beginning with the sunset Catiline calls to the attention of the Allobroges at the close of the play's opening scene and ending with the dawning with which the play concludes. This dawning symbolically represents Catiline's being saved by and for the realm of light, an outcome that, in terms of the direction in which the play is heading (to the extent that it can said to be "heading" anywhere), would seem to be a sentimental turn-around, a saving of the hero at the fifty-ninth minute of the eleventh hour. In the symbology of the inner action, however, this ending has some validity. Since life is a constant battle between the warring forces of the soul, and since we are doomed to assert ourselves and thus make ourselves vulnerable to destruction, death is necessarily a source of peace, rest, release, the oblivion that brings repose.

I have described much of the outer action of *Catiline* as pseudo-action. I want to go even further by applying this label to what might seem to constitute a genuine action-sequence, although one that assigns the burden of acting to someone other than the protagonist: Furia's relentless pursuit of revenge against Catiline because of his past crime against her sister. This sequence, not found in Sallust or Cicero, is Ibsen's own contribution, taken no doubt from the melodramas with which he was familiar. I see it as an attempt by him—an ultimately unsuccessful one, given its clichéd nature—to construct some sort of seemingly valid action from the materials of his symbolic inner action, specifically by creating a concrete substitute for the more symbolic "crime" of yearning and aspiring, of being compelled to assert the self in an arena where self-assertion has self-destructive consequences. The outer action of *Catiline* is inconsequential because the play's symbolic core, the substance of its inner action, continues to be the little drama of Ibsen's poems, and Ibsen has not yet managed to find a way to render it in normal dramatic terms.

iii. Catiline *as Tragedy*

In his Preface to the second edition, Ibsen observes that *Catiline* deals with "the opposition between ability and aspiration, between will and possibility, humanity's and the individual's tragedy and comedy at one and the same time." This is, I submit, a profound statement about the play, the essence of both tragedy and comedy, and (since he also says that this is largely what his "later writing has been concerned with") his own deepest tendencies as an artist, not only up to 1875 but all the way through to his final play. Ibsen was throughout his career essentially a writer of tragedy, and this tendency of his work is fully initiated with his first play. The symbolic core of *Catiline*, its inner action, entirely justifies the judgments of the majority of its first reviewers, who took for granted that they were dealing with a tragedy. Existence, according to the terms of this symbolic core, is flawed by a fundamental discrepancy between our vision of things as they ought to be and the ultimate reality of things as they are. We find ourselves, as a result, in the grip of a conflict between ourselves and outer reality that is also mirrored within our own souls. This conflict suspends us temporarily, but, unless we give up in despair and adopt some form of actual or spiritual suicide, it ultimately makes action unavoidable. And yet, because we can never negate this conflict, action, even mental action, inevitably leads to catastrophe. In all these respects, the symbolic core of *Catiline* is unequivocally tragic. It is not, however, merely its core that likens *Catiline* to tragedy, for several of its other features also conform to familiar conventions of traditional tragedy.

As an aristocrat, Catiline brings with him from history the traditional tragic protagonist's elevated social status—although Ibsen does not (apparently could not) do very much with this. He does, however, as in traditional tragedy, place his protagonist at the top of the play's character-hierarchy by endowing him with traits and motives far superior to those of his co-conspirators and, supposedly, the shadowy tyrants ruling Rome. More important, as Catiline's scenes with Curius and Lentulus in Act Three particularly demonstrate, Ibsen also likens Catiline to the typical protagonist of tragedy by making him able—indeed, compelled—to resist the patterns humanity has devised to ensure itself safe existence and, instead, probe the gray area of human understanding of reality by pushing against the boundaries of the known and plausible. In his divided soul, Catiline possesses the possibility for tragic experience that the others, in their certainty about what they want, completely lack, and in the juxtaposition within him of both noble, admirable qualities and other tendencies normally categorizable as evil, he has the potential to arouse in us the opposing responses of pity and fear that ordinarily characterize our relationship to the tragic protagonist.

Catiline's "ambiguous and enigmatic" dreams and the Ghost's riddling prophecy constitute two signs of how the universe Catiline inhabits corresponds to the typical universe encompassing and opposing the protagonist of tragedy in its remaining mysterious, its ultimate nature known only through its effects and only retrospectively. And Catiline's inability to grasp the Ghost's riddle or to recall the ending of his dream, the darkness in his soul preventing him from seeing what is stirring there, and his fatal attraction for Furia despite his fear of what she represents are all signs of his suffering from the "blindness" of the typical tragic protagonist, a blindness owing partly to the invisibility of the universe, partly to the ultimate limitations of even those endowed with a capacity to see beyond the human norm.

The action characteristic of tragedy usually consists of a sequence of particular stages: some initial act or acts of provocation by the protagonist (perhaps set in the past), one or more phases of suffering (often for others as well as for the protagonist), discovery or recognition by the protagonist (often concerning his or her own nature or the implications of what he or she has done), temporary loss of identity for the protagonist, and an ultimate catastrophe (in most post-classical tragedy, normally the death of the protagonist). Most of these stages are recognizable in *Catiline*. Catiline's seduction/rape of Furia's sister, as factitious as it is in terms of the play's real substance, is Ibsen's attempt to provide the initial provocative act. Catiline's suffering is frequent and many-sided. Significantly, as several have pointed out, he evinces virtually no suffering in relation to his past crime or his having sworn to bring vengeance on his own head, easily dismissing, for example, his brooding on these matters at the beginning of the fourth scene of Act One. He does suffer genuinely, however, from his inability to give himself wholly to either his Aurelia-side or his Furia-side when one or the other of these is dominating him, from the incompatibility he perceives between his motives and those of his fellow conspirators, from the implications of destruction for others in his plans to rebel, from his troubling dreams, and from other kinds of mental agony. Furia's tormenting of Catiline in the garland episode of Act Three with reminders of her sister's death and the other desctructions he has supposedly caused might be said to constitute some sort of recognition for Catiline since Furia is within him as well as exterior and autonomous. But there are also more unequivocal instances of recognition on his part. He prefaces his summation of life as a "constant battle," for example, with "It's now all clear / to me, what I so long have dimly felt." And, at the very end of the play, he recalls the ending of his dream, he characterizes his past life as "night-like, foully lit by lightning's glow," and he acknowledges Aurelia's ultimately triumphant role in both the inner and outer actions. Just prior to the first of these unequivocal recognitions, he reveals in a speech to Furia that his fatal stabbing of Aurelia has caused him to experience the sense of self-disintegration often felt by the tragic protagonist:

Now it is done, soon I'll exist no more;
death's peace already settles in my soul;

what's wrong with me? I do not understand it;
—it seems to me my heart-strings burst asunder
upon her dying groan—I'm so uneasy,
—as if the ample Earth had suddenly
become a vast and monstrous wilderness
where only you and I were left behind.

A few lines later, still speaking to Furia, he adds: "Well, then, I am no longer Catiline; / here, take my dagger, quench the lamp's last flame."

These resemblances between aspects of *Catiline* and major characteristics of tragedy occasion a question of considerable importance to a full evaluation of the play: does *Catiline*, which looks so much like tragedy, actually succeed as tragedy? My answer to this question is a slightly qualified "no." In writing *Catiline*, Ibsen's bent was already in the direction of tragedy, and most of the features of the play show that he was trying to shape his work accordingly. However, three of its features prevent it from succeeding as tragedy.

The first of these relates to tragedy's peculiarity among literary forms. We are prepared to withhold the label from works that look as if they meet its specifications, as we are not, for example, with the label "sonnet" or even "comedy," because we have become accustomed to think of tragedy in terms of a certain level of excellence. We discover the authentic existence of tragedy only through its impact, an impact that depends on a full, intense, genuine, and sufficiently artistic rendering of its materials. And in this respect *Catiline* fails. I do not have in mind the metrical flaws and the ubiquitous verbal filler of the first version—these infelicities were, after all, eliminated from the second edition, which, despite its being in most respects a much better piece of work, is scarcely more successful as tragedy. I am thinking, rather, of such far more substantive matters as the thinness of texture, the absence of any genuine political and social context, the airy nature of many of the characters, Ibsen's fondness for the clichéd diction and other literary clichés of his poetic masters, his occasional tendency to write weak and sentimental scenes like that of Curius' arrival in camp in Act Three, his failure to get full control over the various dimensions of Catiline's soul or to render certain aspects of his experience convincingly, and the general inadequacy of the outer action.

The second, and more important, of these features is Ibsen's yielding, at the end of his play, to the unfortunate (for tragedy) tendency of romantic tragic dramatists to save their protagonists in death. This ending, as I have said, makes sense in terms of the symbolic drama at the core of *Catiline*, and Ibsen is therefore not merely yielding to cliché. But his decision to render this ending as the conclusion of the outer action has nearly fatal consequences for the play's success as tragedy. Cox attempts, in his book on romantic tragic drama, to justify this kind of ending, but it undermines the tragic effect. It converts tragedy to affirmation, a difficult to define and assess by-product of tragedy that far too many theorists of the form have confused with the form itself.

Furthermore, this ending is but one example of an unusual phenomenon of the third act of *Catiline*: its dramatization of Ibsen's apparent difficulty in killing off his protagonist. Catiline survives Lentulus' plot against him, the battle in which all the other conspirators are cut down, and Furia's stabbing him with his own dagger— both temporarily, in his living on for a while after the blow in order to continue verbalizing his situation, and ultimately, through Aurelia's intervention.[44] In what is perhaps his most interesting and thought-provoking essay on tragedy, "The Fate of Athaliah—and Racine," Lionel Abel argues that one of the foremost requirements of the writer of tragedy is the ability to kill the protagonist and to do so in a way that is related to the inevitability of the tragic action as it is governed by "an inflexible order."[45] For Abel the "inflexible order" involves a conception of the universe consisting of definite and implacable values, such as those supposedly implicit in the cosmos of Greek tragedy, and therefore I cannot endorse his entire argument as an authentic statement about tragedy. I wholly endorse, however, his insight that the tragic dramatist needs to be able to kill his protagonist according to the laws of inevitability, which I take to mean neither killing the protagonist through tricks and gimmicks nor failing to kill a protagonist when the death is inevitable. And by this criterion, *Catiline* falls short.

Ultimately, for me the most important of the three features preventing *Catiline* from succeeding as tragedy is Ibsen's inability to shape the tragic substance of his symbolic core into a genuine action. Action, not lyric intensity, is the essence of drama, and in tragedy it is the action that dramatizes the sense of inevitability so typical of the form. We need to experience a recognizable sequence of connected and necessary events that move the protagonist from a potential starting-point step by step toward a goal implicit in it but not fully realizable until the protagonist's own course has been crossed—or, perhaps more accurately, blocked—by the workings of an absolute reality that is incompatible with the purposes of the protagonist and whose existence and nature can be fully experienced (as opposed to fearfully glimpsed or intuited) only retrospectively, through its effects. *Catiline* fails in this respect because in it the elements of this typical tragic action remain fused together in the simultaneity of the symbolic core.

iv. Catiline *and Later Ibsen*

One undeniable value of *Catiline* lies, as Ibsen himself saw, in its relevance to the rest of his work. His first play introduces, sometimes only in embryonic form, sometimes far more thoroughly, most of the action sequences, structural patterns, character types, and dramatic and verbal devices that he was to employ throughout his career and continue to refine. Ibsen was correct, then, in suggesting that those who wished to "master" his work must know *Catiline*, a suggestion he did not make about the early plays he omitted from the first collected edition of his works in 1898 (*The Burial Mound, St. John's Night,* and *Olaf Liljekrans*), for which the suggestion would be far less valid. At the very least, knowing *Catiline* provides the reader of Ibsen with some confirmation of the centrality of certain features of his work as a whole and with an opportunity to see exactly how those features evolved during his career. Some of the devices of *Catiline*, moreover, can serve as controls to help facilitate understanding of the use of similar devices in other, and better, plays. And at least one aspect of *Catiline* seems to me to be crucial for fully grasping the substance and dynamics of Ibsen's best work.

The feature of *Catiline* most frequently singled out by those commenting on its relationship to later Ibsen is the Aurelia-Catiline-Furia combination. This is the forerunner of the triads found throughout Ibsen in which a male protagonist is flanked by two contrasting women, who, no matter how precisely Ibsen endows them with a plausible, life-like psychology, always possess some capacity to reflect symbolically dimensions of the male protagonist's nature and/or situation. Major instances of these triads occur prominently in *The Feast at Solhaug, The Vikings at Helgeland, The Master Builder, Little Eyolf, John Gabriel Borkman,* and *When We Dead Awaken;* in *The Lady from the Sea,* the triad flanks the female protagonist with two males, and in *Hedda Gabler* the triad is extended so that the female protagonist is surrounded, and to some extent reflected, by three males. As the device of the triad recurs in Ibsen so also do the two female characters who help form the earliest example of it, often in connection with triads but sometimes independently. Furia has been seen to undergo reincarnations in Hjørdis of *The Vikings at Helgeland,* the title character of *Hedda Gabler,* and Irene of *When We Dead Awaken,* and surely she is also perceptible in Hilde of *The Master Builder,* to mention no others. Aurelia recurs in Blanka of *The Burial Mound,* Anne of *St. John's Night,* Eline of *Lady Inger of Østråt,* and Alfhild of *The Grouse in Justedal/Olaf Liljekrans.* Her character-type is sometimes thought to die out at about this point, but it survives in Solveig of *Peer Gynt* and is still unequivocally alive and well in Thea of *Hedda Gabler* and Ella of *John Gabriel Borkman.* Aline Solness of *The Master Builder* and Maja of *When We Dead Awaken,* moreover, display Ibsen's maturing sense that the Aurelia-type can be, in its own way, as dead and as threatening as the Furia-type.

The primary dynamic of the outer action of *Catiline*—Furia's discovery that the man to whom she is attracted is also the man who caused her sister's suicide and, because of this discovery, her devoting her whole existence to destroying him in vengeance—is melodramatic and, as I have argued, only pseudo-action in terms of the play's real substance. It is nevertheless an embryonic version of what Ibsen was to make his most characteristic action-sequence, the sequence in which the protagonist gradually forms, normally at least in part by realizing something about the past, a particular understanding of his or her situation and then, in response to this understanding, performs an appropriate and decisive act. In *Catiline,* the proportions are still all wrong, with the discovery coming too early and the bulk of the play given over to the carrying out of the decisive act, whereas in most of Ibsen's best work the process of discovery takes up virtually the entire play, and the decisive act becomes a climactic, culminating, and often redemptive gesture designed to transform reality by imposing on it the implications of the discovered knowledge. In *Catiline*, moreover, the object of the discovery is a finite truth, whereas in later Ibsen finite truth usually remains unavailable and the discovery is most often an idiosyncratic reading of the evidence, so that the truth involved is subjective and psychological rather than finite and absolute. Sometimes even, in later Ibsen, the discovery can be a gross, if seemingly plausible, distortion, as in Hjalmar Ekdal's self-indulgent conclusion, in *The Wild Duck*, that Hedvig is really Old Werle's daughter (she may be: Ibsen doesn't say and doesn't care) and therefore looking for an opportunity to betray him. Or the discovery may be a deliberate fiction, as in *The Master Builder*, where very late in the play Solness suddenly "remembers" his defiance of God up on the church spire ten years earlier.

Catiline also features a number of lesser dramatic devices that gradually become recognizable aspects of Ibsen's signature. I have already mentioned, when discussing Paludan-Müller's "*Vestalinden*," the careful anchoring of Furia's symbolic roles in the "realistic" level of the play's action. The repetition of "key words" in *Catiline* is a somewhat obvious and clumsy version of a device that Ibsen continues to employ but with far more subtlety and sophistication, so that the key words acquire new and shifting implications with each repetition. Aurelia's picking up and expanding upon Catiline's image of the shipwrecked man in the fourth scene of Act One specifically anticipates an exchange between Mrs. Linde and Krogstad in Act Three of *A Doll House*, when the two dramatize their new, mutual harmony by building together a fully-evolved explication of the image of shipwreck that one of them has introduced, but there are also numerous other examples of this kind of exchange in Ibsen. Aurelia's act stems from a larger pattern of language in the play, in which Ibsen dramatizes Catiline's current allegiance toward one or the other of his two women by having him adopt her characteristic images, and this pattern anticipates the later Ibsen's tendency to give his male and female twosomes a private language that links them and shuts out all others, the most thorough-going and sustained example of which makes up the conversations between Solness and Hilde in *The Master Builder*.

Beyond all question, however, the most important anticipation in

Catiline of later Ibsen is the play's symbolic core, for this continues to be the basic substance of most of the plays Ibsen was to write, and the starkness with which it is presented in his first play is what makes *Catiline* so crucial to understanding his best work. To become the major dramatist that he soon was, Ibsen had, of course, to learn how to evolve from this core an appropriate, meaningful action and to create for it an authentic conclusion that would not betray its complexities through sentimental cliché.

To show how well he succeeded in accomplishing these necessary requirements, I want to glance briefly at his last play—not because it took him that long (by no means!)—but because of this play's specific links to *Catiline*. Ibsen labeled *When We Dead Awaken* "a dramatic epilogue," which is most often taken to mean that the play relates to and perhaps even sums up his last twelve prose plays of contemporary middle-class life. And in many respects it does—for example, its preoccupation with an artist, its echoing of the "child" image for creative work from *Hedda Gabler*, and its near reduplication of the lifeless marriage in *The Master Builder*. But its unequivocal echoes of *Catiline* make very clear that *When We Dead Awaken* is also an epilogue for Ibsen's entire output.

The most unequivocal echoes connect Irene with Furia, and this connection has been well traced by Fraenkl (see especially 173 ff.). Irene has spent time in mental asylums and even now is accompanied by a "*diakonisse*" (a nurse affiliated with a religious order), who is prepared, whenever necessary, to suppress her with a strait jacket. Irene claims to have gone into the "darkness," she keeps insisting that she is dead, and at one point she describes her horrible, traumatic experience in a "grave-chamber" (some kind of sunken padded cell in one of her stays in a mental asylum). She pursues the male protagonist in order to exact revenge. Unlike Furia, she wears white, but the *diakonisse* is clad in black, and Irene refers to her as her "*skygge*," although she also objects to this, claiming to be her own "*skygge*"; here this word probably means "shadow" but it can also mean "ghost" or "spirit," in which senses it occurs innumerable times in *Catiline* (in my translation, I have normally used the word "shade" for these occurrences). Irene also resembles Furia in her capacity to represent symbolically the striving of the male protagonist, Rubek. Rubek is an artist, specifically a sculptor, although Irene also contemptuously refers to him as a "poet." The artist figure, as I have said, is frequent in Ibsen's late plays, but the connections between *When We Dead Awaken* and *Catiline* suggest that in privileging that figure Ibsen is going all the way back to an important element of the little drama of the Grimstad poems that he suppressed in *Catiline*, the identification of its "protagonist" as an artist, so that the act of self-assertion, of aggression against reality, is the urge to create. Rubek is still an artist professionally, but he was most truly an artist only when he was working in idyllic harmony with Irene, his model for the female figure in his masterpiece, "Resurrection Day," and, as he admits, the "source of his creativity." Her disappearance coincided with Rubek's growing disenchantment with his art and his decision to turn toward "life," just as her reappearance coincides with an awakening desire to resurrect his genuine commitment to his art.

These connections with *Catiline* make it easy to read Maja, the woman toward whom Rubek has turned in his attempt to enter life fully, as a much-transformed reincarnation of Aurelia. Life with Maja—and *for* Maja—is an empty, dead existence, a full-blown version of Catiline's fear that retreating with Aurelia would mean death-in-life for him. Maja herself needs to break out of this empty existence, and so she is attracted to the half-bestial hunter, Ulfheim. Rubek's discontent is expressed through his essential ignoring of her, since she cannot provide him with what he yearns for, and more importantly by the suppressed, concealed rebellion of the hidden animal images that he sardonically engraves into the commercial portrait-busts through which he makes his living. The state he acquired in seeking to enter into life is one of death, as Irene informs him and he himself amply realizes, and like her he needs to awaken from it, to undergo "resurrection."

It should be easy to see from this summary how the action of *When We Dead Awaken* improves on that of *Catiline* by shaping its sequences from the raw material of the symbolic core rather than by imposing pseudo-actions on it. More particular examination of the action of his last play also demonstrates Ibsen's greater understanding of and control over the symbolic core's individual elements. Maja, for example, receives enough attention to allow her to dramatize fully her own situation, but, in terms of the play's central action, Ibsen subordinates her and keeps her to one side. He has recognized that the two female figures of the triad are not coequals and that the protagonist's involvement with the Aurelia-figure is not really a part of his tragic progress but rather an alternative to it, a swerving from it, which he temporarily adopts out of frustration and fear. This change also eliminates the appropriateness of the vacillations, the seesawing back and forth, that Catiline undergoes and makes possible an action consisting of a single continuous forward movement in which the protagonist's striving, initially in force, is abandoned for a period and then once again entered into, this time with full commitment. In *When We Dead Awaken*, the initial striving and the temporary swerving are located in the past, with the second continuing into the present, so that the action actually dramatized within the play consists almost entirely of the return to the tragic progress.

With the Aurelia-figure shunted to one side, the genuine action emanating from the symbolic core can be represented exclusively by the protagonist's involvement with the Furia-figure, the embodiment of the tragic dimension of his experience. Ibsen's inclination to give Furia so much prominence in the action of *Catiline* shows that he was even then already drawn to this truer reading of his material, but in *When We Dead Awaken* he consciously and deliberately develops it, improving its details as he does so. The "crimes" for which Irene seeks revenge are not crimes against another but against herself and what she represents. The crime that sent her into madness and finally into pursuit of Rubek is his betrayal of her in the past, his failure to respond to her beauty and openness, a crime he has committed not in ignorance, like Catiline, but partly out of a fear of defiling his art and partly in a kind of indifference characterized by his calling his time with Irene an "episode." The crime she learns about in the play, which increases her urge for vengeance, is his betrayal of their "child" by his constant altering of it so that the original pure artistic impulse that was a product of their spiritual collaboration is scarcely any longer visible. The first crime, to oversimplify a bit, is a crime against love. The second, clearly, is a crime against art. The complex intermixture here of love and of the medium that constitutes the protagonist's self-assertion is a much more effective dramatization of this element of the symbolic core than Ibsen managed to achieve in *Catiline*, where it amounts to little more than Catiline's attraction to Furia despite the danger she represents and Furia's perhaps having as a partial motive for luring Catiline a genuine wish to help him fulfill his dreams. More important, the nature of Rubek's crimes—failing to embrace fully the source of his creativity and then deliberately defiling his creativity—establish a much more complex understanding of the protagonist's culpability than do either *Catiline* or the Grimstad poems it draws on. In these, the culpability lies wholly in the striving itself, but in *When We Dead Awaken* the failure to strive with full commitment is also culpable. Rubek, as he says, was "born to be an artist"; to strive in this way is a given of his nature and to refuse to strive is a betrayal of his true self. As Ibsen has discovered, there really is no alternative, no escape from the protagonist's tragic destiny: striving leads to catastrophe, but resistance to striving brings about the even more devastating catastrophe of death-in-life.

Irene's reappearance initiates the play's action by fully renewing in Rubek his desire to strive; this is, indeed, the only appropriate word, for although Rubek begins his reawakening by talking about his need to produce more art, by the end of the play his goal is rather "for once to live life thoroughly." But if it is Irene who renews his desire, it is Rubek himself who, as we expect of a protagonist but do not find in Catiline, wills to convert the desire into action. And he does so by pursuing a variation of the journey motif that Ibsen developed after *Catiline*, the climbing of a mountain, the goal in this case being to experience at its top "all the glories of the world."

The ending of *Catiline* evades tragedy as Ibsen wills a false triumph by attributing to the alternative course more efficacy than it has in actuality. He subsequently came to realize that, in the terms of his symbolic core, the only possibility for triumph lies in the tragic progress itself, with the triumph coming through not yielding, even though not yielding also means eventual destruction. This realization necessitates, of course, an ending with ambiguous resonances, and it is exactly this kind of ending that Ibsen gives *When We Dead Awaken*. Irene's desire for revenge never diminishes, and, in effect, she has it fulfilled, for Rubek is destroyed by the avalanche, along with herself. Nevertheless, the outcome is also triumphant, for Rubek achieves his goal, and though he dies the play has insistently redefined death as an awakening from life-as-death. In dying with Irene, moreover, he is embracing the "peace" that the protagonist of the symbolic core longs for but that, in *Catiline*, Ibsen could associate only with the unequal antagonist of the figure who embodies his striving.

v. Evaluation

Regardless of its importance to a full appreciation of Ibsen's work as a whole, a true evaluation of *Catiline* must also judge it on the basis of its own success or failure as a work of art. It would be pointless, however, to judge it in relation to the highest achievements in drama, such as the tragedies of the Greeks or Shakespeare and some of his lesser contemporaries (to keep the focus on plays in the tradition from which *Catiline* springs), for by this standard Ibsen's first play has little merit.[46] Proper appreciation of *Catiline*, as I have already argued, necessitates recognizing that it is a dramatic poem. Equally important—if not more so—it is also the product of the tendencies of the drama of its time, and it should be judged in terms of these—and not only because Ibsen knew no other drama when he wrote the play. For this purpose, I will employ a small sampling of romantic tragic drama consisting of Schiller's first play, *Die Räuber* (1782), the plays of Oehlenschläger (to select works particularly relevant to *Catiline*), Byron's tragedies, and Shelley's *The Cenci* (1820) (to select the best achievements in this kind written in English).

The major weaknesses of *Catiline*, from the standpoint of the best drama, including Ibsen's own later work, are an excessively passive hero—at least in terms of the play's outer action—the essential lack of any genuine action, and a tendency toward melodrama. Anyone at all familiar with romantic tragic drama as a whole, including plays besides those in my sampling, will readily recognize these weaknesses as typical characteristics of the particular kind of drama to which *Catiline* belongs.

Most typical with respect to the passive hero is Byron. The title protagonist of his first historical tragedy, *Marino Faliero, Doge of Venice* (written in 1820, published in 1821), acts initially in deciding to join the planned rebellion against the Venetian Senate, but from then on he is only acted upon and can only react, as the rebellion is betrayed before it actually gets under way, and he is seized and condemned. The father and son title protagonists of Byron's other play based on the history of Venice, *The Two Foscari* (1821), cannot even act initially but are from the beginning passive victims of the authorities, including one patrician, Loredano, who seeks revenge against them because of the older Foscari's supposed murder of his father and uncle. Between these two plays, Byron wrote his Assyrian tragedy, *Sardanapalus* (1821), which is especially revealing of his inclination for elegy rather than tragedy. Sardanapalus consciously resists the kinds of overt action available to him as monarch, forceful political decision-making and leading his troops in battle. Yet his reluctance to act decisively by condemning two rebel leaders exposed by his more aggressive brother-in-law is itself an act having significant dramatic consequences, for it allows the rebels to gather their forces and launch a major attack, forcing Sardanapalus to go into battle in defense of his realm. In this action, he is initially successful, repelling and all but destroying his opponents in the first engagement—and, in the process, occasioning, in the third act, the best dramatic climax in all of Byron's plays. Abruptly, however, and for no clear reason, the play's forward motion comes to a standstill, as Sardanapalus and his supporters suddenly start talking as if their defeat is inevitable, and the wound Sardanapalus received in battle, regarded as minor at the time, becomes regarded as fatal. From this point on, moreover, Sardanapalus has nothing further to contribute in the way of genuine dramatic action. Byron's least passive protagonist is the title character of his best play, *Cain* (1821), whose murder of Abel is the heart of the play and constitutes an effective climax because Byron has so carefully and tellingly motivated it. But here, of course, Byron is given his active protagonist by the original version of the story in *Genesis*, and his own contribution to expanding the meager material of this story also includes a long act (the second of the play's three) in which Cain has nothing to do except marvel at and ask questions about the wonders shown him by Lucifer.

For reasons I will explain below, Oehlenschläger has many active protagonists, but he is also capable of creating a fairly passive figure like the Axel of *Axel and Valborg*. Schiller's protagonist, Karl Moor, forms a robber band, engages in ferocious battle, and fatally stabs his sweetheart after indirectly causing his father's death by shock, but despite this roster of seemingly major acts, he really has very little impact on the play's action, which is shaped almost entirely by the manipulations of a master villainous intriguer, his brother Franz. Shelley's Beatrice Cenci acts forcefully to bring about the killing of her father and thus, as a consequence, her own destruction, but she is driven to it by her father's monstrous villainies, and Shelley so emphasizes her innocence (in proper proportion, a quite legitimate dimension of what she has done) and the pathos of her situation that she, too, comes to seem unusually passive.

All of the dramatists in my sampling are far more adept than the author of *Catiline* in managing to provide a smooth and seemingly plausible surface narrative.[47] Oehlenschläger, for example, tends to create very complicated plots, with many interwoven strands of action, but he has a sure sense for clean dramatic lines; he can make his points sharply and time them well enough to produce effective moments of decisive confrontation or abrupt but likely changes of circumstance. His characters are all clearly-defined and adequately integrated into a sufficiently delineated historical and political context. He has a good command of the particulars of the worlds he is dramatizing, and, while this often manifests itself in his constant allusions to classical and, especially, Scandinavian mythology, he can also use specific historical details as key plot devices. Something similar could be said about the other dramatists in my sampling, although, given one of the criticisms of *Catiline*, I should add that neither the co-robbers of *Die Räuber* nor the co-conspirators of *Marino Faliero* exhibit much more in the way of independent life than do Catiline's "friends" in Ibsen.

But whether the smooth narrative surface the others are able to produce constitutes genuine dramatic action is another matter entirely. In several of his plays (*Marino Faliero*, *The Two Foscari*, and at least the two final acts of *Sardanapalus*), Byron produces virtually no action whatsoever. *Marino Faliero*, in fact, in which the ringing of the bells of St. Mark's is to be a signal for the rebels to start their attack on the Senate, has for its climax the *failure* of a significant action to take place, and while such a failure could well be the core of a tense and exciting dramatic action, this is not the case in Byron's play. More typical of his art, I think, is the 112-line monologue opening Act IV, which is spoken by a character who has not appeared before and relates to the "action" only in the sense that it provides a lyrical contrast to the expected events of the narrative. Furthermore, by "genuine dramatic action" I mean, using the terms prompted by the sharp distinction in *Catiline* between its outer and inner actions, an outer action that is itself strong and engaging and *at the same time* fully dramatizes the issues of the play's inner action, and by this criterion the other dramatists are not much more successful than Ibsen was in writing *Catiline*. Byron's *Manfred* (1817), like *Catiline* more a dramatic poem than a poetic drama, tends to be all inner action (and is superior to *Catiline* in this respect in not trying to disguise the fact). Oehlenschläger's success in creating smooth surface narratives is largely the result of his seeking to accomplish something different from the others and, ultimately, something much less; most of his plays have no inner action. Schiller's real interest is the rebel Karl Moor, but all the energies of the surface narrative involve the intriguings of his brother Franz. Shelley most nearly satisfies this criterion, but he also clutters up his action, obscuring the focus on Beatrice, with the extraneous activities of her brother Giacomo and of Count Orsino, another example of the omnipresent intriguer.

What I have written about Oehlenschläger in the preceding paragraphs should have indicated that, despite his producing a successful tragedy in *Hakon Jarl*, he normally settled for melodrama, a familiar kind of popular melodrama with readily identifiable characters, lots of thrills and excitement, young love, heroic doings, villainous intrigue, and happy endings (even when the protagonists die)—all dressed up in verse and other poetic devices of a kind capable of beautifying the material without making it too difficult. Though Schiller and Shelley aimed higher than Oehlenschläger's usual mark, something of this kind of melodrama is evident in *Die Räuber*, in Franz Moor's manipulations and in Schiller's own manipulations of the audience, as he leads it to believe, erroneously, that the father of Karl and Franz is dead, and in *The Cenci*, in the doings of Count Orsino. These two plays also exemplify another sort of melodrama, a more extreme kind, characterized by exaggeration and excess bordering upon and often fully entering into the Gothic; in Schiller it is particularly evident in the scene where the Old Moor is discovered still alive, in Shelley in the basic conception of Count Cenci and a few of Beatrice's speeches. Byron normally avoided melodrama, even at the cost of having no action at all, but I have already noted his use of the villainous intriguer in *The Two Foscari*. In *Werner* (1822), moreover, with its secret passageways, extreme coincidences, robberies and murders, and contrived suspense, he takes the full plunge. Even so, the protagonist of *Werner* is no less passive than the protagonists of Byron's relatively actionless plays.

My accounts of the plays in my sampling have been designed not to tear them down so that *Catiline* will seem less small in their company but simply to demonstrate that its major apparent weaknesses are typical of romantic tragic drama. However, as I have pointed out in the preceding discussion, *Catiline* is certainly inferior to the plays in my sampling with respect to one requirement for achieving a genuine dramatic action, the producing of a smooth and adequately-detailed surface narrative. And *Catiline* also has other weaknesses that are genuine enough and that cannot be explained away by appealing to the practice of the dramatists in my sampling, especially Schiller, Shelley, and Byron. That is, at least the 1850 *Catiline* has these weaknesses, for Ibsen considerably reduced them for the 1875 edition, as I shall discuss more fully in the next section. The first version of the play has many defective verses, though fewer in the manuscript than in the printed text; some lines are too long or too short by a foot, others substitute trochaic meter for iambic and as a result are too long or too short by a syllable, and a small number of lines simply do not scan all the way through. The basic diction is too clichéd and too repetitious. More serious, the verses often have flabby moments because Ibsen overused certain adjectives almost as filler to eke out the meter, especially "*høi*" ("high," "loud"), "*stolt*" ("proud," "noble"), and "*vild*" ("wild"), with the first two sometimes appearing together.[48] There are also, as I have said, some weak, even sentimental, scenes, as in the Act-Three sequence in which Curius' arrival in Catiline's camp is followed by Lentulus' failed attempt to assassinate his leader. And Aurelia has nothing to do between the first scene of Act Two and her confrontation with Furia in Act Three except exclaim anxiously and imploringly or helplessly inquire what is happening. Fortunately, she appears only twice during this time.

But *Catiline* also has a number of genuine virtues. The verse, despite its irregularities and its moments of flabbiness, has basically a firm, strong, energetic structure, with the weight carried by forceful verbs, so that it maintains a sure sense of the individual line as a decisive unit, whether the line is end-stopped or part of a run-on sequence; this is the kind of verse that critics like to call "muscular."[49] As Fraenkl (221) has pointed out, this is highly dramatic verse, and because it is, it can be argued that *Catiline*, although a dramatic poem, is by no means closet drama. Partly because of the basic strength of the verse, there are also a number of very effective speeches in the play, especially most of Catiline's long monologues and his addresses, in the second scene of Act Two, to his co-conspirators; and many of the set-pieces of Act Three—or all of them, depending on one's taste for the thirteen-syllable trochaic passages—rise to genuine poetry. All of Catiline's scenes with Furia are good, both as drama and as poetry, and his episode with her in the first scene of Act Two, the climax of both the outer and the inner action, is excellent. This is partly because Furia herself is such a powerful and impressive character—or, given the nature of her role, "figure" or "creation."

Catiline's greatest virtue, however, the one that makes it most worth reading, is its splendid symbolic core, which contains in embryo what romantic tragic drama too often lacks: a genuine tragic essence. By itself, this symbolic core raises *Catiline* far above almost the entire output of its author's primary master, Adam Oehlenschläger, and puts it in serious competition with the other plays in my sampling, the real energies of which—such as the instinct for rebellion in Schiller and Byron—tend for the most part to be peripheral and incidental rather than central.

The 1875 Version

Ibsen made no major changes, as he tells us himself in his Preface to the second edition, in the basic conception and the scenario of *Catiline* when he reworked it in 1874–75. He did, however, extensively revise the play on a line-by-line basis, add a considerable number of lines, and provide a good many minor alterations that affect the play's narrative surface, its dramatic power, its characterizations, and, to some extent, its thematic ideas.

The extensive line-by-line revisions are of several kinds. He corrected the errors and incongruities in meter, except for eliminating the fifteen-syllable lines and couplets in the normally thirteen-syllable trochaic passages of Act Three. He cleaned up and system-atized the punctuation, greatly reducing in the process the number of exclamation points; he also strengthened the punctuation by frequently substituting semicolons for commas and periods for semicolons. He removed the rhymes from one eight-line stretch in the episode between Curius and Furia toward the end of Act Two, apparently because the existing rhymes were imperfect and, in one case, extremely awkward (rhyming the third syllable of "Furia" with "Ha!"). He changed the diction in a number of ways. He updated it to bring it in line with the practices that had evolved in Dano-Norwegian grammar and orthography since 1849 and with the personal preferences in diction that he had developed by 1874. He "purified" it to conform with contemporary ideals of a "true" Norwegian diction by fairly systematically purging words conspicuously showing their Greek, Latin, German, and Danish origins.[50] He eliminated all of the virtually omnipresent "Ha"s, sometimes changing them to "Ah," but more often rewording the passage. And, most significant of all for the poetic quality of the retained lines, he tried to substitute more concrete, active phrases for abstractions and polysyllabic words for clusters of monosyllabic ones, especially doublet adjectives, and he severely cut back on the filler adjectives and other often-repeated words. Of the forty-five instances of "*høi*" ("high," "loud") in 1850, he cut thirty-four and added only four new ones. Of the twenty-seven of "*stolt*" ("proud," "noble"), he cut thirteen and added none. Of the thirty of "*vild*" ("wild"), he cut thirteen and added only three. Of the thirty-three of "*sjæl*" ("soul"), he cut twelve and added only two.

The extent of this reduction of filler adjectives and other frequently-repeated but not especially significant words comes to seem even more remarkable when one realizes that the 1875 text is longer than the 1850 text by one hundred lines. The raw number tells only part of the story, however, for it is the net result of Ibsen's having eliminated seven of the original lines and adding 107 new ones, and this calculation ignores all the instances in which he so completely rewrote speeches that, although the number of lines remains the same, the resulting effect is of the old lines having been cut and new ones added. Furthermore, virtually all the new lines come in the second half of the play, from just beyond the midpoint of Act Two on, with the pace of their being added accelerating as Ibsen obviously got more and more inspired by his original text and more and more inclined to go beyond simply rendering it, as he says in the Preface, "in a completed form." To be more specific, he cut two lines from Act One while adding none, two lines from Act Two while adding thirty-two, thirty of them in the second half, and three lines from Act Three while adding seventy-five.

Many of these new lines result from changes and additions that improve, although without greatly altering, the play's success as a drama. Ibsen got rid of the confusion caused by his three Tullias (the mistress who deserted Cethegus, Furia's sister, and the legendary Roman woman who "sought the throne over her father's corpse") by changing the first of them to Livia and the second to Silvia. He sharpened the narrative surface by adding a number of details necessary to full clarity but missing in 1850, such as having the Allobrogian ambassadors indicate in the third scene of Act Two that their interest in joining Catiline is in large part the result of the Senate's having rejected their requests for redress. He also corrected a few errors in the narrative surface. These corrections are usually effective, as when, in the third scene of Act One, the "must with blushing" of Furia's "are you, too, one of those / who must with blushing Rome's great past recall?" becomes "without blushing." But at least once the correction calls more attention to the original error: in 1850, in the third scene of Act Two, Catiline, not wanting to drag his beloved Curius "down into danger's maelstrom," makes him promise to remain in Rome, apparently forgetting for the moment that he plans to attack Rome; in 1875, Ibsen amends this to "Promise me,—remain / within the city, if I should attack / some other place,— which is quite possible."

A few scenes, such as the Curius-Furia episode toward the end of Act Two and the much briefer episode with the Allobrogian ambassadors following it, become more dramatic through additions to the dialogue and heightening of the interplay between the characters. The most important alteration in this respect involves the entrance of the Ghost of Sulla in Act Three. In 1850, Catiline tells Manlius to get some rest, and the time between Manlius' exit and the slow entrance of the Ghost is filled up by Catiline's pacing up and down silently. In 1875, after Ibsen had had the opportunity to see a good many plays onstage, Catiline has a brief monologue after Manlius' exit in which he continues to brood upon his eerie dreams (always plural, even though he has told Manlius only one of them), and the Ghost's abrupt appearance, "as if shooting up from the earth," interrupts this monologue. This change, of course, gets rid of a moment in which the action comes to a virtual standstill, covered only by the gestural filler of Catiline's pacing. More important, it transforms the Ghost's entrance into an occasion like all of Furia's later appearances, suggesting that it arises in response to—and as a representation of—what Catiline is brooding about. In this way, the episode with the Ghost gains much more relevance to the dramatization of Catiline's psyche than it had in 1850.

Some of the changes and additions affect characterization in subtle ways. Lentulus becomes more consistent as his "Yes, yes, we'll follow you!" (in response to Catiline's long, passionate proclamation of his intentions in the second scene of Act Two) is reassigned to Statilius and as, in the 1875 version of Act Three, he urges the Gladiators to cut Catiline down "from behind." He also becomes slightly more interesting through a line that Ibsen adds to Catiline's scornful taunting of this trembling wretch for having the audacity to imagine he could topple someone of Catiline's stature: "You think that *you* are called to be a ruler?" This new line is of interest in and of itself, for it introduces into the 1875 version a thematic concept central to much of the work Ibsen had written since 1850, that of the "call." But it also specifically affects Lentulus: by prompting us to think about the two characters in relation to this concept, it provides some warrant for responding to Lentulus as a foil character rather than merely as a melodramatic villain.

One of the adjectives frequently repeated in the first version of *Catiline*, though not to provide filler, is "*mørk*" ("dark," "gloomy"). In 1875, Ibsen cuts fourteen instances of this word, but he also adds eleven new ones. What he is doing here is making the conception of Furia more precise by getting rid of the word in insignificant or inappropriate contexts so that it will remain more strictly associated with her and her influence (two of the cuts are from speeches by Aurelia, even though she is speaking to Furia). In keeping with this kind of refining, he also removes from Furia's speeches one of her two references to "the realm of light," a phrase more appropriate to the language of Aurelia (the remaining use occurs in the final scene of

Act One, when Furia is, in effect, in the process of permanently passing—or turning—into darkness). And something similar is involved in the elimination from Furia's vocabulary of Aurelia's word "*venlig*" ("friendly"), as her 1850 Act-Three speech, "No, just one / who, like a friend, reminds you of your past" becomes "I'm your own eyes, you see— / I'm your own memory and I'm your own doom" in 1875. Since she is here telling Catiline why she strives to make him think about the friends he has led to death, the blood he has shed, and the sister of hers that he caused to commit suicide, the change is also significant for underscoring the idea that her attempt, in the outer action, to instill remorse in him is a symbolic representation of his own internal and spontaneous experiencing of remorse. Ibsen's revision of Furia's final speech, from "Fall, then, by my hand, and I'll go with you / even beyond the shadows of the grave" to "I shall, you soul whom I in hatred loved! / Shake off your dust and join me in oblivion," is also worth noting. It replaces the overly-explicit linking to the Ghost's prophecy of her stabbing Catiline with an effective expression of her exact feeling for him. It also eliminates an image she has uttered numerous times in favor of a key idea central to the symbolic dimensions of their relationship.

Some of the changes affecting Catiline himself are readily understandable. Ibsen makes him a bit more decisive by indicating that in the second scene of Act Two he has already formulated a plan of action for the rebellion (in the first version the conspirators were to gather at his house "for further consultation"), and he makes him a bit more heroic by removing an 1850 Act-Three line in which he says, "I felt so limp just now, so deeply downcast." But other changes affecting Catiline are less easy to grasp and suggest that Ibsen did some complex rethinking of his protagonist and his experience. He removed from Catiline's reflections after the exit of the Ghost the image of "the radiance / of terror" that subtly linked him in 1850 to the aura of evil emanating from the Ghost—whether deliberately or because he no longer realized the import of the image is not clear. He also shifts the focus, in Catiline's exchange with Furia between his return from battle and his killing of Aurelia, from Catiline's longing for oblivion to his desiring to repent, an entirely new idea in 1875.

Moreover, in what most commentators regard as the single major difference between the two versions of the play, Ibsen eliminates from Catiline's late speeches in Act Three the motif of the battle. Gone in 1875 is "I long to find repose, / my soul has grown so weak in life's hard battle," spoken by Catiline to Furia when he finally accepts her garland, and so also is the more important summation of what he long had dimly felt and now sees clearly, that life itself is "a constant battle / between the warring forces of the soul" (cf. Koht, I, 43–44, and Johnston, 40, both of whom lament this loss). Ibsen replaces this summation with Catiline's cry to Furia, "Don't you see, / I bear the corpse of Catiline upon my back?" and his subsequent urging of her to release him from the corpse by impaling it with his dagger as a "stake." The image may merely convey Catiline's sense of being already dead but lacking—and longing for—the repose that should go with death. But the new image also suggests an image that Ibsen had used in *Peer Gynt* (1867), that of the Fellah with the mummy on his back, and another image he used shortly after the second edition of *Catiline* in a poem called "A Rhyming Letter," that of Europe as a ship sailing along with a corpse in its cargo.[51] The mummy and corpse of these other images represent the past, and it is possible that Catiline's image has similar implications, that the corpse on his back to some extent symbolizes the burden of his entire past. If so, Ibsen may have been trying through this substitution to get away from—or to mask—the static quality of the play by replacing the motif of the battle, a motif with no real beginning or ending in a narrative sense, with a more action-oriented motif based on the impact of the past on the present, a motif central to a primary action-sequence he had been developing in several of the plays he had written since the first version of *Catiline*.

Despite these many minor changes and additions, a large number of the new lines in 1875 result merely from Ibsen's expanding upon the several set-pieces and near set-pieces of the third act. He adds four lines to the Ghost's speeches, six to Furia's monologue imagining the aftermath of the battle, four to Catiline's account of the sleeping warriors, seven to his description of the battle, seven to his expression of the impact on him of his killing Aurelia, and a line or two to numerous briefer speeches. These passages were already the best thing in the play in its first version, and they are even better in the second.

All in all, with the possible exception of the loss of Catiline's summation of life as a battle between the warring forces of the soul, the 1875 version of *Catiline* is markedly superior to the first without losing any of its virtues. If one wants merely to read a version of the play, rather than to become familiar with Ibsen's first extended piece of writing or to see him at work in revision, the 1875 version is the one to turn to.

This Translation

The only English translation of the 1850 version of *Catiline* prior to the present one is that by Graham Orton in Volume I of the Oxford *Ibsen*. This translation is based on the printed text, and although it regularizes the punctuation of that text, it tends to retain the great abundance of dashes, usually rendering them as three dots, as if the speakers are trailing off in what they say. This translation does a fairly consistent job of reproducing the metrical variations and irregularities, but it avoids the rhymes.

The present translation of the 1850 version is based on the manuscript, which, as I have argued in the first section of this introduction, is a much better text. I have punctuated the present translation according to my interpretation of Ibsen's intentions with the dashes or the non-punctuation ending individual lines—that is, inserting commas or periods where punctuation is lacking and semicolons, question marks, exclamation points, or even some dashes where Ibsen has ended lines with dashes. The result provides a lighter style of punctuation than is now conventional, with commas frequently appearing where we would expect semicolons or periods, but it seems to me that this lighter-than-usual punctuation effectively helps to define the rhythms and pacing of the speaking voice. More important, I have also consistently reproduced the rhyming passages. This practice strikes me as being absolutely mandatory to conveying the effect of the original text. As I have shown above, the rhyming passages serve as essential keys to the play's structure. They are also central to its form as a dramatic poem. A version of *Catiline* without them is much thinner in texture than the original and, in fact, is only a distant reflection of the play Ibsen wrote.

Volume I of the Oxford *Ibsen* also contains Orton's translation of approximately the second half of Act Three of the 1875 revision. The

only complete English translation of this version is that by Anders
Orbeck in *Early Plays by Henrik Ibsen*. Orbeck, who offers no trans-
lation of the first version, does reproduce the rhyming passages in his
rendering of the 1875 version. On the whole, however, his translation
has a rather archaic ring, even to the extent of occasionally employing
diacritical marks to call for syllabic stresses other than those normally
pronounced.

Neither version of *Catiline* is particularly archaic in terms of the
period in which it was produced, and I have responded to this quality
of the play by trying to render it in reasonably contemporary English.
In order to do so, I have tended to reduce, without entirely
eliminating, the poetic inversions of the original. I reproduce the
rhyming passages in the second version as well as the first, and I also
reproduce Ibsen's punctuation for the second version. Its combining
of semicolons or commas with dashes is unconventional from the
point of view of standard punctuation in English texts, but these
unfamiliar combinations allow for more nuance in defining speech
rhythms than standard punctuation makes possible. The most im-
portant feature of my translation of the second version, however, is
that I render it as a revision of the 1850 text by keying it, on a line-
by-line basis, to my translation of that text.

The one feature of the original texts of *Catiline* that I have not
been able to reproduce with any consistency is their tendency to
alternate masculine and feminine line endings, especially in the abab
rhyming passages. Dano-Norwegian, with its rendering of the definite
article as an unstressed suffix of the relevant noun, its abundance of
verbal forms ending in unstressed syllables, and its declining of
adjectives in certain syntactical formulations by the addition of an
unstressed syllable (as in *høi, høie, stolt, stolte,* and *vild, vilde*), is far more
generous than English to the versifier who wants to employ frequent
feminine endings. I have, however, been able to capture Ibsen's
practice in this respect in the first eight lines of the first rhyming
passage in *Catiline* and fairly consistently throughout the bulk of my
translations of *The Burial Mound*. The mispronunciation of Cethégus
(as Céth-e-gús) is my fault, not Ibsen's; I plead, in my defense, the
formula "Lentulus and Cethegus" and other requirements of meter.
With regard to other names, I usually follow Ibsen's usual practice of

giving full weight in the meter to the two final light syllables in names like Furia and Aurelia (i-a) and Lucius (i-us).

Notes to Introduction to *Catiline*

1. My chief sources for this section are Chapters 3, 4, and 5 of the first volume of Halvdan Koht's *Henrik Ibsen, eit diktarliv,* Ny, omarbeidd utgåve, 2 vols. (Oslo: H. Aschehoug & Co. [W. Nygaard], 1954), which has been translated by Einar Haugen and A. E. Santaniello as *Life of Ibsen* (New York: Blom, 1971), and the first three chapters of Michael Meyer's *Ibsen, A Biography* (Garden City, NY: Doubleday & Company, Inc., 1971). Meyer's work is the more detailed, and it quotes liberally from the relevant sources, but Koht's formulations of the relevant issues seem to me more incisive, and he is certainly far more critically perceptive than Meyer on Ibsen's writings. The quotations from Koht are my own translations, and, unless otherwise noted, all translations from Danish and Norwegian in these introductions are my own.

2. According to evidence turned up by Per Kristian Heggelund Dahl and reported in his article, "Ibsen-data fra Skien og Grimstad," *Ibsenårbok,* 1985/86, 207–14, the boat that Ibsen most likely took to Grimstad left Skien for Brevik, on the coast a few miles down river from Skien, two days before Christmas and departed from Brevik shortly after the holiday. Ibsen could have gone on board at either location.

3. Christopher Due, *Erindringer fra Henrik Ibsens ungdomsaar* (København: Græbes Bogtrykkeri, 1909), p. 39.

4. My account of the manuscript and my speculations about Due's fair copy of it— which follow—are based on Didrik Arup Seip's textual notes for *Catiline* in Volume I of Henrik Ibsen, *Samlede verker,* Hundreårsutgave, ed. Francis Bull, Halvdan Koht, and Didrik Arup Seip (Oslo: Gyldendal, 1928), pp. 207–42, and on my own examination of the manuscript in Oslo in September 1989.

5. See Seip (211); he attributes this interpretation of the revised word order to the first scholars to discuss the manuscript, Halvdan Koht and Julius Elias, the editors of Henrik Ibsen, *Efterladte Skrifter,* 3 vols. (Kristiania og Kjøbenhavn: Gyldendalske Boghandel, Nordisk Forlag, 1909).

6. On the other hand, the synopsis for the second scene gives its location as "The Forum," the location for the original version of the scene. This synopsis reads, "Forum. Lentulus, Cethegus et al. Reference to the conspiracy[.] Decision to approach Catiline," and in the scene as first written, Cethegus is listed second in the opening stage direction (after Lentulus), but his name is crossed out and he does not appear in the text. Hence, an alternative, and perhaps more correct, interpretation of the evidence than the one I have given is that Ibsen initially planned to make Cethegus a prominent character in the second scene, wrote the synopsis, changed his mind about Cethegus and wrote the original version of the scene without him, and then changed his mind again to write the revision with Cethegus reinstated. Full translations of the two synopsis-outlines appear in an appendix.

7. Since there is no existing copy of a synopsis-outline for Act Three, it is impossible to tell, of course, whether Ibsen deviated from his plan in writing that act.

8. These other deviations consist of changes in or additions of stage directions, changes in words, phrases, and word order, a very few slight changes making the given lines more correct metrically, and—though not in the list of characters— changing the character in the fourth scene of Act One to whom Catiline gives his remaining money from "En Olding" ("an old man") to "En gammel Soldat" ("an old soldier").

9. Contributing to this uncertainty about the extent of Ibsen's involvement with Due's fair copy is the impossibility of knowing—because of the missing final leaf of the manuscript—whether Ibsen's concluding "Notes" to the play already existed in the manuscript or were added at some later time.

10. Unless otherwise indicated I quote Ibsen's letters on *Catiline* from volumes XVI and XVII of the Hundreårsutgave (published, respectively, in 1940 and 1941).

11. The date of Ibsen's departure from Grimstad, usually given as April 13, is pretty definitely fixed by Dahl (213).

12. The 1850 reviews of *Catiline* are conveniently reprinted by Karl Haugholt in "Samtidens kritikk av Ibsens *Catilina*," *Edda*, 52 (1952), 74–94, but only snippets from them have been previously translated.

13. It seems to me that both Koht (I, 57–58) and Meyer (56–57)—Meyer follows Koht *very* closely here—somewhat misrepresent this on the whole intelligent and on the whole fair review by making it appear more negative than it is. For some reason, neither of them discusses the next review I take up, and both of them write that Vibe's review was the only one to appear in a public newspaper. Oddly enough, the brief introductory remarks with which Haugholt prefaces his transcriptions of the reviews are written as if he, too, was unaware of the following review, even though he includes it in its appropriate place chronologically.

14. I do not find in Müller's review the first two of the three quotations from it in Meyer, 57: "absurd contradictions in the characters" and "comprehension of formal requirements"; these seem to be imaginative translations of certain of Koht's remarks (I, 58) about Müller's piece.

15. "Om Førsteutgaven av Ibsens *Catilina*" (Kristiania, 1922), pp. 11–12; this is a small pamphlet providing a separate printing of Thuesen's article in *Morgenbladet*, No. 80, 11 March 1922. Thuesen apparently wrote his article out of a feeling that the rare-book dealers were conspiring to perpetuate the idea that all but a few of the copies of the first edition of *Catiline* had been destroyed.

16. The list of the recipients of the presentation copies and the letter to af Edholm, not available at the time of publication of Volume XVII of the Hundreårsutgave, can be found in Henrik Ibsen, *Brev 1845–1905, Ny Samling*, ed. Øyvind Anker, *Ibsenårbok*, 1979 (Oslo: Universitetsforlaget, 1979), pp. 174–75.

17. *Det nittende Aarhundrede, Maanedskrift for Literatur og Kritik*, April-September, 1875 (København, 1875), pp. 245–47.

18. *Tids-Tavler*, Vol. IV (Kristiania, 1875, 1876), pp. 172–76.

19. It was a frequent charge in Denmark that *The Feast at Solhaug* was virtually a plagiarism of this play by the Danish dramatist Henrik Hertz. Ibsen was enraged by the charge, partly because it was grossly unfair, and he addressed it in his Preface to the second edition of *The Feast at Solhaug* in 1883.

20. Much of the information in this and the following paragraph is based on "*Catiline*: Commentary," Appendix I of Volume I (*Early Plays*) of the Oxford *Ibsen*, edited and translated by James Walter McFarlane and Graham Orton (London: Oxford University Press, 1970), pp. 583–84.

21. Since Archer was in his time the most knowledgeable English-speaking reader of Ibsen and, not without some justification, a critic of repute, his explanation for not including *Catiline* serves as a sample turn-of-the-century attitude toward the play of no little interest: "The eleven volumes of this edition contain all, save one, of the dramas which Henrik Ibsen himself admitted to the canon of his works. The one exception is his earliest, and very immature, tragedy, *Catilina*. . . . This play is interesting in the light reflected from the poet's later achievements, but has little or no inherent value. A great part of its interest lies in the very crudities of its style, which it would be a thankless task to reproduce in translation. Moreover, the poet impaired even its biographical value by largely rewriting it before its republication. He did not make it, or attempt to make it, a better play, but he in some measure corrected its juvenility of expression. Which version, then, should a translator choose? To go back to the original would seem a deliberate disregard of the poet's wishes; while, on the other hand, the retouched version is clearly of far inferior interest. It seemed advisable, therefore, to leave the play alone, so far as this edition was concerned." From Archer's "General Preface" to *The Works of Henrik Ibsen*, The Viking Edition (New York: Charles Scribner's Sons, 1911), Vol. I, p. ix.

22. *The Flower and the Castle: An Introduction to Modern Drama* (New York: Grosset & Dunlap, The Universal Library, 1966 [first published by Macmillan in 1963]), p. 124.

23. *Ibsens Verden* (Oslo: Gyldendal Norsk Forlag, 1978), pp. 60–63.

24. *To the Third Empire: Ibsen's Early Drama* (Minneapolis: University of Minnesota Press, 1980), pp. 29, 32, 34–6, 48.

25. Ibsen's use of these sources, especially the first and third, is discussed in detail by Eiliv Skard ("Kjeldone til Ibsens *Catilina*," *Edda*, 21 [1924], 70–90), who seems to have discovered the third. I have made some use of Skard's account (he is particularly good on identifying in *Catiline* likely echoes of Sallust's language), but I have also reviewed these sources independently. My account, as a result, differs from his in several important respects, and I disagree with some of his findings and especially his judgment about Ibsen's use of "*Vestalinden*." There are also some good observations on Ibsen's use of Sallust by Hans Eitrem in "Om 'Catilina,'" an appendix to his *Ibsen og Grimstad* (Oslo: H. Aschehoug & Co. [W. Nygaard], 1940), pp. 103–26.

26. I quote Sallust from the translation by S. A. Handford in Sallust, *The Jugurthine*

War; The Conspiracy of Catiline (Baltimore: Penguin Books, 1963). The quotations in this sentence are from pp. 184–85 (section 15 in Sallust); subsequent references to Sallust will appear in my text in parentheses, either as section numbers or, in the case of quotations, with the section numbers followed, after a semicolon, by the page numbers from Handford's translation—i.e., in this system the present reference would be (15; 184–85).

27. Skard (84) points out that even the "opposition between ability and aspiration" that Ibsen associates with Catiline in his Preface to the 1875 version has its possible origin in Sallust's "*nimis alta semper cupiebat*," which Handford translates as "hankered . . . after things extravagant . . . beyond his reach" (5; 178).

28. Cicero, *The Speeches*, with an English translation by Louis E. Lord (Cambridge, MA: Harvard University Press; London: William Heinemann, 1959), p. 69.

29. I translate from Paludan-Müller's *Ungdomsskrifter*, Revideret Udgave (Kjøbenhavn: C. A. Reitzels Forlag, 1859).

30. Eitrem (111) also regards the treatment of Aurelia and Furia as "truly original," adding that it is "truly brilliant" as well.

31. *In the Shadows of Romance: Romantic Tragic Drama in Germany, England, and France* (Athens: Ohio University Press, 1987). Cox's summary description of the characteristics of the form he is studying runs from p. 12 to p. 25, but his comments on the several plays that he individually analyzes are also important for their restatement and particularizing of his various points.

32. Many have called attention to *Die Räuber* as a source for *Catiline*. Ibsen may well have modeled his co-conspirator scenes on Schiller's scenes involving the robber band, especially Spiegelberg's easily frustrated attempt in Act Four to kill Karl Moor and take his place as leader. The treatment of Aurelia and the relationship between her and Catiline may perhaps owe something to Schiller's Amalia, the beloved of Karl Moor, who finds it necessary to kill her at the end of the play. And the scene in Act Four in which Karl Moor finds his father virtually entombed is chock-full of the kind of Gothic imagery that Ibsen exploits throughout *Catiline*. The argument for Goethe is advanced by Theodore T. Stenborg in "Ibsen's *Catilina* and Goethe's *Iphigenie auf Tauris*," *Modern Language Notes*, 39 (1924), 329–36, and that for the Hegelian model by John C. Pearce in "Hegelian Ideas in Three Tragedies by Ibsen," *Scandinavian Studies*, 34 (1962), 245–57.

33. "On *Catilina*: A Structural Examination of Ibsen's First Play and its Sources," *Scandinavian Studies*, 55 (1983), 39–54.

34. Ibsen may have seen *Axel and Valborg* staged as early as his time in Skien; see Koht (I, 26).

35. I translate from *Oehlenschlägers Udvalgte Tragedier* (København: Litteraturens Mesterværker Kunstforlaget, 1913).

36. The following discussion of Ibsen's early poems is based on my own reading and analysis of them, but it is very strongly indebted to Pavel Fraenkl, *Ibsens Vei til Drama: En undersøkelse av dramatikerens genesis* (Oslo: Gyldendal Norsk Forlag, 1955), in which he has already argued, in abundant detail, the relationship

between these poems and *Catiline*—indeed, the virtual influence of the poems on the play. Fraenkl is a little careless about chronology, his work is often prolix and repetitious, and I do not find all of his psychological and theoretical conclusions persuasive, but his book is, nevertheless, an extremely valuable one, not just for its study of *Catiline* (and for its frequent insights about the later plays) but also for its suggestive consideration of how the creative mind works.

37. In quoting from the Grimstad poems in what follows, I refrain from trying to reproduce their rhymes and an *exact* echo of their meter in order to provide as literal as possible a rendering of their words and images. Anker (70) dates the letter accompanying the poems that Ibsen sent to Clara Ebbell on New Year's Day, 1849/50, but he gives no reason for this dating, and it cannot be right. In his introduction to Volume XIV of the Hundreårsutgave, Seip (18) indicates that Ibsen sent her the poems later in 1850, after he had been in Christiania for some time. Seip's dating is confirmed by the subheading for one of the poems, "Sonnets," which reads, "Introduction to a Lecture to the Literary Association [i.e., Students Association]"; Ibsen was not eligible for membership in this Association until August 1850 (Koht, I, 61).

38. Cf. Fraenkl, especially pp. 117, 247.

39. The personal content of *Catiline* has been pointed out by numerous commentators. One of the most thorough discussions of it—written, however, with commendable restraint—is that by Eitrem (103–11).

40. It is possible, of course, that *Julius Caesar* helped Ibsen realize that the story of Catiline might be a good subject for a play.

41. The versification has been thoroughly and carefully discussed by Åse Hiorth Lervik in "Ibsens Verskunst i *Catilina*," *Edda*, 63 (1963), 269–86.

42. I ignore, in this account, the song sung by the conspirators in the second scene of Act Two. It is not a "substitution" in the sense I am using the term but rather an entity completely separate from the characters' speech and explicitly introduced as such.

43. The imagery and verbal motifs of Aurelia and Furia are discussed in two articles by Sigurd Bretteville-Jensen ("Lys og Mørke i *Catilina*," *Edda*, 66 [1966], 225–35 and "Blomstersymbolikken i *Catilina*," *Ibsenårbok*, 1967, 61–71) and by Fraenkl (149–54, for Furia; 198–202, for Aurelia).

44. Fraenkl (229–42) also traces Ibsen's apparent inability to kill Catiline off, but he mistakenly reads the scene in which Curius informs Catiline of his betrayal of the conspiracy as a first attempt and, for some reason, fails to note Aurelia's ultimate saving of Catiline as the last and most decisive indication of Ibsen's inability.

45. *Metatheatre: A New View of Dramatic Form* (New York: Hill and Wang, 1963); the essay is on pp. 11–38, the quotation from p. 31.

46. On the other hand, I do not think I would be alone in preferring Ibsen's play on Catiline to that by Ben Jonson, with its pedantic and tedious renderings of long extracts from Sallust and Cicero in extremely crabbed, almost unspeakable verse.

47. Three of them, of course, had the model of Shakespeare to draw on—many would say that Schiller in *Die Räuber* and Shelley in *The Cenci* drew too excessively—and the fourth of them, Byron, could have had it had he not deliberately rejected it.

48. This feature of the diction undergoes a marked decrease in Act Three, which has the best poetry of the acts in other respects as well. Although Act Three is only slightly shorter than Act Two and considerably longer than Act One, these three adjectives occur only twenty-four times in it as opposed to forty-one times in Act One and thirty-seven in Act Two. In contrast, "soul," another word whose frequency Ibsen reduced for the 1875 version, occurs fifteen times in Act Three as opposed to ten in One and eight in Two; but "soul" is of course a more substantive word (in fact, *a* substantive), and however much it may be overworked, it is not filler. Incidentally, Ibsen's repetitions of these "filler" words are not as noticeable as they should be in my translation of the 1850 version, because different contexts often call for different words in English and, more frequently, because, given Dano-Norwegian grammar, these adjectives often appear in a two-syllable form necessitating a search for appropriate English synonyms (such as "savage" for "wild").

49. In contrast, both Oehlenschläger and Byron have a tendency to end lines weakly in run-on sequences, Oehlenschläger because of an over-fondness for feminine endings, Byron because he is inclined to start the run-on sequence with the tenth syllable of a line, often using an unemphatic word like "and" or "of" to do so.

50. See Ragnvald Iversen, "Henrik Ibsen som Purist i 'Catilina' 1875," *Edda*, 30 (1930), 96–100. Ibsen's treatment of allusions to classical mythology was more mixed, however, for although he removed Curius' allusion to Hercules in the poisoned shirt of Nessus in the third scene of Act Two and references to Luna and Aurora, he added an allusion to Actaeon in one of Catiline's speeches late in Act Three.

51. Ibsen apparently wrote the poem in July 1875, for he sent it to Georg Brandes on July 14, 1875, for publication in Brandes' journal, *The Nineteenth Century* (Anker, 180).

Catiline

(1850)

Drama in Three Acts

by

Brynjolf Bjarme
[Henrik Ibsen]

Lucius Catiline, Roman nobleman

Aurelia, his wife

Furia, a vestal

Curius, Catiline's kinsman, a young man

Manlius, an old warrior

Lentulus
Coeparius
Gabinius } young Roman noblemen
Statilius
Cethegus

Ambiorix } envoys of the Allobroges
Ollovico

A Vestal

An Old Man

Servants in the Temple of Vesta; Waiters, Gladiators, Warriors, and the attendants of the Allobroges

A Ghost

The first and second acts take place in and near Rome, the third act in Etruria.

ACT ONE

A highway near Rome; in the background loom the towers and walls of the city. It is evening. CATILINE *stands leaning against a tree to the left, deep in thought.*

CATILINE
(*after a pause*)

I must, I must, a voice commands me thus
from my soul's depths, and I will follow it;—
I feel the strength and heart for something better,
for something higher than this present life,
a simple round of pleasures unrestrained.
No, no, they do not sate the heart's desire.
—I wildly dream;—oblivion is my yearning,
it is because my life's without a goal.[1]

(*after a pause*)

Ha! what became of all my youthful dreams?
Like flimsy forms of air they disappeared;
just bitter disappointment have they left,
I'm robbed of every daring hope by fate.

(*with vehemence*)

Despise, despise yourself then, Catiline!
the noble power you feel within your soul,
and what's the goal indeed of all your striving?
Mere sating of your sensual desires.

(*calmer*)

Yet sometimes still, as in this very hour,

a secret notion smolders in my breast.
—Ha! when I look upon the city there,
the proud, the lofty Rome,—and the corruption
and wretchedness, to which it long has sunk,
appear so sharp and clear unto my soul,—
there cries aloud a voice from deep within me:
"Wake, Catiline! wake up and be a man!"—
                    (*He breaks off.*)

Yet it is mere delusion, nighttime's dreams,
and phantoms born of solitude, no more;
the least sound from reality's domain
and down they flee into the soul's still depths!
(AMBIORIX, OLLOVICO, *and their attendants enter from the right without
noticing* CATILINE.)

AMBIORIX

Look there, our journey's end, the walls of lofty Rome;
toward heaven arches up the towering Capitol.

OLLOVICO

So that indeed is Rome? The queen of Italy,
soon Germany's, and Gaul's as well, perhaps.

AMBIORIX

Unfortunately, yes, it may be so,
and harsh and burdensome is Rome's dominion,
unto the earth it crushes the subdued;
hence we've come hither, sent forth by our people,
to seek redress for wrongs toward us at home
and peace and quiet for our Allobrogia.[2]

OLLOVICO

It will be granted us.

AMBIORIX

That we will hope,
for surely we don't know the contrary.

OLLOVICO

You're fearful, are you not?

AMBIORIX

Perhaps with justice:
For Rome was always jealous of her power.
And then, Ollovico, consider, this proud realm
is not, as we are, ruled by tribal chiefs;
back there at home we choose the wisest man, the best,
the shrewdest in advice, the bravest in a battle;
it's him we choose, the foremost in our tribe,
for leader—for the ruler of our people;—
but here—

CATILINE

(*stepping forward quickly*)

—here filthy egoism rules!
It's cunning, bribery that make a ruler here!

OLLOVICO

O gods on high! he has been spying on us!

AMBIORIX

Is such the high-born noble Romans' way?
Back home it is a woman's occupation.

CATILINE

Be free from fear, to spy is not my trade,
by chance it was I heard your conversation;
is it in Allobrogia you belong?

You think that justice here in Rome can flower?
Turn back, bedazzled fools! here tyranny and wrong
far more than ever hold the reins of power,
in name, of course, it's a republic still,
yet every citizen's a slave in chains,
in debt, and subject to the Senate's will,
a group that is for sale for gifts and gains.
Here rules no more the lofty Roman drift,
the liberalism Rome enjoyed of old,
security and life, you see, are but a gift
from Senators and must be bought with gold!
Not justice but the voice of power matters,
—the noblemen to might have lost the day.

AMBIORIX

Then tell me, who are you whose speech thus shatters
. the fervent hope that brought us all this way?

CATILINE

A man who feels with passion freedom's cause,
an enemy of all misrule by wrong,
a friend of everyone oppressed by laws,
with strength and courage to unseat the strong.

AMBIORIX

The noble Roman people? answer me!
To fool us strangers surely you thus speak,
are they no more what they were formerly,
the tyrant's fear, protector of the weak?

CATILINE

(with gravity)

Look, Allobrogian! toward the west and gaze
upon the splendid Capitol on high,
how it with evening radiance is ablaze
from the last glowing of the western sky.

Rome's evening luster blazes much the same,
its freedom is enwrapped in slavery's night,
—yet in its heaven soon a sun shall flame,
dispelling darkness with its sudden light.

(*They leave.*)

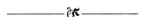

A colonnade in Rome

LENTULUS, STATILIUS, COEPARIUS, *and* CETHEGUS *enter in ardent conversation.*

COEPARIUS

Yes, you are right, it steadily grows worse,
—and what the end will be I do not know.

CETHEGUS

Hey, it would not occur to me to think
of things like that, the moment *I* delight in,
each fruit of joy I keenly pluck and let
the sum of things go sliding as it will.

LENTULUS

That's fine for those who can, I was denied
the knack to so indifferently await
a future when there's nothing more remaining,
when no claim can be duly satisfied.

STATILIUS

And never any prospect for improvement;
it can't, though, be denied, a way of life like this—

CETHEGUS

Enough of that!

LENTULUS

The last of all my heirlooms,
for debt, this very day was robbed from me.

CETHEGUS

Away with sorrow, follow me, we will
forget it in a merry Bacchanal.

COEPARIUS

Yes, yes, we'll do that,—come, you jolly friends, let's go!

LENTULUS

No, wait a minute, there comes Manlius,
our good old friend, he'll surely come with us.

MANLIUS

(coming in angrily)

To hell with them, the dirty, rotten dogs,
they haven't any sense of justice left!

LENTULUS

What's happened? Why are you so furious?

STATILIUS

Have creditors been plaguing you as well?

MANLIUS

Quite different. Listen! as you all well know,
in Sulla's army I with honor served,
a piece of farming land was my reward;
and when the war was over, there I lived
in calm content, it fed me, though just barely;
now it's been stolen from me, as I'm told,
as state-owned property it's to be seized

for equal distribution to all comers;
it's just a robbery and nothing else,
they're only thinking of their own advantage.

COEPARIUS

That is exactly how they treat our rights,
the mighty ones rule over us like tyrants!

CETHEGUS
(*merrily*)

That is bad luck, all right, and yet a worse
has struck me down, as you at once shall hear;
just think, my friends, my young and lovely mistress,
my Tullia, disgracefully has left me,[3]
just now when everything of mine that still
remained, for her sweet sake alone, was squandered!

STATILIUS

Your wild excess is what's to blame for that.

CETHEGUS

Blame it on anything you wish, I won't
neglect a one of my desires, no, those
I'll gratify as long as I am able.

MANLIUS

Ha![4] I, who fought so bravely for the glory,
the might, that now the proud ones boast about!—
—I shall—ha! my old gang of fellow soldiers,
if only those brave men were still around;
but no, the most of them are dead, of course,
and those still living on are spread about the world,—
—and what are you young men compared to them?
When faced with might, you bow down in the muck;
you haven't got the guts to break your chains,
this life of bondage is what you prefer!

LENTULUS

By all the gods! Though he is insolent,
there's truth enough in what he said just then.

CETHEGUS

Indeed, indeed, we have to grant him that,
but how to go about it, see, that's just the point.

LENTULUS

Yes, it's the truth, look fellows, we have long
endured oppression, now's the time to cast
away the bonds that have been woven round
us by injustice and sheer lust for power!

STATILIUS

I understand you, Lentulus, but look,
for that we need a strong and forceful leader,
—with courage, insight; where can he be found?

LENTULUS

I know a man with what it takes to lead us.

MANLIUS

Do you mean Catiline?

LENTULUS

The very man!

CETHEGUS

Yes, Catiline, o yes, he is the only one!

MANLIUS

I know the man; I was his father's friend,
and by his side I fought a lot of battles;

his little son came with him to the strife;
he was already wild then, out of hand.
And yet rare gifts were to be found in him,
his soul is noble and his courage firm.

LENTULUS

I think we'll find him rather more than willing,
tonight I met him very much depressed,
he's brooding on some secret plan or other,
some daring goal he's long since had in sight.

STATILIUS

O yes, he long has sought the Consulship.

LENTULUS

He won't succeed in that, for bitterly
today[5] his enemies spoke out against him;
he heard them speak himself, and in a rage
he left the Council, planning his revenge.

STATILIUS

Then surely he'll agree to our proposal.

LENTULUS

I hope you're right; we'll go and seek him out,
accompany me;—the time is in our favor!
(They leave.)

———————— ?✶ ————————

The Temple of Vesta
The holy fire burns in a niche in the background. CATALINE *and*
CURIUS *slip in and stand behind the columns in the foreground.*

CURIUS

What, Catiline! it's here you're leading me,

in Vesta's temple?

CATILINE
(*laughing*)

Yes, as you can see!

CURIUS

You gods! what recklessness! why, Cicero,
your foe, this very day raged out against you;
and still you can—

CATILINE

O, let that be forgotten!

CURIUS

You are in danger, and you just forget it,
by blindly dashing into further danger!

CATILINE
(*merrily*)

Variety's my joy, I've never numbered
a mistress from among the Vestal virgins,
so here I've come to try my luck at it!

CURIUS

You gods on high! but surely that's a joke!

CATILINE

A joke? o yes, indeed, like all my loves,
but what I said to you just now I meant;
—when during the last festival along Rome's streets
I saw the priestesses in grand procession,
by accident on one of them I chanced
to fix my glance, and with a fleeting look

136

her eyes met mine—they pierced right through my soul,
and the expression in those night-dark eyes
I never saw before from any woman.

CURIUS

I well believe it—tell me, then what happened?

CATILINE

Into the temple here I've wormed my way,
already seen and spoken to her often;
ha! what deep difference is there between her
and my Aurelia!

CURIUS

And both of them you love
at once, no, that I can't conceive at all!

CATILINE

It's strange, I do not understand it either,
and yet, it is exactly as you say;
but ha! how various is this love of mine!
Aurelia is tender, often bringing
this heart tranquility through gentle words,
but Furia—but hush, there's someone coming!

FURIA

(entering)

Detested halls! that witness all the pain,
and the anguish under which I bow;
each glorious thought I once did entertain,
each hope, extinguished in this heart, which now
with fever is pervaded, now with fire
more hot and burning than the Vestal flame.
Ha, what a fate!—what was the fault so dire
that put me in this prison in all but name,

that robbed me of my every youthful pleasure,
in life's fair spring each innocent delight?
Yet not a single tear my cheek shall measure;
—revenge and hate alone this breast ignite!

CATILINE

(*stepping forth*)

And not at all for me a different flame,
a gentler one, you cherish, Furia?

FURIA

You gods! ha! rashness—are you here again?
You're not afraid?

CATILINE

I know no taste of fear,
to meet with danger always was my joy.

FURIA

O glorious, glorious! that is my thought, too,
and so I hate this temple all the more,
because in safety quietly I live,
and danger never dwells behind its walls—
and this employment, empty, without action,
a life as dull as is the lamp's last flare,
what an arena for this multitude
of proud and lofty plans within my breast;
I am pressed in and crushed between these walls,
where life grows stagnant, hope becomes extinguished,
where drowsily the dreary day sneaks on,
where no thought's purpose ever sees the light.

CATILINE

Ha, Furia! how strange is what you say!
it has the music of my own heart's core,

as if with words of fire you would portray
my every yearning, fervent in its store,
affliction thus oppresses this heart, too,
like yours, from hate it hardens into steel,
like you, I'm robbed of every hope I knew,
my life, like yours, lacks any clear ideal!
—Yet I mutely hide the pain I drew,
and no one senses what burns deep within me
—they disregard and scorn me, all those wretches!
they don't know how intensely my heart beats
for right and freedom and for everything
that nobly stirred in any mortal breast.

FURIA

O glorious! o, this soul, not any other,
was made for me, in that a voice cries out
from the heart's core, which never can deceive;
then come! o come! we will obey that voice!

CATILINE

What do you mean, my lovely visionary?

FURIA

Ha!⁶ let us flee away from this low place,
a better native land is where we'll tarry;
the spirit's high, proud flight is here subdued;
here baseness quenches every glorious spark
before it can blaze high, a flaming brand!
Come, let us flee! for those inspired by freedom
the whole earth's circle is a fatherland!

CATILINE

Ha! how enchanting sound your words to me!

FURIA

Then let us flee this very moment; over

those mountains beyond the sea's expanse,
far from Rome we'll make our flight's first stop;
a horde of friends will follow at your heel;
we'll settle down upon some distant shore,
there we shall rule and shall no more conceal
that no hearts ever beat like ours before!

CATILINE

O beautiful! but speak, why should we flee?
—look, here as well can freedom's flame be cherished;
here, too, there is occasion for achievement,
as vast as even that your soul demands!

FURIA

Here, do you say, here in this wretched Rome,
where slavishness and tyranny are all?
Ha, Lucius! are you, too, one of those
who must with blushing Rome's great past recall?
what was it once, and what does now ensue?
a troop of heroes then, and now a heap
of wretched slaves!

CATILINE

Do you sneer at me, too?
Then know, the freedom of great Rome to keep,
for yet once more to see its lofty splendor,
with joy, like Curtius, I'd hurl myself
into the gulf!

FURIA

Be still! a fire most strange
is glowing in your eyes, you've spoken truth;
but go, the priestesses will be here soon,
their custom is to come here at this time.

CATILINE

I'll go, but soon you'll see me here again,
a magic force enthralls me to your side;
a woman proud as you I never saw!

FURIA

(with a wild smile)

Then promise me one thing, and swear that you
will keep your promise—will you, Lucius?

CATILINE

Yes, anything my Furia demands;
within this heart just you alone hold sway!

FURIA

Then know, although I live here in this temple,
in Rome among you others there is one,
toward him I've sworn hostility till death,
and hatred even beyond the grave's dark shadows.

CATILINE

Well, then?

FURIA

So swear, my enemy shall be
your own till death—speak, will you, Lucius?

CATILINE

I swear you that by all the gods on high,
by my mother's memory, by my father's name,
I solemnly do swear it—speak, what's wrong?
—my Furia! your eyes so strangely glow,
your cheek, like death itself, is white as marble!

FURIA

I do not know myself, it burns like fire
within my veins—continue, swear once more!

CATILINE

Pour out, you gods on high, upon my head
your well of vengeance, let the lightning of
your wrath destroy me, if I break my oath,
I shall pursue him like a very demon!

FURIA

Enough, I do believe you, ha! that eased
my breast—in your hands rests my vengeance now.

CATILINE

I shall perform it, but now tell me, Furia!
who is he, what exactly was his crime?

FURIA

By Tiber's banks, far from the Roman walls
my cradle stood—my peaceful home was there
before I was ordained to be a vestal,
a well-beloved sister lived there with me;
—a villain came then to our peaceful dwelling,
he saw the pure and lovely lily there!

CATILINE
(astonished)

You gods on high!

FURIA

And he seduced her then!
In Tiber's waves she sought herself a grave!

CATILINE
(*uneasy*)

You know him?

FURIA
No, I never saw him there;
I didn't know a thing until too late!
But now I know his name.

CATILINE
Then say his name!

FURIA
You surely know him, listen, it is Catiline.

CATILINE
(*shrinking back*)

Ha! dreadful—Furia!—what are you saying?

FURIA
What's wrong? come to your senses! you're so pale—
speak, Lucius! is he perhaps your friend?

CATILINE
My friend? no, Furia!—not any more,
—I've cursed, and sworn eternal hatred toward—
myself!

FURIA
Yourself? you—you are Catiline?

CATILINE
I am, yes.

FURIA

You're my Tullia's seducer?
Ha! Nemesis indeed has heard my prayer;
yourself you've called down vengeance over you!
o woe to you—seducer!

CATILINE

Ha! your eyes,
how horridly they stare—ha! in the moon's
pale light you seem so like the dead one's shade.[7]
(*He hurries out.*)

FURIA

(*after a pause, with wild vehemence*)

Ha! now I understand—before my eyes
the veil has fallen—and I see it all.
So it was hatred that, when first I saw
him in the street, took hold within my breast;
so strange a feeling, like a wild, a blood-red flame!
Yes, he shall feel what hatred of my sort,
eternally aflame and limitless,
without a goal, shall bring down over him!

A VESTAL

(*coming in*)

Go, Furia! the hour's soon at its end,
for I've come—holy goddess! what is this
I see—o woe to you, the flame is out!

FURIA

(*wildly*)

It's out—you say?—it's burning wildly still,
—it isn't out!

THE VESTAL

You gods! o, what is this!

FURIA

No, hatred's burning fire does not go out
so easily; o, love's flares up and sinks
as suddenly, but hatred—

THE VESTAL

Goddess of the heavens!
O help! bring help!—o, this indeed is madness!
(*A number of* TEMPLE SERVANTS *rush in.*)

SOME

What's wrong in here?

OTHERS

The vestal flame is out!

FURIA

Here in my heart the flame is burning still!

THE VESTAL

Away with her, away with the offender!
(*They lead her away.*)

CURIUS

(*stepping forth*)

Ha! they're leading her away to death.
No, no, by all the gods, it must not be!
Shall she, this splendid, yes, this noble creature,
suffer the shame of an offender's death?
O, never have I felt this way before,
how deep her image has impressed itself

within my heart, ha! what is wrong with me?
I wonder, is this love? Yes, it is that.
—I'll save her;—o, but what of Catiline?—
With endless hatred she will hunt him down;
aren't there enough of those who hate him now,
shall I his enemies still more augment?
For me he long has filled a father's place;
duty commands I offer him protection;—
but love? Ha! what does it command I do?
And would this man, this Catiline so proud,
cringe trembling at a woman's anger? No,
—it must be carried out this very moment!
Yes, Furia! I, I shall rescue you
from death, although it cost me my own life!

(*He goes out hurriedly.*)

———————— ?⚚ ————————

A room in Catiline's house

CATILINE

(*coming in greatly agitated*)

"Ha! Nemesis indeed has heard my prayer;
yourself you've called down vengeance over you!"
—indeed, that's what the visionary uttered;
—how strange it is—perhaps it was a sign—
an omen of what the future will bring.
—So with an oath I've bound myself forever
to be avenger—of my own offense.
Ha, Furia! it seems that still I see
your fiery look, as wild as that of some
avenging goddess, while your words still fall
in hollow lingering echo in my soul,
and ever more my oath I shall recall.

(*He breaks off. During the following speech,
AURELIA approaches him unnoticed.*)

Yet it is foolish to waste further thought
upon this madness—it is nothing less;

—a better course, indeed, my brooding has,
a greater object should my soul assess.
—My plans exert a mighty claim on me,
on them my every thought I now must turn.
Within I'm surging like a storm-tossed sea!

AURELIA

(*seizing his hand*)

May your Aurelia the cause not learn;
may she not know what you within engender,
what struggles there in savage disarray;
may she not friendly comfort to you render
and cause your soul's deep gloom to fade away?

CATILINE

(*gently*)

O my Aurelia! how good you are and loving,
yet why should I embitter life for you,
why should you share my every grief with me?
ha! pain enough I have provided you,
is it not quite enough that on my head
a dark and hostile-minded fate has heaped
the whole oppressive curse inherent in
the linking up of noble strength of mind,
of ardent fervor for a life of deeds,
with abject bonds that curb the spirit's striving?
Shall you as well, with deep and grievous draft,
my sorrow's bitter cup be forced to drink?

AURELIA

A loving comfort is the woman's craft,
though she cannot, like you, of greatness think.
When the man is fighting for his glorious dream
and can but grief and disappointment reap,
to him her words then kind and tender seem,
and soon she lulls him to a restful sleep;

then he discovers that the quiet life
has pleasures that the raging turmoil lacks.

CATILINE

Yes, you are right—I deeply feel that, too;
and yet I cannot from its din tear free,
an endless ferment seethes within my bosom,
and nothing but life's turmoil brings it quiet.

AURELIA

If your Aurelia's not enough for you,
if she can't bring contentment to your soul,
then let your heart admit a friendly word,
a loving comfort from your dear wife's lips.
If I can't satisfy this wild desire,
if I can't follow where your thoughts fly forth:[8]
believe me, I know how to share your sorrows,
have strength and courage to assuage your burdens.

CATILINE

Then I shall tell you, my Aurelia,
what is so deeply troubling me just now;
you know that I've long sought the Consulship—
without success—indeed, you know it all—
how I, in order to procure the votes,
have squandered—

AURELIA

O my Catiline! be still!
It gives me pain.

CATILINE

Do you reproach me, too?
What other means, indeed, had I remaining?
—but uselessly has everything been lost;

disdain and infamy are all I've won;
just lately in the Senate my keen foe,
Marcus Cicero, defamed me harshly;
his speech was a portrayal of my life
so dreadful even I was forced to shudder;
in every look I read their mute contempt;
the name of Catiline is said with loathing,
for all posterity it will become
the symbol of a foul, a beastly blend
of dissoluteness and of wretchedness,
of mocking scorn for all that's high and noble,
and not a single deed can shield my name[9]
and testify against these shameful lies,
for people will believe what rumor says.

AURELIA

But I, my Catiline!—I don't believe it.
Let all the world be ready to condemn you,
let it heap up dishonor on your head,
I know you nourish in your lofty soul
a seed that still can bear some noble fruit;
but here it scarcely has a chance to grow,
and noxious weeds will quickly choke its spear;
o, let us leave this home of grief and woe;
what binds you to it, why must we stay here?

CATILINE

What do you mean, that I should simply leave?
I should abandon all my glorious goals?
—the drowning man—though lacking hope to live—
clings to his broken vessel as it rolls,
and when the wet grave swallows up the wreck—
and every hope of rescue from him leaps,
the last of all the planks with his last strength
he grapples, sinking with it to the deeps.

AURELIA

But when a friendly seacoast smiles upon him
with leafy groves beyond the billows' crest,
then hope again awakens in his bosom,
he struggles thither—toward that cheerful nest;
—it's lovely there—there peaceful quiet reigns,
there pleasantly the waves splash shoreward now,
there he can ease his weary limbs from pains,
and cooling evening breezes fan his brow;
they chase away each gloomy cloud of care,
a quiet peace then settles in his mind;
there he remains and finds a soothing lair,
oblivious to the gloomy days behind;
the distant echo of the world's great din
is all that reaches his still place of rest;
—it cannot break the peace that he is in,
it brings more joy and calm into his breast,
it calls back to his mind the bygone days,
his failed designs and joys that made him sorry;
—the quiet life now doubly wins his praise,
he would not change for any Roman's glory.

CATILINE

O, beautifully you speak! and at this moment
from life's mad turmoil I could go with you,
but tell me, where indeed are we to flee to,
yes, where are we in quiet peace to live?

AURELIA
(joyful)

You will, my Catiline! o, what great joy!
o, more, indeed, than what my breast can hold!
—why do we linger?—o, this very night—
we can depart.

ACTONE

CATILINE

And where are we to go—
where lies the place where I can lay my head
in peace?

AURELIA

How can you speak that way? have you
forgotten, then, our little country place,
where once my cradle stood and where we two,
so joyful and so happy in our bliss,
spent all those many cheerful summer days?
Where was the grass more green than in those leas?
Where were there forest shades more cool than those?
The little villa mid the dusky trees
peeks out and offers comforting repose.
Thither we'll flee and dedicate our life—
to rustic peacefulness, to quiet joy;
you'll be made cheerful by a loving wife,
with kisses she shall all your griefs destroy,
(smiling)

and when, your arms with meadow flowers aflame,
you come back home your rural queen to find,
then I'll cry out my flower prince's name,
and round his brow the laurel wreath I'll bind!
—But tell me, what's the matter? With wild might—
you squeeze my hand, your eyes so strangely glow!

CATILINE

Alas, Aurelia!—lost is your delight,
I cannot take you where you want to go,
I am not able.

AURELIA

Gods! you frighten me!
yet surely you are joking, Catiline!

CATILINE

I joke! ha! am I capable of that,
when every word, like vengeance's keen dart,
transfixes wholly this tormented breast,
to which stern fate will never rest impart?

AURELIA

You gods! o speak, what do you mean?

CATILINE

                Look here;
here is your villa, here's your future's joy!
        (He pulls out a purse filled with gold
        and violently tosses it on the table.)

AURELIA

O, you have sold—

CATILINE

      Yes, just this very day.
—And for what purpose?—ha! so I could bribe—

AURELIA

O silence!—silence!—let us think no more—
about this matter, it only causes pain.

CATILINE

Ha! so much more your mildness crushes me
than would a bitter accusation from
your lips.

AN OLD SOLDIER

(coming in and approaching CATILINE)

Forgive me, sir! for coming in

your home like this, at night and unannounced.
Forgive—

CATILINE

Speak out, what do you want?

THE SOLDIER

My errand is a humble boon,—I'm sure
you'll listen to it; I'm a poor man, who[10]
has sacrificed my strength for Rome's great glory;
now I'm infirm—and I can serve no more,
and there my weapons hang at home all rusty;
the only hope I had lay in my son,—
he has supported me through his own work;
alas! for debt he sits in prison now—
and there's no rescue—help me! help me, sir!
(kneeling)

A little coin—I've wandered here from door
—to door, alas! they've all long since been locked,—
I can't do any more.

CATILINE

Ha![11] it is like them!
Look, Aurelia! yes, that is how they treat
the old and valiant troop of veterans;
o, gratitude exists in Rome no more!
there was a time when I in righteous anger
would fain have had revenge with sword and flames,
but o! I cannot do it at this moment;
my mind's a gentle child's, I can't avenge it;
—relieving sorrow's an achievement, too;
—take this, old fellow!—you can pay your debt.
(He hands him the gold.)

THE SOLDIER

O! gods on high!—can I believe your words?

CATILINE

Yes, hurry, old man, go—undo his chains!
(THE SOLDIER leaves quickly.)

—A better use—not so, Aurelia?—
than spending it for bribes and for injustice!
it's beautiful to overthrow a tyrant,
—but quiet comfort also has rewards.

AURELIA

(throwing herself in his arms)

O! great and noble still your soul remains!
now once again I know my Catiline!

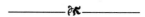

An underground vault
A lamp burns weakly. In the background a large iron door. FURIA
*stands in the middle of the vault, dressed in black and listening to some
sound.*

FURIA

A hollow boom, it's thundering up there,
the distant noise is echoing down to me;
—but here, down in the underworld, it's still.
—Am I to drowsy calm forever doomed?
—am I not even here through labyrinths
to wildly roam, as always was my wish?
(after a pause)

It was so strange a life, so strange a fate,
that, like a comet, quickly came and vanished.
He met me—then a mighty magic force—
an inner sympathy brought us together,
I his avenging goddess, he my victim;
—but punishment soon followed the avenger!
(a pause)

It's hushed up there;—am I already being
removed still farther from the realm of light?
ha! good, if it be so—if my abiding
in this dark hole is but a downward flight—
on wings of lightning toward the land of gloom,
if I'm already nearing the wild Styx!
There leaden waves are rolling toward the shore,
there Charon noiselessly his boat is rowing;
—soon I'll be there—there I will mutely sit
beside the ferry place, will ask each spirit,
each passing shadow, who from life's dominion
with weightless steps approaches Death's terrain—
will ask him earnestly how Catiline
—is faring up among the living souls,
—will ask how he is keeping to his oath!
—I'll shine a bluish sulfur-torch into
the sheenless depths of every specter's eyes;
among the thousands I will pick out Catiline,
—and when he comes, then I shall go with him,
—we two together then shall make the crossing,
together enter Proserpine's great hall;
a shade myself, I'll follow on his steps;
where Catiline is, Furia, of course, must be!
                    (*a pause*)

Ha! more and more the air's becoming stifling,
—and breathing is much harder than before;
then I am getting near the dark morass
where silently the streams of Hades flow;
            (*She listens; a faint sound can be heard.*)

a muffled boom—just like the stroke of oars,
the ferrier of the dead's already coming
to get me—ha!—but here—here I shall wait.
        (*The iron door in the background is opened quietly, and* CURIUS
                appears, quietly beckoning.)

FURIA

Hail, Charon, hail! are you prepared already

`        `to take me as a guest to Death's great halls?
Here I shall wait.

CURIUS

Be still! just come with me!

———————— ❧ ————————

ACT TWO

A room in CATILINE's house
CATILINE *is pacing up and down.* LENTULUS *and* CETHEGUS.

CATILINE

No—I'm telling you, you clean miss the point,
you don't understand me,—ha, am I
to treacherously begin a civil war,
—with blood of citizens defile my hands?
no, no, I will not do it, no; let Rome
condemn me.

LENTULUS

So you will not, Catiline!

CATILINE

I will not.

CETHEGUS

Tell me, have you nothing to
revenge, nor nothing to acquire from it?

CATILINE

Let those who wish seek vengeance, I won't do it;
yet mute contempt, of course, is also vengeance;
and that shall be my only one.

CETHEGUS

Ha, ha!
I see this is an inconvenient moment,
and yet assuredly tomorrow will
put you in rather different thoughts.

CATILINE

Why so?

CETHEGUS

Oh, quite a lot of funny rumors are around;
—just now a Vestal has been led to death.

CATILINE

(*startled*)

A Vestal virgin? ha! what's that you say?

LENTULUS

Indeed! a Vestal virgin!—and as rumor says—

CATILINE

Ha! what does it say?

CETHEGUS

That you are very far
from being unacquainted with this matter.

CATILINE

That's being said?

LENTULUS

Yes, yes, so goes the rumor.
Oh, well, for us, for all your loyal friends,

such things, of course, can be quite unimportant;
—the people, though, judge strictly, Catiline!

CATILINE
(deep in thought)

And she is dead!

CETHEGUS

She is most certainly;
an hour's interment in the offender's tomb
is quite enough.

LENTULUS

Well, let it be forgotten;
that wasn't why we spoke to you about her,
—but listen, Catiline! bear well in mind,
you sought the Consulship—and all your hopes
were leveled at a happy issue of
your seeking it, now also that is done with.

CATILINE
(as before)

"Yourself you've called down vengeance over you!"

CETHEGUS

Enough of this vain brooding, it is useless;
—act like a man, it all can still be salvaged;
—a quick decision—you have friends enough,
quite ready to obey your slightest hint;
so, will you, Catiline? Come, answer!

CATILINE

No, I say!
and why indeed would all of you join in this plot;

perhaps the reason's noble love of freedom,—
perhaps it's to restore Rome's greatness that
you'd topple everything?

LENTULUS

I can't quite say,
but hope for one's own greatness is, of course,
an adequate incentive, Catiline!

CETHEGUS

And means enough to rightly relish life—
are not so wholly to be sneered at either;
—that's what I aim for, I am not ambitious!

CATILINE

Ha! I knew it, only base regard for
your own advantage is what urges you;
no, friends, o no, I have a better goal;
—it's true that I used bribery in my
attempt to get the Consulship; yet my
intention was a better one than could
be judged from such a method. Freedom and
the good of all was what I strove for,—but
I was misjudged, appearance was against me;
—my fate decreed it so, it had to be.

CETHEGUS

You will not, Catiline! you will not save
your friends from utter ruin, from disgrace?
—there's many of us who will soon be forced
to ply the beggar's staff by our wild passions.

CATILINE

Well, stop in time, then, that is my decision.

LENTULUS

What, Catiline! what's that? you plan to change
your way of life, but no, you're joking, aren't you?

CATILINE

I am in earnest, by the gods on high!

CETHEGUS

Ha! there's no further recourse with him, then!
Come, let us hurry—and report to all our friends
the upshot of our meeting; they're now sitting
at Bibulus', in a merry feast.

CATILINE

At Bibulus'? ha, so many nights
I have caroused down there with you, my friends!
but now there'll be no more of that,
I will be going away this very night.

LENTULUS

What's that you say? away?

CETHEGUS

This very night?

CATILINE

This very night with my Aurelia
eternal leave of Rome I will be taking;
—in Gaul's far valleys we will settle down;
a piece of farming land will feed us there.

CETHEGUS

Ha, Catiline! you will be leaving us?[12]

CATILINE

I will, I must, disgrace assails me here;
—ha, I've the courage to bear my poverty,
but to read scorn in every Roman's look,
and deep contempt, no, no, it is too much!
—There as a colonist I'll live in quiet,
I will forget what I at one time was;
will blot away the thought of all my plans;
will as a hazy dream my past remember.

LENTULUS

Well, then farewell! and may luck follow you!

CETHEGUS

Do not forget us, Catiline, we'll always
remember you; and now we will report
to all our friends what you have thus decided.

CATILINE

And give them, too, my final hearty greeting!

(LENTULUS and CETHEGUS leave. AURELIA comes in but stops short
apprehensively when she sees LENTULUS and CETHEGUS; when they are
gone, she approaches CATILINE.)

AURELIA
(gently reproaching him)

Still, my Catiline, your rough and rowdy
comrades?

CATILINE

It's the final time, I was
but taking leave of them—now every bond
that kept me bound to Rome is cut asunder,
—for ever, ever more.

AURELIA

I have packed up
the little bit we own, it isn't much,—
enough, though, Catiline! for frugal needs.

CATILINE

(deep in thought)

Yes, yes, enough, since all is lost for me.

AURELIA

O, think no more of what cannot be changed;
—forget.

CATILINE

Ha! well for me, if I could do it,
if I could tear my memory from my soul,
all my dreams forget and all my plans;
o no, I'm not yet capable of that,
but I will strive to.

AURELIA

I will give you help;
and you will find a cure for all your pain;
but we must leave as soon as possible,
—for here your memory always haunts your soul,
—it's true, this very night we'll go away?

CATILINE

Yes, yes, this very night, Aurelia!

AURELIA

The little bit of money that was left
I've gathered, for our journey it's enough.

CATILINE

Well, now;—my sword I'll trade in for a spade,
ha! how's my sword of further use to me?

AURELIA

You dig the ground, and I shall be planting it,
and soon before your feet will sprout and flower
rose bushes and some nice forget-me-nots—
to serve as symbols that the time has come
when you can greet each memory of the past
as an old friend upon a welcome visit.

CATILINE

That time, Aurelia! o no, o no!
it still lies in the future's distant blue!
                    (after a pause)

But go, Aurelia! go in and rest awhile;
at midnight we'll be starting on our way;
when Rome is resting in its deepest slumber,
and no one will suspect where we are fleeing;
—the pale gray light of dawn will find us—far,
o far—from here, amid the lap of nature
we'll rest upon a carpet of soft grass.

AURELIA

A new existence will be dawning for us;
more rich in joy than that we'll soon be leaving;[13]
but I will go—a quiet hour of rest
will give me strength—good night, my Catiline!
                    (She kisses him and leaves.)

CATILINE

Now she is gone—ha! what relief I feel,
I can at last discard this burdensome
dissimulation, yes, this show of calm,

which least of all exists within this heart;
o, she is my good spirit, it would give her pain
to see my sorrow, and I must conceal it;
—yet I shall dedicate this silent moment
to an appraisal of my madcap life;
—but that lamp burning there disturbs my dreams,
—it must be dark here, dark as in my soul!

> (He puts out the lamp. The moon shines in
> through the columns in the background.)

Ha! much too bright here still, but never mind!
the feeble moonlight is well suited to—
this dark and gloomy halflight that enshrouds,
that always has enshrouded all my steps.
Ha, Catiline! consider: this day is—
your[14] last, even tomorrow you will be
no more the Catiline that you have been!
There in that distant Gaul my future life
shall pass obscurely in the gloomy forest.
Ha! this is my awakening from those dreams
of greatness, of a proud, a glorious life,—
which long I've cherished, my soul's inner core
has been their one arena, no one else has known them.
—Ha! it is not that woeful peace and quiet
far from worldly din that brings me terror;
—no—for one moment but to shine out bright—
and flaming like a meteor!
—to consecrate, with just one glorious deed,
my name to greatness, immortality!
ha! I could then in that very hour
leave[15] life behind;—for then I would have lived;
—I could take flight unto a foreign shore,
I could implant my dagger in my heart;
—but this indeed is death without a life!
Ha! Catiline!—are you to perish thus?
A sign, you Gods on high! that it's—my fate,
forgotten and without a trace, to vanish
from life!

FURIA

(*behind the columns in the background*)

No, no, it is not, Catiline!

CATILINE

(*shrinking back*)

Ha! horrible! what voice rings out from there?
A spirit voice from underworldly shades?

FURIA

(*stepping out into the moonlight*)

I am your genius!

CATILINE

(*appalled*)

Ha, Furia!

FURIA

So deep you've sunk, so deep, to be afraid
of me!

CATILINE

Ha! you have risen from
the grave's dark depths in order to torment me!

FURIA

Torment you, do you say? I am your genius!
I must accompany you what way you go.
(*She comes nearer.*)

CATILINE

O gentle gods! o, it is she herself—
and not a spirit!

ACT TWO

FURIA

Spirit or not, it
is all the same, I shall accompany you.

CATILINE

With everlasting hatred!

FURIA

In the grave
hate vanishes, like love—and every feeling
that mortal bosoms cherish—just one thing,
just one, is everlastingly unchanging.

CATILINE

What's that? speak out!

FURIA

Your fate, o Catiline!

CATILINE

My fate is known but to the gods on high—
and no one else.

FURIA

But I, I know it, too!
I am your genius—a bond most strange
links us together.

CATILINE

It is hatred's.

FURIA

No.
Has any spirit risen from the grave

—still feeling hatred? —Listen, Catiline!
in underworldly streams I have extinguished
the fiery hatred flaming in my breast;
—o Catiline! behold! I am no more
that Furia, so wild and full of vengeance—
whom you once knew.

CATILINE

Do you not hate me, then?

FURIA

Not any more! —You see, within that hole,
when I stood on the threshold changing life—
to death, when I, cut off forever from
the realm of light, prepared myself to pay
my visit to the underworld, o, then
a strange mood seized me—I cannot explain it;
—there took place then a wondrous transformation,
my hate, my vengeance, my whole soul then vanished;
each memory vanished, and each mortal yearning;
only the name of Catiline remains—
in fiery script etched in my breast forever.

CATILINE

Most strange! ha, be whatever you may wish,
a human or an underworldly spirit,
there still is a mysterious magic force
in all your words and in your murky glances!

FURIA

Your soul is proud like mine, and yet you will,
despondent and afraid, give up all hope
of future greatness, you will cowardly
desert[16] the stage on which your lofty plans
to full maturity were to unfold.

CATILINE

I must, I must! my fate compels me to!

FURIA

Your fate? Do you then lack the strength and courage
to fight against what you have called your fate?

CATILINE

Ha! I have fought enough, was not my life
a constant battle—and with what reward?
Contempt and scorn!

FURIA

          Ha! deep you've sunk indeed!
You set yourself a goal, so lofty, daring,
you strive to reach it, yet you're terrified
by every hindrance.

CATILINE

          Fear is not the cause.
My goal was bold, yes, lofty were my plans;
—the whole thing was a fleeting youthful dream.

FURIA

No, Catiline! o no, now you deceive yourself;
your every thought pertained but to this goal,—
your soul is great, quite worthy to rule Rome,
and you have friends, why do you hesitate?

CATILINE

(reflecting)

I should—what do you mean; with people's blood—?

FURIA

Ha! weakling, ha! you lack a woman's courage!
have you forgotten that proud Roman woman,
who sought the throne over her father's corpse?
I feel myself a Tullia, but you?
despise, despise yourself then, Catiline!

CATILINE

Despise myself because my bosom is
no more the seat of wild ambitiousness?

FURIA

You stand before a crossroad in your life;
that way a quiet solitude awaits you,
a life half death and half a drowsy slumber,
but down the other way you dimly glimpse
a ruler's throne, just choose, o Catiline!

CATILINE

Ha! your words sound so seductive to me!

FURIA

One daring step and in your hands is laid
the fate of all proud Rome, o Catiline!
look, here await you greatness, sovereignty,
and yet you waver, you don't dare to act!
you're leaving for your woods, and in that place
each hope that you once cherished will depart.
Ha, Catiline! is there no further trace
of your old pride still left within your heart?
Shall such a lofty soul, for glory meant,
there in an obscure nook unknown expire?
—o! leave—and know, for ever you prevent
what here with forceful deeds you could acquire!

CATILINE

Go on—go on!

FURIA

With shuddering your name
will be remembered by posterity;
your life throughout has been a daring game,
yet bright and shining it would flash out free
to distant times, if you with strong control
could through the frantic throng a pathway clear,
and thralldom's cloud could part, through your bright soul,
to let a new-born freedom's sky appear,
if you could once—

CATILINE

O silence! There a chord
you struck that touched the deepest part within me,
an echo in their sound your words afford
of what my heart has whispered endlessly!

FURIA

Now once again I know you, Catiline!

CATILINE

I will not leave! —You have aroused to life
my youth's resolve, my manhood's aspiration!
Ha! I shall shine out for the sunken Rome,
and blaze forth in the comet's radiant terror!
Ha! wretches filled with pride! You soon shall find
that I'm not broken yet, though for a while
my strength was sapped by battle!

FURIA

Catiline!
Hear me! —What fate demands, what spirits of darkness

determine, that we must obey—well, then—
my hatred's left me, fate has willed it so;
it had to be that way;—give me your hand—
in endless league—why do you hesitate?
You will not?

CATILINE

Dreadful gleams are burning in
your look, like lightning in the night's thick gloom;
your smile is foul;—ha, so I have supposed
that Nemesis—

FURIA

What!—her you will discover
deep down in your own breast;—have you your oath forgotten?

CATILINE

O, I remember, yet a spirit of
revenge you seem to me.

FURIA

I am, you see,
an image out of your own soul.

CATILINE

(brooding)

What's that?
Ha! deep within myself obscure forebodings
and strange but hazy images rise forth;
—but I don't understand them, it's too dark in there!

FURIA

That's how it must be—darkness is our kingdom,
it's there we rule—come, give me now your hand
in dark and endless league.

CATILINE

(*wildly*)

O lovely Nemesis!
my genius, you image of my soul!
here is my hand in everlasting league!
(*He seizes her hand violently; she looks at him with a wild smile.*)

FURIA

Now we two part no more!

CATILINE

Ha! like a fire
your handclasp tore a passage through my veins!—
Blood courses there no more, just raging flames!
Ha! it already grows too cramped in here,
and much too dark—yet soon there shall be spread
a dawn of flames upon the city of Rome!
(*He draws his sword from its sheath.*)

My sword! my sword! ha! look, how bright it gleams!
yet soon it shall be dyed with streams of blood!
My brow's on fire, my heart beats violently!
and startling visions dart within my soul!
It is revenge, revenge and proud wild dreams
of greatness, ruling power, a deathless name;
my watchword shall be blood and crimson flames!
Let's go, let's go! at last I am myself!
(*He rushes out and* FURIA *follows him.*)

———— ?ϗ ————

A tavern
STATILIUS, GABINIUS, *and* COEPARIUS *come in, along with several other
young noblemen.*

STATILIUS

Here, friends! in here we can enjoy ourselves,

here we are safe, no one will overhear us!

GABINIUS

Indeed—we will enjoy each moment fully,
who knows how long we'll be allowed to do so?

COEPARIUS

No, first let's wait to hear the news that we're
expecting Lentulus and Cethegus to bring us.

GABINIUS

O, let them bring us anything they will;
we'll while away the time until they come!
Be lively! friends! let's have a cheerful song!
(While waiters pass the cup around, the following song is sung.)

Bacchus we worship,
joyful we nurse up
the cup to the limit,
drinking his praise.
Red wine in flowing
lovely is glowing,
all of us savor
the wine god's fine drink.

Liber our father
frees us from bother,
joy to us beckons,
clear is the grape;
come, let us relish,
wines life embellish,
stirring to gladness
always our minds.

Sparkling Falernian,
better than others,
leads all its brothers,

glorious drink!
You animate us
merry create us,
cheer you disperse through
all of our souls!

Bacchus we worship,
joyful we nurse up
the cup to the limit,
drinking his praise.
Red wine in flowing
lovely is glowing,
all of us savor
the wine god's fine drink!

(LENTULUS *and* CETHEGUS *come in.*)

LENTULUS

Forget this song and merriment!

STATILIUS
What now?
Is Catiline not in your company?

GABINIUS

He's willing, isn't he?

COEPARIUS
What was his answer?
Speak out, speak out!

CETHEGUS
Quite otherwise
than we imagined was his answer.

GABINIUS

Well!

LENTULUS

He has refused our overtures, will not
have any more to do with our great plans.

STATILIUS

Ha, is that true?

COEPARIUS

Tell us, why won't he do it?

LENTULUS

He will not, as I said; he is betraying
us, his friends—he will be leaving us.[17]

STATILIUS

He's leaving, do you say?

CETHEGUS

Yes, this very night
he's going away; but it cannot be censured;
his grounds were good.

LENTULUS

Ha! cowardice was his grounds,
in time of need he treacherously will leave us![18]

GABINIUS

Ha, that's his friendship, is it!

COEPARIUS

No, o no!
false, treacherous was never Catiline!

LENTULUS

And yet—he's going away.

STATILIUS

With him our hope!
For who, indeed, as well as he could lead us?

COEPARIUS

No, that is true, we must give up our plan.

LENTULUS

By no means, friends! just listen first to what
I have to say;—we have resolved to try
to win by force of weapons what a hard—
a most unfriendly fate denies to us;
at present we're oppressed,—we wish to rule;
we suffer want,—and riches are our goal.

SEVERAL

Yes, might and riches are what we desire!

LENTULUS

Well then, for our commander we have chosen
a man on whom as friend we all relied;
he has betrayed our trust—is going away;
ha! friends! come on, we'll show him that we're able
to help ourselves—look, all that is required
is just one man—with steadfastness and courage—
who wants to lead you.

SOME

Yes, but where can he be found?

LENTULUS

Speak, friends, would you, if he were to stand forth,
select him for your leader—well, your answer?

SOME

We would indeed!

OTHERS

Yes, yes, we would indeed!

STATILIUS

So what's his name?

LENTULUS

What if it were myself?

GABINIUS

Yourself!

COEPARIUS AND OTHERS
(doubtfully)

You, Lentulus! you want to lead us?

LENTULUS

I do.

CETHEGUS

But can you do it? look, that needs—
the strength and courage of a Catiline.

LENTULUS

I have no lack of courage—nor of strength;
but quick, let's set to work;—speak up! would you
back out of it just when the moment is
at hand—when everything gives token of
a happy upshot?

STATILIUS

No, we'll follow you!

OTHERS

We'll follow you!

GABINIUS

Yes, yes, if Catiline
is leaving[19] us, then you're the only one
who's capable of leading.

LENTULUS

Well, then listen,
here's what I plan to do;—first off we must—

CATILINE
(*rushing in*)

I'm here, my friends!

ALL

It's Catiline!

LENTULUS
(*aside*)

Ha! damn it!

CATILINE

Speak out, what is it you demand of me?
But no, no, just be still—I volunteer—
to be your leader—will you follow me?

ALL EXCEPT LENTULUS

Yes, Catiline! o yes, we'll follow you![20]

STATILIUS

We've been deceived!

GABINIUS

And you've been shamefully maligned!
Speak, did you want to leave[21] us, Catiline?

CATILINE

I did—but that is over with—look, now
I will be living only for my plans!

LENTULUS

But just what are your plans, if I may ask?

CATILINE

O, they are lofty;—loftier than you
or maybe anyone can guess—o friends!
upon our side we'll muster every Roman,
each freedom-lover, who for Rome's great glory
and for its ancient freedom gave his all!
O friends! the Roman spirit still exists,
—yet is its final spark not quite extinguished!
Ha! it shall be fanned up to shining flames,
more clear and high than any time before;
o, much too long there lay a gloom of thralldom
as black as night outspread above our Rome!
And this our empire, though it seems both proud

and mighty—totters now and soon will sink;
therefore a forceful hand must seize the helm!
but, friends! it must be cleansed, yes, cleansed here first!
our ancient Rome must be called back to life!
we must annihilate the wretchedness
that here exists and very soon will choke
the final remnant of the mood for freedom!
—Yes, freedom, it is freedom I'll create,
as pure as one time in the bygone days
it blossomed here,—indeed, I will call back
the time when every Roman with his life
in gladness bought his fatherland its glory,
and gave his all—to safeguard its rich splendor!

LENTULUS

You're dreaming, Catiline, that wasn't what
we had in mind.

GABINIUS

Indeed, what is the use
of reestablishing those ancient times
with their absurd naiveté?

SEVERAL

O no, o no!
it's might we want, and means for us to live
a merry, carefree life!

OTHERS

Yes, yes! that is our goal![22]

COEPARIUS

What use to us is Rome's great glory, friends?
—enjoyment's what we want!

CATILINE

               Ha! wretched stock!
are you the issue of the noble fathers?
To heap dishonor on the name of Roman
is how you choose to safeguard its rich splendor!

LENTULUS

Ha! do you dare to mock, you who so long
have been a sign of terror?

CATILINE

               Yes, it's true;
I was a horror to the decent—yet
I never once have been so base as you.

LENTULUS

Stop, stop! we will not tolerate your taunts!

OTHERS

No, no, we will not, no!

CATILINE

               (calmly)

               You wretches, cowards!
there's something you still dare to will, then—you?

LENTULUS

Down, down with him!

OTHERS

Yes, down with Catiline!
(They draw their daggers and rush at CATILINE, who calmly pulls his
toga away from his breast and regards them with a smile of cold con-
tempt; they let their daggers fall.)

CATILINE

Thrust home! You dare not? Ha! you coward stock!
I would respect you if you could have pierced
your daggers into Catiline's bare breast;
no spark of courage yet remains in you!

SOME

No, no! he is our friend!

OTHERS

We have deserved his scorn!

CATALINE

You have, indeed—yet now the time has come
when you can blot away all your dishonor.
Ha! let's forget all that has gone before,
a new existence almost beckons to us!
                    (bitterly)

—But no! what can I hope, indeed, from you;
do you have courage—or the Roman spirit?
                    (passionately)

I dreamt such lovely dreams once, and high plans
were darting through my bosom, that is gone!
—Ha! if I could, Icarus-like, equipped
with wings soar through the blueness of the Ether,
and if the gods on high endowed this hand
for just a moment with gigantic strength;
—I would then seize the lightning in its flight
and sling it toward the city down below;
and when the high and brilliant flames rose up,
and Rome sank in disintegrating ruins,
then from the grave I'd call once more to life
the ancient long-since vanished Roman spirits.
—But, o alas! they're only visions! Ha!
The bygone times do not come back again,
and neither do the proud past's vanished spirits.

(*wildly*)

Well then, if the old Rome cannot again
be roused to life, the new shall nonetheless founder!
Ha! soon there'll be, where marble columns stand
in splendid rows, a heap of ashes only!
Ha! deep in ruins shall the temples topple,
the Capitol will soon be found no more.—
Then swear, my friends! o swear, if you agree
to follow me, I'll lead you faithfully!
Do you agree?

LENTULUS

Yes, yes, we'll follow you!

(STATILIUS, GABINIUS, COEPARIUS, *and the others whisper together.*
CATILINE *regards them with a scornful smile.*)

LENTULUS
(*half aloud*)

Yes, yes, we'll follow him, for right behind the ruins
we may most easily find what was our goal.

ALL

Yes, Catiline, yes, yes, we'll follow you!

CATILINE

Then swear to me by all the gods on high
that you'll obey my every order!

ALL

Yes,
we solemnly do swear that we'll obey you!

CATILINE

All right, let us be off this very moment,

you will find weapons over at my house,
we'll gather there for further consultation.
(*They rush out.*)

LENTULUS

Well done, but listen, Catiline, you know,
don't you, that just today from Allobrogia
a delegation has arrived in Rome?

CATILINE

All right, go on, go on, ha! yes, you're right!

LENTULUS

If we get them disposed to our designs,
with them we'll get the whole of Gaul, that would
increase our strength not inconsiderably.

CATILINE
(*brooding*)

Barbarians? With them we should—?

LENTULUS

It is essential.

CATILINE
(*with bitterness*)

Ha! yes, deep has been Rome's fall,
behind its walls are neither strength nor courage
to topple even ruins that are shaky!
(*They go out quickly.*)

———— ?⚔ ————

185

A garden behind CATILINE's *house, which can be seen in the background. To the left a side-building.* CURIUS, CETHEGUS, *and several others come in cautiously from the right in whispered conversation.*

CURIUS

But is it really true what you've been telling?

CETHEGUS

It is—this very moment everything
has been decided.

CURIUS

He is leading you?

CETHEGUS

He's leading us—he's due here any minute.
(*They go into the house except for* CURIUS.)

CURIUS

A night most strange—my thoughts are whirling round
in circles, just as if it were a dream;
yet in the midst of this strange turbulence
I see her image almost everywhere.

CATILINE

(*coming in*)

You here, my Curius! I've greatly missed you!
our episode in Vesta's Temple had
an unexpected outcome.

CURIUS

(*confused*)

Ha, you're right!

CATILINE

I will not give it further thought, it is
a happening most strange, and quite mysterious.
They say, you know, the Furies rise up from
the underworld in order to torment
us mortals;—ha! if that indeed were so!

CURIUS

Speak, have you seen—?

CATILINE

O yes, this very hour!
But let's forget that—listen, Curius!
A weighty venture is in preparation.

CURIUS

I know about it, Cethegus has told—

CATILINE

Good! what the end will be the gods alone
may know, perhaps it is my fate to be
struck down upon my path before I have
attained my goal—well, let it be so, then.
—But you, my Curius, whom I have loved
since when you were a boy, I won't drag you
down into danger's maelstrom, promise me
you'll stay behind in Rome till all is over.

CURIUS

(*moved*)

My father! Catiline! how good you are to me!

CATILINE

You promise it! then we will say farewell;
wait here for me, I will be back quite soon!
(*He goes inside.*)

CURIUS

He loves me as before, he senses nothing.
(LENTULUS *and other friends of* CATILINE *come in.*)

LENTULUS

Say, Curius! Didn't Catiline just go
into the house?

CURIUS

Yes, yes, he's waiting for you.
(*They go inside.*)

CURIUS

(*pacing back and forth in great agitation*)

I can't subdue this great impatience, this
excitement that so restlessly impels me!
Ha, Furia! you strange and wondrous woman,
o, every moment makes my passion greater!
She rushed away with steps as quick as lightning
when I had led her from the hole of death;
and this distracted, terrifying speech,
glances with a dim and wondrous glow;
ha! could it have been madness? no, o no!
it surely isn't that!

FURIA

(*approaching*)

No, no, pale youth!

CURIUS

(*shrinking back*)

Furia!—you here?

FURIA

Here one finds Catiline!
so here, of course, must Furia also be!

CURIUS

O! come with me, my Furia! I'll take
you where it's safe;—what if they found you here?

FURIA

Me, youth! me?—have you quite forgotten then
that I no more belong among the living?

CURIUS

Ha! once again these horrifying words,
compose yourself,—o do, my Furia!
(*He tries to seize her hand.*)

FURIA

(*wildly*)

Audacious youth! are you not frightened then
of gloom's own daughter, who has risen forth
to life for but a single fleeting moment!

CURIUS

I frightened?—yes, but it is just this terror—

this wondrous shudder that is my desire!

FURIA

Be still, o youth, be still!—you speak in vain,
the grave's my home, it's there that I belong;
—I am arisen from Death's dark domain,
at day's approach I flee back to its throng,
there is my home, for ghastly shades a prison,
in Pluto's halls meanders Furia.
Know, Curius! know, lately I have risen
up from the underworld's dark dimness.

CURIUS

                              Ha!
Then lead me there, I'll let you be my guide,
although your path should take me through Death's night!

FURIA

No, youth! o no! what the grave's shadows hide
cannot be reached by any mortal look!
—My time is short, I must make use of it,
I am allotted only night's brief hours,—
my work is gloom's, for I belong to it.—
—Tell me, is Catiline not there—inside?

CURIUS

You're seeking him? Do you pursue him still?

FURIA

Why have I risen from the underworld?
Was it not for pursuing Catiline?

CURIUS

(vehemently)

Ha! frightful! it is madness after all!

yet you are lovely even in your raging!
—O, think no further, Furia, of Catiline,
—come now; I shall obey your every hint,
I shall, a slave before your feet, beg you

(kneeling)

for but a glance—o hear me, Furia!
I love you—but the flame consumes me; much
less suffered Hercules, when in his breast
the flaming poison raged!

FURIA

Audacious one,
be still! Yet, tell me first, what's happening
inside—at Catiline's?

CURIUS

(getting up)

Again! again!
to him your every thought's devoted, ha!
I could—

FURIA

Speak, Curius! is he prepared
to heed the summons?

CURIUS

Then you know?

FURIA

Yes, yes!

CURIUS

All right, then hear! they've chosen Catiline
to be their leader;—but no more of him!

FURIA

Yes, Curius! first answer me one thing;
it is my last—you will accompany him?

CURIUS

I must!

FURIA

(with a wild smile)

Him;—Catiline?

CURIUS

Ha! this very name
fans up again the flame within my bosom!
Detested one! O, I could murder him!

FURIA

You said just now you're ready to obey
my every order?

CURIUS

Yes, I will obey it!
I only beg, forget him—Catiline!

FURIA

What, forget, you say, no, first he must descend—
into the grave.

CURIUS

Ha, Furia! I should—?

FURIA

Not you yourself—just go reveal his plans.

CURIUS

Ha, dreadful! him, my foster father and—

FURIA

You rival!—wretched weakling! ha! you dare
to mention love and haven't got the courage
to topple him—contemptible!

(She is about to leave.)

CURIUS

(holding her back)

No, no!

don't leave[23] me, I am ready to do all!
ha, you are dreadful, Furia, and yet I am
unable to destroy this magic net
in which I'm snared!

FURIA

Well, are you ready, then?

CURIUS

I must, I must! have I still got a will?
your look is like the serpent's when with force
of magic it ensnares a bird, which in
a circle fearfully flits round it, more
and more approaching near the dreadful gulf!

FURIA

All right, go do it, then.

CURIUS

And then when I
have—sacrificed my duty for my love?

FURIA

Then nothing binds me more to Catiline;
then is my task fulfilled. Demand no more.

CURIUS

I shall—ha, Furia—it's raging in my soul!

FURIA

You tarry, coward?

CURIUS

      No, by spirits of darkness!
I will! for he alone keeps us apart;
yes, he shall fall, extinguished is each spark
of what at one time blazed within my heart!
Ha, frightful one! in your proximity
abruptly turns to stone each feeling that
once gently gave my bosom life, even my love
is more like hate than love;—no longer do
I know myself, I blindly plunge into
a bottomless abyss to follow you!
—Yes, he shall fall; this very moment I
shall go reveal his plans—await me here!
          (*He rushes out.*)

FURIA

(*after a pause*)

My task will soon be ended, Catiline!
with rapid strides, you're coming to your goal!
  (AMBIORIX *and* OLLOVICO *come out of* CATILINE'*s house without*
              noticing FURIA.)

AMBIORIX

So then it is decided, yes, in truth
a daring action!

OLLOVICO

It is venturous,
yet the reward awaiting us is well
worth fighting for through even greater dangers
than those that soon will threaten us.

AMBIORIX

Indeed!

OLLOVICO

Emancipation from Rome's tyranny,
our ancient freedom are well worth a fight.

AMBIORIX

As soon as we are able, we'll rush home,
and secretly the whole of Gaul shall arm
itself for battle with its harsh oppressors,
and join up with the troops of Catiline.
It will be costly; Rome is mighty still,
yet it must happen, come, Ollovico!

FURIA
(in a tone of warning)

O woe to you!

AMBIORIX
(frightened)

O all you Gods on high!

OLLOVICO
(also frightened)

It is a supernatural voice we hear!

FURIA

O woe to you!

OLLOVICO

She's standing yonder in
the pale moonlight, a goddess warning us!

FURIA

O woe to you! Don't follow Catiline!

AMBIORIX

Let's go, Ollovico! It is a spirit voice;
let's go, let's go, we must obey its dictate!
(*They hurry out.*)

CATILINE

(*coming out of the door in the background*)

Ha! what a desperate hope, in truth it is!
to think of toppling Rome with such a group
of wretches; it is only want and sheer
rapacity that urge them on;—o, what
have I to gain?

FURIA

(*behind the trees*)

Revenge, o Catiline!

CATILINE

You gods! o, what was that—is this voice from
my own interior? Revenge! all right,
it shall be so; revenge for every hope
that's robbed from me, revenge for every plan
that hostile-minded fate has smashed for me!

ACT TWO

*(The conspirators, now bearing arms, come out
of the door in the background.)*

LENTULUS

Look, darkness still enshrouds the Roman city;
now it is time.

OTHERS

Yes, yes, let's go, let's go!

AURELIA

(coming out of the side-building without noticing the conspirators)

You here, my Catiline?

CATILINE

Ha!—it's Aurelia!

AURELIA

Are you already waiting—
            (stopping, as she notices the conspirators)

high and gentle gods!

CATILINE

(wildly)

Go, woman, go!

AURELIA

O! what does all this mean!
You are not going—!²⁴

CATILINE

(as before)

Yes, by spirits of darkness!

197

a merry jaunt—my sword, see how it gleams!
it'll soon be dyed in crimson streams of blood!

AURELIA

You gods! o, then my hope has been a dream,
and dreadful is my waking up!

CATILINE

Be still!
Come, woman, come, if that's your wish; to stir this breast
your tears no more avail. Look, in the west
bright Luna floods Rome's towers with her light,
ha! ere she rises once again at night,
hot flames shall upwards soar toward heaven's blue,
and Rome into a heap of ruins strew;
and in the distant future when she beams,
some bright-lit night, on crumbling rubble streams,
a lonely pillar mid the waste shall stand,
and show the wanderer where Rome stood grand!
(*They leave.*)

———————— ❦ ————————

ACT THREE

CATILINE's camp in a wooded area. To the right CATILINE's tent can be seen and beside it an ancient oak. It is night. Now and then the moon breaks through the clouds. Outside the tent a watch-fire is burning. Several more are in the background among the trees. STATILIUS *is sleeping by the watch-fire;* MANLIUS *is pacing back and forth outside the tent.*

MANLIUS

It's just like them, those rash and thoughtless fellows;
they're sleeping there so soundly and so calmly,
as if it were their mother's safe, snug lap
they rested in, and not a desolate woods,—
as if they planned to wake up to some sport,
and not to battle, yes, perhaps the last
they're fighting here.

STATILIUS

(awakening and getting up)

      You're still on watch, old man!
Are you not weary? I'll relieve you now!

MANLIUS

No, you just get your sleep, a young man needs
refreshing sleep, his wild enthusiasm
takes energy; it's very different when
the hair has lost its hue, the blood runs thin,
when old age weighs so heavy on our shoulders.

STATILIUS

Yes, you are right, I also someday shall,
an old and hardened warrior—

MANLIUS

Are you then
so sure that fate has thus determined it,—
that you have been allotted an old age?

STATILIUS

Ugh, and why not? tell me, what put all these
forebodings in your head?

MANLIUS

You really think
we don't have anything to fear, young fool!

STATILIUS

Hasn't our force been pretty well augmented?

MANLIUS

By fencers and by slaves, ugh, yes, indeed.

STATILIUS

Well, never mind; for as a group they don't
seem insignificant, and all of Gaul
will send us help.

MANLIUS

Which hasn't come as yet.

STATILIUS

And have you doubts?

MANLIUS

I know these people well.
But that is all the same, soon time will show, you see,
what the high gods have got in store for us.
—But go along, Statilius, and make sure
the guards are staying vigilant at their posts;
we must secure ourselves against a night attack;
well, cautions's a good thing, it harms no one.

(STATILIUS *leaves.*)

The clouds are gathering now, yes, more and more;
it's a dark night and threatening to storm;
a clammy fog is settling heavily,
oppressively, on this old warrior breast.
I have no more the ease of mind with which
I used to rush into the battle's tumult;
it's not old age alone, it's like a burden
weighing on me, but, strange enough, the others
seem much the same to me, so cross and moody.

(*a pause.*)

Yes, let the gods be told, revenge was not
the reason why I followed Catiline.
My anger flared up for a fleeting moment
when I first felt that I'd been wronged, insulted;
no, this old blood is not yet fully cold;
it runs quite hot still sometimes through my veins.
The wrong's forgotten, though, I have forgiven them,
I only came because of Catiline,
I shall with all my care watch over him;
he stands here quite alone among these crowds
of worthless rogues and frivolous good-for-nothings;
not one can understand him,—no, and he
is much too proud to want to fathom them.

(*He lays some branches on the fire and remains standing in silence.*
CATILINE *comes out of the tent.*)

CATILINE

Already midnight, everything's so hushed,
it's only from my eyes sleep flies away;
—the night wind's gust is strong and cold, it will refresh me
and give me strength—ha! it is sorely needed!
                    (*noticing* MANLIUS)

Is that you, Manlius, so faithfully
at watch this frosty night?

MANLIUS

                    It's only fitting;
I guarded you when you were just a boy;
don't you remember that?

CATILINE

                    That time is gone.
With it my calm, and everywhere I go,
I am pursued by strange and shifting forms;
all, Manlius, all houses in my bosom,
save only peace,—that is no longer there.

MANLIUS

Dispel those thoughts, go rest now, Catiline,
just bear in mind, tomorrow will perhaps
demand already all your calm, your strength.

CATILINE

I cannot, Manlius,—if I but close my eyes
to blot out everything in fleeting slumber—
then I am visited by eerie dreams;
just now I, half-asleep, lay on my cot,
when once again these visions came to me,
more weird than ever, more ambiguous
and enigmatic; ha! if I could grasp
their sense, but no—

ACT THREE

MANLIUS

Come, Catiline! confide to me
your anxiousness, perhaps I can advise you.

CATILINE

(*after a pause*)

If I was awake or dozing, I can scarcely tell,
countless thoughts and countless projects crossed my mind pell-mell;
suddenly all things get dimmer, darkness grows in might,
and its ample wings then lowers in my breast a night,[25]
lit by thought's forked lightning only, loathsome to behold;
then I see a vaulted chamber, black as graveyard mold;
high as heaven is its ceiling, filled with thunderclouds,
and a strange array of figures, just like spirit crowds,
whirled about in frantic circles, as in hurricanes,
when in turbulence they're sweeping over foamy mains.
Yet amid the frantic swarming now and then appear
floral-decorated figures from a better sphere;
roundabout them darkness lessens, brightness fills the air,
and within the hall's omphalos stand a wondrous pair,
two lone women, one is tall and black as night's deep shades
and the other fair as daylight when it slowly fades.
Ha! so strangely all-familiar seemed these two, I thought,
gently one was smiling, and her glance contentment brought,
from the other's haughty eye-casts lightning wildly blazed,
horrible, yet at this vision willingly I gazed.
Haughty, one is standing, and the other leans in stress
toward the table where they play a mystic game of chess.[26]
All the while the group of figures billowed up and down.
Then their game is at its finish, and within the earth sinks down
she, the one whose eyes a gentle, loving glance had sent,
and the fair resplendent figures followed where she went.
Lo, the clamor then increases, growing still more dire,
and the eyes of that dark woman flared up like a fire.
Then all disappeared before me, I saw only her,
but what more I dreamt thereafter in my fever-blur

203

lies behind oblivion's curtain in my being's knot,
could I but the rest remember; ah, it's all forgot!

MANLIUS

It's indeed most curious, Catiline!
this dream of yours.

CATILINE

(*brooding*)

If I could but remember;
no, no—I can't succeed.

MANLIUS

Well, let it be forgotten;
don't give it further thought, for what are dreams?
Imaginings and empty fantasies,
devoid of meaning and without foundation.

CATILINE

Yes, you are right, I will dispel the thought,
it is indeed unmanly, brooding on such things;
but sometimes in the quiet hours of night
I find myself in such a curious mood;
it will be over soon, just go now, Manlius!
rest, if that's your wish, I'll wander here awhile
in solitude with but my thoughts, now go!
(MANLIUS *leaves, and* CATILINE *paces back and forth awhile in silence.*
A ghostly figure comes in slowly from the background without being
noticed by CATILINE.)

CATILINE

(*becoming aware of* THE GHOST)

You Gods above, what *is* this!

THE GHOST

      My greetings, Catiline!

CATILINE

What do you want? who are you, old one, speak!

THE GHOST

Be still! it is for me alone to ask
and you to answer; don't you recognize
from long-since vanished times this voice of mine?

CATILINE

It seems I do, but tell me whom you seek—
here in this place at midnight's quiet hour?

THE GHOST

It's you I seek; no other hour but this
is granted me, I must make use of it.

CATILINE

By all the gods! speak out, who are you?

THE GHOST

                     Silence!
I've come up here to call you to account;
why won't you let me be in peace down there;
why is it that you force me to arise
from the grave's depths at midnight's hour so that
I may protect my dearly-purchased glory?

CATILINE

Ha, what presentiments are rising in my soul!

THE GHOST

What yet remains of all my sovereign power?
mere nothing; no, it joined me in the grave;
ha! it was costly, dearly I acquired it,
my calm in life and in the grave my peace
I traded for it—yes, it was enough!
And now you want, with rash, foolhardy hand,
to steal from me what I still have remaining!
Are there not paths enough to great achievements;
why must you tread the very one I paved?
My power I gave up while still alive,
my name, so I believed, would always stand,
not like a star, a-twinkle pleasantly,
no, like a lightning in the night sky fixed;
I didn't want, like hundreds else before me,
for gentle virtues, magnanimity
to be remembered, didn't want to be
admired, so many have already had
this lot and will as long as time shall last;—
no, in a bloody radiance I wished
to be remembered by the distant future;
they, with a shudder mixed with admiration,
were to look up to me, whom no one ever
before or since had dared to emulate.
So had I dreamt, but it was just a fancy;
I knew you well; why didn't I suspect
what lay concealed within your soul's recesses?
Beware though, Catiline! for I see through
the curtain of the future what you have
in store for you, what fate has predetermined.

CATILINE

(*eagerly*)

You know that, do you? state it, state it, then!

THE GHOST

Only behind the grave's dark gate

shall fade the twilight that enwraps
whatever dreadful is or great
that future waves shall make collapse.
But hear what from your fate's full sum
a ghostly voice to you will say:
"By your own hand your fall will come,
and yet another shall you slay."[27]

(THE GHOST vanishes.)

CATILINE

(after a pause, looking around)

Ha! he has vanished!—was it then a dream?
No, no, he stood here,[28] and the moonbeams fell
upon his visage; ha! I recognized him,
it was the Dictator, the ancient man
of blood, come from the grave to frighten me.
He was afraid that I should pillage him,
not his glory, no, the radiance
of terror keeping bright his memory;
does then ambition last even beyond
the grave's dark shadows?

(a pause.)

O, how everything
assails me;—first Aurelia speaks in words
of gentle warning, and again I hear
re-echo in my breast what Furia has said,—
and o! now even rise up from the grave
the pallid shades of those from times gone by;
they threaten me, they want me to turn back!
No, I won't falter, bravely I'll stride forth
until my goal's attained,—I'll soon have reached it.

CURIUS

(rushing in, greatly agitated)

Catiline!

207

CATILINE
(*surprised*)
What, you—you here, my Curius?

CURIUS
I had to—

CATILINE
Speak, why aren't you still in Rome?

CURIUS
I couldn't stay, I had to look for you!

CATILINE
That was rash of you! But come into my arms,
because of me you hurtle into danger.
          (*He is about to embrace him.*)

CURIUS
(*shrinking back*)
No, Catiline, o no—you must not touch me!

CATILINE
You gods, what's this?

CURIUS
         Flee—flee!—you are surrounded
by enemies!

CATILINE
Compose yourself, my Curius,
you're talking wildly—has your journey tired you?

CURIUS

O no, but save yourself while there's still time;
you've been betrayed!

(*He kneels down before him.*)

CATILINE

(*starting*)

Betrayed! what's that you say?

CURIUS

—It was a friend!

CATILINE

O no—no, Curius,
o no, my friends are all as loyal as you.

CURIUS

Alas, then, Catiline, if that is so.

CATILINE

Compose yourself;—it is your love for me,
your care for my security, that has
you seeing danger where there isn't any.

CURIUS

These words you speak pierce through me like a sword;
but flee, by Heaven's mighty gods, o flee!

CATILINE

Get yourself in hand—speak calmly; why
am I to flee, am I not safe here? speak!

CURIUS

(*in despair*)

No, no, you've been betrayed, your plan's revealed!

CATILINE

You must be mad—no—that's impossible!

CURIUS

Yes, it is true—but flee this very moment,
you can perhaps still save yourself by fleeing.

CATILINE

O, should it, then—! no, that's impossible!

CURIUS

(*pulling out his dagger and offering it to* CATILINE)

There, Catiline! o, take it, drive it in my breast;
—thrust home, thrust home—by me you've been betrayed!

CATILINE

Ha! this is madness!

CURIUS

No, I solemnly swear
by all the gods, it's I who have betrayed you;
don't ask the reason; o, it crushes me!

CATILINE

(*bitterly*)

Must I be robbed of trust in friendship, too?

CURIUS

O, pierce me through! do not torment this breast

with mercy longer!

CATILINE

(gently)

No, my Curius!
Stand up—you erred—and I forgive you for it.

CURIUS

(overwhelmed)

O Catiline! be still—you break my heart;
but hurry, flee!—it soon will be too late;
the Roman army will attack you soon;
it's on its way, o, soon it will be here!

CATILINE

And what about my friends in Rome?

CURIUS

Alas!
they've been imprisoned and perhaps are slain.

CATILINE

(sorrowfully)

O fate, o fate.

CURIUS

(in despair, again offering his dagger to CATILINE)

Here, thrust it in my breast!

CATILINE

(gently)

You were the means, that's all—could you have helped it?

CURIUS

O, let me with my life pay for my crime!

CATILINE

No, I forgive you,

(*as he is leaving*)

only one thing now

remains for me.

CURIUS

(*getting up*)

Flight!

CATILINE

No, heroic death!
(*He leaves.*)

CURIUS

O, it is fruitless—death awaits him! Ha!
this mildness is a dreadful punishment!
—I'll go and look for him;—one thing won't be denied me,
to fall while fighting by the hero's side.
(*He rushes out.* LENTULUS *and two* GLADIATORS *come in stealthily from
behind the trees.*)

LENTULUS

(*softly*)

Someone was talking here just now.

FIRST GLADIATOR

But now
it's still, perhaps it was the night watch after
being relieved.

LENTULUS

Perhaps;—we'll wait right here;—
make sure you're ready,—I suppose your swords
are sharp and gleaming?

SECOND GLADIATOR

Just like lightning, yes!
it has some bite,—at the last contest I
cut down two stout and stalwart warriors with it.

LENTULUS

Then place yourselves beside that bush right there;
rush forward quickly when the sign is given—
and cut him down.

FIRST GLADIATOR

Yes, yes, it shall be done!
(*They remain where they have been standing.*
LENTULUS *comes downstage, reconnoitering.*)

LENTULUS

(*half aloud*)

It is a daring move, there's no denying;
yet it must happen now, this very night—
if it's to be performed;—if Catiline
should fall, there's no one else but me can lead them;
tomorrow we already push toward Rome;
we'll pick up new adherents everywhere.
(*He goes in among the trees.*)

FIRST GLADIATOR

But who is, then, this unknown fellow that
we are to murder?

SECOND GLADIATOR

Quiet!—that's a matter
of no concern to us—since Lentulus
has paid us, he's the one who must defend it.

LENTULUS

(coming back hurriedly)

Make sure you're ready, he'll be here abruptly.
(THE GLADIATORS *and* LENTULUS *place themselves behind the bushes.*
CATILINE *comes in immediately afterwards.*)

LENTULUS

Go, cut him down, quick, run your swords through him!
(LENTULUS *and* THE GLADIATORS *rush at* CATILINE.)

CATILINE

(drawing his sword and defending himself)

Ha! you base wretches! dare you—

LENTULUS

Cut him down!

CATILINE

(recognizing him)

You, Lentulus, you'd murder Catiline?

SECOND GLADIATOR

(terrified)

It's he!

First Gladiator
(the same)

It's Catiline!—no, we won't fight
with him,—let's flee!
(They run away.)

Lentulus

So fall by my hand, then!
*(They fight. Catiline knocks Lentulus' sword from his hand;
Lentulus tries to run away, but Catiline holds him firmly.)*

Catiline

You traitor, murderer!

Lentulus
(imploringly)

Mercy, Catiline!

Catiline

I perceive your plan, you meant to murder me
and make yourself the leader of my friends.

Lentulus

I did, yes, Catiline!

Catiline
(aside)

Then he doesn't know
what has occurred!
(aloud, with dissimulation)
Well, let it be!

LENTULUS

Explain, what do you mean?

CATILINE

    I'm stepping down;
lead them yourself,—you're worthy to.

LENTULUS

(*surprised*)

      You are?

CATILINE

I am, but you be careful, Lentulus!
—your post is dangerous, our plan's betrayed,
—but I will go and call our friends together,
I will present to them their new commander
and then resign.
    (*He is about to leave.*)

LENTULUS

(*taken by surprise and holding him back*)

   No, wait—wait, Catiline!

CATILINE

Our time is precious—for the Roman army
will soon be here.

LENTULUS

(*uneasy*)

   No, hear me, Catiline!
you're surely joking; why, it can't be so!

CATILINE

Our plan has been betrayed, just as I told you!
Now let us see your strength, your competence.

LENTULUS

O woe to us!

CATILINE

(scornfully)

You're trembling, wretched coward!
and you would topple me—would lead my friends.

LENTULUS

Forgive me, Catiline!

CATILINE

Go seek your safety
in rapid flight, if you can get away.[29]

LENTULUS

Ha, you'll allow me to—

CATILINE

Do you believe
I seriously meant to quit this post
in time of danger? —You don't know me, then.

LENTULUS

(dissimulating)[30]

O Catiline!

CATILINE

(loftily)

Don't waste the moment idly;
just seek your rescue,—I'll know how to die.

LENTULUS

(aside, as he is leaving)

I thank you for this handy information,—
I shall make use of it for my own safety.
I know this area,—I shall go lead
the Roman army here on hidden pathways.
—The serpent that you trample in the dust
with such disdain has not yet lost its sting![31]
(He leaves.)

CATILINE

(after a pause)

This is the loyalty that I relied on,
thus they betray me, one by one; o gods!
It's only treachery and cowardice
that dwells within these base and wretched souls;
I am, indeed, a fool with all my plans;
—I would destroy that nest of vipers yonder;
—ha! Rome indeed is long since just a ruin!
(The approaching noise of weapons can be heard.)

O, there they come, there still is bravery
among them;—hear that sword, how merrily
it clinks; it gives me all my strength again;
I felt so limp just now, so deeply downcast;
—but now it's over;—danger wakes my courage
to life again;—and I shall face it bravely!
*(MANLIUS, STATILIUS, GABINIUS, and a number of
other conspirators come in.)*

MANLIUS

Here, Catiline! your friends have come to you;
they are prepared to follow you in all.

STATILIUS

Yes, Catiline! we will accompany you
in life and death, wherever you command!

CATILINE

I thank you all, my valiant comrades; but,
you see, for us there is no more the choice
of life or death,—just that between a death
in valiant battle, facing hostile swords,
and, under torment, being hunted down
ferociously like wild beasts of the woods.
Speak, do you choose in cowardly flight to bear
a wretched life for yet a brief time more,
or else as bravely as your noble fathers
to fall in battle with your sword in hand?

SOME

It's that we choose!

OTHERS

Yes, yes, with sword in hand!

CATILINE

Well, then, let's go! our death shall consecrate us
to immortality, the distant times shall think
of us with admiration!

FURIA

(*who has been approaching him unnoticed*)

Or with horror!

SOME

(*shrinking back in wonder*)

Ha, a woman!

CATILINE

(*taken by surprise*)

Furia!—you here?
what do you want!

FURIA

I must accompany you
unto your goal.

CATILINE

Where *is* my goal, speak out!

FURIA

Each one seeks not his goal the selfsame way;
you seek your goal through wild and frantic battle,
and battle yields a crop of death, destruction.

CATILINE

But also glory and eternal name!
go, woman! noble is this hour, and fair;
my bosom is shut fast to your hoarse shrieks!

AURELIA

(*coming out of the tent and showing surprise when she
sees the assembled group*)

My Catiline!

CATILINE

O, it's Aurelia!

AURELIA

What's happening?

CATILINE

(*sorrowfully*)

To think I could forget you!
O, what will your fate be?

FURIA

(*scornfully*)

In your high purpose
do you already falter, Catiline!
—is *this* your courage?

CATILINE

(*vehemently*)

No, by all the Gods!

AURELIA

O Catiline—o speak, what's going on?

FURIA

Is it now time for whining and complaining?

MANLIUS

No, no—let's go!—don't waver, Catiline!

CATILINE

(*struggling with himself*)

O, what a storm is in this heart, but yet—
no, no, it can't be otherwise—well, then—
come, follow me, let's go!

AURELIA

(*throwing herself in his arms*)

O Catiline!
don't go;—or else I will accompany you!

CATILINE

No, no, Aurelia!

FURIA

(*scornfully*)

O yes, let it be so,
it's worthy your base weakness that you fall
in battle by a woman's side!

CATILINE

(*thrusting* AURELIA *away violently*)

Ha!—ha!
I weak!—no, no, by spirits of darkness, no!
(*wildly*)

Out of my bosom I'll rip every feeling;
just bloody lust for battle blazes there!

FURIA

Just so, just so, my noble Catiline!

CATILINE

Let death await me, imminent and sure;
—it's my desire!

AURELIA

O, hear me, Catiline!
don't cast me off, by all your love for me[32]
I do implore you!

CATILINE

(*wildly*)

Silence! in this breast
love can no more be found!

AURELIA

O gentle gods!
(*She leans weakly against the tree beside the tent.*)

CATILINE

But now, let's go!

MANLIUS

There's noise from weapons yonder!

SEVERAL

They're coming!

CATILINE

Boldly meet them, then; I'll lead!
The voice of honor in our bosoms thunders,
we'll follow it—before the sword we'll bleed!
—Let's go!—by Roman swords with Roman mettle
the last of Rome in their own blood shall settle!
(*They rush out.*)

FURIA

He is gone—and I have triumphed, I've achieved my goal,
on the field he'll soon be lying, death's prize booty, stiff and cold!

AURELIA

(*deep in thought, without noticing* FURIA)

In his heart all filled with anger, love, it seems, can no more dwell!

Was I dreaming? No, I heard it from his angry lips too well.

FURIA

Swords are clinking; he already wanders in the grave's terrain.
Soon he shall, a fleeting shadow, hasten into death's domain.

AURELIA

(becoming aware of FURIA*)*

Ha! whose is that horrifying voice resounding now,
like an owl that's wildly shrieking from a hemlock bough;
are you risen from the murky land where shadows roam
to lead Catiline to dwell there, in your somber home?

FURIA

Home's the goal of every wandering—and his chosen way
went through life's abysmal swamps.

AURELIA

       But only for a day!
Once his heart was great and noble, he was good and true,
but then evil in his bosom sank its root and grew.

FURIA

Also once the flower flourished, colorful and fair,
but its petals fade and death then takes it in its snare.

AURELIA

Dreadful creature! far too well this voice's sound I know,
o, from Catiline's own lips it often seemed to flow.
Gloomy spirit, you have stolen life's best fruit from me,
forced my Catiline's pure heart my tenderness to flee;
from among my dreams' dark visions, you I recognize,
how you placed yourself between us, menace in your eyes.
O! beside my Catiline I dreamt with joy possessed
of a life by love embellished, of a peaceful nest;

in his lovely heart I planted once a flower bed,
as its richest ornament with care my love I bred;
—but your hostile hand yanked up the flower, root and all,
and it's lying in the dust, where once it stood so tall!

FURIA

You weak fool! and *you* would guide the steps of Catiline,
don't you know his heart was never yours to so entwine?
Woman! your weak flowers in such soil cannot hold out,
only in the spring's warm sunshine can the lily sprout,
while the henbane's chalice blossoms under skies of gray,
and his soul has been long since a cloudy autumn's day.
Light will soon within his bosom fade with his last breath,
and he'll lie, as gloom's rich booty, in the arms of death.

AURELIA

(with passion)

No, by all the gods of heaven, no, that's not to be!
to his heart my tears will somehow find a way still free.
Even if he now lies bloody at the battle's crest;—
I will fling my arms around his cold and lifeless breast,
breathe upon his pallid lips my love's unending store,
soothe the tempest in his bosom, give him peace once more.
Gloomy spirit! what you've seized I'll wrest from your grim hands,
bind him to the realm of light with love's eternal bands.
And when his last heartbeat ceases, at his last grimace,
we will go from life together in a fast embrace.
Grant me then, you gods on high! for what I've had to brave,—
there beside my Catiline, the still peace of the grave!
(*She leaves.*)

FURIA

(*staring out through the trees in the background*)

Just go, deluded fool!—I have no fear,
my triumph rests secure within my hand,
—hark, sounds of battle—soon the hour is come;

—the cries reverberate, he's fighting still,
—soon shall the field become a silent graveyard.
The moon's in hiding, lovely is this hour.
Soon he'll be lying there with eyes aglaze;
I shall behold him thus before I go
to look for him among the pallid shades.

(listening)

Ha! it's becoming quieter already,
—the battle's almost still, perhaps already
his soul on airy wings flies toward its home.
O, it is lovely in these half-dark woods,
in gloomy night to hear the final sigh
escape a breast as it contends with death.

(with wild joy)

It is a beautiful, a pleasing music,
—the owl is joining in—it's wishing them
a joyful welcome to its somber kingdom!

(after a pause)

Now rests the grave's full silence all around;
those who have won already leave the field,
and now the dead alone rest hushed out there,
—there they will slumber many, many days,
while scorching sunbeams bleach their rotting bones,
and greedy ravens flutter overhead!

(a pause.)

Ha! look, what's hovering upon the meadow,
like mist of morning when it, humid, gray,
in close-packed swatches, glides above the swamp?
It's coming nearer, now I see it clearly,
—it is a warrior, staggering and weak,
ha! one who's from the shades of fallen heroes!

(She withdraws somewhat. CATILINE comes in with lowered head and a
distracted look.)

226

CATILINE

(*without noticing* FURIA)

"By your own hand your fall will come,
and yet another shall you slay."
Those were his final words before he vanished.
What did he mean? I cannot grasp the riddle!

FURIA

O, welcome from the battle, Catiline!

CATILINE

Ha! who are you?

FURIA

Do you no longer know me?

CATILINE

It's you, then—Furia!—you offer me a welcome.

FURIA

I am your genius, your goddess of rewards!
Look, take the victor's garland from my hand!
(*She picks some flowers and braids them into a garland during the*
following speeches.)

CATILINE

What do you mean?

FURIA

I will enwreathe your temples;
but say, why come you hither so alone,
why have your friends not followed after you?

CATILINE

They're sleeping, Furia.

FURIA

They're sleeping, do you say?

CATILINE

Yes, yes, they're sleeping;—go beyond those woods,
they're lying there so quiet in the moonlight;
—you'll find them there, stretched out in row on row;
they went to sleep from the swords' lullaby;
but listen to me, Furia, can you conceive it?
I thought before that slumber would be peaceful
when once the fount of heart-blood had dried out.

FURIA

Well, isn't it then so?

CATILINE

No, listen to me!
At my troop's head I fought ferociously,
I looked for death beneath the sword's keen edge,
and round about me all my friends sank down
in death's last doze, but I—I didn't find it,
and when they lay there stretched out on the earth,
and all the enemy troops had marched away,
I stood there still half-stunned, where just before
the battle echoed; everything was hushed,
the moon shone down between the broken clouds,
faintly lit up the dead men's pallid features;
they lay there round me with their eyes aglaze,
with savage smiles on foully twisted mouths;
it seemed as if they lay there dreaming, seemed
they grinned at me with mockery and menace—
as if they were demanding back their blood.

FURIA

No, Catiline! o no, it was not so;
—they merely beckoned you to come with them.

CATILINE

Happy for me could I have done so.

FURIA

Think
no more of that, come, I'll adorn you with
the victor's garland, with your victor's wages.
                    (*She offers him the garland.*)

CATILINE

Ugh, what is that—a poppy garland?

FURIA

(*with wild gaiety*)

Well,
are they not pretty flowers? look, see how
they glisten in the moonlight, like fresh blood.

CATILINE

Away with them, they have a dreadful luster.

FURIA

(*with laughter*)

Well, if you love the feeble, pallid colors,
I'll let you have the garland of green seaweed
that Tullia wore upon her dripping tresses,
when her corpse floated on the Tiber billows!

CATILINE

Ha! what foul images!

FURIA

Shall I perhaps
then fetch you from Rome's fields some grass all stained
in brown by the life-blood of its citizens,
which your hand caused to flow, my Catiline!

CATILINE

Leave off, leave off!

FURIA

Or shall I bring you, then,
a garland from the brown leaves of the woods,
which withered at their witnessing the curse
that issued from the ravished victim's lips?

CATILINE

Ha! are you then a demon?

FURIA

No, just one
who, like a friend, reminds you of your past.

CATILINE

Why now?

FURIA

The weary wanderer, you know,
when at his goal, looks back upon his way.

CATILINE

Do I stand at my goal?

FURIA

If you so wish.

CATILINE

So wish?—indeed!—ha! your foul talk a host
of images has called up in my soul!

(vehemently)

What do you want with me, you pallid shades?
leave me in peace; what is it you demand?

FURIA

Compose yourself, your mind is in an uproar,
come, let me braid the garland in your hair.
It has a strong, effective healing force,
it lulls to rest, it brings oblivion.

CATILINE

(deep in thought)

Ha! oblivion! you say?—ha! that's the word,
then press the garland tightly round my brow.

FURIA

(putting the garland on his head)

Now you're adorned, and that is how you must
appear before Gloom's Prince, my Catiline!

CATILINE

Yes, yes—I will;—I long to find repose,
my soul has grown so weak in life's hard battle;
—now it would slumber;—it's all black in there,
like this dark night, and yet I still can glimpse
a single star that's gleaming through the darkness here.

(He lays his hand on his breast.)

FURIA

(aside)

Ha! it is she!

CATILINE

It hinders me; o, I
can't go along with you before its radiance
is wholly quenched—o yes! there was a time
when it was bright and shining like that star
in heaven there, behind the cloud's dark edge.
Now it is faint, it glimmers hid by mist.

FURIA

Then wholly quench it.

CATILINE

Ha! what do you mean?

FURIA

You have your dagger yet, an inch or two
of steel is all it takes to still that heart
that came between us in hostility.

CATILINE

I understand—Aurelia—no, no!
I had forgotten her, I don't know why,
—it seems that everything would be both good
and peaceful in my soul could I but lay
my head upon her bosom and forget,
—blank out everything.

FURIA

No, it is foolish
to give more thought to that, but, as you wish;
—I'm leaving now, just see if you can find
with her your long-since-vanished peace and quiet.
                    (with increasing vehemence)

Ha, fool! do you believe the pallid dead
will let you be in peace—no, no, they shall

232

in savage multitudes be gathered round you;
disgustingly they'll stare with hollow eyes
and call for bloody vengeance!

CATILINE

Ha! you're right!
(*looking around; wildly*)

Peace cannot sprout for me upon the Earth;
I'll go with you to Death's grim land of shades;
—yes, she shall fall—she is the only bond
still linking me to life.

BOTH

Yes, she must fall!
(*A flash of lightning lights up the stage, and the thunder rolls.*)

FURIA

The Powers on high have heard what you just swore;
—look, Catiline!—there comes your sacrifice!

AURELIA

(*coming in from the background and looking around anxiously*)

Where shall I find him? Nowhere do I see him!
You gods on high! o, grant me strength!
(*noticing him*)

O Heaven!
(*rushing toward him*)

My Catiline!

CATILINE

(*wildly*)

What do you want here, woman!

AURELIA

You're still alive!
> (*She is about to throw herself into his arms.*)

CATILINE

> (*pushing her away*)

Go, go, I hate you, go!

AURELIA

O gentle heaven!

CATILINE

Do you seek to snare
me once again in chains—it won't succeed;
don't gaze at me in that way, woman, know,—
I cannot tolerate these tender looks;
they pierce into my heart like tapered daggers;
I won't endure it longer—you shall fall!
> (*He draws his dagger and seizes her arm violently.*)

AURELIA

O gods on high! you must watch over me!

CATILINE

> (*with increasing vehemence*)

You shall—you must—my only bond to life
is you, that bond will soon be smashed to pieces!
> (*A powerful thunderclap can be heard.*)

> (*in a rage*)

There, woman!—listen to the thunder echo;
you hear it, do you not? the gods now speak
their final parting words to Catiline!
> (*He rushes toward her; she flees offstage; he pursues her.*)

FURIA

(watching them with wild joy)

My triumph is now sure! he's raising up his dagger;
in vain she stretches forth her hand to heaven!
—he's thrusting home—she sinks down in her blood!

CATILINE

(coming in slowly)

Now it is done, soon I'll exist no more;
death's peace already settles in my soul;
what's wrong with me? I do not understand it;
—it seems to me my heart-strings burst asunder
upon her dying groan—I'm so uneasy,
—as if the ample Earth had suddenly
become a vast and monstrous wilderness
where only you and I were left behind.

FURIA

It's so, my Catiline!

CATILINE

(brooding)

It's now all clear
to me, what I so long have dimly felt.
Is life not after all a constant battle
among the warring forces of the soul?
this battle is the soul's distinctive life.
But now my battle hushes in my bosom.
(vehemently)

Well, then, I am no longer Catiline;
here, take my dagger, quench the lamp's last flame.

FURIA

(seizing the dagger)

Fall, then, by my hand, and I'll go with you
even beyond the shadows of the grave.

> *(She thrusts the dagger into his breast;*
> *he sinks down at the foot of the tree.)*

CATILINE

(after a pause, in a weak voice)

Ha! you enigmatic spirit, now I understand!
"half by my own hand I fall, half by another's hand."[33]
When her tender heart I'd broken, from my soul took flight
every trace of good and beauty, just a foul midnight
then remained, in there soon only endless gloom will dwell.
Murky Styx, now let your billows strike the shore and swell
up the bank, soon you'll be leading Catiline alone
toward that murky Tartarus, yes, toward his future home.
Dual paths go down there, but for me there's only one,
to the left.

AURELIA

(coming in, pale and staggering, her breast all bloody)

No, to the right, toward fair Elysium!

CATILINE

(horrified)

Ha, her pallid shade makes horror in my soul revive;
speak, are you from death arisen, or are you alive?

AURELIA

(kneeling by his side)

O, I see your soul is churning, like a sea tossed high;
let me press my heart so fondly to your breast, and die.
Just a slumber, Death's quick herald, took my soul in thrall,

but my weakened eyes could follow you, I saw it all;
and my love at death's approach to me new power gave;
breast to breast, my Catiline, we'll sink into the grave.

CATILINE

(sorrowfully)

O, how gladly! yet such hope no longer can apply;
in my heart resounds with horror vengeance's wild cry.
No, Aurelia! you are soaring into bright eternity;
downward toward the darkness Nemesis leads me.
(The day dawns in the background.)

AURELIA

(kindly, as she points toward the East)

No, when faced by love, Death's horrors and its night all disappear,
look, the thundercloud retreats, the star is twinkling, weak but clear;
(weakly)

light is winning,—look, Aurora smiles as at a guest,
come with me, beloved! Death already grips my breast.
(She sinks down. CATILINE seizes her hands.)

CATILINE

(with his last strength)

Ha, how lovely! now quite clearly I recall my dream,
how the hall's thick darkness scattered in a dazzling stream
of the sun's bright emanations, from the dawning day.
O, my eyes are growing dimmer, and my strength gives way;
but as never once before my soul sees light appear,
and my life, my past's wild orbit, is to me now clear.
Yes, my life was night-like, foully lit by lightning's glow,
but a rosy-colored dawning through my death I know!
From my soul the gloom you've driven, peace now fills my breast,
see, with you I'm going to the realm of light to rest!
(He pulls the dagger quickly from his breast and
speaks with his dying voice)

Looks of reconciliation show the gods above;
you have vanquished gloom's great forces with your mighty love!

(During the final speeches FURIA *has withdrawn gradually toward the
background, and during the conclusion she vanishes.* CATILINE's *head
sinks down on* AURELIA's *breast. They die.)*

NOTES
As for the facts that provide the basis for the present play, these are
much too familiar for it not to be immediately obvious what
departures have been made from historical truth and that the
historical material has been only partially used, so that it must, rather,
be considered as only a framework for the idea running throughout
the play. That the author has made use of historical names for
characters who in regard to their natures as well as other circum-
stances behave differently from what one has learned to know about
them from history will, it is to be hoped, be excused, all the more so
since these names are scarcely eminent enough that confused impres-
sions will be created by their behavior under circumstances that they
never met with in history.

Notes to *Catiline* (1850)

1. I adopt the reading of the manuscript, which has *"fordi"* instead of the *"forbi!"* of the printed text. Using the printed text, the line would be translated as "it's done with me! my life's without a goal!" The following line is merely a string of dashes in the printed text; I adopt the stage direction from the manuscript.

2. "Allobrogia" is my coinage (apparently: I can locate no reference to it or that the lands inhabited by the Allobroges even had a name) in response to Ibsen's *"Allobrogerland,"* literally: "Allobroges-land." He *may* have meant "the land [or "lands," for the neuter noun *"land"* is not inflected in the plural] of the Allobroges," and, indeed, in 1875 he amends to *"Allebrogers land,"* which does mean "the land [or "lands"] of the Allobroges." The Allobroges were a Celtic tribe inhabiting the areas of modern Dauphiné and Savoy in southeast France bordering on Switzerland and Italy.

3. The verb *"forlade,"* which Ibsen uses here, does mean "leave," but it also means "desert," "abandon," and "forsake"; the double sense of this verb is very important in the text of *Catiline*, especially in the second act.

4. I adopt the reading of the manuscript; the printed text has "Og" ("And").

5. I incorporate this word from the manuscript; its omission from the printed text is clearly in error, since it is needed to complete the meter of the line.

6. I adopt the reading of the manuscript; the printed text has *"Vel"* ("Indeed").

7. In the printed version this line is only eight syllables, because the manuscript's *"blege"* ("pale") has been overlooked—obviously unintentionally. This deviation from the manuscript is not indicated in the textual notes of the Hundreårsutgave.

8. In this and the preceding line the original *"hun"*("she") of the manuscript was changed to *"jeg"* ("I"), but the printed text has *"hun."* I adopt the revision in the manuscript.

9. I adopt the reading of the manuscript, which has *"mit"* ("my") for the *"hans"* ("his") of the printed text.

10. By jumbling the word order of the first three words of this line, the printed text has made the line metrically flawed; it is correct in the manuscript.

11. I adopt the reading of the manuscript; the printed text has *"Ja"* ("Yes").

12. This is the first instance of the frequent occurrence of *"forlade"* in Act Two (Catiline has used *"drage afsted"* ["go away"] to refer to his departure); the additional senses of *"forlade"* ("abandon," "desert," "forsake") are very much in the minds of the conspirators in this and the following scene.

13. *"Forlade."*

14. I adopt the reading of the manuscript, which has *"din"* ("your") for the *"den"* ("the") of the printed text (a possible misreading of the vowel).

15. *"Forlade."*

·16. *"Forlade."*

17. *"Forlade."*

18. *"Forlade."*

19. *"Forlade."*

20. The words "EXCEPT LENTULUS" do not occur in the manuscript. They constitute an example of the slight building up and modifying, or clarifying, of Lentulus' role between the manuscript as we have it and the printed version—and they provide evidence that Ibsen may have made at least some contribution to the "fair copy" from which the play was printed. I discuss both issues in the first section of the introduction.

21. *"Forlade."*

22. In the manuscript, the first "yes" is clearly crossed out, suggesting some effort— incomplete—toward reducing this line to the ten-syllable norm.

23. *"Forlade."*

24. I add the "not" from the *"ei"* of the manuscript; its omission in the printed text is clearly an error, since it is needed for the meter.

25. The printed text has a period after "night" and a capital letter beginning the next line; on the basis of the manuscript (which has no punctuation after "night" and a lower-case letter beginning the next line), I have altered this punctuation so that subsequent line modifies "night"—as is the case in Ibsen's 1875 revision of the printed text.

26. This is one of the lines in this speech that has fifteen rather than thirteen syllables in the printed text; but that text includes a trochee (*"begge"*: "both") that had been crossed out in the manuscript.

27. The word I have translated as "another" is *"fremmed,"* which would normally be translated as "stranger," a word that would be misleading here; Ibsen seems to be using *"fremmed"* much in the sense of "one different from, separate from yourself."

28. I follow the manuscript, which has *"her,"* although the printed text reads *"der"* ("there").

29. The manuscript reading would call for the second half of this line to be translated as "if you can manage to."

30. The stage direction originally read "moved" in the manuscript but was changed to "dissimulating" by another hand than Ibsen's in a late revision. I discuss this in the first section of the introduction.

31. This is another passage building up Lentulus' role that was added between the manuscript as we now have it and the printed text. I discuss this in the first section of the introduction.

32. I translate Aurelia's speech on the basis of the manuscript, which has "*din Kjærlighed*" ("your love") instead of the "*min Kjærlighed*" ("my love") of the printed text. Catiline's response confirms this choice.

33. Except for changes from "your" and "you" to "my" and "I," the passage within quotation marks is an exact echo of the original form of the Ghost's "riddle." It was changed in the manuscript to what appears in the printed text; this change must have occurred before Ibsen wrote Catiline's echo of the riddle upon his return from battle, but, for some reason, he used the original form in the echo here.

Catiline

(1875)

Drama in Three Acts

by

Henrik Ibsen

Second, Revised Edition

Preface to the
Second Edition

The drama *Catiline*, the work with which I embarked on my literary career, was written in the winter of 1848–49, that is, in my twenty-first year.

I was at that time in Grimstad, being obliged to earn by my own efforts what I needed for subsistence and for tuition in order to prepare myself for the matriculation examination at the University. The times were extremely turbulent. The February Revolution, the uprisings in Hungary and elsewhere, the Slesvig war—all this had a powerful and formative effect on my development, however incomplete it even long afterwards continued to be. I wrote resounding poems to the Magyars, encouraging them, for the good of freedom and humanity, to hold out in their just struggle against "the tyrants"; I wrote a long series of sonnets to King Oscar, essentially, insofar as I recall, containing an appeal to set aside all petty considerations and forthwith, at the head of his army, advance to the aid of our brothers on the frontiers of Slesvig.[1] Since I nowadays, as opposed to then, doubt that my winged proclamations would have benefited to any substantial degree the cause of either the Magyars or the Scandinavians, I consider it fortunate that they remained within the manuscript's semi-private domain. But I could not refrain, on more intoxicating occasions, from expressing myself in an impassioned manner in keeping with my poetry, which, however, did not yield me—from either my friends or my non-friends—anything other than the dubious profit of being hailed by the former as prone to being unintentionally amusing, while the latter found it extremely remarkable that a young person in my inferior position could take it upon himself to discuss things that not even they themselves presumed to have any opinions about. I owe it to truth to add that my behavior, in various circumstances, did not at all justify any particular hopes that the community could count on an accession in me of middle-class virtues, since I also with epigrams and caricature-sketches quarreled with many who had deserved better from me and whose friendship, by the way, I valued. Altogether, while a great age was raging outside, I found myself in a state of war with the little community within which I sat cramped in by my living conditions and by circumstances in general.

Such was the situation when, in preparing for my examination, I went through Sallust's *Catiline* and Cicero's orations against Catiline. I devoured these writings, and a few months later my drama was finished. As one will see from my book, I did not at that time share the two ancient Roman authors' conception of Catiline's character and conduct, and I am still inclined to believe that there nevertheless must have been a good deal that was great or significant about a man whom the majority's indefatigable advocate, Cicero, did not find it expedient to tackle until things had taken such a turn that there was no longer any danger connected with the attack. It should also be borne in mind that there are few historical figures whose reputation has been more exclusively in the power of their adversaries than has Catiline's.

My drama was written during the nighttime hours. From my employer, a good and decent man but entirely preoccupied with his business, I virtually had to steal free hours for studying, and from these stolen study hours I in turn stole moments for writing. There was, thus, little other than the night to turn to. I believe that this is the unconscious cause that almost the whole of the play's action takes place at night.

The fact that I was occupying myself with writing plays—a most incomprehensible fact, given my circumstances—had to be kept secret, of course; but a twenty-year-old writer can scarcely get by without having at least some others who are privy to what he is doing, and I therefore confided in two friends of the same age about what was secretly occupying me.

We three attached great expectations to *Catiline* when it was finished. First of all, it was to be fair-copied so that, under a pseudonym, it could be submitted to the theater in Christiania, and after that it was to be published. One of my devout and faithful friends undertook to produce a handsome and legible copy of my rough and uncorrected draft, a task that he carried out to such a scrupulous extent that he did not even forget a single one of the innumerable dashes that, in the heat of production, I had put in wherever the right expression would not at the moment occur to me. The second of my friends, whose name I mention here since he is no longer among the living, Ole C. Schulerud, at that time a student and later an attorney, went to Christiania with the copy. I still remember one of his letters, in which he informed me that *Catiline* had been submitted to the theater; that it would soon come to production, about which there could of course be no doubt, since the management consisted of very discriminating men; and there could be as little doubt that all the booksellers of the city would gladly pay a considerable fee for the first edition; it was just a matter, he thought, of finding the one that would make the highest offer.

After a long and tense period of waiting, however, a few difficulties began to manifest themselves. From the theater management, my friend received the play sent back with an extremely polite but equally definite rejection. He then went with the manuscript from bookseller to bookseller; but to a man they all responded in the same fashion as the theater management. The one making the highest offer demanded so and so much to print the play without a fee.

All this, however, far from discouraged my friend in his belief in triumph. He wrote to me, on the contrary, that it was exactly for the best this way; I myself should act as publisher of my drama; he would advance me the necessary money; we were to share the profits, in return for his attending to all the relevant business matters—except for proof-reading, which he considered superfluous, since there was such a handsome and legible manuscript to print from. In a later letter, he declared that in view of these promising prospects for the future he was thinking of giving up his studies in order to be able to devote himself fully to the publication of my works; he thought that I ought easily to be able to write two or three plays a year, and according to a calculation of the probabilities he had made he concluded that from the profits we should before long be able to undertake the journey through Europe and the Orient that we had frequently agreed on or at least talked about.

For the time being, however, my journey was to take me no farther than to Christiania. I arrived there at the beginning of spring 1850, and shortly beforehand *Catiline* had made its appearance at the bookstore. The play attracted attention and aroused interest among the students; but the critics dwelt rather on the faulty verse and in other respects found the book immature. A more appreciative judgment was given out from only a single quarter; but this opinion came from a man whose appreciation has always been dear and momentous to me, and to whom I take this opportunity to express my renewed thanks. To be sure, not very much of the small edition was sold; my friend had a number of the copies in his keeping, and I remember that one evening, when our joint domestic plight seemed to pile up insurmountable difficulties for us, this heap of printed matter was converted to waste paper and fortunately disposed of to a dealer. For the next few days, we lacked none of life's primary necessities.—

During my stay up at home last summer, and especially after my return down here, the varying images from my career as an author appeared before me more clearly and sharply than ever before. Among other things, I also picked up *Catiline*. I had almost forgotten the details of the book's contents; but on reading through it anew, I found that it nevertheless contained a great deal that I could still acknowledge, especially if one bears in mind that it is my maiden effort. Much that my later work has been concerned with—the opposition between ability and aspiration, between will and possibility, humanity's and the individual's tragedy and comedy at one and the same time— already appears here in hazy intimations, and I therefore conceived the intention of arranging for a new edition as a kind of jubilee publication, an intention to which my publisher with his usual willingness gave his approval.

But, of course, it would not do simply to reprint the old first edition, for this is, as previously indicated, nothing other than a printing of my unfinished and uncorrected rough draft or the very first sketch. On reading it through, I recollected clearly what originally had been vaguely present in my mind, and I saw in addition that the form virtually nowhere afforded an adequate expression of what I had wanted.

I decided therefore to rework this writing of my youth in a way that, I believe, I even then would have been able to do it, provided that time had been at my disposal and circumstances had been more favorable for me. The basic ideas, the particular representations,[2] and the over-all development, on the other hand, I have not touched. The book remains as it was originally, except that it now appears in a completed form.

In the light of what I have said, I hope it will be welcomed by my friends in Scandinavia and elsewhere; I hope that they will accept it as a greeting from me at the conclusion of what has been for me a period full of changes and rich in contrasts. Much that I dreamed of twenty-five years ago has been realized, even if not in the manner or as soon as I then hoped. Yet I now believe that it was all for the best; I do not wish that any of what lay between should have been unexperienced, and when I look back on what I have experienced as a whole, I do so with gratitude for everything and gratitude to everyone.

Dresden, 1 February 1875
Henrik Ibsen

1. The "long series of sonnets" survives as a poem called "Wake, Scandinavians"; it is dated 1849 in the manuscript containing it, but it may have been written in its first form the year before. It is a multi-stanza poem in a pattern of two four-line stanzas followed by two three-line stanzas with the lines of the fourth stanza rhyming with those of the third; hence it is a series of sonnets, although there are no divisions separating the individual four-stanza, fourteen-line groups. It is addressed only in part to King Oscar of Sweden-Norway. For clarifications of other references in this Preface, see the first section of my introduction to *Catiline*.

2. The "*ideerne, forestillingerne*" of the original is usually translated as "the ideas, the thoughts." However, it seems to me that "ideas" and "thoughts" lack adequate differentiation in English to convey exactly what Ibsen has in mind. Moreover, in writing "*forestillingerne*" rather than "*tankerne*" (the more common Dano-Norwegian word for "the thoughts"), he uses a noun whose related verb has as a primary sense "to present, to represent" and is often so used in contexts having to do with performing a play onstage.

The Characters

LUCIUS CATILINE, a noble Roman

AURELIA, his wife

FURIA, a vestal

CURIUS, Catiline's kinsman, a young man

MANLIUS, an old warrior

LENTULUS
COEPARIUS
GABINIUS } young noble Romans
STATILIUS
CETHEGUS

AMBIORIX } envoys of the Allobroges
OLLOVICO

A VESTAL

AN OLD MAN

PRIESTESSES and SERVANTS in the Temple of Vesta

GLADIATORS and WARRIORS

ATTENDANTS OF THE ALLOBROGES

SULLA'S GHOST

(The first and second acts take place in and near Rome, the third act in Etruria.)

ACT ONE

By the Flaminian way outside Rome. A tree-covered hillside by the highway. In the background loom the heights and walls of the city. It is evening.

CATILINE *is standing on the hillside among the bushes, leaning against a tree-trunk.*

CATILINE
I must! I must; a voice commands me thus
from my soul's depths,—and I will follow it.
The strength I have, and heart, for something better,
for something higher than this present life.
A simple round of pleasures unrestrained—!
No, no; they do not sate the heart's desire.
   I wildly dream! Oblivion is my yearning.
It's done with me! My life's without a goal.
      (after a pause)

   What has become of all my youthful dreams?
Like flimsy summer clouds they disappeared.
Just gall and disappointment have they left;—
I'm robbed of every valiant hope by fate.
      (striking his brow)

   Despise! Despise yourself then, Catiline!
You feel these noble powers in your mind;—
and what's the goal of all your endless striving?
Mere sating of your sensual desires.
      (calmer)

   Yet sometimes still, as in this very hour,

253

a secret yearning smolders in my breast.
Ah, when I look upon the city there,
that splendid, wealthy Rome,—and the corruption
and wretchedness, to which it long has sunk,
appear as clearly as the sun before me,—
there cries aloud a voice from deep within me:
wake, Catiline;—wake up and be a man!
                    (breaking off)

        Alas, it's mere delusion, nighttime's dreams,
and phantoms born of solitude, no more.
The least sound from reality's domain,
and down they flee into the soul's mute depths.
        (The envoys from the Allobrogians, AMBIORIX and OLLOVICO,
            enter with their attendants and come along the highway
                        without noticing CATILINE.)

                    AMBIORIX
        Look there, our journey's end! The walls of Rome!
Toward heaven juts the towering Capitol.

                    OLLOVICO
        So that is Rome? The queen of Italy,
soon Germany's,—and Gaul's as well, perhaps.

                    AMBIORIX
        Unfortunately, yes;—it may be so
someday; and merciless is Rome's dominion;
the cowed it crushes to the earth. We'll soon
see what our people can expect: if there's
to be a stop to wrongs at home, and peace
and justice for the Allobrogians' lands.

                    OLLOVICO
        It will be granted us.

AMBIORIX

Let us so hope;
as yet we don't know anything for sure.

OLLOVICO

You're fearful, are you not?

AMBIORIX

On valid grounds.
For Rome was always jealous of her power.
And you must bear in mind that this proud realm
is not, as we are, ruled by tribal chiefs.
Back home the wiseman or the warrior governs,—
in cunning the most shrewd, in strife the strongest;
it's him we choose for leader of our tribe,
to be the judge and ruler of our people.
But *here*—

CATILINE

(*calling down to them*)

—here force and egoism govern;—
it's tricks and plots that make you ruler here!

OLLOVICO

O woe, my brothers,—he was spying on us!

AMBIORIX

(*to* CATILINE)

Is such the high-born noble Romans' way?
Back home it is a woman's occupation.

CATILINE

(*climbing down to the highway*)

Be free from fear;—to spy is not my trade;

by chance it was I heard your conversation.—
    Is it in Allobrogia[1] you belong?
You think that justice here in Rome can flower?
Turn back! Go home! Here tyranny and wrong
far more than ever hold the reins of power.
In name, of course, it's a republic still;
yet every citizen's a slave in chains,
in debt, and subject to the Senate's will—
a group that is for sale for gifts and gains.
Quite vanished is the former social savor,
the liberalism Rome enjoyed of old;—
security—mere life—require the favor
of Senators and must be bought with gold.
Not justice but the voice of power matters;
the noblemen to might have lost the day—

AMBIORIX

    But tell me,—who are you whose speech thus shatters
the fervent hope that brought us all this way?

CATILINE

    A man who feels with passion freedom's cause;
an enemy of all misrule by wrong;
a friend of everyone oppressed by laws,—
with will and courage to unseat the strong.

AMBIORIX

    The noble Roman people—? Answer me;—
to fool us strangers surely you thus speak.
Are they no more what they were formerly:
the tyrant's fear, protector of the weak?

CATILINE
(*pointing to the city*)

    Look, Allobrogian,—great upon its hill,
the Capitol tyrannically glares.

Look how, lit up with evening radiance still,
it's blazing from the setting sun's last flares.—
Rome's evening luster blazes much the same;
its freedom is enwrapped in slavery's night.—
Yet in its heaven soon a sun shall flame,
dispelling darkness with its sudden light.

(*He leaves.*)

————— ᚨᚾ —————

A Colonnade in Rome

LENTULUS, STATILIUS, COEPARIUS, *and* CETHEGUS *enter in ardent conversation.*

COEPARIUS

Yes, you are right; it steadily grows worse.
And what the end will be I do not know.

CETHEGUS

Hey! It would not occur to me to think
about the end. The moment *I* enjoy.
Each cup of pleasure I gulp down—and let
the sum of things go sliding as it will.

LENTULUS

That's fine for those who can. I was denied
the knack to so indifferently await
the day when we have nothing more remaining,
and no claim can be duly satisfied.

STATILIUS

And not one glimpse of prospects for improvement!
Still, it is true: a way of life like ours—

CETHEGUS

Enough of that!

LENTULUS

The last of all my heirlooms,
for debt, was just this morning robbed from me.

CETHEGUS

Away with sorrow and complaints! Come, friends!
We'll drown them in a merry drinking bout!

COEPARIUS

Yes, yes; we'll do that! Come, my happy brothers!

LENTULUS

Hold on; I see old Manlius coming there;—
I think he's seeking us, as usual.

MANLIUS

(coming in angrily)

To hell with all these dirty, rotten dogs!
They haven't any sense of justice left.

LENTULUS

What's happened? Why are you so furious?

STATILIUS

The money-lenders plaguing you as well?

MANLIUS

Quite different. Listen! As you all well know,
I have with honor served in Sulla's army.
A piece of farming land was my reward.

And when the war was over, through this land
I kept myself; it fed me, though just barely.
Now it's been taken from me! As I'm told—
all state-owned property is to be seized,
for equal distribution to all comers.
It's just a robbery, and nothing else!
They only want to satisfy their greed.

COEPARIUS

They do just as they please with all our rights!
The mighty ones can practice what they wish.

CETHEGUS

(merrily)

That's hard on Manlius, all right! Yet I've
received a harder blow, as I'll now tell you.
Just think, my friends,—my young and lovely mistress,
my Livia, most faithlessly has left me,
just now when everything of mine that still
remained, for her sweet sake, I've fully wasted.

STATILIUS

Your wild excess's to blame for your misfortune.

CETHEGUS

Blame it on anything you wish; I won't
neglect a one of my desires; no, those
I'll gratify as long as I am able.

MANLIUS

And I, who fought so bravely for the glory,
the might, that now the proud ones boast about!
I shall—! Ah, my old gang of fellow soldiers,
if only those bold men were still around!
But no;—the greatest part are dead, of course;

and all the rest live spread through every land.—
O, what are you young men compared to them?
When faced with might, you bow down deep in muck;
you haven't got the guts to break your chains;
you bear this life of bondage patiently!

LENTULUS

By all the gods,—although he is offensive,
there's truth enough in what he said just then.

CETHEGUS

O yes; indeed;—we must admit he's right.
But how to go about it? That's the point.

LENTULUS

Yes, it's the truth. For far too long we have
endured oppression. Now's the time to cast
away the bonds that have been woven round
us by injustice and sheer lust for power.

STATILIUS

I understand you, Lentulus! But look,
for that we need a strong and forceful leader—
with courage, insight. Where can he be found?

LENTULUS

I know a man with what it takes to lead us.

MANLIUS

Do you mean Catiline?

LENTULUS

The very man.

CETHEGUS

Yes, Catiline; he is perhaps the man.

MANLIUS

    I know the man. I was his father's friend,
and fought beside him in a lot of battles.
His little son came with him to the war.
He was already wild then, out of hand;
and yet rare gifts were to be seen in him;—
his mind was noble and his courage firm.

LENTULUS

    I think we'll find him rather more than willing.
Tonight I met him very much depressed.
He's brooding on some secret plot or other;—
some daring goal he's long since had in sight.

STATILIUS

O yes, he long has sought the Consulship.

LENTULUS

    He won't succeed in that; his enemies,
with thunderous vehemence, spoke out against him;—
he heard them speak himself, and in a rage
he left the Council—planning his revenge.

STATILIUS

Then surely he'll agree to our proposal.

LENTULUS

    I hope you're right. But first in private we
must weigh our plan. The time is in our favor.
            (*They leave.*)

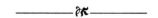

In the Temple of Vesta in Rome. On an altar in the background a
lamp is burning with the holy fire.
CATILINE, *followed by* CURIUS, *comes in stealthily between the columns.*

CURIUS

What, Catiline,—it's here you're leading me?
In Vesta's temple!

CATILINE

(*laughing*)

Yes; as you can see!

CURIUS

You gods,—what recklessness! Why, Cicero
this very day denounced you in the Council;
and still you can—

CATILINE

O, let that be forgotten!

CURIUS

You are in danger, and you just forget it—
by blindly dashing into further danger.

CATILINE

(*merrily*)

Variety's my joy. I've never had
a vestal virgin's love,—forbidden fruit;—
so here I've come to try out fortune's favor.

CURIUS

You what? Impossible! It's just a joke!

CATILINE

A joke? Oh, yes, indeed,—like all my loves;—
but what I said to you just now I meant.
At the last spectacle the priestesses
I saw pass through the square in grand procession.
By accident, on one of them I chanced
to cast my eye,—and with a fleeting look
her eyes met mine. They pierced right through my soul.
Ah, the expression in those jet-black eyes
I never saw before from any woman.

CURIUS

I well believe it. Tell me,—then what happened?

CATILINE

I knew a way to slip into the temple,
and I have seen and spoken to her often.
O, what a difference lies between this woman
and my Aurelia.

CURIUS

You love them both
at once? No,—that I cannot understand.

CATILINE

It's strange. I do not understand it either.
And yet—I love them both, just as you say.
But yet, o yes, how various is this love!
Aurelia is tender, often bringing
my mind tranquility through gentle words;—
while Furia—. Go, go; there's someone coming.
            (*They hide among the columns.*)

FURIA

(coming in from the other side)

Detested halls,—that witness all my pain,
home for the anguish under which I bow!
Each glorious hope I once did entertain,
each thought, extinguished in this heart,—which now
with fever is pervaded, now with fire
more hot and burning than the Vestal flame.—
    Ah, what a fate! What was the fault so dire
that put me in this prison in all but name,—
that robbed me of my every youthful pleasure,—
in life's warm spring each innocent delight?
    Yet not a single tear my cheek shall measure;
revenge and hate alone this breast ignite.

CATILINE

(stepping forth)

And not at all for me a different flame—
a gentler one—you cherish, Furia?

FURIA

You gods! What rashness—are you here again?
You're not afraid—?

CATILINE

                    I know no taste of fear.
It always was my joy to challenge danger.

FURIA

O glorious; glorious! That is my joy, too;—
and so I hate this temple all the more,
because I live in constant safety here,
and danger never dwells behind its walls.
    O, this employment, empty, without action,
a life as dull as is the lamp's last flare—!

How narrow an arena for my store
of lofty aims and passionate desires!
To be pressed in and crushed between these walls;—
here life grows stagnant; hope becomes extinguished;
here drowsily the day sneaks toward its end,
and not one thought can be fulfilled through deeds.

CATILINE

Ah, Furia, how strange is what you say!
It's like an echo from my own heart's core,—
as if with words of fire you would portray
my every yearning, fervent in its store.
Resentment thus oppresses this heart, too;
like yours—from hate it hardens into steel;
like you, I'm robbed of every hope I knew;
my life—like yours—lacks any clear ideal.
And yet I mutely hide my pain, my lack;
and no one senses what burns deep within me.
They scorn and ridicule me,—all those wretches;
they don't grasp how intensely my heart beats
for right and freedom and for everything
that nobly stirred in any Roman's mind.

FURIA

I knew it! O, your soul, not any other,
was made for me,—in that a voice cries out
that never fails and never can deceive.
Then come! O come—and let us heed that voice!

CATILINE

What do you mean, my lovely visionary?

FURIA

Come,—let us flee this place, go far away;
a new-born fatherland is where we'll tarry.
The spirit's pride and flight is here subdued;

here baseness quenches every glorious spark
before it can blaze forth, a flaming brand.
Come, let us flee;—for those inspired by freedom,
the whole earth's circle is a fatherland!

CATILINE

O, how enchantingly you draw me on—

FURIA

Then let us seize this moment! High across
the mountains; way beyond the sea's expanse,—
far, far from Rome we'll make our flight's first stop.
A thousand friends will surely follow you;
we'll settle down upon some distant shore;
there we shall rule; and there it shall prove true,
that no hearts ever beat like ours before!

CATILINE

O beautiful! —But flee? Why should we flee?
Look, here as well can freedom's flame be cherished;
here, too, there is a field for deeds and action,
as vast as even that your soul desires.

FURIA

Here, do you say? Here in this wretched Rome,
where slavishness and brutal force are all?
Ah, Lucius, are you, too, one of those
who without blushing Rome's great past recall?
Who ruled here in the past? Who rules today?
A troop of heroes then,—and now a heap
of slaves to slaves—

CATILINE

O yes, just sneer away;—
but know,—the freedom of great Rome to keep,
for yet once more to see its vanished splendor,

with joy, like Curtius, I'd hurl myself
into the gulf—

FURIA

I trust you; you alone;—
your eyes are burning; you have spoken truth.
But go; the priestesses are coming soon;
this is the time they usually gather here.

CATILINE

I'll go; but just to meet you here again.
A magic force enthralls me to your side;—
so proud a woman have I never seen.

FURIA

(with a wild smile)

Then promise me one thing; and swear that you
will keep your promise. Will you, Lucius?

CATILINE

Yes, anything my Furia demands;
command me, tell me what I am to promise.

FURIA

Then listen. Though I live here like a captive,
I know there is a man frequenting Rome,
toward whom I've sworn hostility till death—
and hatred even beyond the grave's black shadows.

CATILINE

And so—?

FURIA

So swear,—my enemy shall be

your own till death. Will you, my Lucius?

CATILINE

I swear you that by all the mighty gods!
Let it be sworn upon my father's name
and on my mother's memory—! Furia,—
what's wrong with you? Your eyes glow wildly,—and
your cheek, as on a corpse, is white as marble.

FURIA

I do not know myself. —A fiery torrent
is rushing through me. Swear! Complete your oath!

CATILINE

Pour out, you mighty ones, upon this head
your well of anger, let the lightning of
your wrath destroy me, if I break my oath:
I shall pursue him like a very demon!

FURIA

Enough; I do believe you. Ah, that eased
my breast. In your hands rests my vengeance now.

CATILINE

It shall be carried out. But tell me now,—
who is your enemy? What was his crime?

FURIA

By Tiber's banks, far from the city's noise,
my cradle stood; my peaceful home was there.
A well-beloved sister lived there with me,
chosen to be a vestal as a child.—
A villain came then to our distant region;—
he saw the young, already-chosen priestess—

CATILINE

(*astonished*)

What? Priestess? Tell me—! Speak—!

FURIA

He ravished her.
She sought herself a grave within the Tiber.

CATILINE

(*uneasy*)

And do you know him?

FURIA

No, I never saw him.
It all had passed when sorrow's tidings reached me.
But now I know his name.

CATILINE

Then say his name!

FURIA

The name is famous. It was Catiline.

CATILINE

(*shrinking back*)

What are you saying? Horror! Furia—!

FURIA

Come to your senses! What is wrong? —You turned
so pale. My Lucius,—is this man your friend?

CATILINE

My friend? No, Furia,—not any more.

I've cursed,—and sworn eternal hatred toward—
myself.

FURIA

Yourself! You—you are Catiline?

CATILINE

I am, yes.

FURIA

You my Silvia dishonored?
Ah, Nemesis indeed has heard my cry;—
yourself you've called down vengeance on your head!
O woe to you, you man of violence,—woe!

CATILINE

Your eyes, how bright their stare is! In the lamp's
weak light you seem so like the shade of Silvia!
(*He hurries out; the lamp with the holy fire goes out.*)

FURIA

(*after a pause*)

Yes, now I understand it. From my eyes
the veil has fallen,—in the night I see.
So it was hatred that, when first I saw
him in the square, swelled up within my breast.—
So strange a feeling; like a blood-red flame!
O, he shall feel what hatred of my sort,
eternally fermenting, never sated,
can hatch of vengeance and of ruination!

A VESTAL

(*coming in*)

Go, Furia; your watch is at its end;

for I've come—. Holy goddess,—what is this
I see! O woe to you! The flame is out!

FURIA

(*confused*)

It's out, you say? It never burned so wildly;—
it isn't out.

THE VESTAL

You Powers,—what is this?

FURIA

No, hatred's fiery sea does not go out
so easily! O, love flares up—and dies
as suddenly; but hatred—

THE VESTAL

All you gods,—

this is sheer madness!

(*crying out*)

Come! Bring help; bring help!
(VESTALS *and* TEMPLE SERVANTS *rush in.*)

SOME

What's wrong in here?

OTHERS

The vestal flame is out!

FURIA

But hatred's burns; revenge's blazes bright!

THE VESTALS
Away with her;—to doom and punishment!
(*They lead her out among them.*)

CURIUS
(*stepping forth*)

They're leading her to prison. Then to death.—
No, no, by all the gods, it must not be!
Shall this most splendid of all women end
in shame by being buried still alive?—
        O, never have I felt this way before.
Can this be love? Yes, surely it is that.—
By me she shall be saved! —But Catiline?
With hate and vengeance she will hunt him down.
Has he not enemies enough already?
Dare I add yet another to their number?
Toward me he's been just like an older brother;
my gratitude commands that I should shield him.—
But love? Ah, what does it command I do?
And would this man, this valiant Catiline,
cringe trembling from a woman's plot? O no;—
an act of rescue now, this very moment!
Wait, Furia;—I'll drag you from the grave
to life,—although it cost me my own life!
                (*He goes out hurriedly.*)

———————— ✗ ————————

A hall in CATILINE's house

CATILINE
(*coming in greatly agitated*)

    "Ah, Nemesis indeed has heard my cry;
yourself you've called down vengeance on your head."
Indeed, that's what the visionary uttered.
How strange it is! Perhaps it was a sign,—
an omen of the fruits that time shall yield.

So with an oath I've bound myself to be
bloody avenger of my own offense.
Ah, Furia,—it seems that still I see
your fiery look, as wild as that of some
death-goddess! All the while your words still fall
in hollow lingering echo in my ears;—
and all my days I shall that oath recall.

> (*During the following,* AURELIA *comes in and*
> *approaches him without his seeing her.*)

Yet it is foolish to waste further thought
upon this madness;—it is nothing less.
Much better paths my brooding can pursue;
a greater purpose calls upon my strength.
The time's unrest puts forth its claim on me;
toward that my every thought I now must turn;
hope, doubt,—they hurl me like a storm-tossed sea—

AURELIA

(*seizing his hand*)

May your Aurelia the cause not learn?
May she not know what you within engender,
what struggles there in savage disarray?
May she not wifely comfort to you render,
and cause your brow's deep gloom to fade away?

CATILINE

(*gently*)

O my Aurelia,—how good and loving—.
Yet why should I embitter life for you?
Why should I share with you these griefs of mine?
Because of me you've suffered pain enough.
From now on I will bear on my own head
what hostile fate has chosen to allot me,—
the whole oppressive curse inherent in
the linking up of ample strength of mind,
of ardent longing for a life of deeds,

with abject means that curb the spirit's striving.—
Shall you as well, with deep and lengthy draft,
my fate's embittered cup be forced to drink?

AURELIA

A loving comfort is the woman's craft,
though she cannot, like you, of greatness think.
When the man is fighting for his glorious dream,
and can but grief and disappointment reap,—
to him her words then kind and tender seem,
and soon she lulls him to refreshing sleep;
he comes to see then that the quiet life
has pleasures that the raging turmoil lacks.

CATILINE

Yes, you are right; I deeply feel that, too.
And yet I cannot from its din tear free.
An endless ferment seethes within my bosom;—
and nothing but life's turmoil brings it quiet.

AURELIA

If your Aurelia's not enough for you,—
if she can't bring contentment to your soul,—
then let your heart admit a friendly word,
a loving comfort from your dear wife's lips.
If she can't satisfy this ardent craving,
if she can't follow where your thoughts fly forth,—
believe me, she knows how to share your sorrows,
has strength and courage to assuage your burdens.

CATILINE

Then I shall tell you, my Aurelia,
what has depressed me so these last few days.
You know that I've long sought the Consulship—
without success. Indeed, you know it all;—

how I, in order to acquire the votes,
have squandered—

AURELIA

O my Catiline, be still;
it gives me pain—

CATILINE

Do you, too, censure me?
What better means were there for me to choose?—
But uselessly I've lost my property;
derision, infamy my only gain.
Just lately in the Senate my keen foe,
the crafty Cicero, dragged me through the mud.
His speech was a portrayal of my life
so shocking even I was forced to shudder.
In every look I read both fear and horror;
the name of Catiline is said with loathing;
for all posterity it will become
the symbol of a foul and beastly blend
of dissoluteness and of wretchedness,
of scornfully defying all that's noble.—
And not a single deed can cleanse this name
and strike to earth these sly and ugly lies!
For people will believe what rumor says—

AURELIA

But I, my husband, don't believe such rumors.
Let all the world be ready to condemn you;
let them heap up dishonor on your head;—
I know you nourish deep within your mind
a seed that still can blossom and bear fruit.
Yet here it scarcely has a chance to grow;
and noxious weeds will quickly choke its spear.
O, let us leave this home of vice and woe;—
what binds you to it? Why must we stay here?

CATILINE

I should desert the field,—and simply leave?
I should relinquish thus my greatest goals?
The drowning man—though lacking hope to live—
clings to his broken vessel as it rolls;
and if the wet grave swallows up the wreck,
and the last glimpse of rescue from him leaps,—
the last of all the planks with his last strength
he clutches, sinking with it to the deeps.

AURELIA

But if a gracious seacoast smiles upon him
with leafy groves beyond the billows' crest,
then hope again awakens in his bosom,—
he struggles thither, toward that cheerful nest.
It's lovely there; there peaceful quiet reigns;
there silently the waves roll shoreward now;
there he can ease his weary limbs from pains,
and cooling evening breezes fan his brow;—
they chase away each gloomy cloud of care;
a cheering calm then settles in his mind;—
there he remains and finds a soothing lair,
oblivious to the grievous days behind.
The distant echo of the world's great din
is all that reaches his snug place of rest.
It cannot break the peace that he is in;—
it brings more joy and calm into his breast;
it calls back to his mind the bygone days,
with failed designs and joys that made him sorry;
the quiet life now doubly wins his praise—
he would not change for any Roman's glory.

CATILINE

You speak the truth; and at this very moment
from strife and turmoil I could go with you.
But can you name me any place so hidden
that we can find a quiet haven there?

AURELIA

(*joyful*)

You will, my Catiline! O, what great joy,—
more rich, indeed, than what this breast can hold!
Then let us do it! Yet this very night
we shall depart—

CATILINE

Depart for where? Name me
the spot where snugly I may lay my head
in peace!

AURELIA

How can you speak that way? Have you
forgotten, then, our little country place,
in which my childhood passed and where we two,
in love's first happy time, so joyfully
spent all those many cheerful summer days?
Where was the grass more green than in those leas?
Where were there forest shades more cool than those?
The snow-white villa mid the dusky trees
peeks out and offers comforting repose.
Thither we'll flee and dedicate our life
to rustic duties and to peaceful joy;—
you'll be made cheerful by a loving wife;
with kisses she shall all your griefs destroy.
(*smiling*)

And when, your arms with meadow flowers aflame,
you come back home your rural queen to find,
then I'll cry out my flower prince's name,
and round his brow the laurel wreath I'll bind!—
But why do you grow pale? With such wild might
you squeeze my hand,—your eyes so strangely glow—

CATILINE

Alas, Aurelia; lost is your delight;—

I cannot take you where you want to go.
I never can again!

AURELIA

You frighten me!
Yet, surely,—you are joking, Catiline?

CATILINE

I joke! O, if it only was a joke!
Your every word, like vengeance's keen dart,
transfixes wholly this tormented breast,
to which stern fate will never rest impart.

AURELIA

You gods; o speak! What do you mean?

CATILINE

Look here!

Here is your country place,—your future's joy!
(He pulls out a purse filled with gold and tosses it on the table.)

AURELIA

O, you have sold—?

CATILINE

I sold it just today;—
and for what purpose? Ah, so I could bribe—

AURELIA

Say nothing more! Let us not think about
this matter; it will only cause us sorrow.

CATILINE

Your quiet patience crushes me ten times

as much as would a scream of suffering from
your lips!
(An OLD SOLDIER *comes in and approaches* CATILINE.)

THE SOLDIER

Forgive me, sir, for coming in
your home like this, so late and unannounced.
Do not be angry—

CATILINE

What's your errand here?

THE SOLDIER

My errand is a humble boon. I'm sure
you'll listen to it. I'm a poor man, who
has sacrificed my strength for Rome's great glory.
Now I'm infirm and can no longer serve,
and there my weapons hang at home all rusty.
The hope of my old age lay in my son.
He has supported me through his own work.
Alas,—for debt he sits in prison now.
And there's no rescue—. Help me; help me, sir!
(*kneeling*)

A little coin! I've wandered here from house
to house; but every door's long since been locked.
I know no other remedy—

CATILINE

It's like them!
Look at this image of most people's need.
Thus they reward the old and valiant troop.
O, gratitude exists in Rome no longer!
There was a time when I in righteous anger
would fain have punished them with sword and flames;
but soothing words were spoken to me lately;
my mind's a gentle child's; I will not punish;—

relieving sorrow is itself a deed.—
There,—there, old warrior;—clear your debt with that.
(*He hands him the purse filled with gold.*)

THE SOLDIER

(*getting up*)

O good my lord,—dare I believe your words?

CATILINE

Yes; hurry; free the hope of your old age.
(THE SOLDIER *leaves quickly.*)

CATILINE

A better use,—not so, Aurelia?—
than spending it for bribes and buying votes.
It's beautiful to crush the bully's might;
but quiet comfort also has rewards.

AURELIA

(*throwing herself in his arms*)

O, rich and noble still your soul remains.
Now once again I know my Catiline!

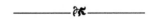

An underground burial chamber with a freshly walled-in opening
high up on the back wall. A lamp burns weakly.
FURIA, *dressed in long black robes, is standing in the burial chamber,
listening to some sound.*

FURIA

A hollow boom. It's thundering up there.
I hear it even here, down in this grave.
And yet the grave itself is still—so still!
Am I to drowsy calm forever doomed?

Am I not even here in tangled paths
to wander forth, as always was my wish?
                    (*after a pause*)

    It was so strange a life;—so strange a fate.
It all came like a shooting star—and vanished.
He met me. Then a secret magic power,
an inner concord, drew us toward each other.
I his avenging goddess,—he my victim;—
but punishment soon followed the avenger.
                    (*another pause*)

    It's clear up there. —Am I then—gradually—
being taken downward from the realm of light?
Ah, it is good, if so,—if this abiding
in the grave's womb is but a downward flight
on wings of lightning toward the land of gloom,—
if I'm already nearing the broad Styx!
There leaden waves are rushing toward the shore;
there Charon noiselessly his boat is plying.
Soon I'll be there! There I will mutely sit
beside the ferry place,—will ask each spirit,
each passing shadow, who from life's dominion
with weightless strides approaches Death's great river,—
will ask him earnestly how Catiline
is faring up among the living souls,—
will ask how he's been keeping to his oath.
I'll shine a bluish sulfur-torch into
the glassy depths of every specter's eyes,—
determining if it be Catiline.
And when he comes, then I shall go with him;—
we two together then shall make the crossing,
together enter Pluto's silent hall.
A shade myself, I'll go beside his shade;—
where Catiline is, Furia must be!
                    (*after a pause, weaker*)

    Alas, the air's becoming close—so stifling,—
and breathing steadily more difficult.—
Then I am getting near the black morass

where sluggishly the streams of Hades flow—
(*She listens; a muffled sound can be heard.*)

A muffled boom? Just like the stroke of oars.
It is the ferrier of the dead, who's coming
to get me. Ah! No, here—here I shall wait!
(*The stones in the recently walled-up opening are broken apart.* CURIUS
comes into view outside; he beckons to her.)

FURIA

Hail, Charon, hail! Are you prepared already
to take me as a guest to Death's great halls?
Here I shall wait!

CURIUS

(*whispering*)

Be still;—I'll rescue you!

ACT TWO

A hall in CATILINE's house with an open colonnade in the background. The hall is lit up by a lamp.
CATILINE *is pacing up and down.* LENTULUS *and* CETHEGUS *are with him.*

CATILINE
No, no! I tell you, you don't understand
yourselves what you demand of me. Am I
to treacherously begin a civil war,—
with fellow Romans' blood defile my hands?
I'll never do it! Let the city just
condemn me—

LENTULUS
So you will not, Catiline?

CATILINE
I will not.

CETHEGUS
Tell me,—have you nothing to
revenge,—nobody that you'd like to get?

CATILINE
Let those who wish seek vengeance; I won't do it.

283

Yet mute contempt, of course, is also vengeance;—
and that shall be my only one.

CETHEGUS

Aha,—
we chose, I see, an inconvenient hour.
And yet tomorrow will, I'm sure, put you
in different thoughts.

CATILINE

Tomorrow? Why is that?

CETHEGUS

A lot of funny rumors are around.
Just now a Vestal has been led to death—

CATILINE

(startled)

A Vestal virgin? Ah, what's that you say?

LENTULUS

Indeed; a Vestal virgin. Many mutter—

CATILINE

They mutter what?

CETHEGUS

That you are very far
from having had no part in this dark matter.

CATILINE

Do they think that of me?

LENTULUS

                    So runs the rumor.
Oh, well,—for us, for all your loyal friends,
such things can be, of course, as they will be;—
the people, Catiline, will judge more strictly.

CATILINE

(deep in thought)

And is she dead?

CETHEGUS

                    She is without a doubt.
An hour's interment in the offender's tomb
is quite enough—

LENTULUS

                    That's no concern of ours;
that wasn't why we spoke to you about her.
But listen, Catiline! Consider this.
You sought the Consulship. All your well-being
hung on that single fragile thread of hope;—
now it is broken; everything's now done with.

CATILINE

(as before)

"Yourself you've called down vengeance on your head."

CETHEGUS

                    Get rid of thoughts like those; they're of no use.
Act like a man; the game can still be won;
a bold decision—; you have friends enough;
we'll follow you upon your slightest hint.—
Are you not tempted? Answer!

CATILINE

No, I say!
And why would all of you join in this plot?
Speak honestly! Does love of freedom urge you?
Is it to reinvigorate Rome's greatness
you'd topple everything?

LENTULUS

No, not at all;
but hope for one's own greatness is, of course,
an adequate incentive, Catiline!

CETHEGUS

And means enough to richly relish life
are not so wholly to be sneered at either.
That's what I long for;—I am not ambitious.

CATILINE

I knew it. Only narrow, base regard
for your advantage is what urges you.
No, friends, o no; toward greater goals I aimed!
It's true that I used bribery in my
attempt to snatch the Consulship; yet my
design involved much more than could be judged
from such a method. Civil freedom and
the welfare of the state was what I strove for.
I was misjudged; appearance was against me.
My fate decreed it so. It had to be!

CETHEGUS

All right; but what about the flock of friends
that you can save from ruin and disgrace—?
You know it won't be long before we're forced
to ply the beggar's staff by our loose ways.

CATILINE

Well, stop in time, then; that is *my* decision.

LENTULUS

How's that, eh? Catiline,—you plan to change
your way of life? Ha-ha; you're joking, aren't you?

CATILINE

I am in earnest,—by the mighty gods!

CETHEGUS

Well, there's no further recourse with him, then.
Come, Lentulus; we must inform the others
what answer he has given. They are all
at Bibulus', in a merry feast.

CATILINE

At Bibulus'? How many lively nights
I have caroused with you at Bibulus'!
But now my madcap life is over with;
before the dawn I will have left² the city.

LENTULUS

What's that you say?

CETHEGUS

You're going away from here?

CATILINE

This very night, accompanied by my wife,
shall I and Rome forever say farewell.
In Gaul's far valleys I will found a home;—
the field I clear myself shall feed me there.

CETHEGUS

Then you will leave the city, Catiline?[3]

CATILINE

I will; I must! Disgrace assails me here.
Ah, I've the courage to bear my poverty;
but to read scorn in every Roman's look,
and bold contempt—! No, no; it is too much!
In Gaul I can live hidden and in quiet;
there I'll forget what I at one time was,
will blunt my instinct for the great designs,
will as a hazy dream my past remember.

LENTULUS

Well, then farewell; and may luck follow you!

CETHEGUS

Remember us with friendliness, as we
will you, eh, Catiline! And now we'll tell
our brothers of your new and strange intention.

CATILINE

And give them, too, my own fraternal greeting!
(LENTULUS and CETHEGUS leave. AURELIA has come in from the side
but stops short apprehensively upon seeing the departing figures; when
they are gone, she approaches CATILINE.)

AURELIA

(gently reproaching him)

Again your rowdy friends here in your house?
O Catiline—!

CATILINE

It was the final time.

Just now I took my leave of them. All bonds
that kept me bound to Rome are cut in two
for once and all.

AURELIA

I have already packed
the little bit we own. It isn't much;—
enough, though, Catiline, for frugal needs!

CATILINE

(*deep in thought*)

More than enough for me who has lost all.

AURELIA

O, do not brood on what cannot be changed;—
forget—

CATILINE

Happy the man who could forget,—
who could tear out his memory from his soul,
and all his hopes, and the goal of all his wishes!
It will take time before I come so far;
but I will strive to—

AURELIA

I will give you help;
and you will find relief for all your loss.
Yet we must leave as soon as possible.
For here life wheedles with you like a tempter.—
It's true,—we will depart this very night?

CATILINE

Yes, yes,—this very night, Aurelia!

AURELIA

A scanty bit of money that was left
I've gathered; for our journey it's enough.

CATILINE

Good, good! My sword I'll sell to buy a spade.
Ah, how's my sword of further use to me!

AURELIA

You clear the ground and I shall cultivate it.
And soon around our home will sprout and flower
rose bushes and some nice forget-me-nots
as tokens that the time will soon be near
when you can greet each memory of the past
as an old friend upon a welcome visit.

CATILINE

That time, Aurelia? I fear, beloved,—
it still lies in the future's distant blue.
                    (in a lighter tone)

But go, my wife; go in and rest awhile.
Right after midnight we'll be starting out;—
the city naps then in its deepest slumber,
and no one will suspect where we are fleeing.
The first gray light of dawn will find us far—
o far from here; within a laurel grove
we'll rest upon a carpet of soft grass.

AURELIA

A new existence will be dawning for us,—
more rich in joy than that we've ended here.
Now I shall go. A quiet hour of rest
will give me strength—. Goodnight, my Catiline!
                    (She embraces him and goes out.)

CATILINE

(looking after her)

Now she is gone. Ah, what relief I feel!
I can at last discard this burdensome
dissimulation, yes, this show of ease,
which least of all exists within this heart.
O, she is my good spirit. She would grieve
if she should see my doubt. I must conceal it.
Yet I shall dedicate this silent moment
to an appraisal of my wasted life.—
Ah, that lamp burning there disturbs my thoughts;—
it must be dark here,—dark as in my soul!

> (He puts out the lamp; the moon shines in
> through the columns in the background.)

Too bright,—it's still too bright! But never mind;—
the feeble moonlight is well suited to
this dark and gloomy halflight that enshrouds,—
that always has enshrouded all my ways.

Hm, Catiline,—consider: this day is
your last; tomorrow you'll already be
no more the Catiline that you have been.
Far in that desolate Gaul my future life
shall pass obscurely like a forest river.—
Now I have woken up from all my dreams
of might, of greatness, of a glorious life;—
like dew they disappeared; the night within me
has been their one arena;—no one knew them.

O, it is not this dull, lethargic stillness
cut off from worldly din that frightens me.
If only for one moment I could shine
and flame out like a star in falling flight,—
if only once I with a glorious deed
could link myself and the name "Catiline"
to fame and to a grand, immortal legend,—
then I with joy would in the hour of triumph
leave[4] all behind,—head for a foreign shore;
I would implant my dagger in my heart;

die free and glad;—for then I would have lived!
But this sad lot is death without a life.
Can this be possible? I'm thus to perish?
(with uplifted hands)

A sign, you wrathful Gods,—that it's my fate,
forgotten and without a trace, to vanish
from life!

FURIA

(outside behind the columns)

No, no, it is not, Catiline!

CATILINE

(shrinking back)

Who speaks? What inauspicious voice is that?
A spirit voice from underworldly shades!

FURIA

(stepping out into the moonlight)

I am your shade.

CATILINE

(appalled)

The Vestal virgin's ghost!

FURIA

So deep you must have sunk, if you're afraid
of me.

CATILINE

Speak! Have you risen from the grave
to torment me with hatred and revenge?

FURIA

Torment you,—do you say? I am your shade.
I must accompany you what way you go.
                    (*She comes nearer.*)

CATILINE

She's living? Gods,—o, it is she herself
and not a spirit!

FURIA

            Spirit or not,—it
is all the same; I shall accompany you.

CATILINE

With bloody hatred!

FURIA

                In the grave hate dies,
like love and like all other inclinations
that mortal bosoms cherish. Just one thing
stands fast in life and death and can't be changed.

CATILINE

What's that? Speak out!

FURIA

            Your fate, o Catiline!

CATILINE

My fate is known but to the all-wise gods—
not any human.

FURIA

Yes, I know it, too.
I am your shade;—for enigmatic bonds
link us together.

CATILINE

They are hatred's.

FURIA

No!

Has any spirit risen from the grave
still urged by hatred and revenge? Just listen!
In underworldly rivers I've extinguished
all earthly fires once raging in my breast.
As you here see me, I'm not any longer
that Furia,—so wild and fired with anger,—
whom you once loved—

CATILINE

Do you not hate me, then?

FURIA

Not any more. When I was in the grave,—
when at the crossroad changing life to death
I tottered, any hour prepared to pay
my visit to the underworld,—o, then
a strange thrill seized me; I cannot explain it—;
there took place then a wondrous transformation;—
my hate, my vengeance, my whole soul dissolved;
each memory vanished, and each mortal yearning;—
only the name of "Catiline" stands written
in red-hot script, as always, in my bosom.

CATILINE

Most strange! O, be whatever you will be,—

a human or an underworldly shade,—
there's still a dreadful magic fascination
in all your words and in your jet-black eyes.

FURIA

Your mind is strong like mine; and yet you will,
despondent and in doubt, give up all hope
of victory and might. You cowardly turn
your back upon the stage where your dim plot
in bright maturity could soon unfold!

CATILINE

I must! Inexorable fate so wills it.

FURIA

Your fate? Why were you given hero's strength,—
if not to fight against what you call fate?

CATILINE

Ah, I have fought enough! Was not my life
a constant battle? And the battle's fruits?
Contempt, dishonor—!

FURIA

Deep you've sunk indeed.
You're yearning toward a lofty, daring goal;
desire to reach it; yet you're terrified
by every hindrance.

CATILINE

Fear is not the cause.
The goal I sought is unattainable;—
the whole thing was a fleeting youthful dream.

FURIA

Now you deceive yourself, my Catiline!
You're still preoccupied with that one purpose;—
your soul is great,—quite worthy to rule Rome,—
and you have friends—. Why do you hesitate?

CATILINE

(reflecting)

I should—? What do you mean—? With people's blood—?

FURIA

Are you a man,—and lack a woman's courage?
Have you forgotten that brave Roman woman,
who sought the throne over her father's corpse?
I feel myself a Tullia;—but you?
Despise;—despise yourself then, Catiline!

CATILINE

Shall I despise myself because my mind
no longer harbors wild ambitiousness?

FURIA

You stand before a crossroad in your life.
That way an empty, deed-less role awaits you,—
a half-way thing of death and drowsy slumber;—
but down the other way you dimly glimpse
a ruler's throne. Just choose then, Catiline!

CATILINE

You're luring and you're tempting me to ruin.

FURIA

Just cast the die,—and in your hands is laid
the welfare of proud Rome for all of time.

Your silent fate holds glory, sovereignty;
and yet you waver,—you don't dare to act!
You're leaving for your woods, and in that place
each hope that you once cherished will depart.
Ah, Catiline, is there no further trace
of lust for glory left within your heart?
Shall this high ruler's soul, for glory meant,
there in a nameless waste unknown expire?
Yes, leave! But know,—for ever you prevent
what here with daring deeds you could acquire.

CATALINA

Go on; go on!

FURIA

With shuddering your name
will be remembered by posterity.
Your life throughout has been a daring game;—
yet in atonement's light it would flash free,
by legend borne, if you with strong control
could through the frantic throng a pathway clear,—
if thralldom's cloud could part, through your great soul,
to let a new-born freedom's sky appear,—
if you could once—

CATILINE

Enough! O, there a chord
you struck that resonated deep within me;—
an echo in their sound your words afford
of what my heart has whispered day and night.

FURIA

Then once again I know you, Catiline!

CATILINE

I will not leave! —You have aroused to life

my youth's resolve, my manhood's aspiration.
Yes, I shall shine out for the sunken Rome,—
strike them with terror like the meteor's whip!
You wretches filled with pride,—you soon shall learn
you haven't broken me, though for a while
my strength was dulled by heat of battle!

FURIA

Listen!
What fate demands,—what mighty spirits of darkness
determine for us, that we must obey.
Well, then! My hatred's gone;—fate ordered it;
it had to be that way. —Give me your hand
in endless league! —Why do you hesitate?
You will not?

CATILINE

Will—? I'm looking at your eyes.
They glow,—like lightning in the night's thick gloom.
You smiled just now! Ah, so I have supposed
that Nemesis—

FURIA

What? If you would see *her*,—
look in yourself. Did you forget your oath?

CATILINE

O, I remember;—yet a spirit of
revenge you seem to me—

FURIA

I am, you see,
an image out of your own soul.

CATILINE

(brooding)

What's that?
I sense unclearly what I can't get hold of;—
I catch a glimpse of enigmatic visions,—
but I can't make them out. It's much too dark here.

FURIA

It must be dark here. Darkness is our kingdom;—
we rule in darkness. Come; give me your hand
in endless league!

CATILINE

(wildly)

O lovely Nemesis,—
my shade,—you image out of my own soul,—
here is my hand in dark and endless league!
(He seizes her hand violently; she looks at him with a rigid smile.)

FURIA

Now we can never part!

CATILINE

Ah, like a fire
your handclasp tore a passage through my veins!
Blood courses there no more, just red-hot flames;—
It grows too cramped around my breast's tight vault;
grows dark before my eyes! Now there'll be spread
a fiery dawn upon the city of Rome!
(He draws his sword and brandishes it.)

My sword; my sword! Do you see how it gleams?
It soon shall be deep-dyed with lukewarm blood!—
What's happening to me? My brow's on fire;
A multitude of visions rushes past me.—

It's vengeance, victory for all my dreams
of greatness, ruling power, and deathless name.
My password shall be: death and crimson flames!
To the Capitol! At last I am myself!
(*He rushes out;* FURIA *follows him.*)

————— ჯ —————

The inside of a dimly-lit tavern.
STATILIUS, GABINIUS, *and* COEPARIUS *come in, along with several other*
young Romans.

STATILIUS

Here, friends, we can disport the night away;
here we are safe; no one will overhear us.

GABINIUS

Indeed; now we shall drink, carouse, enjoy!
Who knows how long we'll be allowed to do so?

COEPARIUS

No, first let's wait to hear the news that we're
expecting Lentulus and Cethegus to bring us.

GABINIUS

O, let them bring whatever news they will!
Wine's being brought; we'll try that while we're waiting.
Be lively, brothers,—raise a merry song!
(WAITERS *come in with jugs of wine and cups.*)

ALL THE FRIENDS
(*singing*)

Bacchus we worship;
joyful we nurse up
the cup to the limit,

drinking his praise!
Red juice in flowing
lovely is glowing.
All of us savor
the wine god's fine drink.

Liber our father
frees us from bother;
ecstasy beckons,
clear is the grape.
Come, let us relish!
Wines life embellish,
stirring to gladness
notions and minds.

Sparkling Falernian,
better than others,
leads all its brothers,
glorious drink!
Courage you buy us;
strength you supply us;
cheer you let fall through
all of our souls.

Bacchus we worship!
Joyful we nurse up
the cup to the limit,
drinking his praise!
Red juice in flowing
lovely is glowing!
All of us savor
the wine god's fine drink!

(Lentulus *and* Cethegus *come in.*)

LENTULUS
Break off this song and merriment!

STATILIUS

What now?

Is Catiline not in your company?

GABINIUS

He's willing, isn't he?

COEPARIUS

What was his answer?

Speak out; tell everything!

CETHEGUS

Quite otherwise

than we imagined was his answer.

GABINIUS

Well?

LENTULUS

He waved away our every overture;—
of our design he wouldn't hear a thing.

STATILIUS

Is this the truth?

COEPARIUS

And just why won't he do it?

LENTULUS

Because he won't. He is betraying us;
he's leaving all his friends,—leaving the city.[5]

STATILIUS

He's leaving, do you say?

CETHEGUS

He's going away
this very night. Well,—he cannot be censured;
his grounds were valid—

LENTULUS

Cowardice was his grounds!
In the hour of danger he's betraying us.

GABINIUS

Ah, *that* to Catiline is friendship!

COEPARIUS

No;—

no, he was never false nor cowardly!

LENTULUS

And yet he's going away.

STATILIUS

With him our hope.
Where are we now to find the man to lead us?

COEPARIUS

He can't be found; we must give up our plot.

LENTULUS

By no means, friends! Just listen first to what
I think about the matter. What have we
resolved? To try to win by force of weapons
what's been denied to us by unjust fate.

They are oppressing us;—we wish to rule.
We suffer want;—and riches are our goal.

MANY VOICES

Yes, might and riches! We want might and riches!

LENTULUS

Well, then;—for leader we picked out a friend,
on whom, we thought, we safely could rely.
But he betrayed our trust; he runs from danger.
Ah, friends,—don't be dismayed! For he shall learn
that we know how to help ourselves. What's needed?
Only one man with steadfastness and courage
who'll take the lead—

SOME

Name us a man like that!

LENTULUS

And if I give his name and he stands forth,—
will you then choose that man to be your leader?

SOME

Yes, we will choose him!

OTHERS

Yes; we will indeed!

STATILIUS

So name him, friend!

LENTULUS

What if it were myself?

GABINIUS

Yourself!

COEPARIUS

You, Lentulus—!

OTHERS
(*doubtfully*)

You want to lead us?

LENTULUS

I do.

CETHEGUS

But can you do it? Look, that needs
the strength and courage of a Catiline.

LENTULUS

I have no lack of courage; nor of strength.
But let's get going! Or would you back out
of it just when the moment urges us?
It's now or never! Everything betokens
a happy upshot—

STATILIUS

Good;—we'll follow you!

OTHERS

We'll follow you!

GABINIUS

Oh, well,—if Catiline
is leaving[6] us, then you are surely next
in line to take control.

LENTULUS

Then listen to
the plan of action I have thought of. First—
(CATILINE *comes in hurriedly*)

CATILINE

I'm here, my friends!

ALL

It's Catiline!

LENTULUS

(*aside*)

Him! Damn it—

CATILINE

Speak out,—what is it you demand of me?
But no; indeed, I know what it concerns.
I'll be your leader. Will you follow me?

ALL EXCEPT LENTULUS

Yes, Catiline! o yes,—we'll follow you!

STATILIUS

We've been deceived—

GABINIUS

And you've been lied about!

COEPARIUS

We have been told you wished to go away
and rid your hands completely of our cause.

CATILINE

It's so; I wanted to. But now I don't;
I now live only for this one great purpose.

LENTULUS

But just what is your purpose, by the way?

CATILINE

My purpose is much loftier than you—
or maybe anyone—can guess. O hear
me, friends! First, to our cause I'll win
each citizen who is disposed to freedom,
who values far above all other things
the people's glory and his country's welfare.
The ancient Roman spirit's still alive;—
its final spark is not yet quite extinguished.
It now shall be fanned up to brilliant flames,
more bright by far than any time before.
Ah, much too long there lay a gloom of thralldom,
as black as night, outspread above our Rome.
O, this our empire—though it seems both proud
and mighty—totters and will fall abruptly.
Therefore a forceful hand must seize its reins;
it must be cleansed here, cleared out to the roots;
the drowsy people must be roused from sleep;
We must annihilate the base ones' might,
which strews its poison in our minds and chokes
our final chance for recreated life.
Look,—civil freedom is what I would further,—
and civil spirit, as in former times
it flourished here. The golden age I will
call back when every Roman gladly for
his country's glory gave his life, and for
the people's happiness gave all he owned!

LENTULUS

You're dreaming, Catiline! That wasn't what
we had in mind.

GABINIUS

What use is there to us
of reestablishing those ancient times
with their absurd naiveté?

SOME

O no!

It's might we want—

OTHERS

—and means for us to lead

a free and happy life!

MANY VOICES

Yes, that's our goal!

COEPARIUS

Are we for others' happiness or freedom
to set our lives upon the dice's cast?

THE WHOLE GROUP

We want the victory's fruits ourselves!

CATILINE

You wretches!

Are you the issue of the mighty fathers?
To heap dishonor on the fathers' name
is how you choose to safeguard its rich splendor!

LENTULUS

You dare to mock us,—you who for so long
have been a sign of terror—

CATILINE

Yes, it's true;
I was a horror to the decent; yet
I never once have been so base as you!

LENTULUS

You hold your tongue! We won't endure your taunts.

SEVERAL

No, no,—we will not—

CATILINE

(*calmly*)

Oh? You cowardly brood,—
there's something you still dare to will, then, *you*?

LENTULUS

Ah, down with him!

MANY VOICES

Yes, down with Catiline!
(*They draw their daggers and rush at him;* CATILINE *calmly pulls his
cloak away from his breast and regards them with a smile of cold
contempt; they let their daggers fall.*)

CATILINE

Thrust home! You dare not do so? O friends, friends,—
I would respect you if you could have pierced
this undefended breast that you have threatened.
Have you no longer any spark of courage?

SOME

He means us well!

OTHERS

We have deserved his scorn.

CATILINE

You have, indeed. —Yet—now the time has come
when you can blot away dishonor's brand.
Whatever lies behind we will forget;—
a new existence almost beckons to us.
(*bitterly*)

I am a fool! To hope to win with you!
Is victory's spirit in this drooping crowd?
(*enrapt*)

Such lovely dreams I dreamt once, and great visions
rushed through my mind and passed before my eyes.
I dreamt that I, like Icarus, equipped
with wings flew high up under heaven's vault;
I dreamt the gods with giant's strength my hand
endowed and offered me the lightning's bolt.
And this hand grasped the lightning in its flight
and slung it toward the city deep below.
And when the crimson flames licked out and rose,
and Rome sank into brown remains of dust,—
then I cried out with loud and mighty voice,
and conjured Cato's kinsmen from the grave;
a thousand spirits came upon my call,—
took life again—and raised Rome from its ashes.
(*breaking off*)

It was but dreams. Gods do not conjure up
the buried past into the light of day,—
and vanished spirits rise not from the grave.
(*wildly*)

Well then; if the *old* Rome cannot be raised
up with this hand,—this Rome of *ours* shall perish!

Soon now, where marble columns stand in rows,
columns of smoke shall whirl amid the flames;
temples and palaces shall fall in ruins,
and the Capitol shall vanish from its hill!
        Swear, friends, that you will dedicate yourselves
to this great deed! I'll be your leader in it.
Speak,— will you follow me?

STATILIUS

We'll follow you!
(*Several of the others seem doubtful and whisper together.* CATILINE
regards them with a scornful smile.)

LENTULUS

(*in an undertone*)

It's best we follow him. Among the ruins
we may most easily find what was our goal.

ALL

(*shouting*)

Yes, Catiline, yes, we will follow you!

CATILINE

Then swear to me by all our fathers' gods
that you'll obey my every hint!

THE WHOLE GROUP

(*with raised hands*)

Yes, yes;
we solemnly swear, in all to follow blindly!

CATILINE

Then singly steal your way, by different paths,

into my house. You will find weapons there.
I'm coming shortly; then I'll let you know
what plan of action I have chosen. Go!

> (*They all leave.*)

LENTULUS

(*holding* CATILINE *back*)

A word in haste! Are you aware that to
the Senate the Allobrogians have sent men
to air their grievances?

CATILINE

Yes, I'm aware.
They reached the city just today.

LENTULUS

Quite right.
What if . . . we prompted *them* to join our plot?
With them the whole of Gaul will rise in might
and kindle up a storm against our foes.

CATILINE

(*reluctant*)

Are we to league up with barbarians?

LENTULUS

A league like that is necessary for us.
With our own strength the victory can't be won;
help from outside—

CATILINE

(*smiling bitterly*)

Ah, deep has been Rome's fall!
Its walls contain no men with strength enough

to topple even ruins that are shaky.
>   (*They go out.*)

———————— ?ĸ ————————

A garden behind CATILINE's house, which can be glimpsed among the trees. To the left a side-building.
CURIUS, CETHEGUS, *and other conspirators come in cautiously from the right in whispered conversation.*

CURIUS

>   But is it really true what you've been telling?

CETHEGUS

>   In every word. The matter was decided
this very moment.

CURIUS

>   He is leading all?

CETHEGUS

>   Yes, everything. Just speak to him yourself.
>   (*They all go into the house except for* CURIUS.)

CURIUS

>   A night most strange! My thoughts are tumbling round
in circles! O, could I have dreamt it all?
Experienced or dreamt,—awake I see,
wherever I may turn, her image only.
>   (CATILINE *comes in from the right*)

CATILINE

>   (*going towards him*)
>   You here, my Curius? I've greatly missed you.—

My meeting with the Vestal virgin had
an unexpected outcome—

CURIUS

(*confused*)

Yes, you're right!

CATILINE

I will not give this matter further thought.
It was for me a highly fateful meeting.
(*brooding*)

They say, you know, the Furies come up from
the underworld in order to torment
us throughout life. —Indeed, if that were so!

CURIUS

(*uneasy*)

What? Have you—

CATILINE

She herself was here tonight.—
But let's forget that. Listen, Curius,—
a weighty venture is in preparation—

CURIUS

I know about it. Cethegus has told—

CATILINE

Who knows what end the gods have settled for
this work? Perhaps it is my fate to be
struck down upon my way by spiteful powers—
and never reach my goal. Well, let it be!
But you, my Curius, whom I have loved
since you were young,—you mustn't be dragged down

in danger's whirlpool. Promise me,—remain
within the city, if I should attack
some other place,—which is quite possible;
don't aid us till success has crowned our work.

CURIUS

(moved)

My fatherly good friend! O, such concern—!

CATILINE

You promise it? We'll say farewell, then, here;
wait just a moment; I'll be coming soon.
(He goes into the house.)

CURIUS

(looking after him)

He loves me as before. He senses nothing.
(LENTULUS and other conspirators come in from the right.)

LENTULUS

Say, Curius, didn't Catiline just now
go through the garden?

CURIUS

Yes, he is inside.
(They go into the house)

CURIUS

(pacing about restlessly)

What can I do to curb this avid yearning?
A restless ferment seethes within my blood.
Ah, Furia,—you strange and wondrous woman!
Where are you now? When shall I see you again?—

What has become of her? She slipped away
just like a shade when I had freed her from
the grave. And those obscure, mysterious words,—
her eyes, so dull and shining both at once—?
Could it be madness? Has the horror of
the grave made dark her soul—?

FURIA

(behind him, among the trees)

O no, pale youth!

CURIUS

(with a shriek)

My Furia! Here—?

FURIA

(approaching)

Here one finds Catiline.
Where *he* is,—there must Furia also be.

CURIUS

O come, beloved! I will take you where
you will be safe. Just think—if someone saw you—!

FURIA

The dead can have no fear. Have you forgotten—
you took my corpse and bore it from the grave?

CURIUS

Again these horrifying words! I beg you;—
compose yourself,—and come now, Furia!
(He tries to seize her hand.)

FURIA

(*pushing him back wildly*)

Audacious fool,—do you then feel no horror
at death's own daughter, who has risen from
the underworld for but a fleeting while?

CURIUS

I feel the horror. But it is this horror,
this wondrous shudder, that is my desire.

FURIA

What do you want of me? You speak in vain.
The grave's my home; it's there that I belong;—
I am a fugitive from Death's domain;
at day's approach I must rejoin its throng.
You don't believe me? Don't believe I've sat
in Pluto's hall among the pallid shades?
I tell you,—I was there quite recently,—
beyond the river and the inky swamps.

CURIUS

Then lead me there!

FURIA

You?

CURIUS

I'll go willingly,
although your path should take me through Death's night!

FURIA

That cannot be. For we must part up here;—
no corpse and human may go there together.—
Why rob me of my time, which is so short?
I have but gloom's own hours in which to act;

317

my work is gloom's; I am gloom's messenger.—
But where is Catiline?

CURIUS

You're seeking him?

FURIA

I'm seeking him.

CURIUS

Do you pursue him still?

FURIA

Why have I risen from the dead tonight,
if it were not because of Catiline?

CURIUS

Alas, this madness that has taken you—!
Yet you are lovely even in your passion.
O, think no further now of Catiline!
Come now! Rule over me, and I will serve you!
                    (throwing himself down before her)

Here like a slave before your feet I beg
for but a glance! O hear me, Furia!
I love you so! A sweet and poisonous fire
consumes my soul, and no one else but you
can soothe my torments—

FURIA

(looking toward the house)

                    Yonder there are lights—
and many men. What's happening in there
at Catiline's?

CURIUS

(*leaping up*)

Again I hear that name!
To him your every thought turns ceaselessly.
O, I could hate him now—!

FURIA

Has he resolved
to set in motion soon the daring purpose
he long has cherished?

CURIUS

Then you know—?

FURIA

The whole.

CURIUS

So then you also know that he's agreed
to be the leader of this dangerous league?
Yet I implore you, ask no more about
him—Catiline!

FURIA

First answer me one thing;—
it is my final question. Will you join him?

CURIUS

He's like a loving father to me—

FURIA

(*smiling*)

He?

My Catiline?

CURIUS

Alas!

FURIA

The man to whom
my thoughts keep turning?

CURIUS

Faintness seizes me!
I hate him—yes! O, I could murder him!

FURIA

Did you not swear to me just now that you're
prepared to heed my will?

CURIUS

Ask what you wish;
in all I'll serve you and obey you blindly!
I only beg, forget him—Catiline!

FURIA

I shall forget him—when he has descended
into his grave.

CURIUS

(shrinking back)

Do you demand that I—?

FURIA

There is no need of steel; you're only to
betray his undertaking—

CURIUS

Treachery

and murder both at once! Remember he's
my foster father and—

FURIA

—my thoughts' one goal!
Ah, you weak fool,—you dare to speak of love,—
and lack the courage to destroy the one
who's standing in your way? Be gone, then!
(*She turns her back on him.*)

CURIUS

(*holding her back*)

No;—

don't leave[7] me! I am willing to do all!—
Some horror coming from you chills my blood;
yet I'm not able to destroy this net
in which you've snared me.

FURIA

Are you willing, then?

CURIUS

Why do you mock me so by asking that?
If I am willing? Have I any will?
Your look is like the serpent's when with force
of magic it ensnares a bird, which in
a circle fearfully flits round it, more
and more approaching near the dreadful gulf.

FURIA

Then set to work!

CURIUS

And when I've sacrificed
my friendship for my love,—what then? What then?

FURIA

Then I've forgotten Catiline existed.
My task is then concluded. Ask no more!

CURIUS

For this reward I should—?

FURIA

You hesitate?
Is then your hope so weak that it can't build
on what a thankful woman can bestow
when time—?

CURIUS

By all the powers of the night,—
I'll do it! He alone keeps us apart.
Then let him fall! Extinguished is each spark
of tenderness for him; all bonds are broken!—
Who are you, lovely vision of the night?
Your nearness petrifies me and consumes
me both at once. My yearning freezes me,—
my fear enkindles me; my love's like hate
with witchcraft blended. O, and who am I?
I know myself no more. I only know
one thing: I am not who I was before
I saw you. Gladly would I leap into
the depths to follow you! —Ah, Catiline
is doomed! I'm going to the Capitol.
The Senate's there tonight. A written slip
betrays this act of Catiline's. —Farewell!
(He goes out quickly.)

FURIA

(to herself)

The clouds amass; the lightning soon will glitter.

322

The end is fast approaching, Catiline;—
with giant strides, you're walking toward your grave!
*(The Allobrogian ambassadors, AMBIORIX and OLLOVICO,
come out of the house without noticing FURIA, who is
standing half hidden in shadows in among the trees.)*

AMBIORIX

So then it is decided. It was risky
for us to join this daring league.

OLLOVICO

Yes; but
refusal by the Council of our just
demands left us no other means of rescue;
and victory's reward,—if our friends win,—
makes up for, does it not, the dangerous combat
that soon awaits us now.

AMBIORIX

That's so, my brother!

OLLOVICO

Breaking away from Rome's authority,—
our vanished freedom are well worth a fight.

AMBIORIX

Now we must hasten home the shortest way;
throughout all Gaul rebellions we must spark.
All tribes there easily can be incited
to rise against the oppressors, follow us,
and join up with the troops of Catiline.

OLLOVICO

The battle will be hard. Rome's mighty yet.

AMBIORIX

It must be risked. Let's go, Ollovico!

FURIA

(*calling out in a tone of warning*)

O woe to you!

AMBIORIX

(*starting*)

By all the Gods!

OLLOVICO

(*terrified*)

O listen!
A voice is warning us in night's deep darkness!

FURIA

Woe to your people!

OLLOVICO

There she stands, my brother,—
that ominous and pallid shade; o look!

FURIA

O woe to those who follow Catiline!

AMBIORIX

Home; home! Take flight! We break all promises.

OLLOVICO

A voice has warned us;—we'll obey the voice.
(*They go out quickly to the right.* CATILINE *comes
out of the house in the background.*)

CATILINE

A desperate hope—to think of toppling Rome
with this array of knaves and wretched cowards!
What urges them? They brazenly admit it,—
just want and lust for plunder drive them on.
Is it, then, worth the trouble, to shed blood
for such a purpose? What have I to gain?
What to acquire?

FURIA

(invisible behind the trees)

Revenge, o Catiline!

CATILINE

(starting)

Who spoke! Who wakes the spirits of revenge
out of their sleep? Is this voice from my own
interior? Revenge? Yes, that's the word—
my watchword and my warcry! Bloody vengeance!
Revenge for every hope and every dream
that hostile-minded fate has smashed for me!
Revenge for all my devastated life!
(The conspirators, now bearing arms, come out of the house.)

LENTULUS

The dark of night still broods above the city;
now it is time for us to start.

SEVERAL

(whispering)

Let's go!
(AURELIA comes out of the side-building without noticing the conspirators.)

AURELIA

Beloved,—are you here?

CATILINE

(*with a shriek*)

Aurelia!

AURELIA

Have you been waiting for me?
(*She catches sight of the conspirators and rushes toward him.*)

Gentle gods!

CATILINE

(*pushing her aside*)

Go from me, woman!

AURELIA

Catiline,—o speak!
These many men with weapons—? You as well—?
O, you are leaving—

CATILINE

(*wildly*)

Yes, by spirits of darkness,—
a merry jaunt! You see how my sword gleams?
It's dry with thirst; I go—to quench its thirst.

AURELIA

My hope,—my dream! O, blissful was my dream!
And thus I'm wakened from my dream—

CATILINE

Be still!

Stay here,—or come with us! Closed is my breast
to tears and wailing. —Friends, see in the west
the full-moon's disappearing in its flight!
When next it's full and rises in the night,
a flaming deluge mightily shall flow
upon the city and its gilded show.
And when a thousand years from now it beams
again on Latium's crumbling rubble streams,—
a lonely pillar in the waste shall stand,
and tell the wanderer: Here Rome stood grand!
              (*He rushes out to the right; all follow him.*)

ACT THREE

CATILINE's camp in a wooded area in Etruria. To the right CATILINE's tent can be seen and beside it an ancient oak-tree. Outside the tent a watch-fire is burning. Several more can be glimpsed among the trees in the background. It is night. Now and then the moon breaks through the clouds.
STATILIUS *is lying asleep by the watch-fire.* MANLIUS *is pacing back and forth outside the tent.*

MANLIUS

It's just like them, those young and carefree birds.
They're sleeping there so soundly and so calmly,
as if it were their mother's safe, snug bosom
that sheltered them, and not a desolate woods.
They're resting there as if they could expect
to be awakened for some merry sport
and not for battle,—yes, perhaps the last
they'll have a chance to fight here.

STATILIUS

(*awakening and getting up*)

Still on watch?
You're weary, aren't you? I'll relieve you now.

MANLIUS

No, no, you sleep yourself. A young man needs
refreshing sleep; his wild enthusiasm

takes energy. It's very different when
the hair has turned to gray, the blood runs thin,
and old age weighs so heavy on our shoulders.

STATILIUS

Yes, you are right; I also someday shall,
an old and hardened warrior—

MANLIUS

Are you then
so sure that fate has destined you to live
to your old age?

STATILIUS

Why shouldn't I be sure?
What put all these forebodings in your head?
Has some mischance occurred?

MANLIUS

You really think
we don't have anything to fear, young fool?

STATILIUS

Our army's much augmented—

MANLIUS

Very much,—
by slaves who've run away and mincing fencers—

STATILIUS

Well, never mind; for as a group they don't
seem insignificant, and all of Gaul
will send us help—

MANLIUS

—which hasn't come as yet.

STATILIUS

And do you doubt the Allobrogians
will keep their word?

MANLIUS

I know these people well
from times gone by. But that is all the same.
The day that's coming will no doubt disclose
what the high gods have got in store for us.
But go along, Statilius, and make sure
that all the guards are keeping to their duty.
We must protect against a night attack;
we don't know where our foes are, after all.
(STATILIUS *goes into the woods.*)

MANLIUS

(*alone by the watch-fire*)

The clouds are gathering now, yes, more and more;
it's a dark night and threatening to storm;—
a clammy fog is weighing on my breast,
as if it bode some mishap for us all.
Where is it now, the easy, carefree mind
with which I used to romp into a war?
Could it be just the burden of old age
that I'm aware of? Strange enough,—tonight
even the young seemed out of sorts to me.
(*after a pause*)

Well, let the gods be told, revenge was not
the object of my following Catiline.
My anger flared up for a fleeting moment
when I first felt that I'd been wronged, insulted;—
no, this old blood is not yet fully cold;

it often courses through me hot enough.
The wrong's forgotten, though. I followed him,
my Catiline, for his own sake alone;
and over him I'll watch with all my care.
He stands here solitary in these crowds
of madcap friends and worthless good-for-nothings.
They can't begin to fathom him,—and he
is much too proud to want to fathom them.
　(*He lays some branches on the fire and remains standing in silence.*
　　　　　Catiline *comes out of the tent.*)

CATILINE

(*to himself*)

　　It's almost midnight. Everything's so hushed;—
it's only on my eyes that sleep won't linger.
The wind is strong and cold; it will refresh me
and give me strength—. Ah, it is sorely needed!
　　　　　(*noticing* MANLIUS)

Is that you there, old Manlius? At watch
alone here in this pitch-dark night?

MANLIUS

　　　　　I have,
when you were young, watched over you so often.
Don't you remember that?

CATILINE

　　　　That time is gone;
with it my calm; and everywhere I go,
I am pursued by multifarious visions.
All, Manlius,—all houses in my breast;—
save only peace. That's in the distant blue.

MANLIUS

Dispel those melancholy thoughts. Go rest!

Remember that tomorrow may demand
your fullest battle strength to save us all.

CATILINE

    No, I can't rest. If I but close my eyes
to find oblivion in fleeting slumber,
then I am tossed about in eerie dreams.
Just now I, half-asleep, lay on my cot,
when once again these visions came to me,
more weird than ever,—more ambiguous
and enigmatic. —Ah, if I but knew
what this forebodes! But no—

MANLIUS

                Confide your dream
to me; perhaps I can interpret it.

CATILINE

(after a pause)

If I was awake or dozing, that I do not know;
countless thoughts pursued each other in a ceaseless flow.
Suddenly around me gloomy darkness grows in might;
and its ample wings then lowers in my soul a night,
pierced by gleams of lightning only, loathsome to behold;
and I see I'm in a chamber, damp as graveyard mold.
High as heaven is its ceiling, filled with thunderclouds;
troops of spectres, swarms of spectres, spirits in wild crowds,
all are whirling past and soughing, as when seas aroar
send their storm-caps wildly crashing on a stony shore.
Yet amid the frantic swarming now and then appear
flowered children singing of a half-forgotten sphere.
Roundabout them darkness lessens, brightness fills the air,—
and amid the space I glimpse a solitary pair;
two lone women,—one is stern and black as night's deep shades,—
and the other mild as daylight when it slowly fades.
Ah, how strangely all-familiar seemed these two, I thought!
One of them to me by smiling blissful calmness brought;

from the keen eyes of the other, lightning wildly blazed;
I felt fear,—yet at this vision willingly I gazed.
Haughty, upright, one is standing, and the other leans in stress
toward the table where they seemed to play a mystic game of chess.[8]
They are trading pieces, moving others all around;—
then the game has been decided, and within the earth sinks down
she, the one who lost, the woman with the lambent smile;
and the flowered groups of children rush away meanwhile.
Noise increases, darkness thickens; but from this dire sea,
two keen eyes transfix me with a glow of victory;
faintness grips me; those bright eyes are all I can make out.
But what more I dreamt thereafter in my fever-bout
lies behind oblivion's curtain in my being's knot.
Could I just the rest remember. Ah, it's all forgot!

MANLIUS

It is indeed most curious, Catiline,
this dream of yours.

CATILINE

(brooding)

If I could but remember—.
But no, it can't be done—

MANLIUS

Don't make yourself
uneasy with these thoughts. For what are dreams?
Imaginings and empty fantasies,
devoid of meaning and without foundation.

CATILINE

Yes, you are right; I won't brood any longer;—
I'm calmer now. So go then, Manlius;
go rest a bit. I'll wander here meanwhile
alone with but myself and my designs.

(MANLIUS *goes into the woods.* CATILINE *paces back and forth awhile by the watch-fire, which is starting to go out. Then he stops.*)

CATILINE
(*musing*)

If I could only—. Ah, it is unmanly
to be disturbed by such a thing and brood
on it. And yet,—in this still midnight hour,
in this full solitude, what I have dreamt
appears before my eyes so vividly—
(A GHOSTLY IMAGE *in the likeness of an old man in armor and toga appears, as if shooting up from the earth, at a distance from* CATILINE *in among the trees.*)

CATILINE
(*shrinking back from the* GHOST)

You gods above—!

THE GHOST

My greetings, Catiline!

CATILINE

What do you want? Who are you, pallid shade?

THE GHOST

Wait! *I'm* the one with right to question here,—
and you shall answer. Don't you recognize
from long-since vanished times this voice of mine?

CATILINE

It seems I do; but I'm not fully certain—.
Speak out,—who are you seeking here at midnight?

THE GHOST

It's you I seek. No other hour but this
is granted me for time of wandering here.

CATILINE

By all the gods, speak out! Who are you?

THE GHOST

Silence!

I've come up here to call you to account.
Why won't you let me keep the grave's still peace?
Why do you force me up from Death's abode?
Why do you break my calm oblivion,
and make me seek you out with warning whispers
to thus protect my dearly-purchased glory?

CATILINE

Ah, yes, this voice—! I guess and I remember—

THE GHOST

What yet remains of all my sovereign power?
A shade just like myself; yes, scarcely that.
We both went in the grave—and turned to nothing.
And it was dearly purchased; dearly, dearly
acquired. It cost me all my calm in life;
for it I gave up peace within my grave.
And now you want, with rash, foolhardy hand,
to snatch from me what I still have remaining!
Are there not paths enough to great achievements?
Why must you choose the very one I chose?
My power I gave up while still alive.
My name,—so I believed,—should always stand,
not twinkling pleasantly like some pale star,—
no, like a lightning in the night sky fixed!
I didn't want, like hundreds else before me,
for gentle virtues, magnanimity

to be remembered; didn't want to be
admired;—so many have already had
this lot and will until the end of time.
O no, it was from blood and horror that
I'd build the name I meant to leave behind!
In mute dismay, as toward an airy vision,
which comes and vanishes mysteriously,—
they were to goggle back on my behavior
and peep above toward me, whom no one ever,—
before or since,—had dared to emulate!—
Thus was it I had dreamt,—and was deceived.
We were so close; why didn't I suspect
what secret seed was sprouting in your soul?
Beware though, Catiline; you see, I glimpse
what's hidden by the curtain of the future;
there written mid the stars—I read your fate!

CATILINE

You read my fate? So then decipher it!

THE GHOST

Only behind death's darksome gate
shall fade the twilight that enwraps
whatever dreadful is or great
that future waves shall make collapse.
This only, from your fate's full sum,
a spirit freed may to you say:
By your own hand your fall will come,—
and yet another shall you slay![9]

(*The ghostly figure glides away, as in a mist.*)

CATILINE

(*after a pause*)

Ah, he has vanished. Was it but a dream?
No, no; he stood here, and the moonbeams grazed
his sallow visage. Ah, I recognized him!

It was the Dictator, the ancient man
of blood, come from the grave to frighten me.
He feared to lose the crown of victory,—
not honor's garland but the reputation
of horror keeping fresh his memory.
Are therefore even shades devoid of blood
urged on by hope of glory?
                    (*He paces back and forth restlessly.*)
                              Everything
assails me. First Aurelia speaks in words
of gentle warning,—and again the cry
of Furia echoes in me, urging action.
And more than this;—up from the grave arise
the pallid shades of those from times gone by.
They threaten me. Am I to stop here, then?
Turn back? No, bravely I'll stride forth until
my goal's attained;—I'll soon stand there triumphant!
          (CURIUS *comes through the woods in great agitation.*)

                    CURIUS

          O Catiline—!

                    CATILINE
                    (*surprised*)
              What, you,—you here, my friend?

                    CURIUS

          I had to look—

                    CATILINE
              Why have you left the city?

                    CURIUS
        Fear drove me here; I had to look for you.

                    338

CATILINE

For me you hurtle blindly into danger?
How rash of you! But come into my arms!
(He is about to embrace him.)

CURIUS

(shrinking back)

No, Catiline, don't touch me! Don't come near me!

CATILINE

What's wrong with you, my Curius?

CURIUS

Break camp!

Flee, if you can, right now! By every route
the army of your enemies is coming;
your camp's surrounded, Catiline!

CATILINE

Be calm;

you're talking wildly. Did your journey shake you—?

CURIUS

O no; but save yourself while there's still time!
You've been betrayed—
(He throws himself down before him.)

CATILINE

(starting)

Betrayed! What's that you say?

CURIUS

Behind a mask of friendship!

CATILINE

Now you err;
my madcap friends are all as loyal as you.

CURIUS

Alas, then, for the loyalty of your friends!

CATILINE

Compose yourself! It is your love for me,
your care for my security, that has
you glimpsing danger where there isn't any.

CURIUS

O, can't you see that these words murder me?
But flee! I do beseech you and implore you—!

CATILINE

Be calm and speak deliberately. Why should
I flee? My foes don't know where I'm encamped.

CURIUS

They know,—indeed, they know your every plan!

CATILINE

You must be mad. They know—? Impossible.

CURIUS

Would that were so! But there's so little time;
you can perhaps still save your life by fleeing!

CATILINE

Betrayed? No;—ten times no; impossible!

CURIUS

(*seizing his dagger and offering it to* CATILINE)

There, Catiline! O, thrust it in my breast;—
right through my heart! It's I who have betrayed you!

CATILINE

You? This is madness!

CURIUS

Yes, it was in madness!
Don't ask me why; I scarcely know myself;
but I've revealed to them your whole design.

CATILINE

(*distressed*)

Now you have killed my confidence in friendship.

CURIUS

O, thrust it in my breast, and don't torment
me more with mercy—!

CATILINE

(*gently*)

Live, my Curius!
Stand up! You erred;—and I forgive you for it.

CURIUS

(*overwhelmed*)

O Catiline, you see me broken-hearted—!
But hurry; flee! You hear, don't you?—it's urgent.
The Roman force will soon invade your camp;
it's on its way; o, it is everywhere.

CATILINE

My friends within the city—?

CURIUS

They are taken;—
some were imprisoned; most of them were slain.

CATILINE
(to himself)

O fate,—o fate!

CURIUS
(again offering his dagger to CATILINE)

Here, thrust it in my heart!

CATILINE
(looking quietly at him)

You were the means, that's all. You acted rightly—

CURIUS

O, let me with my life atone my crime!

CATILINE

I have forgiven you.
(as he is leaving)

Now but one choice
is left, my friend!

CURIUS
(jumping up)

Flight?

CATILINE

No, heroic death!
(*He goes away through the woods.*)

CURIUS

O, it is fruitless! Ruin waits for him.
This mildness is a tenfold punishment!
I'll follow him;—one thing won't be denied me:—
to fall while fighting by the hero's side!

(*He rushes out.* LENTULUS *and two* GLADIATORS *come stealthily through the trees.*)

LENTULUS

(*softly*)

Someone was talking here—

FIRST GLADIATOR

It's quiet now.

SECOND GLADIATOR

Perhaps it was the night watch after being
relieved.

LENTULUS

That's very likely. Here's the place;
it's here you are to wait. Now, are your weapons
well sharpened?

FIRST GLADIATOR

Gleaming just like lightning, sir!

SECOND GLADIATOR

Mine has some bite. At the last games in Rome,
two stalwart swordsmen fell before this sword.

LENTULUS

Then stay here in this thicket and keep quiet;
and when a man, whom I shall indicate,
goes toward the tent, you must rush forth and, from
behind, you'll cut him down.

FIRST GLADIATOR

It shall be done.
(*The* GLADIATORS *conceal themselves;*
LENTULUS *walks about, reconnoitering.*)

LENTULUS
(*to himself*)

It is a daring game I'm trying here;—
but it must be performed this very night
if it is to succeed. —If Catiline
should fall, there's no one else but me can lead them.
With golden promises I'll buy them all
and push without delaying toward the city,
where, in bewildered fear, the Senate's still
not thought to arm itself against the danger.
(*He goes in among the trees.*)

FIRST GLADIATOR
(*softly to the other*)

Who is he, then, this man as yet unknown,
whom we are to cut down?

SECOND GLADIATOR

What's it to us
who it may be? Since Lentulus is paying,
then he must also answer for our deed.

LENTULUS

(*coming back rapidly*)

Make sure you're ready; he is coming now!
(LENTULUS *and* THE GLADIATORS *place themselves in ambush among
the bushes. Immediately afterwards,* CATILINE *comes through the woods
and heads toward the tent.*)

LENTULUS

(*whispering*)

Go! Cut him down; strike at him from behind!
(*All three rush at* CATILINE.)

CATILINE

(*drawing his sword and defending himself*)

Ah, you base wretches,—dare you—?

LENTULUS

(*to* THE GLADIATORS)

Cut him down!

CATILINE

(*recognizing him*)

You, Lentulus, you'd murder Catiline?

FIRST GLADIATOR

(*frightened*)

It's he!

SECOND GLADIATOR

(*shrinking back*)

It's Catiline! No, I won't try
my sword on him. Let's flee!
(*The* GLADIATORS *run away.*)

LENTULUS

Then fall by mine!
(*They fight;* CATILINE *knocks* LENTULUS' *sword out of his hand;*
LENTULUS *tries to run away, but* CATILINE *holds him firmly.*)

CATILINE

You traitor! Murderer!

LENTULUS

(*imploringly*)

Mercy, Catiline!

CATILINE

I see your purpose written on your brow.
You meant to murder me and make yourself
the leader of my friends. Was that not so?

LENTULUS

I did, yes, Catiline!

CATILINE

(*looking at him with concealed disdain*)

Oh, well, who cares?
If it is might you wish for,—let it be.

LENTULUS

Explain,—what do you mean?

346

CATILINE

                              I'm stepping down;
you lead the army in my place—

LENTULUS
(*surprised*)
You are?

CATILINE

I am. But be prepared for everything;
for you should know,—our enterprise has been
betrayed; the Senate knows our whole design;
its army is surrounding us—

LENTULUS
What's that?

CATILINE

Now I'll go call our friends together. Come
along; present yourself as their new leader;
and I'll resign.

LENTULUS
(*holding him back*)
No, wait then, Catiline!

CATILINE

Your time is precious; you can fear attack
before the day has dawned—

LENTULUS
(*uneasy*)
O hear me, friend!

You're joking, no? It can't be possible—

CATILINE

Our plot has been betrayed, as I have told you.
Now let us see your shrewdness and your skill.

LENTULUS

Betrayed? Then woe to us!

CATILINE

(smiling scornfully)

You wretched coward!
You're trembling now;—and *you* would topple *me*;
You think that *you* are called to be a ruler?

LENTULUS

Forgive me, Catiline!

CATILINE

Go seek your safety
in hasty flight, if that's still possible.

LENTULUS

Ah, you'll allow me to—?

CATILINE

Did you believe
I seriously meant to leave[10] this post
in time of danger? You don't know me well.

LENTULUS

O Catiline—!

CATILINE

(coldly)

Don't waste the moment idly.
Go seek your rescue;—I'll know how to die.
(He turns away from him.)

LENTULUS

(to himself)

I thank you for this goodly piece of news,—
and I shall use it for my own advantage.
It's opportune that I'm familiar with
this area; I'll seek the army of
our foes and lead it here by hidden pathways,
to your destruction and to my salvation.—
The serpent that you trample in the dust
with such disdain still has its piercing sting!
(He leaves.)

CATILINE

(after a pause)

This is the loyalty that I relied on!
Thus they betray me, one by one. O gods!
It's only treachery and cowardice
that animate these lukewarm, slavish souls.
O, what a fool I am with my designs!
I would destroy that nest of vipers, Rome,—
and Rome has long since been a sunken ruin.
(The approaching noise of weapons can be heard; he listens.)

O, there they come! There still are valiant men
among them. Lovely is that clang of steel!
How merrily shields clash against each other!
It kindles up the fire in me once more;
decision's time is near,—the weighty time
resolving every doubt. I greet the time!

(MANLIUS, STATILIUS, GABINIUS, and a number of other conspirators come through the woods.)

MANLIUS

Here, Catiline, you have your friends with you;
in camp I struck the alarm as you commanded—

CATILINE

You told them—?

MANLIUS

Yes, they know our situation.

STATILIUS

We know it and we'll follow you with sword
in hand into a fight for life or death.

CATILINE

I thank you all, my valiant friends-at-arms!
But do not hope that here there's any choice
of life or death;—our only choice is that
between a death in valiant battle, facing
superior forces, and a death in torment
as viciously like beasts we're hunted down.
So what do you prefer? By flight to bear
a wretched life for yet a brief time more,—
or else as bravely as your noble fathers
to fall in battle with your sword in hand?

GABINIUS

We choose the latter!

MANY VOICES

Lead us on to death!

CATILINE

Well, then, let's go! In dying thus we wed
ourselves to immortality's fair life.
Our fall, our names, throughout the distant times,
shall be proclaimed aloud with pride—

FURIA

(crying out behind him, among the trees)

—or horror!

SOME VOICES

Ah, look,—a woman—!

CATILINE

(starting)

Furia! You here?

What drove you here?

FURIA

I must accompany you

unto your goal.

CATILINE

Where *is* my goal? Speak out!

FURIA

Each mortal seeks his goal in his own way.
You seek your goal through wild and hopeless battle;
and battle yields a crop of death and ruin.

CATILINE

But also glory and eternal name!
Go, woman! Noble is this hour, and fair;
my bosom is now deaf to your hoarse shrieks!

(AURELIA *appears in the opening of the tent.*)

AURELIA

My Catiline—!
(*She stops fearfully at the sight of the many who are gathered.*)

CATILINE

(*sorrowfully*)

O, it's Aurelia!

AURELIA

What's going on here? This alarm in camp—.
What's happening?

CATILINE

To think I could forget you!
O, what will your fate be—?

FURIA

(*whispering scornfully without being noticed by* AURELIA)

In your high purpose
do you already falter, Catiline?
Is *this* how you face death?

CATILINE

(*angrily*)

No, no, by gods
of darkness!

AURELIA

(*approaching*)

Dearest, speak; don't give me further
alarm—

FURIA

(*in a low tone behind him*)

Flee with your wife—while your friends die!

MANLIUS

Come, hesitate no longer; lead us to
the plain—

CATILINE

O, what a choice! And yet,—there's no
choice here;—I must pursue my goal,—dare not
stop half-way.

(*calling out*)

Follow me! Out to the plain!

AURELIA

(*throwing herself in his arms*)

Don't leave me, Catiline,—or take me, too!

CATILINE

No, stay, Aurelia!

FURIA

(*as before*)

Take her along!
You'll get a death your life, your name deserve
when you're cut down—within a woman's arms.

CATILINE

(*thrusting* AURELIA *aside*)

Away from me, you'd rob me of my fame!—
With men I'll be when death shall strike. I have
a life to expiate, a name to cleanse—

FURIA

Just so; just so, my noble Catiline!

CATILINE

From my full soul I'll rip out all that binds
me to my past and to its empty dreams!
What lies behind me is as if I never
had lived through it—

AURELIA

O no, don't cast me off!
With all my tender love,—I do implore you,—
don't let us part, my Catiline!

CATILINE

Be still!
My breast is dead, my eyes are blind to love.
From all life's jugglery I turn my gaze
and only look up toward the great pale star
in reputation's heaven!

AURELIA

Gentle gods!
(*She leans weakly against the tree beside the tent.*)

CATILINE
(*to his men*)

And now, let's go!

MANLIUS

There's noise from weapons there!

SEVERAL VOICES

They're coming!

CATILINE

Good! We'll meet them, brave and proud.
Our night of shame was long; dawn's in the air—.
Let's bathe in battle's rosy morning cloud!
Come, then! By Roman swords with Roman mettle
the last of Rome in their own blood shall settle!
(*They rush out through the woods; from the camp noises and cries of
fighting can be heard.*)

FURIA

He is gone. And I've at last achieved my life's one drift.
On the plain the sun's first look will see him cold and stiff.

AURELIA

(*to herself*)

In his heart all filled with anger is, then, love no more to
dwell?
Was I dreaming? No, I heard it from his angry lips too well.

FURIA

Swords are clinking; he already wanders in the grave's terrain;
soon he shall, a noiseless shadow, hasten into death's domain.

AURELIA

(*starting*)

Ah, whose is that voice of boding that I'm hearing now,
like an owl in hollow warning from a hemlock bough!
Are you risen from the clammy land where shadows roam
to lead Catiline to dwell there, in your gloomy home?

FURIA

Home's the goal of every wandering, and his chosen way
went through life's morass and swamps—

Aurelia

But only for a day!
Once his heart was free and noble, strong his soul and good,
till its growth with snakelike roots a poison-seed withstood.

Furia

Fresh and green the plane tree's leaf is, too, in every case,
till its trunk is strangled by the creepers' fast embrace.

Aurelia

You've betrayed now where you come from! This foul voice's
                                                        sound
many times on Catiline's own lips an echo found.
You're the serpent that has poisoned life's best fruit for me,
serpent that has forced his heart my tenderness to flee.
From my wakeful nighttime dreaming, I remember you,
see you clearly, like a menace, placed between us two.
By my darling husband's side I yearned with joy possessed
for a life by calm protected, for a restful nest;
in his weary heart I planted once an herbal bed;
as its richest ornament with care our love I bred.
Ah, your spiteful hand has ripped this herb up, root and all,
and it's lying in the dust, where once it stood so tall!

Furia

You weak fool; and *you* would guide the steps of Catiline?
Don't you see his heart was never wholly yours to twine?
Do you think that your weak flowers in such soil can thrive?
Only in the spring's rich sunshine can the violet strive,
while the henbane grows most lushly under skies of gray;
and his soul has been long since a cloudy autumn's day.
You have lost! And soon life's spark will fade with his last breath,
and he'll lie, revenge's victim, in the arms of death!

AURELIA

(with increasing passion)

No, by all the gods of brightness, no, that's not to be!
To his heart my tears will somehow pave a way that's free.
If I find him pale and bloody from the battle's crest,
I will fling my arms around his cold and lifeless breast,
breathe upon his silent lips my love's unending store,
soothe the suffering in his bosom, bring him peace once more.
Herald of vengeance, what you've claimed I'll wrest from your grim
hands,
bind him to the realm of light with love's eternal bands;
and if his great heart's stopped beating, at his last grimace,
we will go from life together in a fast embrace.
Grant me then, you gentle gods, for what I've had to brave
here beside my husband, all the still peace of the grave.
(She leaves.)

FURIA

(watching her go)

Seek him, deluded fool;—I have no fear;
I hold my triumph safely in my hands.
      The din of battle grows; its roar is mixed
with death-shrieks and the clash of broken shields.
Does he already bleed? Does he still live?
O, lovely is this hour! The moon's in hiding
behind thick thunderclouds in its descent.
It will be night again a moment more
before day comes;—and with day's coming, all
is over. He will perish in the dark,
just as he lived in darkness. Lovely hour!
      (She listens.)

      The din's now soughing past like autumn windstorms
to lose its voice out in the far-off distance;
the swarming troops are sweeping clean the plain.
Unstoppable, and trampling down the fallen,
they're pouring forth like wrathful ocean waves.—

Out there I now hear cries and gasps and groans,—
the final lullaby,—with which they lull
to rest themselves and all their pallid brothers.—
The owl is joining in. It's wishing them
a welcome to the realm of somber shades.
              (*after a pause*)

How still it is. And so he now is mine,—
yes, mine alone, and mine for ever more.
Together we can reach oblivion's river—
and then beyond, to where it never dawns.
But first I shall go seek his corpse out there,
shall glut my eyes with gazing on his fair
detested face before it is disturbed
by rising suns and soaring waiting ravens.
        (*She turns to go but then starts and shrinks back.*)

What now! What glides across the meadow yonder?
Is that but swampy vapors thickening in
the morning-chill to form a solid image?
It's coming nearer. —Catiline's own shade!
His spectre—! I can see his glassy eyes,
his cloven shield, his newly clangless sword;
I see the whole dead man; there's just *one* thing,—
how very strange,—his death-wound I don't see.
(CATILINE *comes through the woods, pale and weak, with lowered head
and a distracted look.*)

CATILINE

(*to himself*)

"By your own hand your fall will come,—
        and yet another shall you slay."
So ran his prophecy. Now I am fallen—
though struck by no one's hand. Who'll solve the riddle?

FURIA

Be welcome from the battle, Catiline!

CATILINE

Ah, who are you?

FURIA

I am a shade's own shade.

CATILINE

It's you, then, Furia! You welcome me?

FURIA

Be welcome to our common home! Now we
can make our way to Charon's boat,—two spectres.
Wait—take the victor's garland from my hand.
(*She picks some flowers and braids them into a garland during the
following speeches.*)

CATILINE

What are you making there?

FURIA

I will adorn
your brow. But why do you come here all alone?
A chieftain's shade should be accompanied by
ten thousands of the slain. Where are your friends?

CATILINE

They're sleeping, Furia!

FURIA

They're sleeping still?

CATILINE

They're sleeping still,—and they'll be sleeping long.
They're all asleep. Go softly through the woods;

Peek out at them,—but hush! do not disturb them!
You'll find them on the plain in long, long rows.
They went to sleep from the swords' lullaby;
they went to sleep,—and did not wake, like me,
when past the distant heights the song died out.
A spectre you just called me. Yes, I am
a spectre of myself. But don't believe
that those men's sleep is so entirely peaceful
and free of dreams. O, don't believe it!

FURIA

Speak!
What is it that your friends are dreaming?

CATILINE

Listen.—
I led them forward with despairing thoughts,
and looked for death beneath the sword's keen edge.
To right and left they all were sinking down;
Statilius fell,—Gabinius, Manlius;
my Curius was killed protecting me;
they all fell down before the Roman swords,—
before those swords rejecting me alone.
Yes, Roman arms rejected Catiline.
With broken sword I stood there, half-benumbed,
and noticed nothing while the battle's waves
washed over me. I only gained my senses
when everything was still, and I looked up
and saw the battle surging—far behind me!
How long was it I stood there? All I know
is this,—I stood alone among my dead.
But there was life in all those glassy eyes;
the corners of their mouths wrenched into smiles;
and all those smiles and eyes were turned toward me,
who stood alone upright among the corpses,—
toward me, who strove for them and Rome,—toward me,

who stood there once again disdained, rejected
by Rome's keen swords. —And Catiline then died.

FURIA

O, falsely you've construed your dead men's dreams,
and falsely you've construed what killed you there.
With smiles and looks they were inviting you
to sleep just like themselves—

CATILINE

Yes, if I could!

FURIA

Be confident,—ghost of a former hero;
your hour of rest is near. Come; bow your head;—
now I'll adorn you with the victor's garland.
(*She holds it out toward him.*)

CATILINE

Ugh,—what is that? A poppy garland—!

FURIA

(*with wild gaiety*)

Well,—

aren't poppies pretty flowers? They will glisten
around your brow just like a fringe of blood.

CATILINE

No, throw that thing away! I hate this red.

FURIA

(*with loud laughter*)

Do you love more the feeble, pallid colors?
Good! I will fetch the garland of green rushes

that Silvia wore upon her dripping tresses,
when her corpse surfaced close by Tiber's mouth.

CATILINE

Alas, what visions—!

FURIA

Shall I bring you rather
from Rome's great forum thistle clumps all stained
in brown by the life-blood of its citizens,
which your hand caused to flow, my Catiline?

CATILINE

O stop!

FURIA

Or would you like a garland from
the winter-oak beside my mother's house,
which withered when a young dishonored woman
leaped, shrieking and distracted, in the river?

CATILINE

O, empty all the cups of vengeance on
my head at once—!

FURIA

I'm your own eyes, you see—
I'm your own memory and I'm your own doom.

CATILINE

Why *now*—?

FURIA

The weary wanderer, you know,

when at his goal, looks back upon his way.

CATILINE

Do I stand at my goal? Is this my goal?
I am not living,—and I'm not interred.
Where lies my goal?

FURIA

Nearby,—if you so will.

CATILINE

I have no will remaining; my will died
when everything was marred I once had willed.
(striking out with his hands)

Get far away from me, all you pale shades!
What do you want with me, you men and women?
I cannot grant you—! O, this multitude—!

FURIA

Your shade is still bound firmly to the Earth.
O, tear to bits this thousand-threaded net!
Come, let me press the garland in your hair;—
it has a healing force that brings oblivion;
it will lull you to rest; it kills the memory.

CATILINE

(toneless)

It kills the memory? Dare I trust your words?
Then press your poison garland round my brow.

FURIA

(putting the garland on his head)

Now you're adorned. And that is how you must
appear before Gloom's Prince, my Catiline!

CATILINE

Come, let us go! Down there I long to be;—
I'm nearing home,—the land of all the shades.
O, let us go together! —What confines me?
What binds my steps? I feel behind me in
the morning-heaven's vault a hazy star;—
it holds me back here in the land of life;
it draws me as the moon's force draws the sea.

FURIA

O, come along!

CATILINE

It beckons and it twinkles.
I cannot come with you before this light
is wholly quenched, or else bedimmed by clouds.—
I see it now! It isn't any star;
it is a heart,—it's throbbing and it's warm;
it binds me; it imprisons and it draws,
as the star of evening draws the eyes of children.

FURIA

Then stop this heart from beating!

CATILINE

What's your meaning?

FURIA

You have your dagger in your belt. One thrust,—
the star's put out, and broken is this heart
that stands between us in hostility.

CATILINE

I should put out—? My dagger's sharp and gleaming—
(with a shriek)

Aurelia! Aurelia, where are you?
If you were near—! No,—I don't want to see you!
And yet—it seems that all would be so good,
that peace would come, if I could lay my head
upon your breast and then repent—repent!

FURIA

What is it you'd repent?

CATILINE

All that I've done!
That I've existed and that I have lived.

FURIA

You would repent too late! Where you now stand
no paths lead back. —Try it, deluded fool!
I'm going home now. You just lay your head
upon her breast and see if you find there
the peace you're seeking for your weary soul.
(with increasing wildness)

They'll soon be rising up, the thousand dead;
dishonored women will be joining them;
and all of them, all shall demand from you
the life, the blood, the honor you have stolen.
In terror you will flee into the night,—
will flee around the Earth to every shore,
Actaeon-like, your hound pack hunting you,—
a shade pursued by all the thousand shades!

CATILINE

I see it, Furia! I'm outlawed here.
Within the world of light I'm homeless now!
I'm going with you to the land of all
the shades;—the bond that binds me I shall sunder.

FURIA

Why does your dagger falter?

CATILINE

She shall die.
(*A flash of lightning strikes and the thunder rolls.*)

FURIA

The mighty Ones rejoice at your intention!—
Look, Catiline,—your wife is coming yonder.
(AURELIA *comes through the woods, anxiously searching.*)

AURELIA

Where shall I find him! Where can he have gone!
He's not among the dead—
(*catching sight of him*)
O you high heavens;—
My Catiline!
(*She rushes toward him.*)

CATILINE

(*confused*)

You shall not say that name!

AURELIA

You're living! Yes—!
(*She is about to throw herself into his arms.*)

CATILINE

(*warding her off*)

Away! I'm not alive.

Aurelia

O hear me, dear one—!

Catiline

Quiet; I won't listen!
I hate you! Go! I see your cunning trick;
you want to chain me to a horrid half-life.
Don't stare at me! Your eyes—they torture me,—
they pierce into my soul like tapered daggers!
Ah, dagger; dagger! Die! Close up your eyes—
(*He draws his dagger and seizes her arm.*)

Aurelia

O gentle gods, watch over him and me!

Catiline

Close up your eyes; close them,—close them, I say;—
the light of stars and morning sky is in them—.
Now I'll put out the morning sky's fair star!
(*The thunder rolls again.*)

Your heart's blood! Now the gods of life call out
their parting words to you and Catiline!
(*He raises the dagger to her breast; she flees into the tent;
he pursues her.*)

Furia

(*listening*)

She's reaching out her arms imploringly.
She's begging for her life. But he hears nothing.
He's thrusting home! —She's fallen in her blood.
(Catiline *comes slowly out of the tent, the dagger in his hand.*)

Catiline

Now I am free. And soon I shall be nothing.

My soul is sinking in oblivion's mists;
I see but dimly and my hearing's blurred
as under churning water. Do you know
what with this little dagger I have killed?
Not her alone,—but all the hearts of Earth,—
yes, everything that lives and everything
that grows and comes to leaf:—all stars I have
put out, and the moon's disk, and the sun's fire.
See for yourself,—see there,—it isn't rising;
it never more will rise; the sun's put out.
The whole vast circle of the Earth is now
transformed into a cold and monstrous grave
with leaden vault,—and underneath this vault
stand you and I, cast out[11] by light and darkness,
by death and life,—two pale and restless shades.

FURIA

We're standing at the goal then, Catiline!

CATILINE

No; one step more—before I'm at the goal.
Release me from my burden! Don't you see,
I bear the corpse of Catiline upon
my back? A stake through Catiline's remains!
(showing her the dagger)

Release me, Furia! Here, take this stake;—
with it I pierced the morning star's fair eye;—
take it,—take it and ram it through the corpse,
then it will lose its might,—and I am free.

FURIA

(seizing the dagger)

I shall, you soul whom I in hatred loved!
Shake off your dust and join me in oblivion!
(She plunges the dagger deep in his breast; he sinks down
at the foot of the tree.)

CATILINE

(regaining his senses after a pause, moving his hand over his brow, and speaking in a weak voice)

Ah, you enigmatic spirit, now I understand!
Half by my own hand I fall, half by another's hand.[12]
Nemesis has claimed her victim. Hide me, Death's dark cell!
Murky Styx, lift now your billows' head up high and swell!
Bear me over; speed the boat on; chase it as it's rowed
toward the silent Prince's kingdom, every shade's abode.
Two disparate paths lead down there! mutely I shall come
down the left—

AURELIA

(coming from the tent, pale and staggering, her breast all bloody)

—no, down the right one! Toward Elysium!

CATILINE

(starting)

O, how this bright form makes horror in my soul revive!
It is she herself! Aurelia,—speak,—are you alive?

AURELIA

(kneeling beside him)

Yes, I live to calm the sea of woe that makes you sigh,—
live so I may lay my bosom on your breast and die.

CATILINE

O, you live!

AURELIA

On me a moment weakness cast its pall;
but my weakened eyes could follow you; I heard it all,—
and my love a wifely power back to me then gave;—
breast to breast, my Catiline, we'll go into our grave!

CATILINE

O how gladly! Yet your hope no longer can apply.
We must part. And I must follow vengeance's deep cry.
You can hasten, free and soaring, forth to light and peace;
I must pass oblivion's river, must gloom's host increase.
(*The day dawns in the background.*)

AURELIA

(*pointing toward the increasing daylight*)

No; when faced by love, Death's horrors and its night all
disappear.
Look, the thundercloud retreats, the morning star gleams, weak but
clear;

(*with uplifted hands*)

Light is winning! Look, the day comes, great and warm and blessed!
Come with me, beloved! Death already grips my breast.
(*She sinks down over him.*)

CATILINE

(*pressing her tightly to himself and speaking with his last strength*)

O, how lovely! Now quite clearly I recall my dream,
how the vault's thick darkness scattered in a sunbeam stream,
how the children's voices sang unto the dawning day.
Ah, my eyes are growing dimmer, and my strength gives way;
but as never once before my mind sees light appear,
and my past's tumultuous wandering lies behind me clear.
Yes, my life was night-storm raging, lit by lightning's glow;
but a rosy-colored dawning through my death I know.
(*bending over her*)

From my soul the gloom you've driven; peace now fills my breast.
See, with you I'm going to the realm of light to rest!
(*He pulls the dagger quickly from his breast and
speaks with his dying voice.*)

Morning's gentle forces grant atonement from above;
you have vanquished night's dark spirit with your mighty love!

(*During the final scene* FURIA *has withdrawn gradually toward the background, where she disappears among the trees.* CATILINE'*s head sinks down on* AURELIA'*s breast; they die.*)

Notes to *Catiline* (1875)

1. See note 2 for the 1850 version. In 1875 Ibsen altered the first use of *Allebrogerland* but left the second unchanged.

2. The word in the original for "leave" is "*forlade*," which also means "abandon, desert, forsake," a sense that is very much in the minds of the conspirators in this and the following scene. In this version, in contrast to 1850, Ibsen allows Catiline to introduce "*forlade*" in connection with his leaving.

3. "*Forlade*."

4. "*Forlade*."

5. "*Forlade*" in both cases.

6. "*Forlade*."

7. "*Forlade*."

8. Although Ibsen slightly revised this line for the 1875 edition, he retained the fifteen-syllable count from 1850; in addition, apparently in order to provide a uniform couplet, he also expanded the preceding line to fifteen syllables. He did not, however, expand the subsequent line to fifteen syllables to accommodate it to the line with which it rhymes, which—also slightly revised—retains the fifteen-syllable count of its 1850 counterpart.

9. See note 27 for the 1850 version.

10. "*Forlade*."

11. "*Forlade*."

12. Catiline's rephrasing of the Ghost's prophecy reflects its original form in the 1849 manuscript of *Catiline*. See note 33 for the 1850 version. Ibsen carried this line over into the 1875 version unchanged.

Introduction to *The Burial Mound*

Composition and Reception

The earliest recorded reference to *The Burial Mound* appears in the letter that Ibsen wrote to Ole Schulerud from Grimstad on January 5, 1850—the letter in which, responding to Schulerud's bad news about the rejection of *Catiline* by the Christiania Theater, he refers to "*Catiline*'s death sentence." After discussing Schulerud's intention of finding a publisher for *Catiline*, Ibsen brings his friend up to date on his "literary activity," mentioning, among other writings, a play that Schulerud must have been familiar with before his departure for Christiania around the beginning of September 1849. "The little one-act play, 'The Normans,'" he writes, "is re-worked—or, to be more exact, shall be re-worked—a project with which I am currently occupied, and in its new form it will become the vehicle for a more extensive idea than that for which it was originally intended."[1] Like all the projects Ibsen mentions, "The Normans" was part of a concerted effort to move his work, as he writes of the short poems he describes, in "a national direction"—that is, to devote himself to producing examples of the "National Romanticism" so popular in Scandinavia at the time. "The Normans" was the only one of the major projects mentioned in this letter that was to be completed. This occurred toward the end of May 1850, after Ibsen had arrived in Christiania, by which time he had also given the play its present title.

Using his early pseudonym, Brynjolf Bjarme, Ibsen submitted *The Burial Mound* to the Christiania Theater. This time he was successful in getting his work accepted, the play was prepared for production during the summer, and on September 26 it received its premiere before a good-sized audience of 557 ticket-holders. Ibsen, who described the experience as "dreadful," hid himself away in the darkest corner of the theater (Koht, I, 60), but the premiere was enough of a success to warrant two further performances on September 29 and

October 24. Partly because of faults in the production itself, the audiences for these further performances were smaller, but all in all *The Burial Mound* was viewed by 1,171 spectators, approximately 4 percent of the existing population of Christiania.[2] The theater management granted Ibsen an honorarium of 15 *spesidaler* for the right to produce his play (Anker, 73)—i.e., 60 Norwegian kroner, or approximately $8.50 at today's rate of exchange—and Ibsen had them turn the money over to Schulerud (perhaps in partial repayment for Schulerud's having financed the printing of *Catiline*).

The theater reviewers amply praised the beauty and resonance of the verse of *The Burial Mound*, but otherwise they condemned both the play and the production. The review appearing in the *Christiania-Post* on page one of the issue for September 28 is unsigned but was probably written by its regular reviewer, Ole Richter (Rudler, 298). This reviewer professes to be sure that Brynjolf Bjarme undoubtedly had a great deal in mind when he wrote the play but lacked "either the patience or the ability" to render any of it successfully. He particularly dislikes the author's attempt to provide an image of "our forefathers' life and customs on their famous Viking raids":

> his description is extremely loose and sketchy, and on top of that in his haste the author has attributed to the ancient Vikings characteristics that neither we nor our forefathers can be served by: the Vikings of the sagas were by no means such inhuman barbarians that, to satisfy their vengeance, they even cut down defenseless women; nor is it at all credible that Norway's ancient sea-heroes should have experienced any satisfaction in burning down a wretched hermit cottage because it happened to lie in an area where an affront was to be avenged: such heroic deeds are most rightfully reserved for the celebrated knight of the windmill.

Nor, the reviewer continues, has the author been any more successful in his attempt to represent "Nordic paganism and Christianity in conflict with one another and the victory of the latter": "the development is inadequate; one gets no notion of how it actually comes about that Christianity, like an Old Norse sorceress, is capable of blunting the heathens' swords; one sees only that the author has been of the opinion that such is the case." The reviewer has to conclude that "the play's contents in and of themselves do not at all seem to be particularly suited for dramatic treatment." He then summarizes these contents, pausing here and there to coat with his sarcasm such details as the old Viking's being converted to Christianity by the five-year-old Blanka and his plan to watch for the northern lights ("a pleasure that without question he will not enjoy very often, since, as is well known, there are no northern lights in France, but that is indeed a *licentia poetica* that one is not to be too particular about"). The story itself, he concedes, "is by no means unpoetic":

> it could reasonably yield excellent material for a couple of romances, and regarded as an epic-lyric poem *The Burial Mound* is without doubt a work of no little poetic worth; for many of the details are most beautiful—almost every speech is distinguished by a lyric flourish, a wealth of poetic thoughts, and one may reasonably find even more of these qualities by *reading* the play than by seeing it performed a single time. Furthermore, the whole work is dressed in a most becoming and melodious verse, in which the author seems to have uncommon strength. As a "dramatic" poem, however, it is manifestly not very successful. Almost everywhere sufficient motivation is lacking, the characters, perhaps with the exception of Blanka, are very loosely delineated, and one feels far too much the lack of true dramatic effect.

Brynjolf Bjarme, the reviewer notes, is also the author of *Catiline*, which, although it is not of particular worth as a dramatic work, "is undoubtedly superior to *The Burial Mound* in this respect." However, he concludes, "both these works attest to a talent for writing that deserves attention and that with time, it is to be hoped, will also be able to gain mastery over dramatic form."

Another review of *The Burial Mound*, entitled "Some Further Considerations of Brynjolf Bjarme's New Drama 'Kjæmpehøien,'" appeared in the supplement to *Krydseren* on October 5, also unsigned. Reminding his readers that Brynjolf Bjarme is the author of *Catiline*, the reviewer observes that "purity of form, ideal worth, and a noble air are to be found throughout this work as well as its predecessor," and he adds that these are no doubt great merits, "which not very many writers can pride themselves on possessing, at least in our days when the weaknesses and the egotistical demands of a powerful audience often seem to exert an alarming effect on the ideals of taste." These merits, he goes on to say, are absolutely necessary for art, but they "are by no means sufficient for the artist," especially for writing drama, which "must also possess a certain *intellectual* richness." For that reason, he continues, "we would rather see in a young talent—as, for example, was the case with Schiller—a subjectivity so rich that it cannot compress the material into the forms that a mere ideal of taste presupposes." This intellectual over-abundance is, unfortunately, what Brynjolf Bjarme does not have:

> He is not weak; for it is not power that he lacks; but what it seems to us he lacks is complexity, richness, perhaps boldness, and—to use a seemingly curious expression—a spirit of literary enterprise. The idea is beautiful; but the subject is not developed; it has too much historical material to be concentrated into one act with a few beautiful tableaus. The consequence of this is that the play, even though there is already tension in the beginning, nevertheless produces a certain emptiness and disappointment that might have been absent if the play had been given a tragic ending (which would of course have had to be prepared for from the beginning); for, as the Greek tragedies show, the tragic effect could provide work for the emotions and thereby fill up the emptiness that is caused by the lack of intellectual material.

These judgments prompt the reviewer to wonder "whether the author is not more predisposed to tragedy":

> *Catiline* seems to us to indicate as much; likewise a certain artistic composure, which is what makes tragedy so sublime, is one of his most substantial merits, just as on the whole the artist is more conspicuous in him than the mere man of letters. It is also certain, however, that where tragedy is concerned . . . those qualities that we established above as advantageous for the writing of drama call for considerable qualification; tragedy is of all genres the one that lies nearest to genuine art, and therefore

it has no need of occupying the spectators to such a degree with all these by-issues and complications that, with a misleading and often misused term, one calls rounding off.

But the reviewer also considers it "perhaps somewhat indelicate to put such pressure on a young author after so brief an acquaintance; let us wait; perhaps time will alter our judgment of him. In the meantime we will urge him to retain in his future works the beautiful arrangement and the beautiful and substantial verse whose pure sound truly gave us an unadulterated pleasure." The reviewer continues to make objections, however, pointing out that the skald "has the appearance of being more a troubadour than a genuine Nordic skald, just as the over-all impression is more romantic than Nordic." He then concludes by recommending that "the author, if he has not already done so, read Keyser's book about the religious practices of the Norwegians in pagan times, since this book provides an account of the deeper poetic foundation in the public as well as the private life of our forefathers that [Brynjolf Bjarme] himself seems to show both the desire and the ability to call attention to and to treat in depth in his subjects."[3]

Production of *The Burial Mound* apparently gave P. F. Steensballe, the book-seller who had printed *Catiline* for a fee, more faith in his author, for on December 19, 1850, he worked out with Schulerud a contract to publish Ibsen's new play, agreeing to provide a fee of twenty-five *spesidaler* for the rights, with ten of them to be paid in advance.[4] The first signature of the play was duly printed and the proof corrected, but at this point, for reasons that remain unexplained, the project was discontinued. The text of the play survived in the prompt book for it of the Christiania Theater, which is now in the holdings of the University of Oslo Library. It was printed by Martin B. Ruud, with several errors, in *Scandinavian Studies and Notes*, 4 (1917), 309–37, and subsequently in a far more accurate version in the first volume of the Hundreårsutgave in 1928.

Ibsen next touched *The Burial Mound* in 1853, after he had assumed his post as technical director and house dramatist at the Norwegian Theater in Bergen. His first effort to fulfill his obligation to provide a new play annually for production on the anniversary of the founding of the theater (January 2) was a prose comedy, *St. John's Night*. The play failed resoundingly and had to be replaced after its second performance by P. A. Jensen's *The Goblin's Home*, a play Ibsen had seen in Christiania and expressed his loathing for in a review of it. The whole experience seems to have left a feeling of deep bitterness in Ibsen, and in later years he completely disowned the play, refusing to allow it to be included in the collected editions of his works and claiming that he had merely re-drafted it from an unfinished version sent to him by a fellow student. To meet his obligation the following year, sometime during the summer and/or fall of 1853 he produced a substantial revision of *The Burial Mound*. This was no more successful than *St. John's Night* had been: it had only one performance, on January 2, 1854, and was revived for one further performance while Ibsen was still in Bergen, on February 15, 1856. However, a local newspaper, the *Bergenske Blade*, stating that the play had aroused considerable interest, printed its text in four successive issues in late January and early February of 1854.[5] Nevertheless, the following year Ibsen fulfilled his obligation by submitting a play that he initially claimed had been written by a friend of his—actually his own *Lady Inger of Østråt*—and Meyer speculates (114) that he did this because of the failure of *The Burial Mound*.

In 1897, Ibsen agreed to allow a translation of *The Burial Mound* to appear in the German collected edition of his works, and he borrowed the prompt book of the revised version from the Norwegian Theater in Bergen for this purpose.[6] When he sent it to the editor of this edition on September 9, he wrote, "I find upon reading it through that there is much that is good in this little work of my youth, and I sincerely thank you for compelling me to include it in the edition" (Anker, 442). He would not, however, allow Hegel, his Danish publisher, to include *The Burial Mound* in the original-language collected edition of his works, informing him in a letter of January 16, 1898, that the play "would have to be thoroughly re-worked first. As the basis for a translation the old text can, of course, be quite adequate. If you wish to have [it] included in the People's Edition, it could perhaps most preferably be in the form of a sort of concluding supplement."[7] The text of the Bergen prompt book was duly included in the supplementary tenth volume of this edition in 1902, and in 1928 this version of *The Burial Mound* appeared in the first volume of the Hundreårsutgave in a text based on that printed in the *Bergenske Blade* in 1854.

The German translation mentioned above came out in 1904 and a Czech translation at some indeterminate time, and there have apparently been translations of the play in the French, Russian, and Dutch collected editions of Ibsen's works. Archer ignored *The Burial Mound* as he had *Catiline*, and the first English translation (of the second version) appeared in 1921 in Anders Orbeck's *Early Plays by Henrik Ibsen* under the title *The Warrior's Barrow*. Translations of both versions of the play, rendered by James Walter McFarlane, appeared in Volume I of the Oxford *Ibsen* in 1970. As one can readily imagine, there have been few productions of *The Burial Mound* since 1856. George B. Bryan cites a production in Vienna in 1900 but provides no further information.[8] McFarlane (606) cites a production, under the title of "The Hero's Mound," by the Ibsen Club in London on May 30, 1910. And in September 1989, actors from Oslo's Norwegian Theater gave a staged reading of the revised version of the play in the courtyard of Akershus fortress; I have been told that their performance aroused considerable interest.

The Burial Mound has little critical history. Few have discussed the play, even fewer in any detail, and apparently no one has expressed much enthusiasm for it. Koht (I, 60, 96) finds both versions "wildly romantic and absurd." For Meyer, "such virtues as the play possesses are poetic rather than dramatic; like *Catiline*, it moves with considerable skill from rhymed to unrhymed verse, and contains several fine passages"; but he concludes that it "is nearer to being worthless than any other play [Ibsen] wrote" (61, 113). McFarlane, referring to its "tired conventionality," sees it as showing "some measure of the extent to which [Ibsen] fell victim to current enthusiasms":

> This second play of his marks an almost complete surrender to the received ideas of the day: determinedly nationalistic . . . ; safely Oehlenschläger-like in language and style . . . ; popularly Viking in its subject matter with its blond and blue-eyed heroism, its skaldic portentousness . . . ; and a reach-me-down dramatic structure that based all on unsuspected identities astonishingly revealed. (12)

And he is even more ferocious on the revised version: "Ibsen's determination to fashion something to the popular taste, to make the play acceptable at all costs to the Norwegian public, strikes one now as rather pathetic, perhaps even somewhat distasteful. In mitigation, one might perhaps remember that in 1854, after the resounding failure the previous year of *St. John's Night* to win favour with the public, he was desperately anxious to achieve a popular success" (13–14).

Johnston finds much to admire in the conception of *The Burial Mound*, but he does not hesitate to list its "all too evident crudities," which include, along with several echoes of McFarlane's complaints, the "facile pairing off of the characters at the end of the play when the northern Gandalf appropriates the southern Blanka and the southernized Bernhard-Audun acquires the northern scald, Hemming. The formalism of the character-pairing reveals the naive dialectical aesthetic of the play in which thematic considerations take precedence over individual character. The poet's concentration upon his southern-northern, pagan-Christian, male-female dualities prevents him from endowing his figures with much dramatic life" (49). He can also be as severe as McFarlane on the revised version of the play, claiming that the "naive Romanticism" is even more obvious in it and concluding a long, sarcastic account of some of its "wildly improbable" stage conventions with "This is purely escapist theater which has neither the discipline imposed by the need to simulate a plausible reality nor that imposed by a demanding theatrical convention" (56–57). Yet he is more ambivalent than McFarlane about this version, for he also sees it as sharpening and clarifying the argument of the play (54), radically changing in valuable ways the character of Blanka (55), and making "more of the struggle within Gandalf's soul" (57). And it is also about the second version that he writes, "There is thematic subtlety in the contrast of the northern, masculine weakness beneath the outward strength of the pagan hero and the feminine strength beneath the outward weakness of the Christian heroine. The considerable extention of Ibsen's thematic material beyond that of *Catiline* may be missed if we consider only the all too evident crudities of the play" (57).

Sources, Analysis, Evaluation

Commentators have mentioned a couple of other Scandinavian poets as possible minor influences on *The Burial Mound*, but everything about its first version clearly demonstrates the Grimstad Ibsen's devoted apprenticeship to his first master in creating drama, the Dane Adam Oehlenschläger, and whatever Ibsen needed to know to work out the details of his play he could have gotten from Oehlenschläger without having to bother to turn to any other source. The play's particular exemplification of National Romanticism—the clash between northern Viking paganism and southern Christianity with the triumph of the latter over the former—was a central preoccupation of Oehlenschläger's, and from him as well Ibsen took, without question, his extensive (and sometimes rather obscure) allusions to Norse mythology, the multiple verse forms, the characteristic diction, the use of poetic rather than dramatic means for heightening, and (to a considerable extent) the particular tendencies of action and characterization—although Ibsen's action is far more schematic and his characterization weaker than Oehlenschläger's. Perhaps we can credit Ibsen with the idea that the fusion of northern strength with southern values advances the modern North to a higher stage of existence than any that, apparently, the world has ever known, but otherwise the first version of *The Burial Mound* exhibits little originality.[9] Bull (246) and Koht (I, 61) propose, as an influence on the play, Ibsen's infatuation with Clara Ebbel at the time he wrote it, but there is nothing about the romance between Blanka and Gandalf that indicates any personal feeling on the author's part; to portray it, Ibsen certainly did not have to have been in love himself—or, for that matter, to have even made the acquaintance of a woman. *The Burial Mound* often echoes *Catiline* when Ibsen is dramatizing moments and feelings similar to some of those in his first play, but perhaps the most significant indication of the non-personal and utterly literary-derivative quality of *The Burial Mound* is its extreme remoteness from the little drama of the poems that Ibsen had been writing, which he had already utilized for the symbolic core of *Catiline*.

Ibsen called *The Burial Mound* a "dramatic poem," and it exemplifies this form even more thoroughly than *Catiline*. As in *Catiline*, the primary medium of blank verse—typically end-stopped because of a tendency to alternate masculine and feminine endings—freely yields to rhyming passages. These are usually decasyllabic rhymes in abab (alternating masculine and feminine endings) or couplets (with the alternating endings extending to the couplet units). But Ibsen also employs octosyllabic couplets and an intermittently rhyming passage in a kind of "Viking" metrical pattern with two or three feet to the line and a basic dactyllic/trochaic meter. In all, 193 of the play's 610 lines rhyme (almost 32 percent), and if one adds the 40 lines of two other passages of obviously heightened poetry in an unrhymed version of the "Viking" meter, the percentage increases to over 38 percent. The tendency of the play to veer more toward poem than drama is also evident in the conscious and deliberate repetitions by characters of what they or others have said and in the highly explicit verbalization typical of many of the speeches. We know that Gandalf is affected by Blanka's talk of spiritual (as opposed to physical) combat, for example, because he articulates a rather precise account of what is happening to him: "No, you are right, I do not grasp your words,— / But feeble lightning bolts gleam in my soul, / And visions stir there that I never saw before."

As with Catiline, proper appreciation of The Burial Mound depends on rightly grasping its particular form. The complaints about the play lose some of their force when one realizes that the pleasures it seeks to provide, focused, as they are, in the verse and the rhyming, tend to be of a different order from those we normally look for in drama. And some of the complaints virtually evaporate when we accustom ourselves to letting the conventions of the dramatic poem help us understand what is going on. From the point of view of drama, for example, the scene between Blanka and Gandalf is both too abrupt and too vague on its central point (the forming of a romantic attachment between them) to lend plausibility, as it must, to what happens later. From the point of view of the dramatic poem, however, their twice sharing extended rhyming passages should successfully indicate that a bond of considerable importance has linked them together.

Like nearly everything that Ibsen wrote, The Burial Mound is of interest and value to a full study of his career. For one thing, it bears on the question of when and how well he knew Shakespeare, in this case The Tempest, which it resembles in both versions and seems to echo in the second.[10] Like Catiline, The Burial Mound also tries out several things Ibsen was to do far more effectively later on—although in this respect *The Burial Mound* has much less significance than *Catiline*, especially as being crucial to a full understanding of later Ibsen. *The Burial Mound* was his first attempt to use his later famous retrospective method to structure an entire play—here, admittedly, with rather crude and melodramatic results. It contains his first uses of the word "call" and thus introduces the concept that was later to be of such importance to his work.[11] It is his first rendering of the clash between a pagan world and a Christian world which plays so prominent a role in such later plays as *The Vikings at Helgeland*, *Emperor and Galilean*, and *Rosmersholm*, and since the play works toward a fusion of the two worlds into a higher union it even anticipates the concept of the "third empire" that is so central to the thought of *Emperor and Galilean*. As Johnston points out (49–50), by creating, in the mound, a "central visual symbol that draws into itself the dominant meaning of the play," *The Burial Mound* establishes "a major poetic breakthrough in [Ibsen's] dramatic method which is to have immense consequences not only for Ibsen's later career as a dramatist but for the development of modern drama itself." And Johnston also argues (55–56) that through the Blanka of the revised version Ibsen introduces the theme "of spiritual inwardness and its resources" and that this formulation, although it "is presented somewhat unsubtly," is nevertheless "the germ of what will be one of the most fascinating aspects of the 'Ibsen heroine,' the inhabitant of an inward psychic realm as impressive as the external world from which she is excluded to such a great extent."

Despite its importance as a step in Ibsen's career, the frequent success of its poetic devices in compensating for dramatic weaknesses, and its genuinely strong and pleasurable verse, *The Burial Mound* is ultimately not a good play. The basic problem is the utter implausibility of its "wildly romantic" scenario. And the first version of the play compounds this problem in two ways. One of these is Ibsen's putting too much emphasis on the poetic devices and thereby failing, even more thoroughly than in *Catiline*, to move its scenario toward at least imaginative plausibility by adequately developing the action and characters. The action proceeds abruptly and with virtually no concessions to the requirement of convincing us that it has to take place, as the characters do what they do more in obedience to the necessities of the scenario than in response to any clearly defined motivations of their own. None of them shows much trace of human individuality or psychology or possesses any substance beyond the trait or two relevant to his or her function; they are not even convincingly present—in the sense that we can witness their actually experiencing what supposedly happens to them. Some of the characters, like Asgaut and Hemming, are little more than embodiments of the theme; others, like Jostein and Hrolloug (the only Vikings with names aside from Gandalf, Asgaut, and Hemming) are mere labelled entities. Further compounding the basic flaw of the weak scenario, Ibsen displays little sense of proper and effective pacing in rendering its individual sequences into units of representation. By line 469, when Blanka declares, "All ends in gentle reconciliation," the play's action has been exhausted: Bernhard has revealed his true identity, Gandalf need no longer sacrifice himself to uphold his vow, and he and Blanka can unite and proceed on their way to transform the North. And yet the play continues for another 141 lines, almost a quarter of its full length. Some of what follows Blanka's line, such as Bernhard-Audun's long narrative of how he survived and was converted, is wholly anti-climactic, and most of the other sequences are made to seem so by Ibsen's drawing them out well beyond the length that any importance they may have can appropriately justify.

It has to be stressed, however, that this double compounding of the basic flaw is true only of the play in its original form. Ibsen completely eliminated these further weaknesses in its second version by carrying out what must, all in all, be called a brilliant act of revision.

The Revised Version

In discussing Ibsen's revision of The Burial Mound, Koht (I, 96) points out the virtual elimination of Oehlenschläger's characteristic diction, and he and other commentators have also stressed two further changes. Ibsen has been reading the Old Norse sources (in a Danish modernization), and this has freed him from dependency on Oehlenschläger for his knowledge of Viking lore; as a result, the revised version has fewer mythological allusions and, in their place, some attempt to capture the specifics of Viking experience.[12] The second change involves what Johnston describes as sharpening and clarifying the play's "dialectical thrust" (54). Ibsen moves the locale from Normandy to an island near Sicily, thus heightening the north-south polarity. The ruins of an ancient temple have been added to the setting, and the revised play opens with a new monologue by Blanka, in which she focuses on the statues of the ancient gods as an indication of the South's decadence. Her monologue as a whole puts at the head of the play a sharpened contrast between northern vitality and southern weakness, and throughout the revised version numerous passages allude to the poisonous nature of the southern air and over-all "atmosphere," thus apparently producing the appeal to contemporary vulgar taste that prompted McFarlane to find the revised version so loathsome. What has not been pointed out is that the complaints about the South's "poison" stem entirely from the Viking visitors, and at the end only Asgaut—the one Viking who remains impervious to the changes taking place—continues to make them. Furthermore, the ancient gods form no part of Christianity, the primary element of the South in Ibsen's scheme, and—despite Blanka's reason for introducing them—the actual purpose of their being mentioned at the beginning may well be Ibsen's trying to prepare for the ending by establishing transitions from one era to another as a fundamental fact of human reality.

I am astonished that the commentators, despite glances at improved characterization and better management of the action, have paid so little attention to the most impressive results of the 1853 revision.[13] The scenario of the play remains the same, but its details have been thoroughly transformed. Less than fifty of the original version's 610 lines survive, even in changed form, and that figure includes its five opening lines and its last fourteen. The first half of the play (up to the return of the Vikings with Bernhard/Roderik in tow) is nearly one and a half times longer in the revised version (489 lines to 323). More surprisingly, the second half of the play (not counting the retained final fourteen lines) is considerably briefer in the revised version (154 lines to 273), while nothing of significance is omitted and much is added. But my dry statistics merely hint at the full effect of this thorough revision, which results in a more gradual, more plausible, more believable (not the same thing), and better-paced action, fuller and richer characterizations (part of and necessary to the improvement in the action), and, as a dimension of the improved characterizations, the endowing to some extent of some of the characters with genuine human voices.

These changes, extensive as they are, could not save the play—what did Ibsen say later about torpedoing the ark?—but they vastly improved it. They deserve careful examination, not only for what they show about the greater richness of the revised version of *The Burial Mound* but also for their indication of how rapidly and in exactly what ways Ibsen's art was advancing when he made them—including his having emerged from his phase of writing dramatic poems, as in *Catiline* and the original version of *The Burial Mound*, to begin to produce the kind of genuine drama he was to write for the rest of his career. And since demonstrations of artistic growth as extreme as this one are rare, the changes Ibsen made in revising *The Burial Mound* are also of interest for what they reveal about the process in general. The exact nature of these changes is especially evident in the sequence from the entrance of the Vikings to the end of Gandalf's scene with Blanka, although I shall also make some additional observations about changes in the play's long concluding episode.

The section of the play from the entrance of the Vikings to the return of Blanka has been nearly doubled in length (from 77 lines to 143), as Ibsen works carefully to give his Vikings fuller and richer characterizations. In the first version, Jostein and Hrolloug speak once each, a half-line apiece, and what they say sounds no different than the half-line assigned to the generic "The Warriors." In the second, Jostein speaks six times and Hrolloug five, much of it substantive: they ask why they are made to trudge about the island like fools; they assure Gandalf that although they swore allegiance to him as their king they joined him for his sea warfare in order to win fame and glory and gold and treasure; they are taken by surprise when they learn that the present purpose is to avenge their former king, Gandalf's father, but even after hearing the details of the earlier raid they manage one more protest before saying that since they are here they may as well contribute to raising a worthy monument for the dead king. I lump them together in this account of what "they" say because there is still something generic about them: they make the same complaints, and if anything differentiates them it is only that Hrolloug more frequently echoes Jostein than the other way around. As the brief speeches assigned to "Several" and "Some" indicate, they also seem to be speaking for the Viking troop as a whole.

While giving these two their first traces of even minimal life, Ibsen also deepens and enriches the characterization of Asgaut. The first version distinguishes Asgaut from the other Vikings by making him clearly in charge of them under Gandalf's leadership; his primary trait is the single-mindedness with which he concentrates on taking revenge the instant it proves possible. In the second version, he is more fully in charge (in ways that I will soon define); he has the opportunity to narrate the aftermath of the earlier raid; in a bitter undertone he characterizes Jostein and Hrolloug as "Wretched lot!"; and when Hemming objects to Gandalf's swearing by the northern gods here in these woods, Asgaut introduces a motif new to this version by asking, "Has the South's plaguy air touched you as well?" Most important of all, when the other Vikings leave him and Gandalf alone, he laments the "musty times" they live in, the fact that their faith and ancient customs are running downhill. Then, after rejoicing that he is old and will not have to witness the North's collapse, he reminds Gandalf that *he* is young and must remember that "it's a kingly deed / To keep your people's gods and strength from fading!"

These enrichments of characterization are significant in themselves, but they are even more important for what they contribute to the major example of character enrichment in this episode, that of Gandalf. The Gandalf of the first version is completely sure of himself and his purpose. He is the first to speak, and his statement of why they have come and his vow take up the first 32 of the episode's 77 lines. Noticing the mound momentarily distracts him, as he wonders if it is his father's grave, but he quickly returns to the issue at hand. If he ever shows even the slightest slackening of purpose, it is at the end of this section, when Asgaut sees Blanka approaching: for Gandalf she is "A woman fair as Freya!", and when Asgaut urges that she be "the first of our revenge's victims," Gandalf briefly expresses hesitation before recalling his vow. In the second version, Gandalf is radically transformed; his "project" throughout the episode is an attempt to seize a control that he does not have and that he can never grasp except momentarily. His lack of control is evident as early as the opening line, for it is Asgaut who speaks first, announcing that they are close to "the place," while Gandalf's initial words suggest his subordination to Asgaut's authority: "Where? let's see!" But Asgaut, confirming his authority, replies, "No, wait a bit till we're beyond the woods."

At this point Jostein and Hrolloug interpose their complaints about wasting their time on this island, and Gandalf summarily orders them to shut up and blindly obey their king's commands—an assertion of authority that is betrayed by its excessiveness and arbitrariness. He then shows some self-possession by joking with Asgaut about his and the other warriors' having done too good a job of cleaning house on the preceding visit: "You might, I would suggest, have left a little / For me and my revenge!" But his establishing of his agenda by this means falls on deaf ears: instead of shutting up as ordered, Hrolloug and Jostein insist on making clear their own purpose for joining Gandalf on his raids, and the other Vikings echo them. So Gandalf changes his tactics; he explains why they are there by referring to the ancient Viking custom of taking blood vengeance when a kinsman has been slain by enemy hands and his corpse lies unburied, and he piques their interest with his abrupt announcement, "You have a king to avenge, and I a father." Their aroused curiosity gives him firm control of the moment, and he produces his first lengthy speech of the episode, a detailed account of what happened on the earlier raid. The speech is also important in another respect. In contrast to the first version, in which we learn all the salient facts of the raid from Bernhard in a passage of unmotivated exposition during the opening episode, Gandalf's narrative—the revised version's first detailed account of the raid—comes only after Ibsen has piqued *our* curiosity through oblique and cryptic references to it by Blanka and in the earlier speeches of this episode. In this, as well as in the episode's characterization of Gandalf, Ibsen—for the first time in his dramatic career—is working *obliquely*, conveying his information not directly through assigned reports but indirectly through plausible and motivated speeches and interactions.

Through his account, Gandalf has appropriated authority from Asgaut, the only one of the Vikings who had been present on the earlier raid. Now Asgaut repossesses authority by telling what he did after the raid: how he searched for Gandalf, finally located him, told him what had happened, and thus occasioned Gandalf's swearing by all Valhalla's gods to take blood vengeance—significantly, in this version it is Asgaut who first mentions Gandalf's vow. Their curiosity apparently satisfied, Jostein and Hrolloug renew their protests: if they had been Gandalf, they would have stayed in Velskland, where gold and glory were to be won. This time Gandalf tries sarcasm—"And that's your loyalty to the fallen king?"—and the two Vikings finally agree to join the pursuit of vengeance, but only, as they make clear, because they decide to do so on their own. Now Gandalf can give his first effective order, as he sends the Vikings to reconnoiter, to which he adds the second half of his vow: "For yet tonight revenge shall be accomplished, / If not, then I must fall myself." This moment is diluted, however, by Asgaut's adding, "He swore it," and by Hemming's interrupting Gandalf, as he is about to repeat his vow, to object to his swearing by his northern gods here in the south.[14] It is, moreover, Asgaut, not Gandalf, who first responds to Hemming's objection, but then Gandalf, apparently finding Hemming easier to manage than the others, silences him with a long speech. He emphasizes Hemming's subordinate position—he was brought along only so that he could sing about Gandalf's exploits in the long winter evenings—and concludes by telling him to throw away his harp and put on a monk's cowl; King Gandalf will get himself a skillful singer. This is Gandalf's most impressive display of authority in the episode. It is immediately followed by Asgaut's stressing to Gandalf that he must assume his kingly obligations.

I have focused on characterization in my analysis of this episode, but it should also be noted that the improvements in characterization are ultimately in the service of better management of the action. By establishing Gandalf as a Viking king unsure of himself and uneasy with the authority that he cannot take full possession of, Ibsen makes him ripe for something to happen to him, better preparing us for the momentous change that is to occur in his upcoming scene with Blanka. The enhanced characterizations of Asgaut, Jostein, and Hrolloug—even Hemming's account of his experience in Velskland—provide the context for this momentous change (as well as for the entire drift of the play) by indicating that the Viking ways are already crumbling, making room for something new to take their place.

The final speech of this section, Gandalf's monologue, constitutes the single most significant addition to the revised version. Its relevance to what I have already said about the section is obvious, for as Gandalf begins he makes explicit Asgaut's authority over him and his uneasiness with this, and as he continues he indicates his awareness of the decline in Viking ways and shows his own openness to the attractions of the South and to experiences quite different from the Viking warrior values. I find this monologue most interesting, however, for how it sounds, for its conveying a necessary quality of any truly full and rich characterization in drama, the sense of a genuine human voice, one that is speaking spontaneously. To show this clearly about the speech, it will be helpful to glance first at Ibsen's practice in *Catiline* and the first version of *The Burial Mound*. The speeches of these two plays—with their end-stopping and the tendency of the characters to *sound* alike, however much they may be differentiated by their individual concerns and the imagery they favor—are consistently formal, and the formality is often made especially extreme by rhyme and the other conventions of the dramatic poem that call attention to the dramatist's controlling hand.[15] Furthermore, although changes occur in the plot and presumably to the characters, we are never allowed to actually witness something happening to the characters. Instead, we learn about it from their speeches, which are reports of fully processed material, even when the report supposedly pertains to something that is going on within the character at that very moment. Gandalf's speech in the original version of *The Burial Mound* about his being deeply affected by Blanka's talk of spiritual combat (quoted in the preceding section of this introduction) is wholly typical in this respect.

To replace this kind of formal reporting, Ibsen first had to clear the ground. Perhaps the most fundamental change in the revised version of *The Burial Mound* is the displacement of lyrical and poetic heightening from the moments of high drama to the margins of the play, to the beginning and the end and to a single passage in the middle when, in a new interlude breaking her episode with Gandalf into two scenes, Blanka sums up in rhyming verse what we have already seen happening to her. But, as Gandalf's monologue shows, clearing the ground was only the beginning. Gandalf goes through a great deal in this speech, and there is little, if any, sense of a formal report. We hear a speaker actually experiencing what he is talking about and can thus accept it—and him—as a convincing representation of human behavior. Several qualities of the monologue contribute importantly to this effect. The verse flows more freely than ever before in Ibsen's drama. More than one passage runs on for several lines—in contrast to Ibsen's earlier practice of having his characters speak in one- or two-line units—and, wherever end-stopping does occur, it coincides with natural pauses in the progression of Gandalf's discourse. The shift from topic to topic reflects the activity of a mind in motion. Sometimes the shifts respond to external stimuli, such as the scent of the grove, the burial mound, and the beauty of the place, and it is clear that Gandalf is noticing these things *as* he reacts to them. Sometimes the shifts respond to internal stimuli—the memories of his father's courtyard and of his boyhood—the existence of which is indicated only by the responses.[16]

The sense of a real speaker actually experiencing something is reinforced by the frequent exclamations and questions, the self-interruptions, and the modulation to a colloquial level of speech in "Well, I'll head homeward! Save whatever still / Is savable before it all collapses." The exclamation "A burial mound here in the South!" brings the mound to life in Gandalf's mind for a second time and thus modifies what has been developing into an almost formal pattern of exclamation or question followed by appropriate reflection. The link between the beauty of the southern grove and the father's joking remark about Freya is especially interesting because it is only partially defined. Gandalf is not simply remembering, he is also—without in any way explicitly calling attention to it—performing the additional act of beginning to understand something about his memory that he could not grasp when the remembered event occurred. It is clear, moreover, that he does not as yet fully understand it, and we believe in his reality all the more because of the limitation he shows in not fully grasping an implication that is clearer to us than to him.

The episode between Gandalf and Blanka, which follows immediately, applies the accomplishments of the monologue to the more difficult form of interaction in dialogue between two characters. The episode is only 36 lines longer than its counterpart in the original version (217 vs. 181), but Ibsen has already begun his process of vastly reducing material in the original version, here eliminating the characters' lengthy formal representations of their conflicting ideologies and Gandalf's detailed accounts of what is going on inside him, so that, in reality, the episode is expanded far more than the line count would seem to indicate. Some of this expansion results from additional material designed to render the linking up of Blanka and Gandalf and the transformation of Gandalf more plausible. Blanka's scene with her foster father has already emphasized her yearning for the Viking north; in this episode, her opening monologue, which Gandalf overhears, concludes with a bit of self-dramatization in which she imagines herself as a young northern bride welcoming her Viking hero back from a sea voyage, and later she urges Gandalf, playfully as it turns out, to take her North with him, so that she can bring mirth to his hall, even volunteering to become his skald. Ibsen also has her describe for Gandalf, without her yet knowing who he is, the earlier Viking raid, thus giving him an opportunity to experience his Viking values in all their brutality and horror from the victims' point of view.[17] Most of the expansion, however, is devoted to making the movement of the episode more gradual, more uncertain, more true to experience. The distribution of the speeches in relation to the verse lines, the varying tones of the speeches, the jokes, the questions and exclamations, the occasional cryptic references and moments of unpredictability, the frequent breakdowns in communication—all contribute to creating the kind of interchange we might expect from two people meeting for the first time and under such unusual circumstances.

To illustrate this briefly presents a problem, for there are so many good moments to choose from, including Gandalf's halting attempts to find out if she knows who the raiders were without inadvertently revealing it, while she continues to misunderstand him,[18] and her sudden cutting off of his outraged rejection of her faith (before knowing much about it) with "O, take me with you there!" But I choose a passage for which there is no counterpart in the original version—oddly enough—an interchange that makes clear they are beginning to respond to one another romantically. Blanka is talking, obliquely, about her dream of being a Viking bride when she is forced to break off abruptly because of something more immediate: "You look at me so stiffly." Gandalf's response ("Do I?") is of an uncertain tone; he is either trying to conceal his feelings or he is genuinely unaware of his action. Blanka pursues the matter with "Indeed, what are you thinking of?" and his response ("I? Nothing.") indicates that now, at least, concealment is his aim. Her repetition of his word ("Oh?— nothing?") may be expressed skeptically or may merely be her way of prompting him to keep talking. At any rate, he continues, at first stumblingly as he says he does not himself know only to correct that immediately with "But yes, I know," then fluently as he tells her that thinking about her wish to plant her southern flowers in the North makes him recall his own faith. Then he adds: "There is / A saying in it that I couldn't grasp / Before; but now you've taught me how to do so."

Blanka's "What do you mean?" is not at all the kind of empty question Ibsen had frequently used to interrupt an otherwise continuous account so that the second character on the stage might be given something to say; it suggests that Gandalf has stopped, apparently reluctant to go on, and that Blanka wants him to continue, partly because she genuinely has no way of knowing what he means, partly because she wants to hear more. The prompting works, for Gandalf continues:

> It's said Valfader gets
> A half-part only of the fallen warriors;
> The other half of them belongs to Freya.
> I never could quite rightly understand that;
> But now—I grasp it now—I am myself
> A fallen warrior, and my better half
> Is Freya's property.

We understand this far better than Blanka can—which means that we understand much more than the words explicitly convey. We relate what he says to his recollection concerning Freya in his monologue and realize that his understanding of that recollection continues to grow. We also realize that he is trying to tell Blanka that he has become attracted to her but can do so only through this indirect and cryptic means. Blanka now asks another question, not unlike her preceding one: "What does *that* mean?" But, according to the stage direction, she is "startled" by what he has said, so that either his words completely bewilder her or, more likely, she *has* grasped something of what he means, in which case her question does not convey what *she* really means: it is either a way of putting distance between herself and what he is saying or a demand for him to go on.

Gandalf apparently assumes the latter and is encouraged by it; if not, it is his own desire that forces him to proceed, for he tries to speak more clearly: "Well, in plain terms, I am—" Here, however, she "quickly" cuts him off with "No, let it be!", adding that she dare not tarry longer because her father is waiting for her, and she tries to close their conversation with an abrupt "Farewell!" Her motive is obviously quite different from what she expresses; it is clear that she has grasped his meaning and is not prepared to deal with it. Now it is Gandalf's turn to be disconcerted; all he can manage is "You're going?", but we can imagine several different feelings pointed to but left unexpressed in his simple question. Blanka's answer is to pick up the oakleaf garland she has brought with her and toss it on his helmet as she says, "There you are, and you can keep it. / What formerly I gave you in my dreams / I give you now that I'm awake." Because it avoids direct expression in favor of allusion to the content of her dream, Blanka's answer resembles Gandalf's speech about being Freya's property; but while Gandalf could suspect that Blanka would not understand the allusion to his northern religion, Blanka knows that Gandalf has overheard her acting out the part of her dream on which *her* allusion depends: she is, in other words, deliberately indicating that his feelings are reciprocated. Now it is Gandalf's turn to say "Farewell!" abruptly, and he backs it up by quickly leaving. It is possible that Ibsen merely wants to get him off the stage for Blanka's lyrical interlude summing up her feelings, but, given the careful and intricate drama that has led up to it, it is more likely that we are supposed to understand his quick exit as an indication that he, too, is unprepared to deal with the momentous thing that is happening to him.

The revisions in the second half of the play include further additions to the characterizations of Asgaut, Jostein, and Hrolloug and further material on the tenuousness of the Viking faith and warrior values, but, as I have said, these revisions are most noteworthy for the consistency with which Ibsen compresses speeches without eliminating them. Generally speaking, moreover, this compression produces the kinds of results I have tried to demonstrate in my foregoing analyses—that is, the speakers sound more like real people, they experience what is happening to them rather than merely providing reports of having experienced it, and their words tend to convey far more than what they explicitly express.

The last of these effects deserves further comment, because one of the means by which it is achieved—verbal repetition—especially indicates how fully Ibsen has discovered his mature dramatic voice in revising *The Burial Mound*. The Ibsen of *Catiline* and the original version of *The Burial Mound* was aware of the dramatic value of repetition, but in those plays his norm—in keeping with the extreme explicitness of his style—is to repeat whole lines, complete with oral and/or actual quotation marks (as in the repetition first by Asgaut and then by Gandalf of Gandalf's vow to get revenge or fall himself just when his transformation makes it impossible for him to kill Bernhard), or of key words that have been virtually "flagged" for future reference (such as "reconciliation," a word that Gandalf has indelibly burned into our memory by making such an explicit show of failing to understand it the first time Blanka uses it). The repetitions in the revision of *The Burial Mound* are of a subtler kind, similar to, but more abundant and, all in all, more resonant than, the unconscious echoes spoken by some of the characters of *Catiline* (and discussed in my introduction to that play). These repetitions, suddenly linking the present context to an earlier one and with enough of a twist to let loose a flood of meaning, exemplify the kind of verbal repetition that constitutes one of the hallmarks of Ibsen's mature style. I have already discussed one case of this, Gandalf's second reference to Freya, which in recalling the first dramatizes for us not only his feelings for Blanka but also the fact that he is undergoing a continuing development of his understanding of human experience.

The second half of the revised version contains three further examples worthy of attention. When Gandalf says he cannot take vengeance against Roderik, Asgaut's response ("Is our chief a coward?") associates Gandalf with the term Gandalf had used to disparage Blanka's faith at her first mention of it and thus inadvertently suggests what may be going on in Gandalf's mind to help cause his hesitation. Later, as Gandalf explains to Blanka why his oath requires him to die, his words ("It was my call / As king to keep our warrior life safeguarded") echo Asgaut's admonition to him just prior to his monologue and indicate that he has internalized it; in this version, apparently, his transformation is a complex maturation that gives him full commitment to the Viking ideals only when he is already moving in another direction. The last example is also the richest. Hemming's conclusion to his speech about staying with Roderik-Rørek, "Farewell, my king! / Now you have found yourself a better skald," refers to Blanka and recalls both Gandalf's angry dismissal of Hemming and Blanka's joke about becoming Gandalf's skald. By evoking not only the change from one skald to another but also the altered function of the skald necessarily accompanying the change in personnel, this repetition condenses into a single conceit the thoroughgoing transformation in northern life that is the theme of the play.

The plays Ibsen worked on between the first and second versions of *The Burial Mound* provide some precedents for the advancement in his art demonstrated by the revision. In the fragment *The Grouse in Justedal* (1850), which he abandoned somewhere in the second act, Ibsen experimented with his early dramatic style by introducing a couple of scenes in prose and—more important—by associating rhyming verse only with his mysterious, seemingly supernatural characters; the norm of the fragment, as a result, is a more relaxed and somewhat more flexible blank verse. The introduction of prose is apparently to make possible the creation of a character with a highly distinctive voice—the mead-loving Parson Mogens—an achievement Ibsen developed much more fully with the often-admired Julian Poulsen of the mainly prose play *St. John's Night* (written in 1852). The distinctiveness of their voices is entirely a matter of idiom, however, for both characters consistently reprocess whatever they experience into the terms of their customary stances; they do not, in other words, actually experience anything. *St. John's Night* more effectively anticipates the revision of *The Burial Mound* in a couple of monologues by Birk and, especially, the moment late in the play when Birk and Anne realize they love one another, all of them passages in which something immediate and unmediated is happening.

These precedents and, above all, the revision of *The Burial Mound* make clear how much Ibsen was learning from his exposure to performed drama in Christiania, Bergen, and particularly (during his study tour in 1852) Copenhagen and Dresden, where the offerings were better than what he was accustomed to in Norway and included considerable Shakespeare. The plays Ibsen wrote for the next several years after revising *The Burial Mound* do not consistently match or further advance the achievements in the revision, but these achievements provided him with a springboard for both the three masterpieces of verse drama he was still to write (*Love's Comedy*, *Brand*, and *Peer Gynt*) and the even more subtle dramatic effects he was to produce in the long string of prose dramas from *The Vikings at Helgeland* to *When We Dead Awaken*. In terms of the focus of this book, *The Feast at Solhaug* (1856) and, to a lesser extent, *Olaf Liljekrauns* (1857)—with their ballads, authentic and imitated, and their frequent shifts from prose to passages in rhyming verse— approximate the dramatic poem; but for all intents and purposes the revision of *The Burial Mound* also marks Ibsen's liberating himself from the conventions of this form. He did not soon abandon rhyme, as his three later masterpieces of verse drama amply attest, but in them rhyming is not a substitute used to heighten (or create) the moments of high drama; it is intrinsic to their very medium, and its effects are consistently dramatic as well as poetic.

This Translation

The translations of the two versions of *The Burial Mound* by James Walter McFarlane do not reproduce the rhymes of the original texts, and their verse is often disappointingly limp. Anders Orbeck's translation of the revised version reproduces the rhymes and renders the lines into effective verse, so that it conveys a good sense of the experience provided by Ibsen's original, although, as in his translation of the second version of *Catiline*, Orbeck is inclined far too much toward inappropriate archaizing.

In my translations of the two versions of *The Burial Mound*, I have reproduced the rhymes, and in both versions I have been far more successful than in my translations of *Catiline* in also reproducing Ibsen's alternating of masculine and feminine endings in the rhyming passages. A few lines of the first version of *The Burial Mound* have twelve syllables rather than ten, and I have rendered my translations of these lines accordingly. Where applicable, I have translated the second version of the play as a revision of the first. Drawing on the prompt book from the Christiania Theater, I have occasionally corrected the punctuation of the first version as it is given in the Hundreårsutgave. Drawing on the prompt book from the Norwegian Theater in Bergen and the printed text that appeared in the *Bergenske Blade*, I have much more frequently altered the punctuation of the revised version as it is given in the Hundreårsutgave; this text is based on the text in the

Bergenske Blade, but, for reasons that are unclear, its punctuation often differs from that found in any of the original texts. On a few rare occasions, where the original texts of the revised version have punctuation out of keeping with today's conventions, I have normalized it.

Notes to Introduction to *The Burial Mound*

1. Hundreårsutgave, Vol. XVI (1940), p. 28. The content of the play in its final form suggests that its original title was a reference to the Vikings who had conquered Normandy in the tenth century. "The Normans" survives only in its revision as *The Burial Mound*, and it seems unlikely that we will ever know what Ibsen had in mind by the "more extensive idea"; however, Samuel G. McLellan has speculated about this in "Ibsen's Expanded Idea in Kjæmpehøien," *Edda*, 82 (1982), 273–80.

2. The information about the sizes of the audiences and of Christiania's population in 1850 is provided by Roderick Rudler, "Kjæmpehøien—og Ibsens første teaterstudier," *Edda*, 81 (1981), 297. Rudler describes this number of performances under the given conditions as merely a "*success d'estime.*"

3. Rudler notes (295) that contrary to the usual notion that these were the only two reviews of *The Burial Mound*, it was also reviewed in *Morgenbladet*, on September 28. I have not seen this review, and Rudler indicates nothing about its view of the play, but the two reviews I have quoted from should be sufficient to give a good representation of the play's immediate reception by the reviewers.

4. English translations of the contract are in Meyer (68) and in McFarlane's "Appendix III, *The Burial Mound*: Commentary," in Volume I of the Oxford *Ibsen* (605).

5. The play was evidently reviewed by the *Bergenske Blade* in its first issue for 1854, but I have not been able to see a copy of this review nor are its contents indicated by any of the commentators on the play.

6. The prompt book is now in the holdings of the University of Oslo library. Its text also survives, in virtually the same form, in the individual acting parts prepared for the actors who played the roles in 1854; these are in the holdings of the library of the Theater Museum in Bergen.

7. Hundreårsutgave, Vol. XVIII (1939), p. 406.

8. *An Ibsen Companion* (Westport, CT: Greenwood Press, 1984), p. 46.

9. McLellan provides a fairly detailed account of the Oehlenschläger plays, scenes, and character types that Ibsen drew on in writing *The Burial Mound*.

10. The resemblance—chiefly that of the father and daughter living alone on their otherwise deserted coast and visited by a group with an important connection to their past—may well be purely coincidental insofar as the first version is concerned. It may be purely coincidental insofar as the revised version is concerned as well, but by the time he revised *The Burial Mound* Ibsen had very definitely established an acquaintanceship with Shakespeare, having seen several of his plays on a study trip he took in 1852 to Copenhagen, Dresden, Hamburg, and perhaps Berlin. Between that trip and revising *The Burial Mound*, he had, arguably, borrowed from *A Midsummer Night's Dream* in writing *St. John's Night* in 1852, and he was to echo Shakespeare extensively in writing *Lady Inger of Østråt* in 1854. Given the importance Shakespeare was assuming for Ibsen, it

is likely that he increased his knowledge by reading translations of plays he had not had an opportunity to see. It is also possible, therefore, that knowledge of *The Tempest* was in part responsible for prompting him to move the location of *The Burial Mound* in its revised version from the coast of Normandy to a small island in the Mediterranean Sea. And it is also possible that certain passages in this version that seem to echo *The Tempest* are more than merely further coincidences. I am thinking particularly of two passages. One is Blanka's reply when the awed Gandalf praises her as "certainly the fairest [child] on this island"—"The fairest? Yes, that is quite possible; / For no one else is here"— which resembles the frequent witty play in *The Tempest* on the uniqueness of the island's few inhabitants. The other passage comes at the end of the final speech by Blanka's foster father as he blesses the union between Blanka and Gandalf: "You are the children of the coming dawn,— / Go thither where the royal throne awaits you; / I am the last one of the vanished times, / My throne is now the grave—o grant me it!"—which, though the plot circumstances differ, expresses an incisive finality similar to that in Prospero's penultimate speech: "And in the morn / I'll bring you to your ship, and so to Naples, / Where I have hope to see the nuptial / Of these our dear belov'd solemnized, / And thence retire me to my Milan, where / Every third thought shall be my grave" (V.i.307–12; I quote from *The Riverside Shakespeare*, ed. G. Blakemore Evans, et. al. (Boston: Houghton Mifflin, 1974).

11. In the first version, Bernhard-Audun uses the word in urging Blanka to "guard the precious call / That god assigned to woman's lot on earth, / Plant southern flowers in the spruce-tree's halls, / Spread truth's mild, soothing light throughout the North!" In the second version, Gandalf uses it in speaking about his own "call / As king to keep our warrior life safeguarded."

12. The change of Bernhard-Audun's name to Roderik-Rørek is usually seen to be an example of Ibsen's more authentic knowledge of the historical milieu he is trying to dramatize. Meyer (113) thinks that the reduction in the "mythological apparatus" occurs to "the play's detriment," and one would have to agree with him if the second version was the same kind of work as the first—i.e., a dramatic poem.

13. Bryan's brief summary of these results (50) is typical, except that it is more extensive than most such discussions: "A comparison of the two versions of the play shows that Ibsen learned much about dramaturgy between 1850 and 1854. Despite several problems of chronology, the second version is the more theatrically sound. The 1854 characterizations . . . are more strongly motivated and thus are rendered more probable than those in the script of 1850." The "problems of chronology" Bryan refers to stem from Ibsen's decision to change the prior Viking raid from ten years in the past to "three years ago" about halfway through the revised version and neglecting to alter all the time references. I discuss this issue in a note to my translation of the revised version.

14. Hemming's similar objection in the first version has no particular dramatic effect and could be removed without there being any indication that something is missing. His reason for the objection in the first version is far from clear, but in the revised version he explains why he urges Gandalf not to swear by his northern gods here in the South: "In Velskland I have heard the pious priests /

Speaking delightfully of the white Christ, / And what they said still hovers in my mind / By night and day, it will not disappear." This addition enriches the characterization of Hemming by giving him some motivation. It also provides some preparation for his decision to remain with Rørek at the end of the play; in the first version, Hemming had to explain his decision as he pronounces it by reporting that "this hour has deeply stirred my soul," a development that Ibsen has left to the actor to convey during the preceding action by whatever means he can manage to muster.

15. This generalization must be slightly qualified for *Catiline* by acknowledging that Cethegus and Manlius have somewhat distinctive voices and that the brief opening section of Act Three with Manlius and Statilius, Manlius' monologue, and his following interchange with Catiline moves toward human-sounding speech—after which Catiline narrates his dream in thirteen- and fifteen-syllable rhyming verse in trochaic meter!

16. The one possible false note in this monologue is the overly explicit "It calls to mind" (literally, "I have to think about") introducing the memory of sitting on his father's knee. The characterization of Gandalf in the revised version of *The Burial Mound* is also discussed by A. M. Sturtevant in "*Kjæmpehøien* and its Relation to Ibsen's Romantic Works," *JEGP*, 12 (1913), 407–24; but Sturtevant is concerned only with Gandalf's character traits, particularly his possessing qualities appropriate for a conversion to Christianity.

17. This speech corresponds to Bernhard-Audun's account, from the original version, of Blanka's saving his life and inculcating him with Christianity. There it occurs after he has revealed his identity and seriously retards the pace of an action that is rapidly working out its resolution. It is the only passage that, in effect, Ibsen moved from the second half of the play to the first in altering the relative lengths of the two halves. In moving it, he eliminated a long anticlimactic passage from his final episode and gave the material it includes an opportunity to have a dramatic rather than a purely narrative effect. Incidentally, another important change in the revision, which I do not discuss in the text, is Ibsen's attempt to make Bernhard/Roderik's history a bit more plausible. In the original version, Bernhard has concealed his identity from Blanka, but he does not disguise the fact that he is a Viking and presumably a member of the earlier raiding party, although this does not seem to bother Blanka. In the revised version, he has a better "cover." It is not entirely clear, but he has told Blanka that he came to the island on a merchant ship at the same time as the Viking raid and fought against the raiders on her father's side. Other references suggest that he has also told her he is from Normandy and thus once removed from his earlier Viking past. In other words, he is for her a good Viking, who can inspire her with love for the North, without in any way being implicated by the cruel marauders who murdered her father and all the other inhabitants of her island.

18. In the original version, Gandalf identifies himself to her almost at once as a Viking "fuming for revenge."

The Burial Mound

(1850)

Dramatic Poem in One Act

by

Brynjolf Bjarme
[Henrik Ibsen]

BERNHARD, an old hermit.

BLANKA, his foster daughter.

GANDALF, viking chieftain from Norway.

ASGAUT, an old warrior.

HEMMING, Gandalf's skald.

JOSTEIN, standard bearer.

HROLLOUG together with other Vikings.

The action takes place on the coast of Normandy, at that time called Valland, before the introduction of Christianity in Scandinavia.—

A wooded area near the sea, which can be glimpsed in the background between the trees. In the middle of the stage a burial mound with a stone monument; in front of the mound a little moss-covered altar, upon which is a cross decked with flowers. The roof of a cottage can be seen through the foliage.

Under a tree in the foreground BERNHARD *sits writing on a roll of parchment; by his side* BLANKA *stands deep in thought. It is evening.*

BERNHARD

(*writing*)

"Then it is said,—when Ragnarok has calmed
The savage forces, called forth purer life,
Alfader, Balder, and the gentle Freya[1]
Shall govern all the clans in peace once more."
            (*laying the parchment aside and getting up*)
But, Blanka! look, you're lost in dreams again.
You're bored by these old sagas telling of
The northern people, whom you've never known;
You'd rather lose yourself in your own world;
It must be so,—yes, that's what I do, too,
I love these ancient memories of the past,
From when I wandered far and wide throughout
The northern seas, mid Thule's barren mountains;
I stored within my memory every song
From the skald's lips,—the exploits of the clans
From dim but lovely ancient days of yore,
And can no longer tear them from my soul.
Now that I've settled down in peace and quiet
On Valland's shore, they're doubly dear to me;

407

For when I write them down, it seems to me,—
It's like I'm living through my life once more.

BLANKA

(*gaily*)

You think I'm bored? —No, no, that is not so,—
It was indeed the North that filled my dreams,
Toward it my soul in longing strives to go
With rapid strokes of oars on thought's pure streams.
Your every legend, father! seems so real,
My spirit soars and whirls in restless zeal
Until in fleeting dreams it greets the North.

BERNHARD

You are a little fantasist, my Blanka!
For often when you hear these ancient legends
From the far north, your cheeks glow red,—and you
Almost forget the Valland flowers for them.

BLANKA

(*vehemently*)

Of course, I do,—life in the South can't plead
Its case against the North's heroic flight;
They are as different as the feeble reed
Is from the spruce, which braves the tempest's might!
(*amiably, as she seizes his hand*)

But tell me, why do you become so sad
Reminded of your own life in the North?
It almost seems as if long since you had
Forgotten all your youthful faring-forth!

BERNHARD

(*evasively*)

Don't ask about that, daughter! it's enough
You know I found you as a little girl

Forlorn and helpless when, without rebuff,
A band of Vikings had laid waste the coast.
Your father met his death at their grim hands,
His castle's still there, on that cliff in ruins;
But vengeance paid them for their savage conduct,
Their cruel chieftain fell himself in battle;
But ask no more about the North, my life
Among the people there,—it makes me cross—

BLANKA
(quickly)

Wouldn't you like to see once more the vast
Bright glacier where the flowery meadows part
Up North, from which a music of the past
Still vibrates through the harpstrings of the heart?

BERNHARD

O, do not call these wishes back in me,
But let this yearning slumber in my soul;
For thoughts like these my heart must always flee
If I'm to find repose on Valland's shores,—
But speak no more of it;—I'm taking now
My usual evening ramble through the woods.

BLANKA

I'll go along and where the oak-leaves bow
Above the waves I'll pick some flower buds;—
Then here beside the grave my usual prayer
I'll offer for the dead one's peace and rest;
Soon from the cross the garland, fresh and fair,
With hopeful smiles shall greet the radiant west.
(*They go into the woods.* GANDALF *comes in from the opposite side
followed by the Vikings.*)

GANDALF

So here we stand, prepared for deadly war,
With sword in hand on Valland's verdant shore;
Hither the son has led his sea brigades
Where the father's blood was shed by hostile blades!
Straw-covered cottage roofs rise in the air,
But crimson flames shall soon devour them there,—
We hear the sound of song and evening bells,
At once the woman's joy shall turn to knells,
And the man's song in this still evening pause
Shall turn to death-groans from his speechless jaws!
My father's scattered dust I shall collect,
Garland his urn with leaves that newly decked
The oak's green bough, and for his endless peace
His native soil shall be its final lease!

(He draws his sword.)

The goal is achieved, men!
Vengeance has cleaved, then,
A course through the billowing wave;
Swords are all set to
Bloodily wet through
The earth on the Viking chief's grave!—
Thor and Alfader!
Hear now my promise,
Hear now my oath of true worth;
All that we come on,
Man or else woman,
Bloody shall sink to the earth!
Daylight shall witness
Blood before fading,
Or I shall fall here myself;
If I don't keep the
Oath I have sworn to,
Down with me, gods! into Hel!—[2]

(HEMMING, who hitherto has held back in fear, rushes forward excitedly
with his harp in his hand.)

HEMMING

(*crying out*)

Don't swear revenge by gods of heaven, Gandalf!

GANDALF

(*darkly*)

You, Hemming, here? Why aren't you in the ship?

HEMMING

I couldn't stay,—I must accompany you
Upon your course, like an attendant spirit!

GANDALF

This is no place for skalds—

HEMMING

But listen, Gandalf!
How peaceful is this bright and pleasant shore
Among these beeches and these oaktrees high,—
See how the waves, like mirrors, lie adorned
In golden gleams from Odin's father-eye,
While wood-clad cliffs with calm regard explore
The gentle waves that at their feet divide,
Although no glacier-armor has been formed
Upon the mountain's peak and craggy side!

ASGAUT

(*Approaching, as* HEMMING *goes toward the background*)

Soon Odin will descend to Saga's halls,[3]
And darkness will be spread across the land;
Here it is cool and greensward decks the field,
Here is the place to pitch our nighttime camp!

GANDALF

You're right,—but look, I see a cottage there,
Beneath those treetops—

JOSTEIN

Ha, a splendid find!

HROLLOUG

And those who live there?

GANDALF

Them we'll send to Hel!

THE WARRIORS

Yes, yes, to Hel!

ASGAUT

That's just what shall be done,—
With blood and burning we'll avenge our Audun!
Yet go, you men, and carefully check out
The woods to see that no one has observed us.
(*The Vikings go.* HEMMING *remains standing in the background.*)

GANDALF

Look, here's the place that you have told me of;
On that steep point beside the cliff-top castle
Was where he fell, you said,—its walls long since
Have lain in ruins, ha, but that's a comfort!
(*He notices the burial mound.*)

But look,—what's that I see there!—an illusion?
—No, no, by Odin and by Asathor![4]
A bauta stone[5] sticks up above the mound,
It is an ancient northern warrior grave!

ASGAUT

Yes, so it is,—what if,—impossible!

GANDALF

My father's burial mound, you mean?

ASGAUT

                              No, no!
His corpse the forest birds long since consumed,
His dust has vanished on the nighttime winds!

GANDALF

By mighty Thor I swore the solemn oath,
His murderer would sink before my sword,
If he's still living—

ASGAUT

Someone's coming there.

GANDALF

A woman fair as Freya!

ASGAUT

Well, then let
Her be the first of our revenge's victims.

GANDALF

Am I to kill a woman! Yet my oath
Commands me to—

ASGAUT

That's what you've sworn to, Gandalf!
Wait by this oak here, if it pleases you,
While I go out and bring the warriors back.

(He leaves. BLANKA comes back with her skirt full of flowers; she kneels before the altar in silent prayer, then gets up, hangs a fresh garland on the cross, and strews flowers on the mound.)

BLANKA

Now I have made my Viking raid
Within the flower world's fair realms;
Each little blossom has obeyed
The rule of force, which overwhelms!
How rich my plunder is compared
To gold that blood has dearly snared;
You hero sleeping in this grave,
Why did you plow the ocean's wave,
Why did you harry foreign strands,
And peaceful dwellings burn with brands,—
Why was your lust but might and power,
Why did you leave your mountain bower?
O, had you stayed there,—you might well
An old and happy man still dwell,
While gently peace makes bright and cheers
The snowy winter of your years!
—I still remember well that night
The castle there stood all aflame,
And through the woods and thicket tight,
The sound of swords and deathcries came;
Full often still it seems to me
The battle's raging waves I see,—
When in the deep the sun sinks low
While whispering winds through treetops blow,
It often seems my eyes then scanned
A Viking bold with sword at hand;—
        (becoming aware of GANDALF)

Almighty God!—

GANDALF
(approaching)

414

Fear not, young maid!

BLANKA

Is it a vision dreams conveyed!
A shadow-image that will merely
Dissolve? —O, no, I see it clearly;
You're from the North, a hero, too—

GANDALF

Don't let it, maiden, frighten you!
But why so fairly do you dress
That burial mound with spring's largess?

HEMMING

(interrupting, as he approaches)

Come, Gandalf! come,—beware, that woman there
Is not an earthly maid—

GANDALF

(vehemently)

Get back there, Hemming!
(HEMMING *goes back.*)

BLANKA

Who is that boy?

GANDALF

O, just a hapless skald.
At times he's somewhat lacking his full sense,
But when he takes the harp, and its sound swells
Majestically into a funeral song,
Then he awakens from the quiet dream
In which he wanders silently through life.

BLANKA

(*excitedly*)

The Nordic son then also owns a bosom
With ardent yearnings and with quiet dreams!
O, more and more it seems to me that land
Takes on a glorious magic radiance,
The clearer to my inward glance it grows!
—But say, my hero! won't you rest a bit
Within the cooling shadow of this oak,
Its canopy spreads out so thick and green;
I shall keep watch for you while you're asleep,
And if you're thirsty I shall fetch for you
A sweet refreshing drink from yonder spring
That bubbles clear and cool in the bright grass;—
O, tell me, won't you?—

GANDALF

No,—no, woman! quiet;—
I clearly see your guile,—you want to charm
My breast with wheedling words and soothing speech!
But when a Viking's fuming for revenge,
He can't be lulled to slumber by a woman!

BLANKA

(*smiling*)

You do but jest,—you only want to scare me!
It won't succeed,—I know the Nordic sons!

GANDALF

You know them?

BLANKA

Yes, since long ago I've known them;
My father's told so much that's beautiful,
So many lovely legends of those people.

GANDALF

You're not afraid, then, of the grim-faced warrior?

BLANKA

O no, why should I be? Why, you are strong,
And I'm a woman, vulnerable and weak;
Would heroes so debase themselves to stoop
To violence against defenseless—

GANDALF

Ha!

You use your words ingeniously, fair woman!
But since you do not fear me,—answer this:
Who slumbers there beneath that burial mound?

BLANKA

That only father knows,—but I believe
He was a Viking from the distant North.

GANDALF

He fell, then, in heroic combat;—tell me,
Who raised the mound above him in the woods
On foreign shore and planted little flowers
And decked the hero's grave with a grass carpet?

BLANKA

I decorated it and plant there still
The tender flower shoots at spring's approach;
They thrive there splendidly, look how each leaf
Bows gently, intimately toward the next,
And as if hand in hand they form a circle,
A fence of flowers round the barrow's side,
As if they were protecting the still grave,
Ordaining it a vernal flower-home!

GANDALF

Ha, that is strange,—I cannot understand it;
He came an enemy to plunder you,
He drenched your native land with streams of blood,
He led your relatives as helpless slaves
To distant homes, and yet you decorate
The fallen warrior's grave with flowers, maiden!

BLANKA

Our faith so teaches us, it's one of our
Commandments: in forgiveness reach your hand
Out to your foe, urge reconciliation.

GANDALF

(musing)

What's that? That's not a word I understand,
Yet wait, I do believe I comprehend it;
But what we do is quite a different practice!

BLANKA

What do you do, then?—speak, I'm listening.

GANDALF

When in his bosom
Rancor is blazing,
Boldly the hero
Girds him for strife,
Presses the shining
Steel on his forehead,
Bravely to combat
Aiming his steps.
—Swords then are clanging,
Wounds start to redden,
Widely they're gaping
In the foe's breast.—
—Sooner or later

Follows the other
After to Valhal,
Einherjer's[6] home,
Clasps to his bosom
Kinsmen and comrades,
Greets as a brother
His enemy there!

BLANKA

Yes, that is fine, but I have heard it told
That your Valhalla is a home of strife,
That savage combat is your joy in death,
And after death still even there with Odin.

GANDALF

Well, what is life, indeed, without such strife?
A day without the sun, a warrior lacking honor,
A frozen spring in winter's stunted life,
A listless sleep in Hela's gloomy chambers!

BLANKA
(vehemently)

Indeed, the inner strife and spirit's struggle
And light's resplendent triumph over darkness;
This is the strife that is life's purpose, heathen!
But o, you do not comprehend its meaning!

GANDALF
(reflectively)

No, you are right, I do not grasp your words,—
But feeble lightning bolts gleam in my soul,
And visions stir there that I never saw before.

BLANKA

There is a myth in your religious lore,—

Which father has so often told to me,
The lovely legend about Balder's death.
He wandered confident, by love protected,
And your gods guarded him on every flank;
But evil Loki then his wiles injected,
And Balder all at once to Hela sank.—
—Yet after night the day comes shining bright,—
And Balder hailed the gods' home with delight;
The power of evil, like a leaf, retreated,
The giant's guile divine command defeated!

(with fiery vehemence)

And you've come here, a butcher seeking life,
To leave these peaceful valleys filled with terror!
O, don't you know, then, any better strife
Than that in which the sword's red tongue speaks error?
Is there then not a battlefield more fair,
Where love and faith serve as the arms to gird you,
Where the victory cry is but a humble prayer
And God the leader whom we swear our word to!
Is there no better goal for this long trip,
This Viking raid across life's surging billows,
Than that in which blood clots your weapon's tip,
And the cottage burns among the quiet willows.
Is your heart cold, like the steel round your girth,
And is your breast not great enough to measure
The rich and everlastingly high worth
In the spirit's fair and golden heaven-treasure?
Why don't you take *this* booty as your good
Here from the South up to your wintry bower,
And learn a sense of love and brotherhood,
A better sovereignty than the sword's power!

GANDALF

(vehemently)

Be still! Your speech possesses magic charm,
And now your poison in my breast is churning!
Before my pride lay in my sword and arm,

With Valhal the reward I'd fain be earning;
But now my craving is directed toward
Two different goals,—one goal the hero graces,
The glory carved with blood, sung by the sword,
And borne across the sea to distant places;
But as a further goal now softly floats
From Freya's lofty grove a light that varies,
Accompanied by wondrous harp-string notes
And lovely singing from the mouths of fairies!—
(sadly)

If I've betrayed thus Odin, Asathor,
And all the North's strong, ancient gods so holy,
I'd like to slumber deep in earth therefore,
Where just above the mound the birch droops lowly!—
(*The Vikings come in with* BERNHARD, *with* HEMMING *following them.*)

ASGAUT

Look, Gandalf! what a splendid catch we're bringing!

BLANKA

O God! my father in their cruel hands!

GANDALF

Fear not, young maid!

BERNHARD
(*deeply moved and pointing at* GANDALF)
Is that man there your chief?

JOSTEIN

He is, yes.
(*to* GANDALF)
He can give you word about
Your father's death, he knows some things about it!

BERNHARD

(*moved*)

Are you the son of the Viking who once landed
On this coast many years ago and fell
There where those castle ruins yet are standing?

GANDALF

That's so, old man!

ASGAUT

And he's come here to take

Blood-vengeance.

GANDALF

Quiet! let the old man speak!

BERNHARD

Our life the Lord holds in his fatherly hand,
I do not fear those murdering swords of yours;
But spare at very least this helpless child,
Whose foster-father I so long have been.
Her father also fell in that fierce battle,
He was the aged owner of the castle,
Which your wild hordes came sailing here to plunder!

BLANKA

(*to* GANDALF)

O, you're a son of him who killed my father;
Yet God forgive him!

BERNHARD

O behold, *this* vengeance
Is magnanimity's, you savage heathens!
A prayer to Heaven for the fallen foe,

And what is yours? Just bloody deeds anew!—

HEMMING

By Balder, Gandalf! that old man is right!

ASGAUT

Be still, you woman in man's clothes! it's like you,—
You'll never be a warrior—

HEMMING

O indeed,
That is a pathway quite unlike the skald's.

GANDALF

A son of him who killed her father? But
No, woman, no, that really isn't true!
It wasn't by my father's hand he fell,

(*pointing at* ASGAUT)

Look there, there stands the warrior who dispatched him!
But lead me thither where my father fell.

BERNHARD

(*pointing to the burial mound*)

He's sleeping in that mound.

THE WARRIORS

It's Audun's mound!

GANDALF

My father's warrior grave!

ASGAUT

That bauta stone?

BERNHARD

I put it on the hero's mound, and she,
My daughter, decks it every day with flowers.

GANDALF

O, strange, mysterious are the Norns' proceedings!

ASGAUT

And now let's go and seek his murderer,
And take our bloody vengeance!

THE WARRIORS

Bloody vengeance!

GANDALF

No, no,—I won't take vengeance at this time!

ASGAUT

What's wrong with you?

GANDALF

My head is all confused;—
I can't explain,—it's seething so in here!
(*He lays his hand on his chest.*)

BERNHARD

You won't take vengeance?

GANDALF

I'm not able to;
You see, this maid has spoken gentle words,
Which even now are ringing in my soul.
Ah, yes, that glance of hers! that gentle voice!
—It's how I see our meadows' lovely Disa![7]

BERNHARD

You won't take vengeance! O, your mind's made gentle!
Then nothing more shall bind my tongue; then hear,
It was by this hand that your father fell!

GANDALF

(taken aback)

Ha, Loki!

THE WARRIORS

Down with him, yes, down to Hela!

BLANKA

(rushing into her father's arms)

O father! calm yourself,—it isn't true;—
Hear me, you warriors! hear me, hear me, Gandalf!
—I found him weak and bleeding in the woods
That dreadful morning following the battle;
I brought him—

ASGAUT

Silence, woman! that's enough!
On, on, you men!

THE WARRIORS

(with drawn swords)

Go down to Hela's shades!

GANDALF

(placing himself in front of BERNHARD)

Hold, spare him,—do not touch this aged man!

ASGAUT

Ha, this indeed is madness, get yourself
In hand,—he is your father's killer, Gandalf!

GANDALF

I tell you, do not touch this aged man!

BLANKA

O father! quick,—take back those words of horror!
You did not slay the Viking—

BERNHARD

                              Just be calm,
My daughter, all will soon come clear for you!

ASGAUT

(to GANDALF)

Have you forgotten, when you came on shore
You swore a solemn oath by Asathor
To avenge your father's death; thus ran your words:
"O, he or I shall fall, a sacrifice!"

GANDALF

(with feeling)

Ha, he or I shall fall, a sacrifice!
—My heart's so tightly clenched here in my bosom,
As if the Midgard snake[8] had wound its coils
With giant's might around it and crushed flat
The last weak remnant of my strength of will;—
You, maiden! woke this doubt with its fierce claims,
And called to life the storm in which I languish,
My blood is burning hot, like Hela's flames,
And there is nothing that can soothe this anguish.

BLANKA
(*moved*)

O Gandalf! calm yourself,—I now first feel
How fond of you this heart of mine has grown!

GANDALF

Ha, maiden! is their truth in what you say?

BLANKA

O doubt not, Gandalf!

GANDALF

Blanka, speak no more!—
Then I have sworn a most accursed oath;—
I can't take vengeance,—well, then I must fall!

ASGAUT

What do you mean?

GANDALF

Yes, he or I,—so ran
My words,—shall sink, a bloody sacrifice!
He shall not die, for he has fostered her,
That woman, who has wakened in my soul
A world replete with strange and wondrous thoughts!
My oath must hold;—so then prepare my ship,
On Muspel's[9] wings I shall be rising toward
My father's spirit in Valhalla's chambers!

THE WARRIORS

Ha, Gandalf!

GANDALF

Yes, in ancient Nordic wise

I'll meet my death;—look, the evening wind is blowing
Out from the land,—then decorate my bark
With signs of victory, I shall climb on board,
As all those many warriors did before me!

BLANKA

O, do you want—

GANDALF

       For me there is no choice;
My father's gods, you see, I can't betray!
To me this hour seems like a splendid glimmer
From Odin's glance through misty Autumn fogs;
My life throughout was full of war and strife,
Now beckons, like a mild spring day, a life
With golden fruit and lovely vernal blossoms,
And this magnificence I must be gone from!
           (*seizing her hand*)
It must thus be,—so, Blanka, now goodbye,
We'll meet no more—

BLANKA

      O yes, in Heaven's brightness!

GANDALF

No, never, Blanka! for your soul so high
Will lift itself above the stars' pure whiteness,
And mine will vault to Odin's far domain.
There I will rush into the battle's churning,
Perhaps I quickly can forget my pain,
But never will be stilled my ardent yearning!
—Forever kept from you! O, what a notion!
In night's dark hours my shade shall be in motion
With restless turmoil forth from shore to shore
Until the sun shows red on Heaven's floor,

And when my spirit-bark, in foam-grave faring,
The hero's ghost across the sea is bearing,
Then you'll be sitting on soft clouds up high
With the white Christ in moonlight in the sky!
—Ha, cruel fate! how earned I this mistreating;
But now—live well, here is our final meeting,
My death-bed is the North's tumultuous wave,
Far, far from you,—far from your flowery grave!

BLANKA

O, turn away then from your gods of darkness!
—But, Gandalf, no,—your look speaks in its starkness,
A firm resolve has freed your breast from doubt;
Well then, go forth and fight your final bout,—
But when you're sleeping in your dark-blue billow,
Then I can freely my great longing follow,
Hasten across the sea up toward the North,
And to your people bring Christ's gospel forth!
　　(*During the preceding speeches* BERNHARD *has been visibly in combat
　　with himself; now he rushes forward and seizes* BLANKA's *hand.*)

BERNHARD

Hush, Blanka, hush!—I can no more fight back
The violent storm that's raging in my bosom!
　　　　　　　(*sinking to his knees*)

Forgive me, child! if you can manage to!
My every dealing with you was deception—

BLANKA

(*raising him up*)

O mighty God!—compose yourself, my father!

GANDALF

Ha, what is this?

429

BERNHARD

Forgive, forgive me, Blanka!
My son, my Gandalf! yes, I am your father!

GANDALF

O gentle Balder!

BLANKA

God! what are you saying!

ASGAUT

You're lying, old man!

BERNHARD

(*as he bares his arm and holds it out to* ASGAUT)

Asgaut! don't you know
This mark which you yourself once long ago
Engraved here in my arm with rusty steel;—
Just look—

ASGAUT

(*seizing his hand in surprise*)

Thor's hammer!—Audun, it is you!—

BLANKA

O gentle Heaven!

GANDALF

Father! o my father!
(*They sink into his arms.*)

THE WARRIORS

(*striking their shields*)

Hail, Audun! Hail, old warrior of the North!

BLANKA

All ends in gentle reconciliation!

AUDUN

Not yet,—o Blanka! can you offer me
Forgiveness?

BLANKA

(*throwing her arms around him*)

O, how can you ask that, father!
Have you not been extremely good to me,
Have you not lovingly made safe my steps,
And carried me so often in your arms!

AUDUN

O, very little, given what I owe you!

GANDALF

But, father, how am I to understand
That you remained behind on Valland's shore?

AUDUN

Just hear. I sank to earth beside that castle
About the time the battle reached its ending,
I lay unconscious, bleeding, by the cliff,
And leaves concealed me from my warriors' view,
They wailed aloud the dying of their chief,
They left then,—I alone remained behind,
And when the following morning had beamed forth,
There was a rustling near me in the branches,

It was my Blanka, then a little girl,
Scarce five years old,—she stopped short fearfully;
But when she saw me weak and bleeding there,
She fetched me water from a nearby spring
In her small hands, and she took care of me;—
She was the only one who wasn't murdered,
The whole shore had been ravaged and deserted.
With gentle words she soothed away my pain,
I lived in happiness here in the woods,—
I felt no sense of longing for my home;
For you, my Gandalf! wandered far and wide
In Viking raids right from your youth's first days;—
I heard the words of Christ from the child's lips,
And it grew bright and shining in my soul!

GANDALF

And yet this burial mound? My father! how
Am I to understand your recent statement?

AUDUN

I buried there my armor and my sword!
(after a pause)

It seemed to me as if the savage spirit
That reigned within the blood-bespattered Viking
Was torn away completely from my soul.
It seemed to me as if a peaceful calm
Then more and more took root within my being,
When by the altar with her pious prayers
My Blanka sought the Viking hero's peace.

ASGAUT

(seizing BLANKA's hand)

Forgive my harshness toward you, lovely maiden!

GANDALF

My Blanka! let me press you in my arms,

432

You've made me learn a better goal in life!

BLANKA
(*affectionately*)

And your gods?

GANDALF

Them indeed I can't betray!
How could you, after all, trust in my love
If I was faithless to my people's gods?

BLANKA

I see,—I'll put my hope on time, then, Gandalf!
But, surely,—one thing you will promise me;
You will no more go forth on Viking raids!

GANDALF

No, solemnly I swear, that shall not happen!
My kingdom I will safeguard like a hero,
But never, never plunder peaceful coasts.
Answer, my friends! are you not willing to
Obey me?

HROLLOUG

Hail to you, our valiant chief!
We'll loyally obey you now as ever!—

GANDALF

Well, let's be off, then, for the distant North!

BLANKA

The goal of all my heart's most perfect dreams!
You lovely land of snow and northern lights,
You land I'll soon be greeting as my home!

(*to* AUDUN)

And you, our dearest father—

AUDUN

(*with suppressed emotion*)

No, my Blanka!

My Gandalf! I can't go along with you.

GANDALF AND BLANKA

O father!—

AUDUN

No, it is unshakably
Determined,—I can never leave this coast;
That burial mound there gently beckons to me,
There shall this aged Viking soon be sleeping;
Don't think I'll part from you without bereavement,
O, often at the midnight hour I shall
Be sitting there beneath the bauta stone
And staring far away across the sea,
And when the pale and distant Northern lights
Ignite the heavens like a spirit's smile,
Then in true thankfulness I'll fold my hands,
And greet those glimmers as a messenger,
A token that a day of light has come
In all its beauty for my fatherland!
But you, my Gandalf! you have solemn duties
Touching your people,—you can't tarry here,
And yours, my daughter! is the lovely lot
To guide his steps in piety through life.
Fear not, my child,—because, you see, where love
Has made its home, soon also with it faith
Will merge to form a blessed harmony!

HEMMING

(stepping forward with his harp in his hand)

I cannot either, Gandalf! go with you,—
You see, this hour has deeply stirred my soul;
Someday the darkness will be lifted from
My breast by Christendom's bright, gentle flame.

        (He sings, accompanying himself on the harp.)

       Clifftops that tower
       Over the cloudbanks
       Crumble from time's all-
       Treacherous tooth.

       Swords that aforetime
       Clanged in the battle
       Wild as a windstorm
       Rust in the gloom.

       Heroes who plow through
       Sea-level billows
       Someday shall slumber,
       Shrined in their mounds.

       Though mighty powers
       Rule yet in Valhal,
       Ragnarok's storm shall
       Rip them asunder.

       But then behind the
       Blood-spattered gloom of
       Warring combatants
       Dawns a new day!
I lay my harp down at the cross's foot,
My last song was the Asa-faith's[10] lament!

        (He lays his harp in front of the altar.)

GANDALF

And you, my father! won't you go with me?

BLANKA

Are your own children not to close your eyes?

AUDUN

That cannot be;—but Hemming's staying here,
He will take care of me—

HEMMING

With son-like love;—
And then perhaps sometime in future days
My harp shall echo with a holy prayer.

GANDALF

(*downcast but calm*)

It must then be—

BLANKA

O God, are we to leave him!

AUDUN

It's fixed and firm;—so kneel before me, children!
In order that my hands may bless your union!
  (*They kneel, one on each side of him, as they reach out their hands to
    one another.* AUDUN *lays his hands on their heads in blessing.*)

—O, blessed be eternally this pact,
Which couples northern strength with southern mildness.
Be good and pious, Gandalf! guard the treasure
That you are taking home from Valland's woods!
And you, my daughter! guard the precious call
That God assigned to woman's lot on earth,

Plant southern flowers in the spruce-tree's halls,
Spread truth's mild, soothing light throughout the North!
(He embraces them silently as they get up.)

THE WARRIORS

(with a crash of shields)

Hail to our chief! and hail to his young bride!
(AUDUN sits down by the burial mound, HEMMING at his feet.)

HROLLOUG

The sail's already hoist,—the ship is ready!

BLANKA

*(with enthusiasm, seizing the banner from JOSTEIN's hand
as she steps forward)*

Well then, let's go,—up north our voyage leads
Through foamy billows on the sea's blue meads!
Soon daylight shall the glacier's peak enkindle,
Soon sea-raids shall to just a memory dwindle!
The Viking sits already on his mound,
The time is past when, grim, he sailed around
From coast to coast and wildly burned and harried;
In dust the thunder god's great hammer's buried,
And the North itself becomes a warrior grave!
But don't forget the vow Alfader gave:
When moss and flowers shall the mound embrighten,
The hero's ghost on Idavold[11] shall fight then,—
And then the North, too, rises from its grave
To purer strife on thought's slate-bluish wave!

Notes to *The Burial Mound* (1850)

1. Ragnarok, the "twilight [literally "destiny"] of the gods," is the decisive final battle between the forces of good and evil in Old Norse mythology; it culminates with the destruction of the gods and their enemies, but after a period of darkness the Earth is restored and a new order (or "purer life") emerges. Alfader, "father of all," is one of the names for Odin. Balder, the son of Odin and his wife Frigg, is the god of light and peace. Freya is the goddess of love and beauty.

2. The realm of the dead in Norse mythology as well as the name of the goddess who rules there; Ibsen calls her "Hela," either to distinguish her from her realm or for metrical purposes.

3. Saga is one of the names for Frigg, Odin's wife, in her role as the goddess who greets Odin as sun god after his descent below the western horizon in the evening.

4. One of the names for Thor, the Norse god of thunder.

5. A tall, roughly cut stone monument used to commemorate fallen Viking heroes.

6. The term for the fallen warrior dwelling in Valhalla.

7. A "dis" in Norse mythology was a minor goddess, actually a female attendant spirit; "Disa" is apparently a name formed from this concept by Ibsen—or something he got already so formed from Oehlenschläger.

8. The Midgard ("Earth") snake was a monster lying at the bottom of the sea and encircling the Earth.

9. Muspel, a giant, was apparently a personification of Muspelheim, a place of raging flames in Norse mythology. The flames of this realm were known as "the sons of Muspel," and apparently "Muspel's wings" is a poetic allusion to the flames by means of which Gandalf shall effect his self-sacrifice. In the 1854 version of the play, Ibsen revises to "crimson wings."

10. The Asa-faith is the Old Norse mythology.

11. The open green field around which the thirteen halls of the Norse gods stood. They used it for individual combats and other recreational activities. After Ragnarok, it was all that remained, and the surviving gods gathered there; it became the focal point for the "purer life" mentioned in Bernhard-Audun's opening lines.

The Burial Mound

(1854)

Dramatic Poem in One Act

by

Henrik Ibsen

The Characters

BERNHARD, an old hermit.

BLANKA, his foster-daughter.

GANDALF, a sea-king from Norway.

ASGAUT, an old Viking.

HROLLOUG,

JOSTEIN, and

OTHER VIKINGS

HEMMING, a young skald in GANDALF's service.

The action takes place on a little island near Sicily shortly before the introduction of Christianity in Norway.

An open area surrounded by trees close to the shore. To the left in the background the ruins of an ancient temple. In the middle of the stage a large burial mound, upon which is a stone monument with flower-garlands wound about it.

SCENE ONE

RODERIK *sits writing to the right. To the left* BLANKA *in a half-reclining position.*

BLANKA

Glowing sunset's final flaming
Billows like a burning sea,—
Temple-hush drifts over me,
Hush as under leaves' thick framing.
Summer evening's calm content
Like a dove makes its descent,
Like a swan it hovers over
Ocean waves and meadow clover.

Deities of ancient wonder
Doze within the orange-grove's splendor,
Marble remnants that engender
Thoughts about a world gone under.
Virtue, faithfulness, and valor
Stand there turned to stone, inert;
Can there be a more overt
Image of the South's death-pallor?
  (*She gets up.*)

But my father's often told
Of a land past seas far distant,
Where a vigorous life's existent,
Not one chiseled or inscrolled!
Here divinity has faded,
Lasts but in what stone can save,—
There it breathes, with force pervaded,
Like a warrior, strong and brave!

And when evening's sultry quiet
Makes my breast weighed down with woe,
Pictures in my mind run riot
Of the North lit up by snow!
Here are ruins ever crumbling,
Drowsy torpor, listless breath,—
There are avalanches tumbling,
Spring's new life, and winter's death!

If I could take on the swan's form—

RODERIK

(after a pause, writing)

"Then, it is said, when Ragnarok has calmed
The savage forces, called forth purer life,
Alfader, Balder, and the gentle Freya
Shall govern Askur's race in peace once more!"[1]
(after having observed her for a moment)

But Blanka, look, you're lost in dreams again;
You gaze at vacant air so pensively,—
What do you seek?

BLANKA

(approaching)

Forgive me, dearest father!
I was but following a bit the swan
That flew on snow-white wings across the sea.

Roderik

And if I hadn't chanced to stop you in
Your flight, you young and lovely swan of mine!
Who knows how far you might have flown with it,
Perhaps to Thule.

Blanka

       Well, what's wrong with that?
Indeed, the swan flies thither in the springtime,
But back it comes again when it is autumn.
              (*sitting down at his feet*)

But I am not a swan,—no, call me rather
A captive falcon, sitting tame and faithful,
A golden ring about its leg.

Roderik

       What ring?

Blanka

It is my love for you, my dearest father!
With it you've bound forever your young falcon,
It cannot fly, not even if it wished to.
             (*getting up*)

But when, you know, the swan sails free across
The billows like a cloud before the wind,
I must remember all that you have told
About heroic life in distant Thule;
To me it seems then that the bird's a ship
Equipped with dragon head and golden wings;
Upon the bow I see the youthful hero
With copper helmet round his yellow locks,
With eyes of blue, with deep and manly chest,
With sword clutched firmly in his strong right hand.
I join the hero on his rapid voyage,
And then my dreams cavort about the ship

And play, as unrestrainedly as dolphins,
In fantasy's profound and cooling billows!

RODERIK

You are a fantasist, my dearest child,—
I almost fear your thoughts too often dwell
Among the people of the distant North.

BLANKA

And who's to blame, my father, if that's so?

RODERIK

You mean that I myself—?

BLANKA

        O yes, what else?
You live, indeed, but in your memories of
Your youthful life among the North's strong heroes;
And don't deny it, ever when you tell
Of stirring warfare, fights, and single combats,
Your cheeks take fire, your eyes begin to glow,
To me it seems that you grow young again.

RODERIK

It's true, but I have also grounds for that;
I've lived among the heroes of the North,
And all that memory whispers in my ear
Of them, you see, are leaves from my own saga.
But you, who have been fostered in the South,
Who never saw the silvery winter mountains,
Who never heard the lur-horn's clanging sound,—
How can my stories captivate *your* mind?

BLANKA

O listen, does a person need to see

And hear things only with the outer senses?
Does not the soul as well have eyes and ears,
Which it can listen with and see with clearly?
With my corporeal eyes I can discern
The richly glowing color of the rose;
But the soul's look can in its blossom see
A charming elf, winged like a butterfly,
Who coyly hides behind the crimson petals
And hums about a secret force from heaven
That gave the flower its color and its fragrance.

RODERIK

That's true, my daughter!

BLANKA

    I almost believe
That just because I haven't actually seen it
It all becomes more lovely in my thoughts;
That's how it is, at least, with you, my father!
The legends of the gods and songs of heroes,
Those you recall and speak about with joy
And scratch them down on parchment with your runes;
But if I ask about your own life there
Up in the North, your eyes so often darken,
Your lips grow silent, and it sometimes seems
As if your breast were home for grievous memories.

RODERIK

(*getting up*)

Don't speak about that any more, good child,—
Who is the man, pray tell, whose youthful memories
Are not alloyed with many bitter grudges?
The Normans, after all, are savage fighters—

BLANKA

But are the warriors of the South less fierce?

Do you forget that night three years ago,[2]
When all those strangers landed on the coast
And plundered—?

RODERIK

(*with visible disquiet*)

Well, enough of that, let's go;
It's getting pretty close to evening;—come![3]

BLANKA

(*as they are going*)

Give me your hand!

(*stopping*)

No, wait!

RODERIK

What's wrong with you?

BLANKA

For the first time I have today forgotten—

RODERIK

Forgotten what?

BLANKA

(*pointing to the mound*)

Look at the stone and garland!

RODERIK

It is—

BLANKA

The withered one from yesterday;

I quite forgot to make the change this evening;
Yet—I'll go with you to the cottage first,
And later I'll go hunt my flower booty:
The violet's scent is best when evening's dew
Has bathed it with its soft and pearly weeping,
And the rose's bud so fair I never knew
As when it's picked while like a child it's sleeping!
(*They go out to the left in the background.*)⁴

SCENE TWO
GANDALF *and* THE VIKINGS *come in from the right.*

ASGAUT

We're nearly at the place here.

GANDALF
Where? let's see!

ASGAUT

No, wait a bit till we're beyond the woods.
A remnant of the wall still stood upon
The sea side of the cliff when we set sail,—
I would imagine that it stands there still.

JOSTEIN

Look, tell us, King, what use is it for us
To trudge about like fools upon this island?

HROLLOUG

Yes, say what we're to do—

GANDALF
You're to be still!
And follow blindly what your king commands!

(*to* ASGAUT)

It seems to me, however, that you cleaned
The house too well the last time you were here;
You might, I would suggest, have left a little
For me and my revenge!

HROLLOUG

You are our king,
And at the Thing⁵ we swore you our allegiance;
But when we came with you on Viking raids
Our purpose was to garner fame and glory.

JOSTEIN

And gold and treasure, Hrolloug, gold and treasure.

SEVERAL

Yes, Gandalf, that's the law, you must respect it!

GANDALF

I know the law, you men, as well as you;
But hasn't it from ancient times the rule
And custom been with us that when a kinsman
Has fallen to a foe and his remains
Are left unburied,—prey for roving ravens,—
There has to be blood-vengeance?

SOME

Yes, that's so!

GANDALF

So then be ready with your swords and shields,—
You have a king to avenge, and I a father.
(*Commotion among* THE VIKINGS.)

JOSTEIN

A king?

HROLLOUG

    A father?

GANDALF

Wait, I will recount
What happened here. My father was, you know,
A mighty Viking. It's been five years since[6]
The last time he, one spring, went out on raids
With Asgaut there and his old troop of warriors.
Two years he roved about from shore to shore,
And touched at Bretland, Valland, even Blaaland;[7]
At last he chanced to harry Sicily,
And there he heard report about a chieftain
Who lived here on this island in a castle
With massive walls built high upon the mountain,
And there were priceless treasures hidden in it;
During the night he landed on the shore
And then with fire and sword attacked the castle.
He led the onslaught like a goaded bear,
And as he ran amuck he didn't see
His warriors sinking to the earth around him;
And when a glimpse of dawn showed in the east,
All of the castle lay in smoking ruins.
Just Asgaut still remained with a few others,—
My father and indeed a hundred with him
Had ridden to Valhalla through the flames.

ASGAUT

I hoisted high the sail upon our ship,
The prow I headed homeward toward the North;
When I arrived I looked in vain for Gandalf,
For the young eagle, I was told, had flown
Across the sea to Iceland or the Faeroes.

I headed after him, but didn't find him,—
They knew his name, though, everywhere I went;
His dragon flew like clouds before a storm,
But his renown had even better wings.
This summer, as you know, I finally found him,
It was in Velskland;[8] I informed him of
What happened, how his father met his end,
And Gandalf swore by all Valhalla's gods
To take with fire and sword a bloody vengeance.

JOSTEIN

An ancient custom and it ought to be
Respected! Still, if I had been King Gandalf,
I surely would have stayed right there in Velskland,—
For there was gold to win there.

HROLLOUG
                    Glory, too!

GANDALF

And that's your loyalty to the fallen king?

JOSTEIN

Come, no offense intended, I just meant
The dead man could have waited.

ASGAUT
(with suppressed indignation)
                    Wretched lot!

JOSTEIN

But, after all, since we are here now—

452

HROLLOUG

Yes,
Let's raise a worthy monument for him!

SOME

Yes, yes!

OTHERS

With fire and blood!

ASGAUT

That's what I like!

GANDALF

And now let's go and scout about the island;
For yet tonight revenge shall be accomplished,
If not, then I must fall myself.

ASGAUT

He swore it.

GANDALF

Yes, solemnly, by all Valhalla's gods!
And yet once more I swear—
(HEMMING, *with a harp over his shoulder, has come forward among the
warriors during the preceding speeches.*)

HEMMING

(*crying out imploringly*)

Do not swear, Gandalf!

GANDALF

What's wrong with you?

HEMMING

Don't swear here in the woods!
For here our gods can't hear the words you say;
In the ship's prow, up North upon our mountains,
They hear you well enough, but here they can't!

ASGAUT

Has the South's plaguy air touched you as well?

HEMMING

In Velskland I have heard the pious priests
Speaking delightfully of the white Christ,
And what they said still hovers in my mind
By night and day, it will not disappear.

GANDALF

I took you with me, for, from boyhood, you
Showed signs of having ample skaldic powers;
You were to see my daring Viking raids,
And when King Gandalf sat, a gray-haired man,
At the oak board among his loyal warriors,
Then with heroic songs the king's young skald
Was to make short the lengthy winter evenings,
And at the last sing me my funeral song;
The stone the lightning of the skald's tongue raises
Is the best bauta⁹ for a burial mound.
Go, fling your harp away, and put yourself
In a monk's cowl, if you so please. Ha, ha!
King Gandalf shall acquire a skillful singer.
     (THE VIKINGS *go into the woods to the left;* HEMMING *follows them.*)

ASGAUT

(*severely*)¹⁰

It is a musty time we're living in;
Our faith and all our customs from the days

454

Of old are heading downhill rapidly.
My luck! my neck already stoops with age;
These eyes of mine won't see the North's collapse.
But you, King Gandalf, you are young and strong,
And everywhere you go in this wide world,
Just keep in mind that it's a kingly deed
To keep your people's gods and strength from fading!
                    (*He follows after the others.*)

GANDALF

(*after a pause*)

He hasn't any confidence in me.
It's good he's gone! It's just as if a weight
Were lying on my shoulders when he's near me.
That aged man of stone with his harsh features,—
He looks like Thor, who, with his hammer and
His belt of strength, stood hewed from greystone in
The offertory grove by father's courtyard.
My father's courtyard! —Who knows how it looks
At home now in those old familiar sites!
—Mountains and woods, I dare say, are the same;
But people's breasts—? Have they the ancient strength?
No, there has fallen mildew on the times,
And it is that which sucks sap from the North
And poisonously gnaws at its best flowers.
Well, I'll head homeward! Save whatever still
Is savable before it all collapses.
                    (*after a pause, as he looks around*)

It's so delightful in these southern groves;
My spruce-woods haven't got as strong a scent.
                    (*He notices the mound.*)

What's that? A burial mound? No doubt it holds
Some Viking from the ancient, vigorous days.
A burial mound here in the South! —That's just;
Indeed, the South gave us our fatal wound.
How lovely it is here! It calls to mind

A winter night when I, a little boy,
Sat on my father's knee beside the hearth
While he was telling me about our gods,
Of Odin, Balder, and the mighty Thor;
And when I mentioned to him Freya's grove,
He pictured it for me like this grove here,—
But when I asked about Freya herself,
Especially how she looked, the old man chuckled
And put me down upon the floor and answered:
"A woman shall, I dare say, tell you that!"

(listening)

Hush! Footsteps through the woods! Be calm now, Gandalf,—
They're bringing you the first-fruits of your vengeance.
   (*He steps to one side so that he is half hidden among the bushes to the*
right.)

SCENE THREE

GANDALF. BLANKA, *with oak-leaves in her hair and a basket of flowers,*
comes in from the left.

BLANKA

(*busying herself with braiding a flower garland*)[11]

The springs are murmuring in the verdant valleys,
The pearly waves are tossing on the shore;
But the springs' murmuring, the waves' soft voice
Have not so strong a force as those sweet flowers
So sisterly embracing, breast to breast,
In close-packed clusters round the barrow's sides;
They lure me hither every day and night,—
Here it is good for yearning and for dreaming.
Look, now the garland's done. The hero's bauta,
So hard and cold, shall be concealed beneath it.
Yes, it is beautiful!

(*pointing to the mound*)

A life lived through,

With mighty strength, now buried deep in earth,—
Its monument, which speaks to after ages,
An ice-cold piece of granite like that mound's!
And then art comes, and with its friendly hand
It picks the flowers from dear nature's breast
And decorates the monument's hard granite
With snow-white lilies, sweet forget-me-nots.
    (She climbs up on the mound and hangs the garland over the bauta
                    stone. After a pause)

Now once again my host of dreams, like birds
Of passage, sail across the ocean waves;
I'm drawn to where my yearning urges me,
And willingly I follow that dark force,
Which has its kingly throne in the soul's depths.
I'm standing in the North, a warrior's bride,
And peering, like an eagle, from a mountain.
Behind the shining waves the ship appears.
—O, like a gull, fly toward your native shores!
I am a southern child, I cannot wait;—
I snatch the oakleaf garland from my hair;—
Take it, my hero! it's the second greeting
To welcome you,—my yearning was the first.
    (She throws the garland. GANDALF *steps forward and seizes it.)*

What now? There stands—
        (She rubs her eyes and stares at him in amazement.)

                O no, it is no dream.
Who are you, stranger? What is it you seek
Here by the shore?

GANDALF

     Climb down, first, from the mound
So we can talk together.

BLANKA
(climbing down)

Here I am!

(aside, as she looks him over)

Chain-mail across his breast, the copper helmet,—
Exactly as my father has described.
(aloud)

Take off your helmet!

GANDALF

Why?

BLANKA

Just do it, then!
(aside)

Two eyes that sparkle, hair the color of grain,—
Exactly as I saw him in my dreams.

GANDALF

Who are you, woman?

BLANKA

I? A humble child!

GANDALF

Yet certainly the fairest on this island.

BLANKA

(laughing)

The fairest? Yes, that is quite possible;
For no one else is here.

GANDALF

What, no one else?

BLANKA

Except my father,—o, but he is old
And has a silvery beard as long as so,—
Then, yes, I do believe *I* win the prize.

GANDALF

You have a merry mind.

BLANKA

Not always, sir!

GANDALF

But tell me, how I am to understand
That you live here alone with just your father,
When I most certainly have heard report
This island was quite richly populated?

BLANKA

It was so once, three years ago it was;
But—yes, it is a melancholy story—
Still, you shall hear it, if you wish to do so.

GANDALF

Indeed, I do!

BLANKA

You see, three years ago—
(*sitting down*)

But come, sit down!

GANDALF

(*retreating a step*)

No, no, you sit, I'll stand.

BLANKA

Three years ago, God knows from where, a band
Of robbers under arms came to the island;
They plundered all about them as they went
And murdered everyone they found alive.
Those few who managed saved themselves by flight
And sought a refuge in my father's castle,
Which stood upon the cliff beside the sea.

GANDALF

Your father's, did you say?

BLANKA

Indeed, my father's.
It was a cloudy evening when they stormed
The castle gate, forced through the wall, and broke
Into the courtyard, killing without mercy.
I fled out anxiously into the darkness
And sought myself a hide-out in the woods.
I saw our home go whirling up in flames,
I heard the crash of shields and frightened death-shrieks.
—At last all things grew still;—for all were murdered.
—The savage band then headed for the shore
And sailed away. —The following morning I
Sat on the cliff beside the smoking ruins.
I was the only one that they had spared.

GANDALF

But yet you told me that your father lives.

BLANKA

My *foster*-father; wait, and you shall hear!
I sat upon the cliff, bereaved and anxious,
And listened to the horrifying stillness;
And then I heard a kind of muffled sigh
From the deep fissure underneath my feet;

I listened frightened, then at last climbed down
And found a stranger, bleeding, pale, and weak.
I went to him, as frightened as I was,
Bound up his wounds and tended him.

GANDALF

And he?

BLANKA

He told me, as he gradually came to,
That he had come upon a merchant ship
And reached the island on the very day
The castle was attacked,—had headed thither,
And bravely fought against the robber band
Until he, weak and bleeding, tumbled down
Into the fissure where I later found him.
And ever since that time we've lived together;
He built a cottage for us in the woods,
And he's been dear to me, like no one else.
But come, you must go see him.

GANDALF

No—no, wait!
We'll meet each other soon enough, I'm sure.

BLANKA

O well, then, as you wish; but rest assured
He'd welcome you beneath our cottage roof;
For hospitality is not a trait
Belonging only to the North.

GANDALF

The North?
I see you know then—

BLANKA

Where you come from? Yes!
My father has so often told about you
That when I first laid eyes on you—

GANDALF

                    And yet

You weren't afraid?

BLANKA

Afraid? But why afraid?

GANDALF

Well, has he never said,—yes, hasn't he—

BLANKA

Told me that you are daring heroes? Yes!
But why on earth should that make me afraid?
I know that you seek fame on distant shores
In manly bouts with awe-inspiring warriors;
But I have neither armor nor a sword,
So why should I then be—

GANDALF

No, no, indeed!
Those strangers, though, the ones who burned the castle?

BLANKA

What of them?

GANDALF

Well, I only meant has not
Your father told you where they came from?

BLANKA

Never.

They were, you see, strangers to him as well.
But if you like, I'll ask him what he knows.

GANDALF

(*quickly*)

No, let it be.

BLANKA

Ah, now I understand!
You want to know where you can look for them
And take blood-vengeance, as you call it.

GANDALF

Ha,

Blood-vengeance! Thanks! You've called back to my mind
A word I'd near forgotten—

BLANKA

It's indeed

A hideous custom, though.

GANDALF

(*going toward the background*)

Farewell!

BLANKA

You're going?

GANDALF

We'll meet again.

(*stopping*)

But tell me one thing more:
Who's resting underneath that burial mound?

BLANKA

I do not know.

GANDALF

You do not know, and yet
You fling your flowers round the hero's bauta.

BLANKA

My father led me here one early morning
And showed to me the new-made mound, which I
Had never seen upon the strand before.
He bade me say my morning prayers beside it
And in my prayers to think with piety
Of those who harried us with sword and flames.

GANDALF

And you?

BLANKA

Each early morn from that day on
I prayed a silent prayer for their salvation;
And fresh-picked flowers braided every evening
In garlands for the monument.

GANDALF

Strange, strange!
How can you pray so for your enemy?

BLANKA

My faith commands it.

GANDALF

(*vehemently*)

That's a coward's faith!
That is a faith that saps the hero's strength;
That's why the life of battle perished in
Its bed among you in the South!

BLANKA

But if
My coward's faith, as you are pleased to call it,
Could be transplanted to your hearty soil,—
I know full well, from it there would shoot forth
A wealth of flowers rich enough to deck
The naked mountains.

GANDALF

Let the mountains stand
With naked walls until they shall collapse!

BLANKA

O, take me with you there!

GANDALF

What do you mean?
I'm heading homeward—

BLANKA

Yes, I'll sail with you;
So long within my thoughts I've made the trip
Up there where your home lies among the ice
And snow and mighty forests dark as night.
Your hall should soon be filled with gaiety
If I could rule there, you can well believe;
For I am cheerful;—do you have a skald?

GANDALF

I had one, but the humid air here in
The South has slackened his harp-strings. They make
No music now.

BLANKA

O good! then I shall be

Your skald.

GANDALF

And you? —You could go off with us,
Just leave your home and father?

BLANKA

(*laughing*)

Ha, ha, ha!

I think you took it seriously?

GANDALF

Was

It just your joke?

BLANKA

Alas! a foolish dream
I often dreamed before we saw each other,—
And that, I'm sure, I'll dream so many times
When you—

(*abruptly breaking off*)

You look at me so stiffly.

GANDALF

Do I?

BLANKA

Indeed, what are you thinking of?

GANDALF

I? Nothing.

BLANKA

Oh?—nothing?

GANDALF

Well, I don't know what I'm thinking;
But yes, I know—and now you'll have to hear it:
I'm thinking of that wish of yours to plant
Your flowers in the North, and as I do
My own faith falls into my mind. There is
A saying in it that I couldn't grasp
Before; but now you've taught me how to do so.

BLANKA

What do you mean?

GANDALF

It's said Valfader[12] gets
A half-part only of the fallen warriors;
The other half of them belongs to Freya.
I never could quite rightly understand that;
But now—I grasp it now—I am myself
A fallen warrior, and my better half
Is Freya's property.

BLANKA

(startled)

What does *that* mean?

GANDALF

Well, in plain terms, I am—

BLANKA

(*quickly*)

No, let it be!
I dare no longer tarry here this evening,—
My father's waiting; I must go. Farewell!

GANDALF

You're going?

BLANKA

(*taking up the oakleaf garland, which he has let fall, and tossing it on his
helmet*)

There you are, and you can keep it.
What formerly I gave you in my dreams
I give you now that I'm awake.

GANDALF

Farewell!
(*He quickly goes out to the right.*)

SCENE FOUR

BLANKA

(*alone*)

He is gone now! Silent stillness
Rules this coast so dispossessed.
Silent stillness, grave-like stillness
Also rules within my breast.

Like a sunbeam through the vapor,
Has he come but for departing?

Like a gull he'll soon be darting
Far from here when night winds caper!

What for me will be remaining?
Just a flower for my dreaming;
Loneliness to start me swimming,
Like a petrel toward his waning!
(THE VIKINGS' *war-horn can be heard from the left.*)

Ha! what was that! A horn, it's from the woods.

SCENE FIVE
BLANKA. GANDALF *(from the right)*.

GANDALF
(aside)

It is too late!

BLANKA
O, there he is again!
What do you want?

GANDALF
Make haste, away from here!

BLANKA
What do you mean?

GANDALF
Away! For danger threatens!

BLANKA
What danger?

GANDALF

Death!

BLANKA

I do not understand you.

GANDALF

I wanted to conceal it from you; so
I went to call my people to the ship
And sail away; you never were to know—
But that horn sounded, and it's now too late;
They're coming hither.

BLANKA

Who is coming, who?

GANDALF

The strangers who back then attacked this island
Were Vikings like myself.

BLANKA

What, from the North?

GANDALF

Indeed. My father fell, he was their king,—
So he must be avenged.

BLANKA

Avenged?

GANDALF

It is
Our rule and custom.

BLANKA
Ha! I understand!

GANDALF
They're coming! Get behind me.

BLANKA
Back, you butcher!

SCENE SIX

BLANKA *and* GANDALF. ASGAUT, HEMMING, *and* THE VIKINGS (*who are bringing* RODERIK *with them*).

ASGAUT
(*to* GANDALF)

A meager catch—but always something, Gandalf.

BLANKA
My father!

(*She throws herself into his arms.*)

RODERIK
Blanka! O my child!

JOSTEIN
A woman!

He'll have a fellow traveler.

ASGAUT
Yes, to Hel![13]

BLANKA

O father, why,—why have you never told me—

RODERIK

Hush! hush! my daughter, hush!
(*pointing at* GANDALF)

Is that your chieftain?

ASGAUT

He is.
(*to* GANDALF)

The man can give you an account
Of how your father died; for he was there
And got away alive, as he has said.

GANDALF

Be quiet! I won't hear a thing.

ASGAUT

Good, let's
get at it, then.

BLANKA

O God! what will they do?

GANDALF

(*in a low tone*)

I cannot, Asgaut!

ASGAUT

(*similarly*)

Is our chief a coward?
Has the fair woman's oily tongue bewitched him?

GANDALF

Well, be that as it may, I said—

ASGAUT

Consider,
This is a matter of your men's esteem
For you. You gave Valhalla's gods your oath,
And if it's broken, you're a knave to all.
Remember, our old faith is weakly propped,—
It's reeling now; a single push can shake it,
And if that push comes from above,—yes, from
The king,—then it's received its death-blow.

GANDALF

Ha!

It was a most accursed oath I swore.

ASGAUT

(*to* THE VIKINGS)

Get ready, warriors!

BLANKA

Will you murder him,
This old defenseless man?

ASGAUT

Down with them both!

BLANKA

O God!

HROLLOUG

The woman is too fair! Let her
Go with us on our ship.

JOSTEIN

(*laughing*)

Yes, as shield-maiden.[14]

GANDALF

Get back!

RODERIK

Spare her, I beg you, spare my child!
I'll bring to you the slayer of your king
If you will only spare her!

GANDALF

(*quickly*)

Bring him here,
Then she'll be free—all right?

THE VIKINGS

Yes, yes, she will!

BLANKA

(*to* RODERIK)

What are you saying?

ASGAUT

Get him here!

RODERIK

He's here!

SOME

Ha, the old man!

GANDALF

Alas!

BLANKA

No, you shall not—

RODERIK

Yes, by this hand the Viking found his death,
And now he's resting in that burial mound!

GANDALF

My father's gravemound!

RODERIK

He was strong and brave;
So I interred him in his fathers' manner.

GANDALF

Since he's been honored thus, we'll—

ASGAUT

No, the slaying
Of our king still demands blood-vengeance,—strike!

BLANKA

He is deceiving you!

(*to* GANDALF)

Have you not seen
He only says it to save *me*, his daughter?
But what would *you* know of a loving mind
That sacrifices all for—

GANDALF

I don't know?

475

You don't believe I—?

(*to* THE VIKINGS)

He shall not be slain.

ASGAUT

What's that?

BLANKA

O father! he is good like you!

ASGAUT

You'll break your oath?

GANDALF

O no, I'm keeping it!

JOSTEIN

What's your intent?

HROLLOUG

Speak out!

GANDALF

What I have sworn
Is to avenge the king or fall myself.
Well then, that man is free,—I'll go to Valhal!

BLANKA

(*to* RODERIK)

What does he mean?

ASGAUT

That's your intent, you want to—?

GANDALF

You go and have one of my ships kept ready,
With sail hoist high, a fire lit in the prow;
As done in days of old, I'll climb on board!
Look, the evening wind is blowing from the shore,—
On crimson wings I'll make my way to Valhal!
        (JOSTEIN *goes out to the right.*)

ASGAUT

Ha, it's the woman who's enchanted you!

BLANKA

No, you must live!

GANDALF

      Live? No. Because, you see,
I'm loyal to my gods, cannot betray them.

BLANKA

That oath of yours is bloody, Balder hates it.

GANDALF

O, Balder now no longer lives among us!

BLANKA

For you he lives; you have a gentle mind.

GANDALF

To my destruction, yes! It was my call
As king to keep our warrior life safeguarded,—
But now my strength fails me! Come, Asgaut, you
Shall take the royal scepter from my hand;
You are a warrior of authentic metal;
On me the South has long since worked its poison.

However, if I can't live for my people,
Then I can die for them.

ASGAUT

Well said, King Gandalf.

BLANKA

So then the die is cast! Fall as a hero
In true devotion to your gods! But now,
When we must be forever parted, know
That when you fall yourself to meet your vow,
You've also dedicated me to death!

GANDALF

What's that! What, you to death?

BLANKA

My life was like
A flower-bud planted in foreign soil,
So that it slumbered in a swaddled prison:
Then came a sunbeam from the distant home,—
O Gandalf, that was you! The flower opened
Its chalice. Ah, a fleeting moment! Then
The sunbeam dimmed—the flower had to die!

GANDALF

O, have I grasped your meaning? Could you—? —Ha,
So then my vow's a tenfold most accursed!

BLANKA

We'll meet again!

GANDALF

O never, never more!

For you it's heaven and the white Christ waiting.
I go to Valhal; mutely I'll sit by
The table's end, the lowest, near the door,
For the hall's merriment is not for me.

JOSTEIN

(coming back with a banner in his hand)

Well, now the ship is ready, as you ordered.

ASGAUT

You'll get a splendid end! Many a hero
Will surely envy you.

GANDALF

(to BLANKA)

Farewell!

BLANKA

Farewell!
Farewell for life and for eternity!

RODERIK

(struggling with himself)

Stop! stop!

(throwing himself down before BLANKA)

O mercy! O forgive, forgive me!

BLANKA

O God!

GANDALF

What does he mean?

RODERIK

I'll confess all:
My every dealing with you was deception!

BLANKA

O, terror has confused him!

RODERIK

No, o no!
(*to* GANDALF *after he has gotten up*)

Young king, you are released now from your vow;
Your father's shade does not demand blood-vengeance!

GANDALF

Ha, then explain!

BLANKA

O speak!

RODERIK

Here stands King Rørek!

SOME

The fallen king!

BLANKA

O heaven!

GANDALF
(*doubtfully*)

You, my father?

RODERIK

Look, Asgaut, look! Do you recall the scratch
You gave me during our first Viking raid
When we got in a fight about the plunder?
(*He bares his arm and shows it to* ASGAUT.)

ASGAUT

By Thor, it is King Rørek!

GANDALF

(*throwing himself in* RODERIK's *arms*)

Father! Father!
Now for a second time you give me life.
O, take my thanks!

RODERIK

(*to* BLANKA, *downcast*)

And you—what do you give
The aged robber?

BLANKA

Love, just as before!
I am your daughter! Hasn't three years' fondness
Quite wiped out every bloodstain in your shield?

ASGAUT

But tell us how it is you're still alive!

GANDALF

She saved him.

RODERIK

Yes, just like a friendly elf

She healed my wounds and tended me, and all
The while she spoke so finely of the faith
Among the quiet people of the South
That even my hard breast grew soft from it.
And day by day I concealed who I was;
I didn't dare—

GANDALF

But then that burial mound?

RODERIK

I buried there my armor and my sword.
It seemed to me as if the savage Viking
Was also laid to rest then. And my child
Has daily prayed for him beside the mound.

ASGAUT

Farewell!

GANDALF

You're going? Where?

ASGAUT

              North with my ship!
For now I clearly see my time is past—
And Viking life as well. I'll go to Iceland;
This sickness hasn't got that far as yet.
          (to BLANKA)

Young woman, take my place beside the king!
For Thor can do no more—his hammer's out
Of joint; now Balder rules through you. —Farewell!
          (He goes.)

GANDALF

Yes, Balder rules through you, my Blanka! Now

I sense the meaning of my Viking life!
It wasn't only lust for fame and riches
That drove me outward from my fathers' home;
No, that which led me was a secret yearning,
A mute but strong desire for Balder. Look,
My yearning now is stilled; we're heading home;
There I shall live in peace among my people.

(to THE VIKINGS)

And will you go with me?

ALL

We'll go with you!

GANDALF

And you, my Blanka?

BLANKA

I? I also am

An offspring of the North; it was among
Your mountains that, you see, my heart's best flower
Struck down its root. To you I headed in
My dreams, from you it was I drew my love!

RODERIK

And so, be off!

GANDALF

But you?

BLANKA

You go with us!

RODERIK

I'm staying here.

(*pointing to the mound*)

My burial mound awaits me.

BLANKA

Am I to leave you here alone?

HEMMING

O no!

Be without fear! For I shall close his eyes
And sing his funeral drapa from the mound;
It'll be my final song.
(*moved, as he takes* GANDALF'S *hand*)

Farewell, my king!
Now you have found yourself a better skald.

RODERIK

(*with firmness*)

It must thus be! for you are king, my Gandalf,
And you have solemn duties toward your people.
(*laying their hands together*)

You are the children of the coming dawn,—
Go thither where the royal throne awaits you;
I am the last one of the vanished times,
My throne is now the grave—o grant me it!
(GANDALF *and* BLANKA *silently rush into his arms.* RODERIK *climbs up
on the mound.* HEMMING, *with his harp, sits down at his feet.*)

GANDALF

(*with composure*)

And now to Norway!

HROLLOUG

Homeward!

ALL

Home! To Norway!

BLANKA

(enthusiastically, as she snatches the banner from JOSTEIN's *hand)*

Yes, now let's go! Up north our voyage leads
Through storm and foam upon the waves' blue meads.
Soon daylight shall the glacier's peak enkindle,
Soon sea-raids shall to just a memory dwindle!
The Viking sits already on his mound;
The time is past when, grim, he sailed around
From coast to coast in arms and burned and harried!
In dust the thunder god's great hammer's buried,
And the North itself becomes a warrior grave.
But don't forget the vow Alfader gave:
When moss and flowers shall the mound embrighten,
The hero's ghost on Idavold[15] shall fight then,—
And then the North, too, rises from its grave
To purer deeds of spirit on thought's wave!

Notes to *The Burial Mound* (1854)

1. Ragnarok, the "twilight [literally "destiny"] of the gods," is the decisive final battle between the forces of good and evil in Norse mythology; it culminates with the destruction of the gods and their enemies, but after a period of darkness the Earth is restored and a new order (or "purer life") emerges. Alfader, "father of all," is one of the names for Odin. Balder, the son of Odin and his wife Frigg, is the god of light and of peace. Freya is the goddess of love and beauty. Askur is the Norse Adam.

2. The printed text reads "ten years." In revising *The Burial Mound,* Ibsen originally retained the ten-year lapse between the two Viking raids, but most subsequent references to this time span have been corrected in the manuscripts to "three years" and are so given in the printed text; whoever made the changes— presumably Ibsen himself—missed this reference. The details are provided by Seip (314), and I have confirmed them in my inspection of the major manuscript and the printed text in September 1989. Although the Hundreårsutgave prints "ten years" here, I have changed it to "three years" on the assumption that Ibsen would have done so had he noticed this error of omission.

3. The manuscripts, which differ slightly between them, call for this line to be translated as "It's getting on toward sunset now,—come, come!"

4. The manuscripts say "to the right," but this change in the printed text is appropriate, since "to the right" is the direction associated with the Vikings and the coast.

5. A legislative and judicial assembly of free men in the Scandinavian Middle Ages.

6. All texts read "twelve years." This is one of the references that was not changed when the time-lapse between the two Viking raids was reconceived as three years. I make the change for consistency's sake.

7. Old Norse names for, respectively, Wales and West England; France, especially Normandy; and the northwest coast of Africa.

8. Italy.

9. A tall, roughly cut stone monument used to commemorate fallen Viking heroes.

10. I add this stage direction from the major manuscript.

11. The manuscripts have "sitting to the left" at the beginning of this stage direction, but there is no corresponding direction for her to get up, unless it is implicit in the second stage direction following.

12. "Father of the slain"—one of the names for Odin.

13. The realm of the dead in Norse mythology.

14. A Valkyrie taking part in a conflict and helping to determine its outcome.

15. The open green field around which the thirteen halls of the Norse gods stood. They used it for individual combats and other recreational activities. After Ragnarok, it was all that remained, and the surviving gods gathered there; it became the focal point for the "purer life" mentioned in Roderik-Rørek's first lines.

Appendix: Ibsen's Synopsis-Outlines for *Catiline*

[I]

Sequence of scenes.

ACT ONE

1.

The Appian Way close to Rome.
Catiline; conversation with the Allobroges.—

2.

Forum.
Lentulus, Cethegus, et. al. Reference to the conspiracy[.] Decision to approach Catiline[.]

3.

The Temple of Vesta
A Vestal. Catiline and Curius come in without being noticed, the former to have a rendezvous with Fulvia. She comes in[.] Conversation between her and Catiline, Catiline is warned that Aurelia is about to come, he flees [perhaps a comma should be here] Fulvia in great agitation, the holy fire goes out—people rush in[,] she is led away—Curius decides to rescue her—

4.

Catiline's house
Catiline and Aurelia in conversation, he is in agitation—she calms him down, an Old Man comes in to ask for help to release his son from debtors' prison—Catiline gives him the last sum he has remaining—

5.

The underground hole.
Fulvia in mad despair—Curius rescues her—

ACT TWO

Catiline's residence
Catiline alone [and] at odds with himself, Cethegus has been with
him and prepared him for the coming of the conspirators—Aurelia
comes in [and] is informed of [the] reason for his uneasiness.

[II]

ACT TWO

A room in Catiline's house
Lentulus and Cethegus have informed him of the decision of their
friends—and urged him to accept the leadership of the enterprise—
but he refuses and they go away—monologue—Furia appears—he is
inflamed to a frenzy and rushes away to the meeting-place of the
conspirators.—

A tavern.
The conspirators are gathered—L. & C. appear and report the
outcome of their mission and L. volunteers to accept the leadership of
the enterprise—which is also approved. However Catiline rushes in in
a frenzy, volunteers to be commander and all joyfully unite with him,
the conspiracy is discussed, and Cethegus goes to the Allobroges to
persuade them to take part in the conspiracy.—

A garden, in the background Catiline's house.
Curius is pacing back and forth in order to guard the entrance—
Furia appears—vehement conversation—, he declares to her his
burning love and she demands that as a proof of this he shall inform
against the conspiracy—struggle between love and duty—, the first
triumphs and he goes away—Furia alone—the Allobroges come out
talking about the conspiracy—she presents herself—warns them, they
are frightened—and decide to withdraw—Catiline comes out—
monologue. Aurelia seeks him out and wants to induce him to give up

the whole thing—in vain—and she decides to go with him—she goes in—Catiline alone—she comes back, bearing arms—the conspirators gather—Furia is among them—they all hurry away—

Index to Introductions

99–103, 397; *The Wild Duck*, 3, 98; THEMES AND TECHNIQUES: artist figure, 100; central visual symbols, 383; characteristic action-sequence, 97–8, 113; character triads, 96–7, 101; concept of the "call," 111, 383, 400 n.11; justifying symbolic characters in literal action, 58, 98; "key words," 98; pagan-Christian clash, 383; private language of characters, 98; retrospective method, 383; symbolic core of *Catiline* in his later work, 98–103, 381, verbal repetition, 395

Ibsen, Knud, 3–5; financial ruin, 3–4

Iversen, Ragnvald, 121 n.40

Jensen, P. A., 378

Johnston, Andrew, 36

Johnston, Brian, 40, 41, 59, 60, 113, 118 n.24, 383, 385; evaluation of *The Burial Mound*, 380; evaluation of *Catiline*, 41

Jonson, Ben: *Catiline*, 77, 120 n.46

Josephson, Ludvig, 35

Kierkegaard, Søren, 6

Knight, G. Wilson, 39

Koht, Halvdan, 4, 17, 61, 65, 113, 116 n.1,4–5, 117 n.13–4, 119 n.34, 120 n.37, 373, 381, 384; evaluation of *The Burial Mound*, 379; evaluation of *Catiline*, 39

Lervik, Åse Hiorth, 78, 120 n.41

McFarlane, James Walter, 118 n.20, 379, 380, 385, 397, 399 n.4; evaluation of *The Burial Mound*, 379–80; evaluation of *Catiline*, 40

McLellan, Samuel G., 65–6, 67, 77, 119 n.33, 399 n.1,9

Meyer, Michael, 8, 27, 35, 116 n.1, 117 n.13–14, 378, 399 n.4, 400 n.12; evaluation of *The Burial Mound*, 379; evaluation of *Catiline*, 39–40

Monodrama, 64

Monrad, M. J., 25–6, 31

Müller, Carl, 22–5, 26, 117 n.14

National Romanticism, 16, 26, 29, 40, 65, 70, 373, 378–80, 381

Norwegian Theater, Christiania, 28

Norwegian Theater, Bergen, 28, 29, 377–8, 397